A Guide to 100 Tests for Special Education

Carolyn Compton, Ph.D.

Associate Director, Children's Health Council
Co-Director, Morrissey–Compton Educational Center
Palo Alto, California

GLOBE FEARON

Contributing Authors

Joan Bisagno, Ph.D.
 Learning Disability Specialist; Psychologist

Polly Bredt, M.A., C.C.C.
 Speech and Language Pathologist

Barbara Fourt, M.A., O.T.R.
 Registered Occupational Therapist

Beth Harper, O.T.R.
 Registered Occupational Therapist

Marsha Silver, M.S., C.C.C.
 Speech and Language Pathologist

Karen Travis, M.S., C.C.C.
 Speech and Language Pathologist; Lawyer

Printed in the United States of America.   2 3 4 5 6 7 8 9 10 99 98 97 96

ISBN: 0-835-91611-1

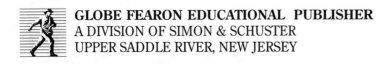
GLOBE FEARON EDUCATIONAL PUBLISHER
A DIVISION OF SIMON & SCHUSTER
UPPER SADDLE RIVER, NEW JERSEY

Contents

Alphabetical Listing of Tests

Acknowledgments

Grateful acknowledgment is made to the following authors and publishers for their permission to reprint copyrighted sample test materials and illustrative matter.

SAMUEL A. KIRK, JAMES J. MCCARTHY, and WINIFRED D. KIRK, for illustrations from *The Illinois Test of Psycholinguistic Abilities*. Copyright © 1968 by the Board of Trustees of the University of Illinois, University of Illinois Press, Urbana. Used with permission of the University of Illinois Press.

MARIANNE FROSTIG, in collaboration with WELTY LEFEVER and JOHN R. B. WHITTLESSEY for illustrations from *The Developmental Test of Visual Perception*. Austin, TX: PRO-ED, 1966.

THE PSYCHOLOGICAL CORPORATION, for illustrations from the standardization edition of the *Basic Achievement Skills Individual Screener*. Copyright © 1983 by The Psychological Corporation, San Antonio, TX. Reproduced by permission. All rights reserved.

ALBERT H. BRIGANCE, for illustrations from *BRIGANCE ® Diagnostic Competence Inventory of Basic Skills*. North Billerica, MA: Curriculum Associates, Inc., 1983. Reprinted/Adapted by Permission.

PHYLLIS L. NEWCOMER, for illustrations from *Diagnostic Achievement Battery*, Second Edition. Austin, TX: PRO-ED, 1988.

THE PSYCHOLOGICAL CORPORATION, for illustrations from the *Wechsler Individual Achievement Test*. Copyright © 1992 by The Psychological Corporation, San Antonio, TX. Reproduced by permission. All rights reserved.

DONALD D. HAMMILL and STEPHEN C. LARSEN, for illustrations from *Test of Written Language*, Second Edition. Austin, TX: PRO-ED, 1988.

BRIAN E. ENRIGHT, for illustrations from *ENRIGHT ® Diagnostic Inventory of Basic Arithmetic Skills*. North Billerica, MA: Curriculum Associates, Inc., 1983. Reprinted/Adapted by Permission.

AUSTIN J. CONNOLLY, for the illustrations from *Key Math Revised, A Diagnostic Inventory of Essential Mathematics*. Circle Pines, MN: American Guidance Service, 1989.

DAVID SHESLOW and WAYNE ADAMS, for illustrations from the *Wide Range Assessment of Memory and Learning*. Wilmington, DE: Jastak Associates, 1990.

BETH SLINGERLAND, for illustrations from the *Revised PreReading Screening Procedures to Identify First-Grade Academic Needs*. Cambridge, MA: Educators Publishing Service, 1977.

KEITH E. BEERY and NORMAN A BUKTENICA, for illustrations from *The Developmental Test of Visual Motor Integration*, Third Revision. Copyright © 1989 by Keith E. Berry and Norman A. Buktenica. Used by permission of Modern Curriculum Press, Cleveland, OH.

RONALD A. COLARUSSO and DONALD D. HAMMILL, for illustrations from *Motor-Free Visual Perception Test*. Novato, CA: Academic Therapy Publications, 1970. By permission of the authors and publisher.

DONALD D. HAMMILL, NILS A. PEARSON, and JUDITH K. VORESS, for illustrations from the *Developmental Test of Visual Perception*, Second Edition. Austin, TX: PRO-ED, 1993.

ELLEN O'HARA WERNER and JANET DAWSON KRESCHECK, for illustrations from the *Structured Photographic Expressive Language Test, Revised*. Sandwich, IL: Janelle Publications, 1983.

MARK BARRETT, LINDA ZACHMAN, and ROSEMARY HUISINGH, for illustrations from *Assessing Semantic Skills Through Everyday Themes*. East Moline, IL: LinguiSystems, 1988.

DONALD D. HAMMILL, VIRGINIA L. BROWN, STEPHEN C. LARSEN, and J. LEE WIEDERHOLT, for illustrations from the *Test of Adolescent and Adult Language*, Third Edition. Austin, TX: PRO-ED, 1994.

LINDA ZACHMAN, ROSEMARY HUISINGH, MARK BARRETT, JANE ORMAN, and CAROLYN LOGUIDICE, for illustrations from *The Word Test–Adolescent*. E. Moline, IL: LinguiSystems, 1989.

LINDA ZACHMAN, ROSEMARY HUISINGH, MARK BARRETT, JANE ORMAN, and CAROLYN LOGUIDICE, for illustrations from the *Test of Problem Solving*, Revised Edition. E. Moline, IL: LinguiSystems, 1994.

GEORGIA DEGANGI and RONALD BERK, for illustrations from the *Test of Sensory Integration*. Los Angeles, CA: Western Psychological Services, 1983.

AMERICAN GUIDANCE SERVICE, for photograph and illustrations used in the review of the *Kaufman Assessment Battery for Children*. Copyright © 1983 by Alan S.

Kaufman and Nadeen L. Kaufman. Reprinted by permission of American Guidance Services, Circle Pines, MN.

AMERICAN GUIDANCE SERVICE, for illustrations used in the
review of the *Kaufman Adolescent and Adult Intelligence
Test*. Copyright © 1992 by Alan S. Kaufman and Nadeen L.
Kaufman. Reprinted by permission of American Guidance
Service, Circle Pines, MN.

LINDA BROWN, SUSAN JOHNSON, and RITA SHERBENOU, for
illustrations from the *Test of Nonverbal Intelligence*, Second
Edition. Austin, TX: PRO-ED, 1990.

DAVID WECHSLER, for illustrations from the *Wechsler
Intelligence Scale for Children*, Third Edition. Copyright ©
by the Psychological Corporation, San Antonio, TX:
Reproduced by permission. All rights reserved.

Preface

A Guide to 100 Tests for Special Education is the fourth edition of this book on testing. It maintains the same basic format as its predecessors, *A Guide to 65 Tests* (1980), *A Guide to 75 Tests* (1984), and *A Guide to 85 Tests* (1990), in that it discusses trends and issues in testing and reviews of specific tests used at the Children's Health Council and the Morrissey–Compton Educational Center.

A Guide to 100 Tests for Special Education has three primary purposes. First, it enables teachers, therapists, and administrators to interpret reports on students evaluated by other examiners. Each Chapter of *100 Tests* concentrates on a specific area of assessment so that the reader can quickly locate a test and find out what skill it measures, how the test measures the skill, and what the test scores mean.

100 Tests can also serve as a selection guide for professionals who are purchasing tests for use with specific types of students. No book of tests is ever complete, and *100 Tests* could easily be *1,000*. Tests have been selected because of their wide usage or their unique strengths in specific areas. Enough information is given to allow professionals to compare several tests that measure a specific skill and select the most appropriate instruments for their population of students or their research needs.

The third purpose of *100 Tests* is to improve communication between the people giving the tests and the people using the test results to plan and implement programs—that is, the teachers and therapists. Although the book was not specifically written for parents, many parents have reported that previous editions have helped them to understand the evaluation reports of their children. A glossary of testing terms is included to facilitate this communication process.

A Guide to 100 Tests for Special Education begins with a section titled "Granddaddies." The test reviews in this section represent tests published in the 1960s when the field of assessment in special education was in a period of rapid growth and expansion. For the first time, tests were being designed specifically for the purpose of evaluating the skills of children with special needs. The tests in "Granddaddies" were exciting contributions to the field of testing and taught us much. Some have been revised and some are no longer published, but they all made great contributions to the field.

Chapters One through Six contain tests for the following areas of special education: Academics; Perception, Memory and Visual Motors Skills; Speech and Language; Bilingual Language; Gross and Fine Motor Skills; and General Intelligence and Developmental Scales. Test batteries often include tests from several skill areas. In such cases, the test reviews appear in the chapter of their primary purpose.

Two new chapters have been added to this edition. Chapter Seven provides an overview of the assessment of children with Attention-Deficit/Hyperactivity Disorder. Descriptions of commonly used behavior rating scales are included. Chapter Eight briefly describes Neuropsychological Assessment, including two well-known batteries for this type of evaluation. These chapters are intended to give the reader an introduction to these two fields, which are expanding rapidly.

A Guide to 100 Tests for Special Education was written by clinicians, each of whom is involved on a daily basis in the assessment of students with special needs. Over the years, my colleagues have authored test reviews and made other valuable contributions to the writing of this book. I appreciate their work not only on the test reviews, but even more in their continuing efforts to use the assessment process to help students obtain the services and teaching they need. These dedicated professionals are:

Joan Bisagno, Ph.D., Psychologist and Learning Disability Specialist

Polly Bredt, M.A.,C.C.C., Speech and Language Pathologist

Barbara Fourt, M.A., OTR, Registered Occupational Therapist and Vocational Specialist

Beth Harper, OTR, Registered Occupational Therapist

Marsha Silver, M.S., C.C.C., Speech and Language Therapist

I would also like to recognize the work of my assistant, Julia Meijer, who brought many organizational skills to this project and, in turn, was introduced to the world of assessment.

Carolyn Compton

Introduction

Educational assessment, in its broadest sense, is the gathering of information about a student's performance in school. When the student's performance is deemed inadequate, educational diagnosis is used to investigate and define the student's particular pattern of academic strengths and skill deficiencies and to translate them into an individualized program. The diagnostician uses many tools—observation, interview, diagnostic teaching, and testing. Testing, then, is just one part of educational assessment.

This book reviews the instruments of educational testing and their uses and misuses, within the total process of educational assessment for students in academic difficulty because of learning disabilities and/or related problems.

tional Record Bureau (ERB) (1992) give teachers and parents important information about students' progress from year to year and about their academic relationship to other students at the same age and grade level.

But questions about an individual student's specific strengths and weaknesses are not easily answered by group achievement tests. Particularly for students with difficulties in academic areas, individual testing is essential to discover the pattern of strengths and weaknesses. This discovery can then lead to the development of an individual instructional program. Educational tests for students in academic difficulty have four main functions: screening, diagnosis, instructional planning, and measuring progress.

PURPOSE OF TESTING

The general purpose of educational testing is to answer educationally relevant questions about a student. Broadly, these questions are:

• What is the student's current functioning level in basic skills?

• What are the student's specific skill deficiencies, if any?

• What are the student's strengths?

• What and how shall the student be taught?

• How well is the student progressing?

The general school testing program attempts to answer these questions through group achievement tests given periodically throughout the grades. Such tests as the California Achievement tests (Tiegs and Clark, 1970), and the Educa-

Screening

The first phase of the diagnostic process is screening. A test or series of tests is given to a group of students who have something in common — age, grade level, or signs of a special problem, such as deficient fine-motor coordination or poor reading performance. The results from screening tests provide a first look at a group of students to determine temporary groupings or to identify students in need of further testing. Kindergarten screening, for example, is popular in many districts as a means of determining which children may have difficulty in first grade. The goal of any screening program is to identify students in need of further individual diagnostic testing. The essence of screening is its quickness; therefore, test items must be carefully selected to measure critical skills.

Because most students who are screened do not receive further testing, we must take care to ensure that the screening procedures will properly identify those students in need of further evaluation. False positives—students identified as having disabilities when they do not—and false negatives—students with difficulties who slip through the screening process—are both serious problems. False positives can be corrected by referrals for individual testing, but false negatives do not get that opportunity.

Diagnostic Testing

In contrast to screening, diagnostic testing is usually a lengthy individual process. A battery of tests assesses the student's functioning not only in basic academic skills but also in processes believed to be essential for all learning—perception, memory, concept development, visual-motor skills, language development, and expressive skills. These tests assess the primary modalities used in the learning process—auditory, visual, and kinesthetic (or motor). Some attention is given to a possible cause for the academic problems, but much more attention is given to a description of their type and degree of severity.

The most common purpose of diagnostic testing is to determine a student's eligibility for special education services and programs. Pursuant to Public Law 94-192 (The Education for All Handicapped Children Act) and its most recent reauthorization, the Individuals with Disabilities Education Act (IDEA, 1990), every state has a set of rules and regulations that specify who is handicapped and what eligibility criteria a student must demonstrate to receive special education services.

In the case of students with specific learning disabilities, the eligibility criteria require that the student's test performance demonstrate a significant discrepancy between ability and achievement. While this discrepancy may be defined differently in different states, the process by which it is determined is diagnostic testing. What results from diagnostic testing is often, then, a placement decision. Students are admitted to or excluded from special programs, retained, placed in private schools, or referred for medical and psychological services on the basis of diagnostic testing. Thus, it must be carried out thoughtfully by experienced professionals who understand the importance of careful diagnostic decisions.

Instructional Planning

Following the diagnostic testing process and the placement decision, the instructional planning phase begins. While the information obtained from diagnostic tests is useful, rarely does it provide information specific enough for individual instructional planning. This planning is usually done by the special education teacher, who often needs to gather more specific information through informal inventories and curriculum-based assessment procedures.

Assessment, including educational testing, is an integral part of special education. It is the process that determines which students we work with, how we work with them, and how long they continue in our programs. Educational testing should never become too routine. Every student tested deserves to have an appropriate, well thought-out assessment planned and implemented. Critical decisions will be based on the result.

Measuring Progress

The final function of educational testing is to assess progress. Measuring pupil progress includes pre- and post-testing on formal and informal tests, daily charting of performance on specific tasks, and observing student performance in the classroom. Standardized tests, informal tests, rating scales, portfolio assessment, and curriculum-based assessment procedures are all used for this purpose.

TYPES OF TESTS

There are many types of tests. To plan an appropriate testing program, one must understand the essential characteristics of each type.

Formal and Informal Tests

Formal tests are more appropriately called *standardized tests*. These may be group or individual tests. They have standardized procedures for administration, timing, and scoring. They are normed on a representative sample of students and may provide age and grade-level scores as well as standard scores, or percentiles, that allow the educator to compare a student with other students of the same age and grade. Once the standardized procedure has been altered, the norms are no longer valid, and legitimate comparisons cannot be made. Another term for formal or standardized tests is *norm-referenced tests*.

Informal testing does not produce normed scores. Informal tests are structured observations that appraise the student's performance without reference to other students. Informal tests are usually administered individually. Because there are no norms, the teacher can modify the test format, the timing, and the administration procedures to allow the student the best opportunity to demonstrate his or her skills. Test items can be selected to best reflect the curriculum being taught. Because the tests are not normed, interpretation of the results is very dependent on the skills of the examiner.

Individual and Group Tests

Some tests are designed to be administered individually, while others may be given to groups of students. Group tests save administration time and student time. They are appropriate instruments for assessing achievement in such skill areas as reading comprehension and math computation. They also measure student behaviors, such as persistence, pacing, and the ability to follow group instruction or to work independently. Often, learning-disabled and other special education students are exempted from group tests. As a result, their repertoires of group test-taking strategies are not well developed.

Individual tests generally allow the student more opportunities to demonstrate his or her skills. The examiner can establish rapport with the student and provide breaks to decrease anxiety or fatigue. The examiner also has more opportunity to clarify instructions and to encourage the student lacking in confidence. If presented skillfully, a test can hold the student's interest, and the examiner can elicit cooperation without deviating from standardized procedures. For these reasons, individual tests are recommended and usually required for the diagnosis of learning disabilities and other academic problems.

Diagnostic and Achievement Tests

Diagnostic and achievement tests can be either standardized or informal, group or individual. Diagnostic tests are designed to determine whether a student has a specific learning disability and, if so, in what skill area or learning process it occurs. Some diagnostic tests, such as the Key Math Diagnostic Arithmetic Test, measure one specific academic skill area in depth. Others, such as the Developmental Test of Visual Perception, attempt to assess several subskills of an important learning process. In diagnostic testing, observations of how the student does a task and the types of errors made are as important as the score. For this reason, individual diagnostic tests are usually more valuable than group tests in determining which students may have learning disabilities and in planning their instruction.

Achievement tests are designed to measure a student's present functioning level in basic academic skills. Items are selected to represent typical curriculum materials at specific grade levels. For example, a spelling test would include a graded list of words to be dictated by the examiner and written by the student. The score would reflect the student's present functioning level in spelling and suggest the instruc-

tional level. Evaluation of the student's error pattern on an achievement test is possible but not as easy as on a diagnostic test designed for that purpose. Achievement tests are often group tests, usually standardized and norm-referenced. They reflect curriculum content in a single area, such as mathematics, or in multiple areas, such as reading, mathematics, and spelling.

Aptitude Tests

Aptitude tests are usually thought to be synonymous with intelligence tests in that they presumably measure innate capacity or potential, in contrast to achievement tests, which measure learning. However, most theoreticians agree that the distinctions between intelligence/aptitude and achievement are not very meaningful. They have come to use the term *developed abilities* to reflect the widely accepted view that aptitude tests also assess learning.

Although theoreticians may choose to blend the terms, test titles continue to imply that the words have different meanings. The Wechsler Intelligence Scale for Children and The Detroit Test of Learning Aptitude are felt to measure broader concepts, while the Wide Range Achievement Tests clearly assess school learning. Also, the aptitude/achievement discrepancy, which demonstrates the belief that the words have different meanings, continues to be the primary characteristic of a specific learning disability. Anastasi's (1980) distinction is probably the most widely accepted. She uses the term *aptitude* to mean the broader, less-controlled learning that takes place both in and out of school, while achievement tests assess the narrower learning typically acquired in school.

FUNCTIONAL ASSESSMENT

Over the years, traditional norm-referenced tests have been repeatedly criticized. These criticisms have focused primarily on three areas. In the 1970s and 1980s, the criticisms centered on the poor technical characteristics of the tests. Standardization samples were not large enough or representative of the U.S. population. Tests that were normed on small, select populations gained widespread use with students for whom the test had never been developed. Test reliability was low, and validity was unproved. Critically important decisions, such as the eligibility for and placement in special education programs of individual children, were made on the basis of technically inadequate tests. Test writers were criticized for their lack of theory and empirical research. Many of these criticisms were justified, and while test construction has definitely improved in the past five to ten years, the fact remains that many poorly standardized, unreliable tests with unproved validity are still in frequent use.

A second area of sustained criticism over the years has been the concern that many tests assess "modality-strengths" or "processing skills," constructs that have no standard definitions and little application to classroom instruction. Several of the tests in the Granddaddies chapter of this book assessed such processes as auditory discrimination, visual closure, and auditory association. Elaborate remediation programs were developed to train such processes, which formed the basis of individualized instruction in special education classrooms. Despite the consistent criticism of modality and process assessment, the concept has not gone away. More than 60 percent of the tests included in this book (and many not reviewed) include the assessment of process modality constructs either as a primary focus or in related subtests. The term *processing disorder* is commonly used in the description of students with learning disabilities. In at least one state, California, a documented processing disorder is required in the determination of eligibility for special education services.

The current criticism of norm-referenced tests focuses on their lack of authenticity and their lack of utility in helping teachers improve instruction (Shepard, 1991). Members of the Executive Committee for Children with Behavior Disorders (1981) emphasized the need to move away from norm-referenced tests to a more "functional assessment" that relates more directly to student performance. The functional approach included:

• direct observation of the learning environment, sometimes called ecological assessment;
• curriculum-based assessment; and
• an analysis of student work products, known as authentic, or portfolio, assessment.

Ecological Assessment

Learning is an interactive process between the student and the environment. While traditional testing approaches focus on the student, ecological assessment focuses on the environment. Information gained from the direct assessment of the classroom can produce information that can be used in designing instructional techniques or modifying the curriculum (Welch, 1994).

Checklists and rating scales are the primary tools of ecological assessments. Such instruments as the Instructional Priority System (Welch and Link, 1991) and the Analysis of Classroom and Instructional Designs (West, 1990) can be purchased, or teachers and other specialists can design their own informal assessments. Observations of such variables as use of materials, teaching format, student grouping, feed-back procedures, and homework are used to develop information that can be used to formulate teaching strategies for an individual student in a classroom. Ecological assessment is a systematized form of classroom observation that, when used in collaboration with teachers, has important information to bring to the instructional planning process.

Curriculum-Based Assessment (CBA)

Curriculum-based assessment (CBA) has become increasingly popular during the past ten years. Its strongest feature—allowing teachers to assess the extent to which the child is learning the curriculum being taught—is intrinsically interesting. CBA methodologies have three common features (Fuchs and Deno, 1994):

1. Student proficiency must be sampled in material from the classroom curriculum.

2. Assessments must occur over a period of time.

3. Information must be used to formulate instructional decisions.

Developing a CBA process requires several steps (Batt, 1990). The first step is to determine what will be taught, i.e., what will be the curriculum in a given subject area. Next, the teacher must analyze the curriculum and formulate behavioral objectives. Then, the teacher must develop appropriate assessment procedures and implement them on an appropriate schedule (daily, weekly, monthly). Determining a way to collect, store, and summarize data is an important next step. Finally, the data must be interpreted and used to make decisions. Given the complexity of the process, it is not surprising that in a survey of teachers with knowledge of the importance of direct and frequent measurement, nearly half did not use CBA in their classrooms (Wesson, King, and Deno, 1984). The primary reason given was that it was too time consuming.

In addition to the investment of time required of teachers, there are other concerns about CBA. Fuchs and Deno (1994) reviewed the research on CBA and summarized the advantages and disadvantages of assessing student progress in the curriculum that they are being taught. The primary advantage seems to be that teacher-made assessments have face validity—they seem sensible to teachers who are more likely to use the assessments to modify instruction. There are, however, several disadvantages to CBA:

1. Curriculum materials have a high degree of variability, and it is difficult to find a passage or problem for assessment that is representative.

2. Students' perceived progress may be due to familiarity with the curriculum format.

3. It is unclear how well decisions within a target curriculum will generalize to other curriculums.

As more teachers are trained to develop CBA procedures in their classrooms and are given the assistance and technology to do it well, CBA may become an increasingly valuable tool.

Portfolio-Based Assessment

Portfolio-based assessment is an alternative to norm-based, standardized testing procedures. The portfolio assessment has been described as a case study approach to assessment. It involves the systematic collection of student work and other documents that reflect change and growth. Swicegood (1994) describes four types of information that a portfolio for a student with learning or behavioral problems might include:

1. Measures of behavior and adaptive functioning, including anecdotal records, behavioral checklists, peer ratings, and sociograms;

2. Measures of academic and literary growth, including classroom work, curriculum-based assessments, writing samples, and photographs of student projects;

3. Measures of strategic learning and self-regulation, including behavioral plans, student self-evaluations, and observations and ratings of study skills; and

4. Measures of language and cultural aspects, including cultural interviews with students and parents and primary language samples.

Students would be actively involved in deciding what information would go into a portfolio and how it would reflect important information. The team of professionals involved in the student's program would review the portfolio to make decisions regarding instructional and behavioral strategies. Portfolios would also provide to parents easily understood information about student strengths and growth.

While portfolio-based assessment provides an alternative assessment procedure that is directly related to classroom performance, it does not provide the objective data on academic skills that is more easily and appropriately obtained from standardized tests.

Many of the criticisms of norm-referenced, standardized tests are well taken. However, these tests also have many advantages. They allow comparisons between an individual student's performance, that of his or her classmates, and that of a group of age-mates in the standardization sample. In practice, eligibility and placement decisions are based on the results of standardized, norm-referenced tests. While the alternative assessment processes described above may provide the teacher with information that is more directly applicable to instruction and classroom management, norm-referenced tests supply an equally important perspective. The combining of a standardized testing process with alternative assessment processes can give the most comprehensive picture of a student's performance.

ABUSES AND MISUSES OF TESTS

Many of the criticisms of educational tests are legitimate; in many instances, tests have been abused and misused. One problem area in educational testing is the confusion of terms. As mentioned earlier, *assessment* is the total process of gathering information about a student's performance in school; *diagnosis* is one part of that process, and the diagnostician uses *testing* as one tool. Basing educational decisions on test results alone, without using the other tools of the diagnostician—observation, interview, and diagnostic teaching—is a misuse of tests. Viewing diagnosis as a once-only process, rather than a continuous procedure, is also a common error.

Anastasiow (1973, p. 349) describes four other consistent abuses of tests:

1. Generalizing the interpretation of test scores to groups not represented in the norming sample;

2. Over-interpreting scores—for example, focusing on a five-point gain in IQ score when five points is not statistically significant;

3. Teaching the answers to test questions in the belief that an improved test score alone will demonstrate pupil progress; and

4. Violating student confidentiality and privacy by revealing test scores to persons not directly involved with the educational program.

Test selection is an important step in the assessment process. A poor choice of instruments may lead to unreliable, invalid, or unuseful data. The following questions should be considered in test selection:

1. Does the standardization of the test include students of the type to be tested?

2. Does the test have strong technical characteristics, such as reliability, validity, and recent norms?

3. Does the test provide a complete measure of the skill being assessed? If not, are measures of different aspects of that skill included in the battery?

4. Has the test been given too recently to be valid?

Hammill (1991, p. 32) reminds us that tests don't diagnose; people do. Test results are simply observations of an individual's performance level at a given time under a given set of circumstances. Students are not mentally retarded because they have low scores on a test of cognitive ability; students are not learning disabled because their scores fit a discrepancy formula. Test results provide useful data, but the skills and experience of the examiner are the most important factors in the assessment process.

Testing is simply one diagnostic tool. When tests are part of a well-designed assessment procedure planned and implemented by skilled, sensitive professionals, they provide important information about a student. But tests selected, administered, and interpreted incorrectly are worse than useless: They lead to incorrect and inappropriate programs and placement.

Table 1. Academic Skill Areas

Reading

Decoding
  Phonic skills
  Sight-word recognition
  Oral paragraph reading

Comprehension
  Oral reading
  Silent reading
  Listening
  Comprehension in specific content areas

Writing

Penmanship
  Manuscript
  Cursive

Written Expression
  Fluency
  Syntax
  Mechanics
  Content

Spelling

Written
  Phonic words
  Irregular words

Recognition of Sight Words
Oral

Mathematics

Concepts
Computation
  Addition
  Subtraction
  Multiplication
  Division

Word Problems
  Oral
  Written

Oral Language

Receptive
  Vocabualry
  Listening comprehension

Expressive
  Articulation
  Morphology
  Syntax
  Semantics
  Pragmatics

THE DIAGNOSTIC BATTERY

A major group of students for whom educational assessment is needed are those in academic difficulty because of suspected learning disabilities. The task of the diagnostician is to determine whether a student's academic problems are related to specific learning disabilities and, if so, what the nature and the degree of the disabilities are. From this information, a specific instructional program may be designed.

In designing a diagnostic testing battery for a student with suspected learning disabilities, the diagnostician must consider academic skill areas, learning processes and modalities, and the time and personnel available for testing.

Academic Skill Areas

If time and personnel are not an issue, what academic skill areas should be assessed in a complete educational evaluation? Table 1 serves as a guide to the major academic skill areas and their subgroups.

Each of these major areas could be further broken down into multiple subskills. Testing could go on forever, and sometimes, from the point of view of the parents, the student, and the teacher who referred the student, it seems as though it does. Fortunately, the constraints of time and personnel force some decisions about what areas should be assessed. Such decisions should be made by considering the following factors:

• *The concerns of the teacher or the parent in the referral or testing request.* If a student is referred because of difficulties in reading and spelling but exhibits superior math skills, the diagnostician may do a quick math screening but focus the evaluation on reading, writing, and spelling.

• *The age and grade of the student.* If the student is in first or second grade, the reading evaluation will focus on phonic skills, sight-word recognition, and oral reading rather than on advanced word analysis skills or silent reading comprehension.

• *Relevance of the area to classroom performance.* Oral spelling and oral math are often omitted because of their low frequency as classroom tasks. Similarly, written expression, an essential skill, should always be included.

Learning Processes and Modalities

The second factor to consider in designing the diagnostic battery for an individual student is the student's pattern of strengths and weaknesses in processing information in the primary learning modalities—auditory, visual, and kinesthetic or motor. As stated above, process/modality assessment has attracted great criticism over the years because the information gained has shown little relationship to academic program planning. However, it is standard practice to include tests of auditory perception, memory, and comprehension, as well as tests of visual perception, memory, and comprehension, in the diagnostic battery for students with known, or suspected, learning disabilities. Measures of visual motor functioning are also widely used. Test instruments for process/modality assessment are improving in technical quality and usefulness to the diagnostician and the classroom teacher.

Time and Personnel Available

The practicalities of time and personnel clearly affect the selection of tests in the diagnostic battery. Two hours of individual educational testing is generally considered a minimum amount of time for a basic educational evaluation; three to four hours would be more usual. Students with major learning disabilities, students who work slowly, or students who need frequent breaks and much encouragement often need several short testing sessions. Overtesting should be avoided: not only is it time consuming, but it rarely leads to significantly more educationally relevant information.

Educational assessment is frequently done by a diagnostic team. The psychologist usually administers general intelligence tests and often tests of visual-motor development. The language therapist assesses receptive and expressive language skill, articulation, and auditory processing. The educational diagnostician tests academic performance and related learning processes. A perceptual-motor specialist examines gross and fine motor skills. When the educational diagnostician is a one-person team, the test battery must include a broader range of tests, particularly in the areas of concept development, language, and motor skills.

SPECIAL ISSUES IN TESTING
The Use of Grade Level Scores

The type of test score most frequently reported by educational diagnosticians is the grade-level, or grade-equivalent, score. Even when percentiles and standard scores are provided in the test manual, many educational reports include only the grade scores. The reason for this is the easy communicability of the grade score; students, parents, and teachers all feel they understand its meaning. Despite repeated criticism of this procedure by experts in test construction, the practice has continued.

In the last edition of this book, *A Guide to 85 Tests for Special Education* (1990), many of the new and revised tests reviewed were dropping grade-equivalent scores from their manuals. Pro-Ed, publishers of many widely used tests, was a primary example. Many of their manuals included the following statement:

"Because the continued use of grade norms is professionally indefensible, the Board of Directors of the International Reading Association in 1980 has asked (1) that examiners abandon the practice of reporting and interpreting test performance in grade equivalents, and (2) that test authors and publishers eliminate such norms from tests (Brown, Hammill, and Wiederholt, 1978)."

In many of the new and revised tests reviewed in this volume, however, grade-equivalent scores are again available. Pro-Ed test manuals explain that they changed their policy because many test users noted that their state guidelines mandated that achievement-test scores be reported in terms of grade equivalents. In these states, eligibility for special education services is determined by the number of months and years a student is "behind" his current grade placement; "two years below grade level" is a commonly accepted criterion for eligibility for services in a program for students with learning disabilities.

Table 2. Process-Modality Chart

Modality	Process				
	Reception (initial receiving of information)	**Perception** (initial organizing of information)	**Association** (relating new information to other information)	**Memory** (short-term, sequential memory)	**Expression** (output)
Auditory					**Verbal Expression**
Visual (primary stimuli are visual)					**Written expression**
Tactile/Kinesthetic (primary stimuli accompanied by motoric input)					**Motoric expression other than written or verbal**

It is unfortunate that grade-level scores continue to be used as measures of a student's level of academic functioning, and it is important for examiners and consumers to know why grade-level scores are inappropriate.

Grade-level scores represent the average score of students in the sampling population at that grade level. In other words, Tom's grade level score of 6.3 says nothing about his ability to read sixth-grade material. It says that his raw score on the test was the same as the average score of all the students in the third month of sixth grade who took the test when it was standardized.

Several other points about grade scores are important to keep in mind:

• They are not an equal-interval scale; the difference between grade levels 3.4 and 3.5 may be very different from the difference between grade levels 8.5 and 8.6, or even between 3.5 and 3.6.

• They cannot be added and subtracted as raw scores, and standard scores can.

• They cannot be compared with a student's current grade placement.

• They cannot be used to measure progress. If a student obtains a grade score of 4.6 in September and on the same test in the spring receives a 5.0, we cannot say that the student has made four month's progress. Months in school are not equal intervals; October is not the same as December; July (when school is usually not in session) is not the same as May. Grade scores cannot be added and subtracted because they are not equal intervals.

The implications of these facts are very clear. An examiner or teacher should never report only grade scores when standard scores and percentiles are available; preferably, he or she should report the standard scores and percentiles and omit the grade scores. If a test yields only grade scores, it should not be used. If it must be used, the results should be reported only through discussion and without scores.

While the above paragraphs deal with the grade-level or grade-equivalent score, it is important to note that the same misinterpretations are equally applicable to the age-level or age-equivalent score.

Evaluating Progress

Evaluating pupil progress is an essential part of every program for students with academic difficulties. Accountability demands that educators evaluate programs in terms of pupil progress, but measuring an individual student's growth is often not a simple process. While there are many classroom-based assessment procedures that are useful in measuring progress, standardized tests can also add important information. The selection of standardized tests that will not only provide valuable diagnostic information but also prove to be effective measures of pupil progress takes forethought and

planning. The following factors may serve as general guidelines:

• Selecting tests that have alternate forms for retesting purposes is helpful only if the two forms have good statistical equivalency. In some tests, Form A or B frequently "seems" easier or usually results in higher or lower scores. Such inconsistencies defeat the purpose of alternate forms. Research studies on "practice effect" are inconclusive with normal children, and even less is known about the practice effect of frequent test administrations with exceptional children, the most tested group.

• Selecting an individual test, such as the Woodcock–Johnson Psycho-Educational Battery, or a coordinated series of tests, such as the Gates–MacGinitie Reading Tests, that covers a wide age range allows for a measure of progress from year to year on the same instrument.

• Selecting tests with an appropriate level of difficulty is necessary in determining student progress. A test that is too hard or too easy gives little information on growth.

• Tests of progress should reflect the curriculum content. For example, oral reading tests usually include a high percentage of sight words. If students have been taught all year in a systematic phonics program, retest scores may not reflect students' progress because exposure to sight words has been minimal. In this case, a measure of phonic skills that reflects the curriculum should be included in the retesting procedures. Testing oral reading with a timed test, when reading speed has not been emphasized by the classroom teacher, is another example of an impractical way to measure student progress.

• Reliability is a critical factor in selecting measures of pupil progress. In addition to the factors within the student and the test that affect reliability (discussed earlier), the teacher needs to be aware of several other reliability factors that affect the measurement of progress. Difference scores are frequently used to document pupil progress; that is, a student is given a test in September and is then given the same test (or its equivalent form) in May. The lower score is subtracted from the higher score, and the resulting difference score is used as an indication of growth or lack of progress. But several precautions are needed for this procedure. First, grade scores and percentile scores are not based on an equal-interval scale and should not be used for calculating differences. Raw or standard scores should be used. Second, difference scores are the most unreliable of test scores because they combine the measurement errors of both test scores. Small gains or losses in achievement may not be reliable or statistically significant. Finally, difference scores that do reach statistical significance may not make any practical difference in instructional level and should not be overplayed.

• Tests with many subtests are particularly difficult to

interpret in terms of student progress. Changes in the total test score often are used to document progress. However, total test scores are usually obtained by summing several subtest scores. Such a procedure often obscures progress in certain skills and lack of progress in others.

• Criterion-referenced tests provide important measures of pupil progress and should certainly be included together with well-selected standardized tests.

Determining Instructional Level

Test scores do not always make clear the level at which instruction should begin. Tests yield achievement scores, which may or may not be helpful when deciding placement in a reading series. "Most series are not constructed according to readability formulas but rather according to a sequence of skills developed by the authors" (Lesiak and Johnson, 1983). Careful study of a student's test protocols yields important information about the type of reading series to select, but having the student read aloud a graded set of paragraphs from that series is the most useful process for determining instructional level.

In 1946, Betts (pp. 445-454) divided reading levels into categories dependent on the student's accuracy rate that are still our best guide for determining instructional level.

1. *Basal or independent level.* Student reads with 99 percent accuracy and 90 percent comprehension. Oral reading is fluent and well phrased. The student is free from tension and free to think about the content because he or she is totally in control of the vocabulary, the sentence construction, and the content.

2. *Instructional level.* Student reads with 95 percent accuracy and 75 percent comprehension. He or she can use word analysis skills and makes good progress with teacher guidance.

3. *Frustration level.* Student reads with less than 90 percent accuracy and less than 50 percent comprehension. He or she becomes easily bogged down, tense, distractable, and sometimes resistive.

Bett's levels are very relevant for planning classroom instruction. Many, many students are being instructed in materials at their frustration level; that is, they are misreading more than one word in every 10. Halting and struggling over almost every word, they become very tense. This is not instruction; it is frustration.

Lesiak and Johnson (1983, pp. 12-17) describe two processes for placing a student in the appropriate reader. They are the informal reading inventory which uses Bett's levels, and a cloze test. In this procedure, graded passages are selected for oral reading and then every fifth word is deleted. The student supplies the word as he or she reads aloud. Independent Level requires at least 50 percent accuracy; Instructional Level is 30-50 percent, and Frustration

Level below 30 percent accuracy. Several reading tests reviewed in Chapter One utilize a similar cloze procedure.

Students with good phonics instructions will often read with approximately the same accuracy rate in materials at a wide range of grade levels. In such cases, instructional level should be the highest level at which the student has 75 percent comprehension. Students with reading disabilities of the dyslexic type often make errors on little words (*the, he, they, from*). Their accuracy rate may also be the same across several grade levels, and they should be instructed at the highest level of good (75 percent) comprehension.

The Diagnostic Report

One of the primary differences between the assessment process in the public schools and assessments performed by private psychologists, speech and language pathologists, or educational specialists is the written report. In assessments completed in public schools, the results of the assessment are usually reported as part of the Individual Education Plan (IEP). The IEP is typically a standard form that provides a space for recording test data and describing the student's eligibility for services. It then goes on to indicate the program in which the student will be placed and instructional goals and objectives.

The written report of a private specialist is very different. Ranging in length from three to ten pages, the report typically contains the following sections:

1. Identifying data
2. Reason for referral; purpose of testing
3. Behavioral observations during testing
4. Tests administered
5. Test results
6. Analysis of test results
7. Summary and diagnosis
8. Recommendations

In addition to the important sections on reason for referral and behavioral observations, the essence of the test report is contained in the analysis of the test results. The examiner discusses the student's performance on each test, summarizes the student's strengths and weaknesses in skills, and analyzes the various learning processes assessed. Examples are given to illustrate the kinds of errors the student has made. The examiner describes in detail the specific tasks the student has not mastered and summarizes the error pattern.

The summary statement then reviews essential information about the student, reasons for referral, and test performance. The summary concludes with a specific statement of classification or a diagnosis (Is the student mentally retarded? Does the student have a specific learning disability?). While the report may recommend that a student be considered for special education placement, only the Individual Education Planning team can determine eligibility.

Recommendations typically include a placement recommendation as well as teaching suggestions. In a well-written report, the recommendations flow logically from the description of the behavior and performance. The suggestions for teaching are based on task analysis and error analysis. They should incorporate analyses of the student's interests and strengths. They lead the teacher directly into curriculum planning. This section may also specify a date for reevaluation.

The purpose of the written report is to communicate information about a student's performance that will enable teachers to plan and implement an appropriate instructional program and to communicate information to parents about their child's performance. As such it is a critical document, one deserving of time and effort in preparation.

Communicating Test Results to Parents

In addition to providing information to the student's classroom teacher, the assessment process should help parents understand their child. Conveying the results of the diagnostic assessment to parents is usually the responsibility of the special educational administrator, teacher, or psychologist. Conducting a parent conference that conveys clear and helpful information to parents is a very important skill.

Parents want to have the right to know whatever you know about their child's abilities and disabilities. They have the right to know your concerns and to express theirs. They need to have all of the information necessary to participate knowledgeably in any decision being made about their child's placement and program. This means that professionals involved in the assessment process have the responsibility to convey clear and accurate information. This does not mean giving the parents a list of numerical scores that have little meaning for them. Nor does it mean describing in detail a child's problems in terms like *perceptual disturbance* or *auditory closure*. Nor does it mean talking with parents in such generalities ("Yes, Tom is a little behind in math") that they leave the office uncertain of the results of the assessment. The balance between being too technical and too general is very difficult, but essential, to achieve.

Some parents ask for specific numbers and terms. What is their child's IQ? At what grade level is he or she reading? Is the child dyslexic? Brain damaged? Others ask few questions. But beneath the specific questions and the unasked questions, parents of all levels of sophistication are basically asking, Is something the matter with my child? What is it? Is the child going to be all right? What is the school going to do? How can we help?

The following guidelines can be used in preparing for a parent conference:

- Think about the most important information you want to share with the parents about their child. Be sure that the information is presented clearly and does not get lost in a morass of numbers and descriptions of behavior.

- Be certain you know what your recommendations will be. If the assessments have been done by a team, come to an agreement about recommendations before the parent conference. Parents want to hear the professional recommendations—not four conflicting views.

- Have all the information ready for the parent conference. Come prepared to answer such questions as, Who is the teacher of the special class? When can we observe? Do you know a good math tutor? How do we go about getting some counseling?

In a recent study titled "What Parents of the Learning Disabled Really Want from Professionals," Dembinski and Mauser (1977, p. 53) found that parents wanted professionals (teachers, psychologists, and physicians) to use terminology they could understand. They overwhelmingly disapproved of professional jargon. But the use of educational and psychological jargon is such a part of the professional role that teachers and psychologists must make a conscious effort not to overwhelm the parents with "jargonese." The following techniques have proven helpful:

- Review with the parents the reasons for referral and the school's concerns about the child. If the parents initiated the assessment, ask them to restate their concerns. Review the assessment process. Name the professionals who worked with the child and explain what they did. Be certain the parents know the names and understand the roles of all the people involved in the assessment process.

- Show the parents a few of the actual test items to demonstrate the task the student was asked to perform and the performance. Be certain to include examples of both the student's strengths and deficits. Rockowitz and Davidson (1979, p. 6) found it was better to present information abaout the child's strengths early in the conference. Too often, parents cannot hear the good news after a discussion of problems.

- Illustrate with examples how the student's skill deficiencies may be noted in the classroom, at home, and with friends.

- Encourage parent questions and comments by your manner. Try to draw both parents into the discussion. Be certain to schedule enough time for questions and discussion.

- Don't avoid using terms such as *mental retardation, learning disability, dyslexia,* or *aphasia* if your evaluation clearly supports the diagnosis. Rockowitz and Davidson (1979, p. 6) echo the finding of several researchers that parents need a name for their child's problems.

- Give parents a written report. With some parents it is better to discuss the report point by point; with others it is better to just talk about the assessment results and have them read the report later. Explain clearly in the body of the report or on an attached sheet the meaning of terms such as *grade score, standard score, stanine,* and *percentile.*

- Before concluding, ask the parents to restate what they have learned from the conference. This gives the professional a chance to clarify any misconceptions.

- End the conference with a clear plan of what will happen next and whose responsibility it is to carry out each part of the process. Be aware of parents' feelings, and don't press them to make decisions until they have had a chance to think it over and talk to others.

TRENDS IN ASSESSMENT

As discussed earlier in this introduction, assessment in special education is placing a significant emphasis on the development of instruments that provide information that is directly related to classroom instruction. Ecological evaluation, curriculum-based assessment, and portfolio assessment are three examples. Directly related to this trend is the development of the technological tools for assessment and data collection.

Technological Assessment

Without question, the most important trend in testing is the use of technology-based assessment. *Technology-based assessment* generally refers to the use of electronic systems and software to assess and evaluate the progress of individual children in educational settings (Greenwood and Rieth, 1994). It encompasses the development of electronic versions of traditional assessment tools through the use of personal computers and videos, as well as innovative assessment procedures designed to utilize electronic technology.

Technology-based assessment provides special educators with the capability to move away from norm-referenced tests to individually designed measures of learning that relate directly to instructional planning. It is the basis of what is called dynamic assessment, the assessment of a student's ability to benefit from instruction. Technological systems provide the data recording and storage that is essential for criterion-referenced testing and curriculum-based assessment. In the field of behavioral assessment, technology is not only used to manage classroom data, such as time on task and independent skills, but computers and video technology are also used for the training of social and work-related skills in all environments.

Technology-based assessment also increases the access of individuals with special needs to the assessment process and broadens the range of possibilities within the assessment field. As with all innovative processes, the incorporation of technology and assessment practices into a field that is traditionally the domain of individual teachers or clinicians will

be a gradual process. As stated by Greenwood and Rieth, access to and integration of technological systems with the necessary training and support is a costly process and one that will move slowly from research labs and special projects into schools and clinics. The process is just beginning, and its impact on assessment practices will change the field.

Inclusion in Assessment

The full inclusion movement in special education primarily affects placement decisions. As it grows in prominence, it will have an increasing effect on assessment practices. From 1987–1988 to 1991–1992, the proportion of special education students receiving some or all of their education in regular classrooms increased from 69 to 71 percent (Hanley, 1995). In addition, the percentage of students in "regular classrooms" as opposed to "resource rooms" increased from 29 to 35 percent. This fact, combined with The Goals 2000: Educate America Act, which focuses on standards for *all* students, has resulted in a decline in special education students exempted from state exams and national achievement tests. New guidelines from the U.S. Department of Education (1990) provide that "only students mainstreamed less than 50 percent of the time in academic subjects *and* judged incapable of participating meaningfully in the assessment" can be exempted. The Goals 2000 focuses on the improvement of education for *all* students, the development of world-class standards, and the adoption of standards-based curricula. The Goals 2000 encourages innovative and nondiscriminatory approaches to assessment and requires that assessments:

- be aligned with a state's content standards,
- involve multiple measures of student performance, and
- provide adaptations and accommodations for participation of all students with diverse learning needs.

These mandates set the stage for technology-based assessments. The mandates will force special education to move away from assessment—which focuses on diagnosis, eligibility, and placement—to instructional concerns. Technology is already providing accommodations in both presentation mode, through Braille, large print, untimed administration, and in response mode, through word processing and other computer responses. Soon, technology will address the specific content and administration of the tests themselves.

Trends in Standardized Tests

While it is likely that we will see substantial changes in the assessment field in the next few years, current practices in schools and clinics still rely heavily on standardized tests. Formal standardized testing is still the gatekeeper that determines eligibility for and access to special education. Test publishers continue to develop tests that will provide the information necessary to determine eligibility. This is exemplified by:

- a return to the inclusion of grade level scores in test manuals to fit state eligibility requirements, and

- the development of new instruments that allow the measurement of aptitude and achievement in the same test and facilitate the process of determining whether a student demonstrates an aptitude–achievement discrepancy.

Despite the criticism of process/modality assessment, old tests are being revised and new tests are being developed regularly that assess learning processes in specific modalities. The field of neuropsychology exemplifies one end of the continuum, as it is based entirely on process analysis.

Standardized tests are improving in their technical characteristics. It is ironic that while the field of test construction advances, providing diagnosticians with more and better tools, diagnosticians have less time to learn and administer them. A clear trend is the shortening of the diagnostic process. Efforts to decrease testing time are seen in two areas. First, many comprehensive batteries contain a screening process, generally the administration of two or three key subtests. The screening is intended as the first step in an assessment process to determine which students will be referred for more extensive testing. Unfortunately, sometimes, the screening test results are used for placement decisions, a misuse of test results. Secondly, computerized scoring and the generation of computerized reports is a popular feature of many new and revised tests. In their efforts to save time, examiners may forget that test results don't constitute a diagnosis. Careful analysis of behavior during testing and data from interviews and observations must be integrated with test results to form a complete assessment. There is an illusion that the computerized report completes the assessment.

In summary, assessment will continue to be an integral part of special education. Testing is a part of our society and, while the forms of the instruments may change, the process of identification of special needs, the determination of their nature and severity, and the measurement of individual progress will continue. It is a field of increasing responsibility and continual challenge.

GRANDDADDIES
A Special Group of Tests

In the early 1960s, special education began to emerge as a clear specialty within the field of education. Innovative curriculum was devised specifically for exceptional students. Prospective teachers in the field were recruited to college and university programs where departments of special education were rapidly developing. Special education began its period of rapid expansion and advancement, culminating in P.L. 94-142 and categorical programs as we know them today. Similarly, the assessment of exceptional children began to be recognized as a specialty, and tests were developed specifically to diagnose the learning and language problems of exceptional children. Many of these tests focused upon language, perceptual-motor, and memory skills, attempting to analyze the sub-skills of these major areas of learning.

Several of these tests are still published today. Their technical characteristics are inadequate for making diagnostic, eligibility, placement, or instructional planning decisions; in some cases the skills they measure have not proved relevant to classroom performance. Despite their currently-recognized inadequacies, they have contributed greatly to the field of special education assessment. These authors provided us with a beginning, the first steps in a new field, and many of our most useful current diagnostic tools are based upon their work.

These five "granddaddies" are grouped together to highlight their contributions to the field:
- Illinois Test of Psycholinguistic Abilities
- Marianne Frostig Developmental Test of Visual Perception
- Myklebust Picture Story Language Test
- Purdue Perceptual Motor Survey
- Wepman Auditory Discrimination Test

Illinois Test of Psycholinguistic Abilities (ITPA)

S. A. Kirk, J. J. McCarthy, and W. D. Kirk
University of Illinois Press, 1961; revised 1968
43 East Gregory Dr., Champaign, IL 61820
(no longer published)

Purpose	To assess how a child communicates with and receives communication from the environment and to provide a framework for planning remediation and developing instructional programs.
Major Areas Tested	Visual-motor and auditory-vocal skills
Age or Grade Range	2–10 years
Usually Given By	Psychologist Speech/language clinician
Type of Test	Standardized Individual
Scores Obtained	Age level Scaled
Student Performance Timed?	Yes (some subtests)
Testing Time	1 1/2 hours
Scoring/Interpretation Time	30–40 minutes
Normed On	962 average children from medium-sized towns and cities in the Midwest; 4 percent Black students
Alternate Forms Available?	No

FORMAT

The Illinois Test of Psycholinguistic Abilities (ITPA) materials consist of a manual, two books of test pictures, objects for description, visual-closure picture strips, and individual student record forms, all packaged in a carrying case.

The ITPA is based on Osgood's model of communication (Osgood, 1957), which postulates three dimensions to cognitive abilities: *channels* (auditory, visual, vocal, motor), *processes* (reception, association, expression), and *levels* (automatic, representational). The subtests of the ITPA represent these dimensions. There are ten basic subtests and two other supplementary tests.

The two levels postulated by Osgood are the representational and the automatic. At the *representational level* (or meaningful level), the processes of *reception, association,* and *expression* are assessed in the two major channels, auditory and visual. Functioning at the *automatic level* is assessed in the two major channels in terms of closure and sequential memory skills. The two supplementary tests provide additional information about automatic functioning

in the auditory channel. The supplementary scores are not included when deriving the total or mean scores for the test.

Precise directions for administrating and scoring each subtest are contained in the manual. Raw scores are converted to age scores and scaled scores and are recorded on the summary sheet. Scaled scores are plotted on the profile sheet to provide a graphic representation of a student's performance.

An individual's test performance may be viewed in several ways. The total of the raw scores from the ten basic subtests is converted into a "psycholinguistic age," which provides an overall index of the student's level of psycholinguistic development. The raw scores are also translated individually into scaled scores. The mean scaled score for the normative population is 36, with a standard deviation of plus or minus 6. The student's own mean is derived by averaging the scaled scores of the ten basic subtests.

Discrepancies of plus or minus 10 from the student's own mean or the median scaled score are considered substantial. Using the student's mean or median scaled score as a reference point assists the examiner in viewing strengths and weaknesses.

SUBTEST	REPRESENTATIONAL LEVEL						AUTOMATIC LEVEL					
	AUDITORY-VOCAL			VISUAL-MOTOR			AUDITORY-VOCAL			VISUAL-MOTOR		
	Raw Score	Age Score	Scaled Score	Raw Score	Age Score	Scaled Score	Raw Score	Age Score	Scaled Score	Raw Score	Age Score	Scaled Score
AUDITORY RECEPTION												
VISUAL RECEPTION												
VISUAL MEMORY												
AUDITORY ASSOCIATION												
AUDITORY MEMORY												
VISUAL ASSOCIATION												
VISUAL CLOSURE												
VERBAL EXPRESSION												
GRAMMATIC CLOSURE												
MANUAL EXPRESSION												
(Supplementary tests) AUDITORY CLOSURE												
SOUND BLENDING												

SUMMARY SCORES:

Sum of Raw Scores	Composite PLA	Sum of SS	Mean SS	Median SS

ITPA Summary Sheet

In addition, patterns of performance may be found by analyzing the results further. Several ways of doing this are described by Kirk and Kirk in *Psycholinguistic Learning Disabilities* (1971). For example:

1. *Comparison of levels of organization.* The representational-level score is obtained by averaging age scores and scaled scores of tests at the representational level. The automatic-level score is obtained by averaging age scores and scaled scores of tests at the automatic level.

2. *Comparison of channels.* The auditory-vocal score is obtained by averaging age scores and scaled scores from auditory and verbal subtests. The visual-motor score is obtained by averaging age scores and scaled scores from visual and motor subtests.

3. *Comparison of psycholinguistic processes.* Scores for reception, association, and expression are obtained by averaging scaled scores for each process.

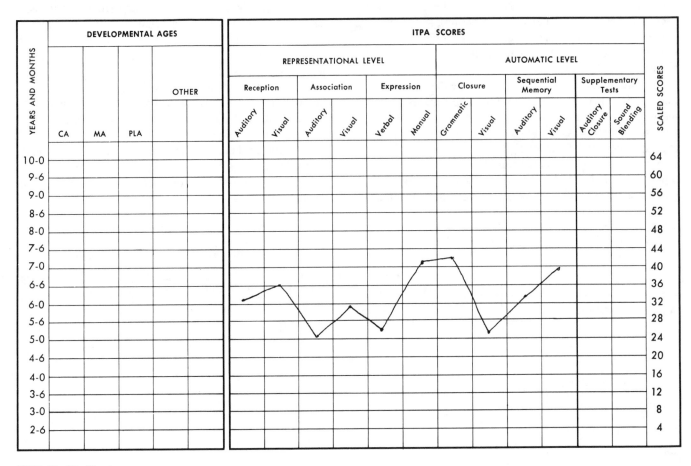

ITPA Profile Sheet

ITPA Subtests

Subtest	Description	Comments
Auditory Reception	Assesses the student's ability to derive meaning from verbally presented material. Questions of controlled length and structure are presented by the examiner. Vocabulary increases in difficulty. A simple yes or no response is required of the student. (*Do dogs eat? Do cosmetics celebrate?*)	The examiner is cautioned not to influence the student's response by inflection or facial expression. The simple response that is required makes it possible to test nonverbal children. However, some students may be tempted to give minimal involvement to the task and thereby respond in random fashion.
Visual Reception	Assesses the student's ability to match concepts presented visually. After brief exposure to a single stimulus picture, the student selects the correct match from four choices on the following page. Objects and situations conceptually similar to the stimulus are to be chosen.	Mild and moderate visual handicaps do not appear to affect performance on this subtest. It appears to measure central rather than peripheral processes (Bateman 1963).
Auditory Association	Assesses the student's ability to complete verbal analogies presented by the examiner. The vocabulary becomes more difficult as the task progresses. (*I sit on a chair; I sleep on a _____ . Years have seasons; dollars have _____ .*)	The student needs to grasp the analogy and to select the correct word that expresses it. Although included as a test of the process of association, the receptive and expressive processes are also involved. Careful analysis of a student's performance is needed to sort out the processes.
Visual Association	Assesses the student's ability to relate associated concepts, such as sock/shoe and hammer/nail. Stimulus and response pictures are presented on one page. At the lower level, the stimulus picture is surrounded by four choices. At the higher level, analogous relationships are employed. They follow the format "If this goes with this, then what goes with this?"	The process of selecting one of the pictures surrounding the stimulus picture is difficult for some children to understand. Some may imitate the examiner's model, pointing to all the pictures. At the higher level, it is possible for a student to choose the correct item without following the two-part analogy. Success at this level does not necessarily indicate an understanding of analogous relationships.
Verbal Expression	Assesses the student's ability to express concepts pertaining to familiar objects. The student is presented four objects individually—a ball, a block, an envelope, and a button—then asked to "Tell me all about this." The score is the number of discrete, relevant, and approximately factual concepts expressed. There is a one-minute time limit for each object.	This subtest, although labeled *Expression,* gives little information about the linguistic development of the student. Sentence use and grammar are not assessed. Rather, it is a test of cognitive awareness regarding objects and of the ability to express those concepts. A calm state, alertness to detail, and the ability to free associate and to respond within a time limit are basic to success on this subtest.
Manual Expression	Assesses the student's ability to demonstrate the use of objects through pantomime. A stimulus picture is presented, accompanied by the verbal request to "Show me what you do with a _____ ." The student's movements are recorded on a checklist of behaviors. Objects pictured include a guitar and binoculars.	Because this subtest assesses observation of and familiarity with objects in the environment, some students may be penalized by lack of exposure to such items as guitars and binoculars. Students respond best to this task when relaxed and uninhibited.

Subtest	Description	Comments
Manual Expression— *continued*		A study by McCarthy, reported in Kirk and Kirk (1971), found Down's Syndrome children to be superior in this area to other retarded children, and in relation to their other abilities. Many children with severe verbal language deficits do well on this measure of gestural language.
Grammatic Closure	Assesses the student's ability to complete verbal statements presented by the examiner. Each item consists of a complete statement followed by one to be completed with the correct word or grammatical inflection. Pictures serve as stimuli. (*Here is a boy. Here are two* _____ . *Each child has a ball. This is hers and this is* _____ .)	The ITPA was standardized on a basically Caucasian population. Standard American dialect was predominant. Therefore, responses of students from other populations may be informative, but they should not be scored. Students with speech defects were found to be deficient on this subtest in studies done by Ferrier (1966) and Foster (1963). This subtest does not provide complete analysis of grammatical form. Language sampling should be employed for more complete information.
Visual Closure	Assesses the student's ability to recognize a pictured object (or objects) when partially obscured in a scene. The task requires visual closure and figure-ground discrimination. A pointing response is used. There is a 30-second time limit.	Scanning ability and a reasonable searching procedure assist the student on this task. Also, an ability to function under time pressure is involved, although not explicitly stated.
Auditory Memory	Assesses the student's short-term memory for digits presented at the rate of two per second. Two trials are allowed. The digit series increase in length from two to eight numbers.	This subtest assesses immediate recall of unstructured, nonsyntactic material. Performance may be unrelated to short-term memory for other material, such as sentences. Because it requires verbal output, it may also be unrelated to tests of short-term retention of directions that are acted out rather than spoken. Performance on this subtest requires attention, a calm state, and retention of sequential material.
Visual Memory	Assesses the student's ability to reproduce sequences of nonmeaningful figures from memory. A pictured sequence is shown for five seconds; then the student places corresponding tiles in the same order. Two trials are allowed. Sequences increase in length from two to eight designs and include such patterns as lines and triangles.	This subtest requires a minimum of accumulated knowledge. Performance may be influenced by the ability to focus attention, function within a time limit, and retain sequential patterns. Patience and tolerance for a frustrating task are an aid. Some students are assisted by their verbal description of the designs. This helps the examiner understand a student's strategy but diminishes the test's value as a discrete measure of visual memory. This subtest only assesses memory of nonmeaningful pictorial material.

Subtest	Description	Comments
Auditory Closure (Supplementary)	Assesses the student's ability to supply mentally, then verbally, the sounds omitted in word(s) presented by the examiner. A progression from easier to more difficult vocabulary is used. Stimuli include "airpla/" (*airplane*) and "auto/o/ile" (*automobile*).	The student needs adequate hearing, good vocabulary, and attentive behavior to accomplish this task.
Sound Blending (Supplementary)	Assesses the student's ability to blend sounds spoken by the examiner at half-second intervals into words. At the lower end of the test, pictures are employed. The test progresses through synthesis of words with no picture clue (*f-i-s-h*) to nonsense words (*t-e-k-o*).	The upper limit for this subtest is below that for the test as a whole, specifically 8 years, 7 months. Adequate hearing, auditory discrimination, and retention of sounds in sequence are required for adequate performance. Performance may also reflect training approaches. For instance, students in the primary grades who have been instructed in a phonic approach often do not reach a ceiling. A recording is provided to ensure correct presentation.

STRENGTHS OF THE ITPA

• The IPTA is widely used and highly respected. It has been carefully constructed, its organization derived from the Osgood and Sebeok (1965) model of communication. This model makes it possible to view an individual's strengths and weaknesses in terms of channels, levels of organization, and processes. The IPTA provides a basis for making observations about an individual's pattern of performance. Supplemented by other diagnostic measures, it assists in accurate diagnosis of learning and language problems.

• Directions for presenting and scoring the ITPA are well stated in the manual. The examiner will find the profile sheet useful in viewing an individual's strengths and weaknesses.

• The variety of tasks included in the test enables the examiner to alter task presentation to meet the needs of the student. Tasks requiring the greatest concentration can be presented when attention and interest are adequate. The visual tests provide a means for evaluating children with poor language skills and give them the opportunity to demonstrate normal functioning.

• The ITPA has been widely studied. Many publications are available to increase the examiner's understanding of the test. Courses are taught on its construction and administration, and a film is available to help prepare examiners.

LIMITING FACTORS OF THE ITPA

• The term *psycholinguistic abilities* used in the title of this test is misleading. The ITPA samples cognitive functioning in verbal and nonverbal areas through different processes, but it does not analyze a student's psycholinguistic abilities.

• The ITPA purports to measure "discrete" functions. However, it is difficult to define and to develop tests that measure "discrete" functions. Subtests that are designed to assess nonlanguage functioning, such as Visual Memory, may still involve the use of vocabulary. Some students use labeling to retain the visual patterns.

• The ITPA was standardized on a limited sample of the population drawn from medium-sized towns and cities in the Midwest. Rural and metropolitan areas were not represented. Only 4 percent of the population was Black, and the number of Spanish-Americans is not even reported. Thus the usefulness of the ITPA for minority populations is extremely limited. The results must be interpreted with caution when used with minorities or students from lower socioeconomic classes. Reference to research on the use of the ITPA with these groups is included in Kirk and Kirk's book (1971).

• Caution is also advised in the interpretation of scores. Within the age range of 2 to 10 years, scores should be compared to the student's scaled score. To do this, all ten subtests must be given. Age scores should not be compared at these ages. Interpretation of scores is difficult at both the lower and upper ends of the age range. Many of the ITPA subtests do not provide a high enough ceiling. Above age 10, language-age scores, rather than scaled scores, should be used to describe performance.

• Accurate administration and meaningful interpretation of the ITPA require good preparation and experience. Its use

by untrained and inexperienced people is fraught with
danger, much as the use of IQ tests is. Its administration is
also more time-consuming than the manual would suggest.
Usually an hour and a half are required for its presentation,
and another hour for scoring and interpretation.

• The ITPA does not, and should not, stand alone as a
diagnostic tool. The examiner needs to know how to
interpret the results and to supplement the testing to obtain
needed information, whether academic, cognitive, or
linguistic.

• Studies on the validity of the ITPA are limited.
Factor-analytic studies of the ITPA have neither proven nor
disproven the construct validity of the test, according to the
authors (Kirk and Kirk, 1978, p. 64). A study by Elkins
(1972) analyzed construct validity and found that the
process and channel dimensions were verified but that the
representational and automatic levels were not clear.
Evidence of predictive validity is not presented. Though
Paraskevopoulos and Kirk (1969) state that scores deviating
from the child's mean make it more likely that the child will
have learning disabilities, no data is provided to support this
conclusion.

• Reliability data is summarized by Salvia and
Ysseldyke in their book on assessment (1978, p. 357).
Internal consistency is generally high in the ITPA, but
particular caution should be taken in interpreting the Visual
Closure and Auditory Closure subtests. Test-retest reliability
is significantly lower than internal-consistency reliability.
Salvia and Ysseldyke (1978) provide a summary of the
reliability data.

Marianne Frostig Developmental Test of Visual Perception (DTVP)

Marianne Frostig, in collaboration with Welty Lefever and John R. B. Whittlessey
Pro-Ed, 1961; manual revised 1966
8700 Shoal Creek Blvd., Austin, TX 78757-6897
(NOTE: See DTVP–2, Chapter Two)

Purpose	To measure certain visual perceptual abilities and to detect difficulties in visual perception at an early age
Major Areas Tested	Visual perception
Age or Grade Range	3–8 years
Usually Given By	Special education teacher Occupational therapist Psychologist
Type of Test	Standardized Individual Group
Scores Obtained	Age level Scaled Perceptual quotient (PQ)
Student Performance Timed?	No
Testing Time	30–45 minutes (individual administration); 40–60 minutes (group administration)
Scoring/Interpretation Time	10–15 minutes
Normed On	2,116 white, middle-class students from southern California
Alternate Forms Available?	No

FORMAT

The Marianne Frostig Developmental Test of Visual Perception (DTVP) is a paper-and-pencil test. The test materials consist of an examiner's manual and monograph, expendable test booklets for the students, demonstration cards, and plastic scoring keys. The examiner must also supply four colored pencils or crayons (red, blue, green, and brown) and a pencil without an eraser for each student. For group administration, access to a blackboard is necessary for demonstration purposes.

During the testing session, the student completes tasks arranged in order of increasing difficulty in five areas of visual perception. The subtests and selected items from each are described below.

1. *Eye-Motor Coordination* (16 items). The student must draw continuous straight, curved, or angled lines between increasingly narrow boundaries or draw straight lines to a target.

2. *Figure-Ground* (8 items). The student must distinguish between intersecting shapes and find embedded figures. The

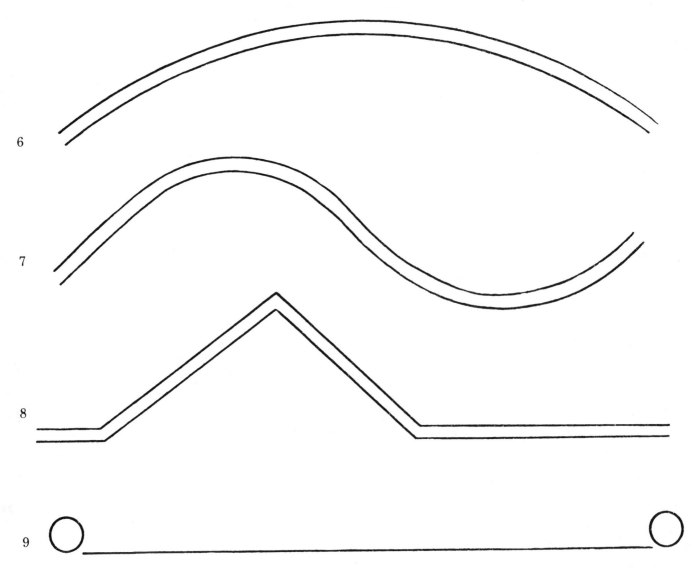

DTVP Eye-Motor Coordination

student must outline the hidden geometric forms with a colored pencil or crayon.

3. *Constancy of Shape* (17 items). The student must discriminate common geometric shapes (circles and squares), presented in different sizes, shadings, textures, and positions, from other similar shapes. The student must outline the recognized figures with a colored pencil or crayon.

4. *Position in Space* (8 items). The student must distinguish between figures in an identical position and those in a reversed or rotated position, marking the different figure.

5. *Spatial Relations* (8 items). The student must copy simple forms and patterns by joining dots.

The DTVP may be administered individually or in groups. The optimum number of students in a group depends on the age of the students. For example, a group of 8 to 10 is appropriate for kindergarten students, whereas 10 to 20 second graders may be tested simultaneously. Large groups require paraprofessionals who can circulate among the students to help monitor the test.

1

2
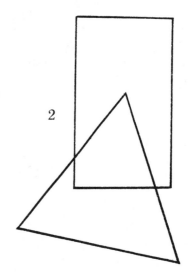

3
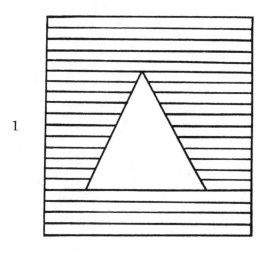

4

DTVP Figure Ground

Instructions for the test are verbal, but there is an adaptation of the manual for hard-of-hearing, deaf, and non-English-speaking students. Additional examples and gestures are used.

Although the items are presented in one test booklet, parts of the test are omitted for nursery school and kindergarten students. The student may not erase, make corrections, or turn the test booklet. The test is not timed. Alternate, equivalent forms of the DTVP are not available.

Raw scores on each subtest are converted to age scores and scaled scores. The scaled scores on the five subtests are added to obtain a total test score; when divided by a student's age, the total score yields a perceptual quotient. Subtest scaled scores range from 0 to 20, with 10 as average and 8 or below indicating need for remediation. A perceptual quotient of 90 is suggested as the cutoff for children entering first grade; lower scores indicate the need for perceptual training.

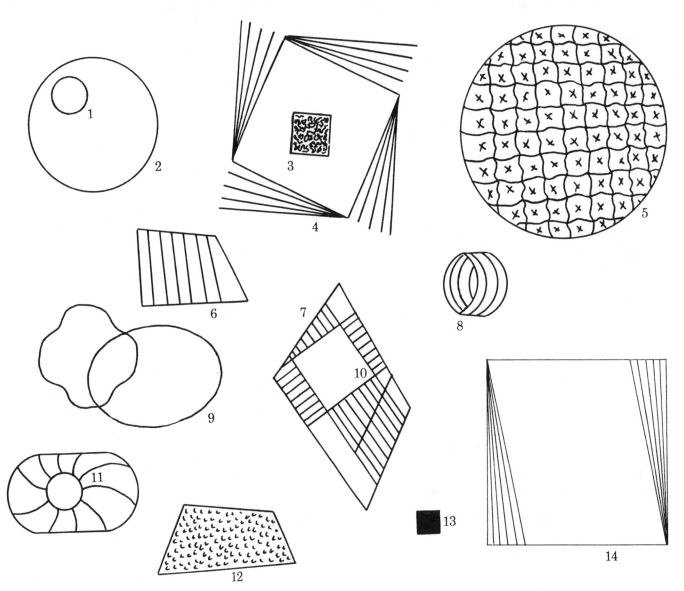

DTVP Constancy of Shape

STRENGTHS OF THE DTVP

• The DTVP is a well-known test, a forerunner in the field. It evaluates both visual perception and eye-hand coordination in young students. No expensive equipment is required. In addition to individual testing, the DTVP is useful as a screening instrument with groups of students. The test can also be used by the experienced clinician to gain diagnostic information on older students who have learning problems.

• The particular tasks on the DTVP are simple in design and arranged in order of increasing difficulty. The subtests can generally be performed quickly. For the most part, the directions for administering the test are clear. Examiner demonstration of each subtest, either on the blackboard or with demonstration materials, is especially helpful for the young student.

• The instructions for scoring the DTVP are fairly explicit. Examples are given that illustrate criteria for scoring each item. Scoring stencils provided for some items further increase objectivity. Time required for scoring is relatively short—approximately 10 minutes.

LIMITING FACTORS OF THE DTVP

• The DTVP purports to measure five distinct aspects of visual perception. Frostig's correlation studies indicate independence of the subtests. However, contradictory evidence has been found in several other investigations.

DTVP Position in Space

Such studies show that the DTVP subtests do not measure five different and relatively independent visual perceptual abilities. The degree to which the subtests measure one or more general visual perceptual factors also needs to be established (Hammill and Wiederholt, 1972).

• The process of transforming raw scores to scaled scores is very confusing. For example, in students over 8 years of age, someone who receives a perfect score on a subtest receives a scaled score of only 10, whereas younger students can make errors and get a higher score. Salvia and Ysseldyke (1978, p. 311) state, "The transformed scores for the DTVP are not only confusing; they are questionably derived and therefore absolutely must not be used in making diagnostic decisions."

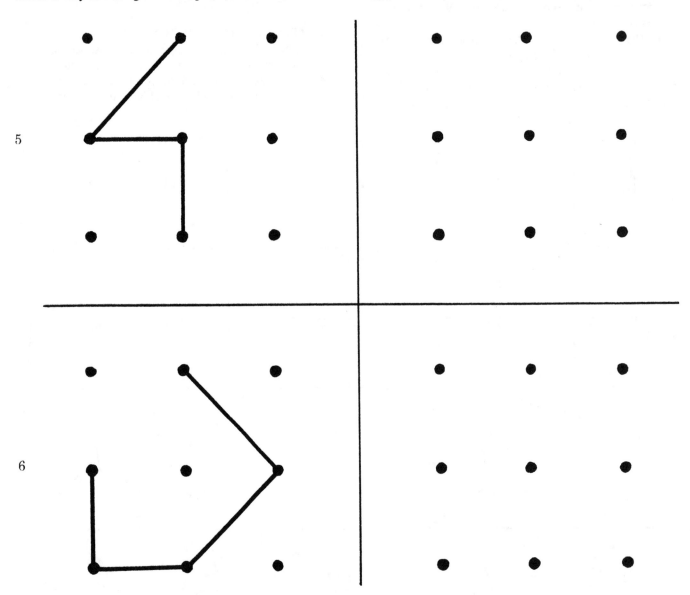

DTVP Spatial Relations

- The test items on the DTVP consist only of geometric forms and shapes; no letters or numbers are used. Although students may be able to distinguish a particular form from other figures presented in an identical, rotated, or reversed position, they still may not be able to differentiate letters having the same form but different positions (for example, *b* and *d*). The examiner should not conclude that a student's good performance on the DTVP automatically rules out difficulties in perceiving the symbols for language.

- Another difficulty with the DTVP is that visual perceptual skills are not measured apart from motor skills. The added motor component (tracing with a pencil), especially on the Figure-Ground subtest, contaminates the purity of the visual perceptual process. Visual perceptual abilities and motor skills should be measured as separate entities as well as integrative functions.

- Reliability results on the subtests range from .29 to .68, too low to be used in differential diagnosis. No reliability studies are given for students below age 5. Reliability on other tests is often low at this age level. This means that the results of a single administration to a preschooler should not be considered definitive of impairments in visual perception and eye-motor coordination.

- Validity studies reported in the manual were poorly designed and controlled (Salvia and Ysseldyke 1978, pp. 314-316).

Myklebust Picture Story Language Test (PSLT)

Helmer R. Myklebust
The Psychological Corporation, 1965; record form revised 1985
555 Academic Ct., San Antonio, TX 78204
(no longer published)

Purpose	To assess various written language skills
Major Areas Tested	Written language
Age or Grade Range	7–17 years
Usually Given By	Special education teacher Speech/language clinician
Type of Test	Standardized Individual Group Norm-referenced
Scores Obtained	Age level Percentile Stanine
Student Performance Timed?	No
Testing Time	20–30 minutes
Scoring/Interpretation Time	20–30 minutes
Normed On	Metropolitan, rural, and suburban school populations in one midwestern state
Alternate Forms Available?	No

FORMAT

The Myklebust Picture Story Test (PSLT) is a test of written language most often administered individually, but it can be given to groups ranging in size from 8 to 10 students. More than 10 students may be tested simultaneously if additional test pictures are available. The test picture is a black-and-white photograph, 10 11/2 by 13 11/2 inches, that shows a young boy playing with dollhouse figures.

Other materials needed to administer the PSLT include the test manual and the printed record forms used for scoring. The manual is a clothbound book *(Development and Disorders of Written Language, Volume One)* containing administration and scoring procedures, as well as chapters discussing the author's ideas about the development of written language skills.

The examiners must supply the type of writing paper and pencils that the students are familiar with. Standard-size writing paper is suggested, because it affords the same potential story length for all students.

Administration of the PSLT requires simple oral directions. The examiner holds up the picture so that all can see, and says, "Look at this picture carefully." The examiner waits 20 seconds and says, "You are to write a story about it. You may look at it as much and as often as you care to. Be sure to write the best story you can. Begin writing whenever you are ready."

The picture is then placed in a central position, where it can be viewed by all students. It is permissible for a student to pick up the picture for close inspection. It should be replaced in a central position after the student finishes examining it.

Questions are answered neutrally. For example, a student might ask, "Should I write about how the boy is dressed?" A typical reply would be, "If you want to. Write the story the way you think is best." The examiner may encourage students to write something if they are having difficulty thinking of a story but must refrain from offering any suggestions that might influence the content of the story.

The PSLT is not timed; the students continue to write until they have completed their stories. Alternate, equivalent forms for test-retest purposes are not available.

STRENGTHS OF THE PSLT

• Tests measuring written expression are virtually nonexistent. The PSLT then, being the first of its kind, is a landmark test.

• The PSLT is easy to administer and requires no special training. The wide age range makes it a particularly good instrument for measuring the progress of a student's writing skills in relation to age. Separate norms are provided for boys and girls, reflecting sex differences in the development of written language at different age levels. Provision has been made for converting the raw scores into age and percentile equivalents and stanine ranks.

• Three attributes of language usage are evaluated by the PSLT. Scores are provided for the following scales: *Productivity* measures the length of the expression and includes counts of total words, total sentences, and words per sentence; *Syntax* measures the correctness of what is expressed and includes accuracy of word usage, of word endings, and of punctuation (errors of additions, omissions, substitutions, and word order are counted). *Abstract-Concrete* measures the meaning of the ideas being expressed on a continuum ranging from concrete to abstract. Norms for each of these measures were established developmentally for both boys and girls.

• The three aspects of language that are measured are useful because they make it possible to obtain a profile of a student's strengths and weaknesses in written language. For example, one student may write a story deficient in syntax but highly imaginative and abstract. Another student may write a syntactically correct story that is limited in ideation, tending toward the concrete. In planning a writing program, the teacher would study the student's performance on each of the three scales.

• Another diagnostic use of the PSLT is to compare the student's facility with the spoken and the written word. Initially the test may be administered by having the student tell a story about the picture. The next day the student is asked to write a story.

• Although the PSLT has not been standardized for spoken language, the findings from an oral test may be significant for remediation.

• The manual includes scored stories (illustrating normal and handicapped children), which are particulary helpful for the examiner who is learning how to score and interpret the PSLT. It will often be necessary to refer to these sample stories for comparison.

• The PSLT answered a critical need for a test of written language. In addition, volume 2 of *Development and Disorders of Written Language: Studies of Normal and Exceptional Children* (Myklebust, 1973) includes further analyses of the PSLT results for normal students and comparative findings for exceptional students—learning disabled, mentally retarded, socially and/or emotionally disturbed, speech handicapped, and reading disabled.

LIMITING FACTORS OF THE PSLT

• The norming procedures described in the test manual are inadequate. The sample came from only one midwestern state, and as yet there is no information available on geographic differences in written language development.

• The author claims that a wide range of socioeconomic levels and cultural backgrounds were included in the standardization sample. However, data regarding the racial breakdown or number of minority students included in the study are lacking. Caution should be the rule when using the PSLT norms with students from different cultural backgrounds.

• Another consideration concerning standardization is that only odd ages from 7 to 17 were sampled. The author interpolates scores for ages not tested. This is a questionable practice, especially because the standard deviations for the sampled ages are quite large.

• The author makes the statement that the PSLT appears to be a valid test but offers no evidence to support this assumption. No attempt was made to evaluate the face validity of the test. How motivating, for example, is the test picture in comparison with other pictures that might have been used?

• The author states that the test-retest reliability coefficients were statistically significant but does not report the data. The coefficients for the syntax scale seem to indicate that there is not sufficient interscorer reliability, especially with untrained examiners. This should be noted in the information on test administration.

Purdue Perceptual–Motor Survey (Survey)

Eugene G. Roach and Newell C. Kephart
The Psychological Corporation, 1966
555 Academic Ct., San Antonio, TX 78204
(no longer published)

Purpose	To assess perceptual-motor abilities, including both gross and fine motor skills
Major Areas Tested	Laterality, directionality, and perceptual-motor skills
Age or Grade Range	Preschool–grade 8
Usually Given By	Classroom teacher Physical education teacher Special education teacher Motor therapist Occupational therapist
Type of Test	Informal Individual Criterion-referenced
Scores Obtained	None (Profile only)
Student Performance Timed?	No
Testing Time	30–40 minutes
Scoring/Interpretation Time	10–15 minutes
Normed On	200 urban and rural elementary school students in Indiana, from grades 1–4 and from all socioeconomic levels; students with known achievement or motor problems excluded; 97 nonachievers of the same age and school used in a validation study
Alternate Forms Available?	No

FORMAT

The Purdue Perceptual-Motor Survey (Survey) is not a test but a series of tasks designed to provide the examiner with a structure for observing a student's motor skills. The materials consist of an examiner's manual and individual student record forms. Materials required are those usually found in a school setting—walking board, broom handle, small pillow, mat or rug, chalk and chalkboard, penlight. The manual includes information on the rationale and development of the test, directions for administering and scoring, and a set of cards for the form-copying task.

The Survey is composed of 11 subtests organized into 5 major skills areas. It provides 22 item scores.

In order to secure the student's best performance, each subtest has four possible levels of administration:

1. *Unstructured Instruction.* The student is given general verbal directions for the task, and the examiner then observes how the student performs. For example, on the Walking Board subtest, the student would be told simply, "Walk to the other end."

2. *Verbal Directions.* If the student cannot perform the task at the unstructured instruction level, the examiner gives more explicit verbal directions, such as, "Step up on the board here and walk forward slowly to the other end."

3. *Demonstration.* At this level, the examiner helps the student by saying, "Do it like this" and then demonstrating the task for the student to imitate.

Survey Subtests

Skill Area	Subtest
Balance and Posture	1. *Walking Board.* Student is asked to walk on a walking board four inches wide and six inches off the ground to obtain a measure of dynamic balance. Three scores are obtained: forward, backward, and sidewise.
	2. *Jumping.* Student is asked to jump and hop on each foot and both feet in a series of eight tasks designed to measure laterality and rhythm.
Body Image	3. *Identification of Body Parts.* Student is asked to point to nine common body parts.
	4. *Imitation of Movements.* Student is asked to imitate a series of 17 arm positions to measure the ability to translate visual information into a motor act.
	5. *Obstacle Course.* Student is asked to step over, step around, and duck under a broom handle to assess spatial orientation.
	6. *Kraus-Weber Test of Physical Fitness.* Student is asked to raise upper body and legs from a prone position to test physical strength and muscular fitness.
	7. *Angels in the Snow.* Student is asked to perform a series of tasks requiring moving specific limbs individually and in pairs.
Perceptual-Motor Match	8. *Chalkboard.* Student is asked to perform a series of four chalkboard tasks assessing visual-motor coordination, with particular emphasis on directionality and mid-line problems.
	9. *Rhythmic Writing.* Student is asked to reproduce a series of eight continuous writing motifs. Rhythm, accuracy, and orientation on the chalkboard are observed and scored.
Ocular Control	10. *Ocular Pursuits.* Student is asked to perform a series of four visual-tracking exercises.
Form Perception	11. *Developmental Drawings.* Student is asked to copy seven geometric forms to assess visual-motor coordination.

4. *Guided Movements*. If the student cannot initiate the task, the examiner physically guides his or her movements.

The level of structure that the student requires for each task is noted, together with other observations of performance, on the individual record forms. Each item is rated on a four-point scale following the guidelines in the examiner's manual. All scores are recorded on the record forms. Because the survey is not intended as a test but as a structured observation, the rating scores are not translated into age scores or percentiles but are simply used as a guide to adequate or inadequate performance.

STRENGTHS OF THE SURVEY

• The Purdue Perceptual-Motor Survey provides a structure for assessing a variety of gross and fine motor tasks in elementary school students. The manual is clearly written, and directions for administration and scoring are easy to follow. Little equipment is necessary, so the Survey is an inexpensive way to assess motor skills. The Survey is intended to be used as a structured observation. The increasing assistance provided for the student in the four levels of task administration is very helpful in determining the type of instruction each student will need, and the profile of strengths and weaknesses helps the teacher plan appropriate perceptual-motor activities.

• The Survey was developed from the theoretical framework described by Kephart (1960) in *The Slow Learner in the Classroom*. This book is very helpful to the teacher who is planning a perceptual-motor program. Also helpful are the checklists of motor performance provided by Chaney and Kephart (1968) in *Motoric Aids to Perceptual Training*.

LIMITING FACTORS OF THE SURVEY

• The Survey should be used as it was intended—as an informal assessment procedure. Normative data was gathered on a limited sample of students. Although the test-retest reliability was high in one study reported in the manual, the four-point rating scale for each item clearly leads to subjective scoring decisions. The five skill areas are general categories rather than discrete motor functions. There is much overlapping, and a differential diagnosis of motor disabilities should not be attempted from this informal scale.

• Validity studies, which were carried out with a very small sample, demonstrated that students who are low achievers academically performed more poorly on the Survey than high-achieving students. Even in the authors' studies, performance of the motor tasks did not improve with age or socioeconomic class. There is not sufficient evidence to document the authors' claim that performance of these tasks is "necessary for acquiring academic skills by usual

instructional methods" (Examiner's Manual, p. iii).

• Although the Survey is an informal test, it requires a skilled examiner. Many of the tests are difficult to administer, and the observations of student performance take the eye of a person trained and experienced in motor skills.

• The manual does not provide any guidelines for interpreting the profiles or subtest patterns. Such information would be very helpful to the teacher who is inexperienced in the area of motor development.

Wepman Auditory Discrimination Test (ADT)

Joseph M. Wepman
Western Psychological Services, 1958; revised 1973; test revised, 1986; manual revised, 1987
12031 Wilshire Blvd., Los Angeles, CA 90025

Purpose	To evaluate the student's ability to recognize fine differences that exist between phonemes in English speech
Major Areas Tested	Auditory discrimination
Age or Grade Range	5–8 years
Usually Given By	Special education teacher Speech/language clinician
Type of Test	Standardized Individual
Scores Obtained	Rating scale
Student Performance Timed?	No
Testing Time	10–15 minutes
Scoring/Interpretation Time	5–10 minutes
Normed On	1,800 children aged 4–8; sample stratified by age, ethnic background, geographic region, and socioeconomic background
Alternate Forms Available?	Yes

FORMAT

The materials for the Wepman Auditory Discrimination Test include a brief manual and forms for recording individual responses. The manual contains some information on test development, directions for administration, and guidance in the interpretation of test results.

The test consists of 40 pairs of monosyllabic meaningful words. The words were selected from the *Lorge-Thorndike Teacher's Word Book* of 30,000 Words (1944). Of the 40 word pairs, 30 differ by only one sound: *muss-mush*. The 10 word pairs that do not differ are included as false choices and aid in the judgment of test validity.

The words in each pair are of equal length. Comparisons are made between 13 initial consonants, 13 final consonants, and 4 medial vowels. Consonants chosen for contrast are within the same phonetic category—for example, the stops /p/,/t/, and /k/. Vowel comparisons are based on such criteria as the part of the tongue that is raised; the height of the tongue; and the position of the lips.

The word pairs are read by the examiner. The student indicates whether the words pronounced were the same or different. No pictures are used, and the examiner pronounces the words with lips covered. Thus, visual skills are not involved. A rating scale is used to interpret a student's performance. The scale provides descriptions of ability ranging from "very good development" to "below the level of the threshold of adequacy" for the ages 5 to 8 years.

STRENGTHS OF THE WEPMAN AUDITORY DISCRIMINATION TEST

• This test is a brief, inexpensive, and relatively simple tool for assessing auditory discrimination ability. The test is carefully constructed. Word length and complexity of test items are controlled.

• Test-retest reliability is high. The existence of equivalent forms provides the examiner with a good reevaluation procedure.

LIMITING FACTORS OF THE WEPMAN AUDITORY DISCRIMINATION TEST

• Some young handicapped children may have difficulty understanding the concept of *same/different*. A low score may represent difficulty in grasping that concept or in sustaining attention for the task, rather than auditory discrimination difficulty. This problem was found in clinical practice and was verified by Blank (1968) in her research.

• This test provides a measure of auditory discrimination of isolated word pairs. Additional testing or observation is necessary to assess discrimination skills of other types and in other situations, such as conversational speech and discrimination of sound against a background of noise.

• Although many phonemic contrasts are presented, others are missing. For instance, the sounds /ng/, /l/, r/, /j/, and /ch/ are not included in the discrimination tasks. In addition, the contrast of voiced/voiceless consonants (for example, *bad-bat*) is not included. Also, only a limited number of vowel discriminations are assessed.

NOTE

The 1986 edition of the Auditory Discrimination Test (ADT, Second Edition) was normed on 1,800 children in 30 states in the United States. The norms reflected the 1980 census in regard to age, sex, ethnicity, and geographic location. Four year olds were included in the sample. Format and administration procedures remained the same. Standard scores and percentiles were added to the qualitative score. The technical characteristics of the test were improved. The Limiting Factors remain.

CHAPTER ONE
Academic Tests

The assessment of skills in basic academic areas is one of the primary purposes of educational testing. This chapter contains 27 tests that assess student functioning in the basic academic skills of reading, writing, spelling, and mathematics.

The first section includes 12 multiple-subject tests in alphabetical order. Examiners frequently select multiple-subject batteries as their initial diagnostic instrument. Multiple-subject tests allow an overview of the student's skills in all of the basic academic areas. As all of the subtests are normed on the same population, it is possible to compare an individual student's abilities in several academic areas at once. Multiple-subject tests usually cover a wide age range and are often used as the required tests for determining a student's eligibility for special education services.

The Basic Achievement Skills Individual Screener (BASIS) assesses reading comprehension, math calculation and word problems, spelling, and written language. The Reading Comprehension subtest uses a cloze procedure with oral reading, which is a very helpful tool. The BRIGANCE® Inventories remain popular criterion-referenced batteries. The author has added a fifth inventory to assess life skills in the older special education population. The newly revised Diagnostic Achievement Battery (DAB–2) was the first multiple-subject battery to include not only reading, writing, spelling, and math, but also the oral language skills of listening and speaking. The Kaufman Test of Educational Abilities (KTEA) provides a quick screening measure as well as a more complete assessment of reading, spelling, and math across the grades. The Norris Education Achievement Test (NEAT) is a relative newcomer to the field. Its unique contribution is the assessment of reading comprehension with controlled vocabulary determined for each student by the word recognition subtest. The well-known Peabody Individual Achievement Test (PIAT–R) uses a multiple-choice format to assess basic skills plus general information. The best-known, most widely used brief test of academic skills, the Wide Range Achievement Test (WRAT3), has been revised, eliminating the two forms for different age levels but retaining the same format for assessing word reading, math computation, and written spelling. Finally, a new multiple-subject battery, the Wechsler Individual Achievement Test (WIAT), enters the field and promises to become very popular. As the name implies, the test was normed on the same population as the Wechsler Intelligence Scale for Children (WISC–III) and allows for convenient, technically sound comparisons of intelligence and achievement. The WIAT includes two reading subtests, two math subtests, spelling, and written language and, as in the DAB–2, measures listening comprehension and verbal expression. Please note that one of the most popular multiple-subject tests, the Woodcock–Johnson Psycho-Educational Battery, Revised (WJ–R) is reviewed in Chapter Six of this book (p. 312). The Achievement Tests of the WJ–R are reviewed together with the Tests of Cognitive Ability in the same battery.

The second section of this chapter contains ten tests specific to reading. The first, the Decoding Skills Test (DST), is a well constructed criterion-referenced test that, according to research, is very helpful in the assessment of dyslexia (Vellutino, 1987). The DST is followed by several older batteries that assess reading skills. The Diagnostic Reading Scales by Spache (DRS–81), the Gilmore Oral Reading Test, the Durrell Analysis of Reading Difficulty, and the Gates-McKillop-

Horowitz (GMH) batteries provide interesting measures of subskills of reading that are helpful in program planning; however, the tests' technical properties are outdated and not strong enough to warrant their use for diagnosing a reading disability. The most recent and best-constructed battery of reading tests is the Woodcock Reading Mastery Tests, Revised (WRMT–R). Three tests of silent reading are included: the Gates–McGinnity Silent Reading Tests, for the K–12 range; the Nelson Denny Reading Tests (NDRT), for older students; and the Test of Reading Comprehension (TORC), for younger students. Finally, the Gray Oral Reading Test (GORT–3) has been recently revised to provide the most comprehensive and well-normed measure of oral reading fluency and comprehension.

In the spelling and writing section of this chapter, only three tests are reviewed, as these skill areas are well covered in the multiple-subject batteries. The Boder Test of Reading–Spelling Patterns is a criterion-referenced test for

identifying dyslexic students. The Test of Written Language (TOWL–2) assesses written language through an original paragraph writing task. The Test of Written Spelling (TWS–3) is just as its name describes.

Math is also assessed in many of the multiple-subject batteries. For that reason, only two separate math tests are reviewed in this section. The ENRIGHT® Diagnostic Inventory of Basic Arithmetic skills is a very comprehensive assessment of computation. The popular Key Math Diagnostic Arithmetic Test covers a wide range of age levels and skills.

Some tests are difficult to categorize. The Slingerland Screening Tests for Identifying Children with Specific Language Disability and the Malcomesius Specific Language Disability Test are clearly tools for assessing academic skills. They include sections related to writing, spelling, and phonics. However, the primary contribution of these tests to educational assessment is in the area of perception and memory. They are reviewed in Chapter Two of this book.

Academic Tests

Tests	Reading	Spelling	Math	Written Language	Listening Comprehension	Oral Expression
BASIS	X	X	X	X		
BRIGANCE	X	X	X	X	X	X
DAB–2	X	X	X	X	X	X
KTEA	X	X	X			
NEAT	X	X	X	X		
PIAT–R	X	X	X	X		
WRAT3	X	X	X			
WIAT	X	X	X	X	X	X
WJ–R*	X	X	X	X	X	
DST	X					
DRS–81	X				X	
GILMORE	X					
DURRELL	X	X			X	
G–M–H	X	X		X		
WRMT–R	X					
G–McKILLOP	X					
NDRT	X					
TORC	X					
GORT–3	X					
BODER	X	X				
TOWL–2		X		X		
TWS–3		X				
ENRIGHT			X			
KEY MATH–R			X			

*Reviewed in Chapter Six, p. 312

Basic Achievement Skills Individual Screener (BASIS)

The Psychological Corporation, 1983
555 Academic Court, San Antonio, TX 78204

Purpose	To provide both norm-referenced and criterion-referenced information in basic academic skills
Major Areas Tested	Mathematics, reading, spelling, and writing
Age or Grade Range	Grades 1–12
Usually Given By	Psychologist Educational diagnostician Counselor Administrator Special education teacher Any trained person
Type of Test	Individual Criterion-referenced Norm-referenced Standardized
Scores Obtained	Grade level Percentile Age level Stanine
Student Performance Timed?	No
Testing Time	45–60 minutes
Scoring/Interpretation Time	15–30 minutes
Normed On	3,296 students in grades 1–12; sample balanced for race and socioeconomic background; 4% mainstreamed disabled students; additional 232 18–23-year-old adults included
Alternate Forms Available?	No

FORMAT

The Basic Achievement Skills Individual Screener (BASIS) is an individual test of reading, math, spelling, and writing achievement. It covers grades 1 through 12 and provides both norm-referenced and criterion-referenced information.

The materials consist of a manual containing directions for administration and scoring as well as technical information; the BASIS content booklet, which includes the reding passages and readiness activities; and BASIS record forms. The student writes directly on these consumable forms for the Mathematics, Spelling, and Writing subtests. The forms also include a summary of the student's performance in both norm-referenced and criterion-referenced scores.

Four subject areas are assessed by the BASIS:

1. *Mathematics*. This subject includes five items at the readiness level: addition; subtraction; multiplication; division of whole numbers, fractions, and decimals; and word problems using basic computation skills.

2. *Reading*. This subtest includes a few items at the readiness and beginning reading levels (letter naming, word matching, word reading, and sentence reading). It primarily assesses reading comprehension through a cloze procedure. The student reads orally a passage with six words missing and fills in appropriate words based on meaning.

3. *Spelling*. In this subtest, the student writes single words dictated by the examiner.

4. *Writing*. This subtest consists of a 10-minute writing sample on a standardized topic ("Your Favorite Place"). The examiner reads the sample for an overall or holistic impression of its content, organization, vocabulary, sentence structure, and mechanics. The impression is then matched against an average sample for the student's grade, and the student's sample is rated average, above average, or below average as compared to the sample.

A student may be given all four subtest areas or single areas selected by the examiner. When the complete test is given, the Mathematics subtest is given first.

The grade-referenced cluster is the basic unit of administration of the BASIS. The content of each subtest area is divided into eight clusters of items, a cluster for each grade level, 1 through 8. All of the items in each cluster for each subject area must be administered at one time. If the student passes the criterion or minimum number of items for each cluster, he or she moves on to the next level. If the student does not pass the criterion, the examiner drops two grade-level clusters to obtain a basal. The basal/ceiling process, then, is done through levels rather than through single items. The basal is the lowest level at which the student passes criterion; the ceiling is the lowest level at which the student

---

$$4283 \times 315$$

$$\frac{2}{3} = \frac{6}{\square}$$

$$67\overline{)7303}$$

$$7.03 \times 4.6$$

$$5.94 + 3.4 =$$

$$.14\overline{)7.42}$$

In the gym, we set up 10 rows of chairs with 12 chairs in each row. 125 more people can sit on the bleachers. How many people can sit in the gym in all?

Jan has $3\frac{4}{5}$ yards of canvas cloth. She needs $1\frac{2}{5}$ yards to make a floor for her tent. How many extra yards of cloth will Jan have?

BASIS Mathematics Cluster

does not pass the criterion.

A grade-referenced cluster in Mathematics consists of six computation items and two word problems.

Criterion is usually five out of eight correct. A grade-referenced cluster in Reading is one paragraph with six omitted words; criterion is usually four out of six. The Spelling grade-referenced cluster is six dictated words with the usual criterion being four correct.

Following the test completion, raw score points for items correct, plus those below the basal level, are totaled in each subject area and converted to a variety of scores: grade equivalents, stanines, and percentile ranks based on grade and age. In addition, a grade-referenced placement is determined. The grade-referenced placement score describes the student's instructional level in each subject area. In Reading, it represents the last level at which a student reached criterion, a level of 50–67 percent accuracy on the cloze procedure. In Mathematics and Spelling, it represents the first level at which the student did not achieve criterion, a level of about 60–70 percent accuracy. In addition to these norm-referenced and criterion-referenced scores, other diagnostic information is elicited by error analysis of math, reading, and spelling performance.

STRENGTHS OF THE BASIS

• The BASIS is obviously designed to provide the quick screening information usually obtained through the Wide Range Achievement Test. Many of the limitations of the WRAT have been eliminated by including reading comprehension, word problems, and written language. The advantages of a single instrument measuring basic skills quickly over a wide age range have been maintained. The BASIS is a good initial screening tool. It is especially useful as a quick survey of a new student's skills.

• The student testing materials are well designed, with large print and in a format familiar to students. The manual is clearly and concisely written.

• The combining of norm referenced scores with criterion referenced information allows for a variety of interpretations of student performance. Actually the interpretation needed is minimal as the BASIS content is directly classroom related.

• The Reading subtest provides an excellent measure of reading comprehension. The cloze procedure requires the student to understand not only individual sentences but also complete paragraphs. Although oral reading accuracy is not scored, the examiner gains very useful information about a student's decoding skills.

• Including two word problems in every level of the Mathematics subtest is a helpful factor.

• Good reliability and validity data are provided in the manual. The BASIS is very reliable for such a short test, and content validity is strong for the narrow range of skills

assessed. Careful attention was given to the standardization sample.

• The manual and the record forms provide good information about procedures for error analysis in each subtest.

The Writing subtest is a unique feature of the BASIS. There are very few, if any, adequate measures of written language skills which actually assess a student's writing (as opposed to grammar or punctuation). It is easy for students to write to the topic "A Favorite Place," and in 10 minutes the examiner can gain important information about the student's skills. The grade level samples provide a useful reference point. The subject area of written language does not allow as precise a measurement as the other basic skills, and the holistic approach of evaluating writing is a useful one.

LIMITING FACTORS OF THE BASIS

• Although the BASIS includes a few items at the readiness level, as in other wide range achievement tests, it is not a good instrument for measuring the skills of first grade students.

• Although the BASIS provides norms for students through high school and beyond, the content of the materials used only reaches eighth grade level. The test is best used in grades 2–8.

• The words for the Spelling subtest were selected from grade-level spelling series, and they reflect all of the inconsistencies of those series. While they may yield an adequate grade referenced score, they give little information about a student's skills and do not reflect the skills of students taught in a systematic phonics approach.

• Although the BASIS manual is clearly written, the organization of the manual with the record forms is confusing. In Reading, the passing criteria are printed on the record forms, in Math and Spelling they are not. The possible correct answers for Reading are in an appendix. The examiner must be very familiar with the materials to administer the test smoothly.

• Although the authors have clearly explained the limitations of grade equivalent scores, their inclusion is questionable. It is too easy for the inexperienced examiner to confuse the grade equivalent score and misuse it as a grade placement recommendation.

BRIGANCE® Diagnostic Inventories
(THE BRIGANCE® SYSTEM)

Albert H. Brigance
Curriculum Associates, Inc., 1976–1983, 1994
5 Esquire Rd., North Billerica, MA 01862

Purpose	To assess preacademic, academic, and vocational skills to provide a systematic performance record to help teachers define instructional objectives and plan individualized educational programs
Major Areas Tested	Reading, writing, spelling, mathematics, language, motor and functional life skills
Age or Grade Range	Birth–Adult
Usually Given By	Classroom teacher Administrator Special education teacher Paraprofessional Psychologist Teaching aide
Type of Test	Informal Individual (some group subtests) Criterion-referenced
Scores Obtained	Grade level (some subtests) Age level (some subtests)
Student Performance Timed?	No
Testing Time	15–90 minutes (depending on purpose of testing)
Scoring/Interpretation Time	15–30 minutes
Normed On	Not normed, but field-tested in 30 states and 2 provinces of Canada
Alternate Forms Available?	No, except for some subtests in the Diagnostic Comprehensive Inventory of Basic Skills

FORMAT

There are six BRIGANCE® Diagnostic Inventories (BRIG-ANCE® Inventories) designed to assess basic competencies at different grade levels. Together, the six instruments evaluate more than 500 skill sequences from preschool through adulthood. The skills assessed in each are outlined at the end of this review. The materials for each BRIGANCE® Inventory consist of an examiner's notebook and individual record books. The notebook is designed to lie flat on the table between the examiner and the student. It includes directions for administering each subtest, test items, scoring criteria, and instructional objectives in behavioral terms. A sample page from the examiner's notebook is shown. When the assessment is oral, the student works directly from the student page; when the test requires writing, or when group testing is done, the student page is reproduced in multiple copies.

The individual student record books provide a means of recording ongoing progress. The student's responses are recorded by the examiner in the record book in a different color each time the test is administered. A grade-level profile is charted after each administration to provide a graphic summary of student achievement. Observation of student behavior can also be noted.

The BRIGANCE® Inventories are informal. Administration directions are given, but the examiner is encouraged to adjust the procedures to meet the needs of the student. The only question asked in each subtest is, "Has the student mastered this skill, or is more instruction needed?" Developmental ages or grade-level scores are provided for a few key subtests in each inventory, but, basically, the tests are not norm-referenced. Their purpose is to assess basic skills, define instructional objectives, assist teachers in program planning, and provide a continuous measure of progress.

Brigance® Diagnostic Comprehensive Inventory of Basic Skills; Student Page

PRONOUNCES WRITTEN INITIAL BLENDS AND DIGRAPHS

SKILL: Pronounces sounds of written initial blends and digraphs.

STUDENT RECORD BOOK: Page 9.

ASSESSMENT METHOD: Individual oral response.

MATERIAL: S-112.

DISCONTINUE: Your discretion, or after failure on two consecutive initial blends or digraphs.

TIME: Your discretion.

ACCURACY: Give credit for each correct response.

DIRECTIONS: *(This assessment is made by having the student look at each blend-vowel and digraph-vowel combination and pronounce the correct sound for each initial blend and digraph.)*

Point to the first item, "sha," and

Say: **I want you to tell me the sound these letters make when they are at the beginning of a word.**

Pause for the student's response. If the student appears confused, explain the first item.

Say: **These letters** *(pointing to the letters "sha")* **have the sound of sha, as in shack.**

Continue with the other items. If necessary, give encouragement and praise.

NOTES:

1. **Give Credit if Blend or Digraph Sound Is Correct:** The purpose of this assessment is to determine if the student can pronounce written initial blends or digraphs. Give credit if this skill is performed even if the vowel sound, long or short, is not correct.

2. **More Than One Sound:** Some of the blends and digraphs have more than one sound. For example, *ch* usually has the *ch* sound, but it also has the *k* sound as in *choir* or the *sh* sound as in *chef*. If the student gives the less common sound of the blend or digraph, you may wish to ask, *"What other sound can the letters "ch" make?"*

   (NOTES: continued on page 114)

STUDENT PAGE FORMAT FOR S-112

1 sha	2 wha	3 tha	4 cho	5 sto	6 gra
7 spo	8 flo	9 glo	10 slo	11 pli	12 clo
13 bla	14 tro	15 cra	16 dro	17 fro	18 pri
19 bro	20 smi	21 sko	22 sna	23 swo	24 sco
25 twi	26 spro	27 thro	28 scro	29 stro	30 squa

(F-9)

OBJECTIVE: By _____ (date) , when shown a list of thirty blend-vowel and digraph-vowel combinations and when requested to do so, _____ (student's name) will give the correct sound of the initial blend or digraph for _____ (number) of the blends and digraphs.

STRENGTHS OF THE BRIGANCE® INVENTORIES

• Each inventory is a comprehensive battery of assessments, including many skills for a wide age range of students. By careful selection of subtests appropriate for each student's age and skill level and for the purpose of the testing, assessment can be completed quickly.

• The BRIGANCE® Inventories are intended to lead directly to instructional objectives and program planning. If used correctly, they do.

• The inventories can be administered by teaching aides or paraprofessionals under supervision.

• The inventories provide a well-organized record-keeping system.

• The inventories include some unique subtests. Skills such as alphabetizing, dictionary and reference book use, interpretation of graphs and maps, and knowledge of geometry are not assessed in other instruments.

• The Spanish Edition is very helpful in assessing the instructional needs of Spanish-speaking students.

• Screening tests are provided at three levels: Early Preschool Screen (2–2-1/2 years), PreSchool Screen (3–4 years), and K & 1 Screen (Kindergarten and Grade 1).

• The BRIGANCE® System includes a number of options that are very helpful in a special education program. In addition to individual student record books, a group record book for each inventory allows the tracing of an entire class. Software to aid in planning IEP goals and objectives is available for most of the inventories. Supplementary curriculum materials, which provide strategies in instruction and reproducible practice activities, are available for Readiness Level, Word Analysis, and Study Skills. Curriculum Associates provides free samples of all its materials, demo disks for software, and a video loan program to introduce materials from the BRIGANCE® system.

Brigance® Diagnotic Comprehensive Inventory of Basic Skills; Student Page

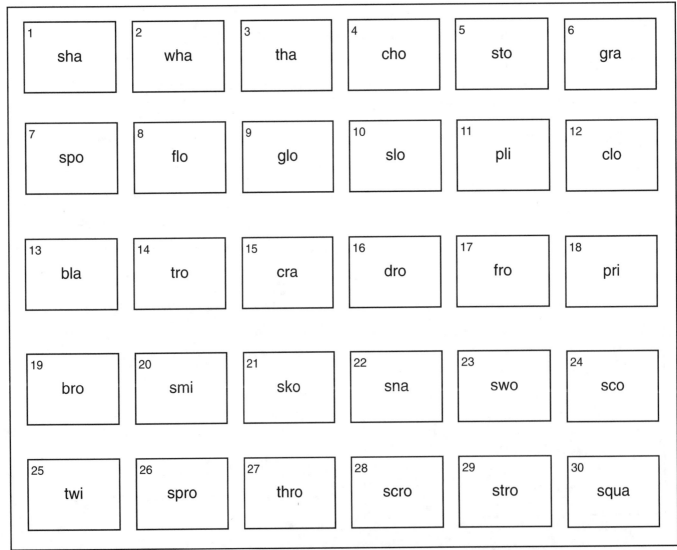

• The Brigance® manuals contain only brief descriptions of the field testing. More complete information about the school districts included would be helpful.

• No reliability data is presented for any of the Brigance® inventories. Reliability is difficult to obtain when the subtests are not administered in a standardized manner. However, at a minimum, data should be presented for those subtests with alternate forms to establish their equivalency.

• Suggestions for discontinuing testing on subtests should generally be ignored. The Brigance® is a criterion-referenced test, and its purpose is to assess exactly what skills a student has mastered. Students tend to know scattered items (some abbreviations, some contractions), so all items need to be assessed. Also, in the Brigance®, item order was determined by examining typical basal series; therefore the order of difficulty will depend upon the instructional program, and it is inappropriate to use ceiling procedures.

• Teachers need to be aware that the Brigance® Inventories assess many specific academic skills; however, they do not tell the user how well or how poorly a student is doing in any subject areas. They should be used in conjunction with good norm referenced tests both at the time of initial assessment and in measuring progress.

• The Brigance® Inventories should not be used for grade placement decisions. The lack of reliability and validity data do not permit the instrument to be used for this purpose.

LIMITING FACTORS OF THE BRIGANCE® INVENTORIES

• Although the BRIGANCE® Inventories claim to be a measure of progress, informal tests should not be used as the only measure of progress. Reliability is difficult to establish, because the tests are not administered in a standardized manner. The grade-level scores should not be used as a measure of progress.

• The informal format may encourage teachers or teaching aides to administer the BRIGANCE® Inventories without preparation. This often results in overly lengthy, inappropriate, or haphazard assessment. Careful selection of tests, preparation of materials, and study of data recording procedures is essential if the instruments are to be valuable.

• BRIGANCE® manuals contain only brief descriptions of the field testing. More complete information about the school districts included would be helpful.

• No reliability data is presented for any of the BRIGANCE® inventories. Reliability is difficult to obtain when the subtests are not administered in a standardized manner. However, at a minimum, data should be presented for those subtests with alternate forms to establish their equivalency.

• Suggestions for discontinuing testing on subtests should generally be ignored. The BRIGANCE® is a criterion-referenced test, and its purpose is to assess exactly what skills a student has mastered. Students tend to know scattered items (some abbreviations, some contractions), so all items need to be assessed. Also, in the BRIGANCE®, item order was determined by examining typical basal series; therefore, the order of difficulty will depend upon the instructional program, and it is inappropriate to use ceiling procedures.

• Teachers need to be aware that the BRIGANCE® Inventories assess many specific academic skills; however, they do not tell the user how well or how poorly a student is doing in any subject area. They should be used in conjunction with good norm-referenced tests both at the time of initial assessment and in measuring progress.

• The BRIGANCE® Inventories should not be used for grade placement decisions. The lack of reliability and validity data do not permit the instrument to be used for this purpose.

NOTE

The BRIGANCE® System includes a number of options that are very helpful in a special education program. In addition to individual student record books, a group record book for each inventory allows the tracking of an entire class. Software to aid in planning IEP goals and objectives is available for most of the inventories. Supplementary curriculum materials that provide strategies in instruction and reproducible practice activities are available for the Readiness Level, Word Analysis, and Study Skills. Curriculum Associates provides free samplers of all of its materials, demo disks for its software, and a video-loan program to introduce materials from the BRIGANCE® System.

Scope of BRIGANCE® Inventories

Inventory	Grade Range	Skills Assessed	Comments
Inventory of Early Development–Revised (Yellow Notebook)–1991	Birth– 7 yrs.	Preambulatory Motor Gross and Fine Motor Self-Help Social Development Speech and Language General Knowledge Readiness Writing Math	Assesses infant and early childhood development, including a separate section on social–emotional development. Developmental ages based upon extensive review of the literature are given for most of the skill sequences. These ages are guides for when a skill is usually learned and should not be used for placement decisions.

Diagnostic Inventory of Basic Skills (Blue Notebook)–1976	K–6	Readiness
		Reading
		    Word Recognition
		    Fluency
		    Analysis
		Vocabulary
		Handwriting
		Grammar
		Spelling
		Math
			Comprises the original BRIGANCE® Inventory with 141 subtests covering a variety of academic tasks in key subject areas. This inventory is available in Spanish. A small pamphlet lists subtests that are appropriate for a particular grade. The grade-level scores provided for some subtests are not based on a standardized sample.

Diagnostic Inventory of Essential Skills (Red Notebook)–1981	6– Adult	Reading
		    Word Recognition
		    Oral Reading
		    Comprehension
		    Analysis
		    Reference
		Writing
		Spelling
		Math
		    Computation
		    Fractions
		    Decimals
		    Percents
		    Measurement
		Study Skills
			Assesses special education students at secondary levels, as well as adults. Measures minimal competencies in academic and vocational skills. Includes rating scales for health practices and attitudes, self-concept, job-interview skills, auto safety, and speaking and listening skills. A guide lists tests appropriate for each grade level. Grade placement scores on some tests are not norm-referenced and their use is questionable. The Reading Comprehension subtest, revised in 1982, can be purchased from the publisher to replace pages in the 1981 edition. The revised form is one of the best measures of passage comprehension available for secondary students.

Diagnostic Comprehensive Inventory of Basic Skills (Green Notebook)–1983	K–9	All skills in Diagnostic Inventory of Basic Skills Speech Listening Percents Metrics Reading Comprehension	Designed for use in elementary and middle schools. Expands Diagnostic Inventory of Basic Skills to grade 9. Adds new subtests, particularly in the areas of speech, listening, and reading comprehension. More than half of the skills can be assessed in groups. A guide lists tests appropriate for each grade level. Has two forms for many subtests to provide for pre- and post-testing; however, no data is provided on the equivalency of these forms and the scores are not norm-referenced. They should not be used as a measure of progress.
Life Skills Inventory (Dark Blue Notebook)– 1994	Secondary Grades– Adult	Speaking Listening Functional Reading Functional Writing Comprehension Functional Math	Designed to assess basic skills in the context of everyday life. For use in vocational, ESL, adult education, and family literacy programs. Assessments range in difficulty from second- to eighth-grade level. Provisions for a quick screen to assess overall competency in major life-skill areas is included.
Diagnostic Inventory of Basic Skills– Spanish Edition (Orange Notebook)	K–6	Readiness Reading Vocabulary	Useful for bilingual, ESL, and special education programs with bilingual students. Can be used to assess language dominance and oral English proficiency. Directions to examiner are in English, directions to the student are in Spanish.

Diagnostic Achievement Battery–Revised (DAB–2)

Phyllis L. Newcomer
PRO-ED 1984, 1990
8700 Shoal Creek Blvd., Austin, TX 78757

Purpose	To identify students who are significantly below their peers in language and academic skills; to determine their strengths and weaknesses; to document progress; and to serve as a research instrument.
Major Areas Tested	Listening, speaking, reading, writing, and mathematics
Age or Grade Range	6–14 years
Usually Given By	Educational; Diagnostician Special educational teacher
Type of Test	Individual Norm-referenced Standardized
Scores Obtained	Percentile Standard Score Age equivalent Grade equivalent
Student Performance Timed?	No
Testing Time	1–2 hours
Scoring/Interpretation Time	20–30 minutes
Normed On	2,623 students from 40 states; sample was balanced for sex, place of residence, race, geographic region, and occupation of parents, and compared with Statistical Abstracts of the United States, 1985
Alternate Forms Available?	No

FORMAT

The DAB–2 is an individual test of academic achievement. The original DAB (1984) was developed to fill the need of a single assessment tool to measure spoken language, written language, and mathematics. This revised edition contains modifications of four subtests and a broader norming sample. The materials consist of the Manual, the Student Booklet, Student Worksheets for the writing and math subtests, and a 12-page Profile/Answer Form for recording responses and recording scores. All of the information needed to administer the test is contained in the student booklet, and the Profile/Answer Form adds to ease administration.

The DAB–2 consists of 12 subtests that measure three major constructs: spoken language, oral language, and mathematics. The two-language constructs are assessed in both the receptive and the expressive modes: listening and speaking, reading and writing. The examiner may administer the entire test or selected subtests in the order described below.

Subtest scores are then combined into seven composite scores and a total test standard score called quotients. Quotients have a mean of 100 and a standard deviation of 15 to allow easy comparison with other tests.

TABLE 1.1
DAB–2 Composites and Subtests

Composites	Subtests
1. Listening	(1) Story Comprehension (2) Characteristics
2. Speaking	(1) Synonyms (2) Grammatic Comprehension
3. Reading	(1) Alphabet/Word Knowledge (2) Reading Comprehension
4. Writing	(1) Punctuation (2) Capitalization (3) Synonyms (4) Writing Composition
5. Mathematics	(1) Math Reasoning (2) Math Calculation
6. Spoken Language	(1) Story Comprehension (2) Characteristics (3) Synonyms (4) Grammatic Completion
7. Written Language	(1) Alphabet/Word Knowledge (2) Reading Comprehension (3) Punctuation (4) Capitalization (5) Spelling (6) Writing Composition
8. Total Achievement	(1) All 12 subtests

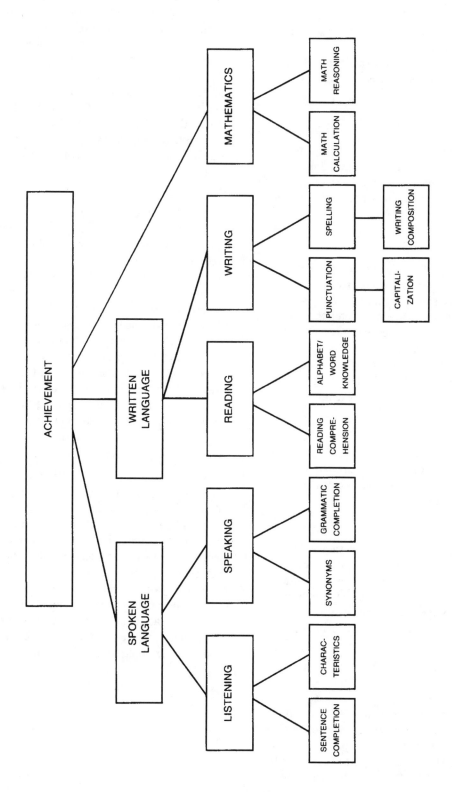

DAB–2 Test Model

Listening

1. *Story Comprehension* (35 items). The examiner reads aloud brief stories of increasing length, and the student answers questions about them.

2. *Characteristics* (35 items). The examiner reads aloud a brief statement, and the student decides whether it is true or false.

Speaking

3. *Synonyms* (25 items). The examiner says a word and the student supplies a word with the same meaning.

4. *Grammatic Completion* (27 items). The examiner reads unfinished sentences and the student supplies the missing morphological form.

Reading

5. *Alphabet-Word Knowledge* (65 items). The first 25 items include matching letters and words, recognizing and naming letters, and recognizing beginning and ending consonants. These items are only administered to students who cannot read at least three of the five words in the 40-word list which comprises this subtest.

6. *Reading Comprehension* (35 items). The student silently reads short stories of increasing length and answers questions about them that are read by the examiner.

Writing

7 and 8. *Capitalization and Punctuation.* The student is given 30 sentences without capitals and punctuation and asked to rewrite them correctly. Separate scores are calculated for each subtest.

9. *Spelling* (20 items). The student writes words dictated by the examiner.

10. *Written Composition.* The student is shown three pictures representing the story "The Tortoise and the Hare." He or she writes a story based on the picture. Vocabulary is measured by counting the number of words with seven or more letters. In addition, the written composition is scored according to nine criteria, including sequence, use of dialogue, and total words.

Applied Mathematics

11. *Mathematics Reasoning* (30 items). The student is asked a question involving a math concept or operation and asked to answer it without using pencil or paper. Pictures are used for the younger students. "Art drove 55 m.p.h. for 10 hours. How far did he drive?" "Which pie is divided into fourths?"

12. *Mathematics Calculation.* The student is given a page of math calculations arranged in order of increasing diffi-culty. A 15-minute time limit is imposed.

Starting levels according to age are indicated on the examiner's form for each subtest. Ceiling levels, which differ for each subtest, are also clearly indicated. In this way students are tested only over an appropriate range for their age. Each subtest begins with one sample item to illustrate the task. The raw score for each subtest is converted into a percentile rank and a standard score with a mean of 10 and a standard deviation of 3. Subtest scores can then be combined into 9 composite scores called quotients. Quotients are standard scores with a mean of 100 and standard deviation of 15.

STRENGTHS OF THE DAB–2

• The DAB–2 is a well-designed and well-normed technically strong test. Test–retest reliability is good, and validity data reported in the manual is strong.

• The DAB–2 manual is comprehensive and clearly written. The administration and scoring procedures are well described. The discussion of the DAB Test Model is interesting to read. The manual also includes a well-written discussion of the problems with group tests.

• The DAB–2 measures a wide variety of skills that are directly related to classroom performance. Interpretation of test results to teachers, parents, and older students is not difficult due to the familiarity of subtest tasks. The comprehensiveness of the test adds to its usefulness for special educators in the public schools.

LIMITING FACTORS OF THE DAB–2

• The DAB is a long test. For students at the upper end of the age norms, it may require two hours to administer. While the tasks are varied on each subtest, they all have a "school-like" quality that could be overwhelming to the student who is not doing well in school. Administering the test in two sessions or selecting only critical subtests or composites is recommended.

• Many of the subtest tasks such as those in Spelling, Math Calculation, Capitalization, and Punctuation are familiar to the students; others such as those in Characteristics require a new type of thinking. For these subtests, additional examples or training items would be very useful.

• As with all test instruments that attempt to assess students' abilities across a wide age range, the DAB–2 has less value for students at the youngest and oldest ends of the norms than for those in the middle range. Some of the subtests assess skills that are not very appropriate to measure in six and seven year olds. For example, Characteristics uses a true–false format; many young children will not have that concept, especially when applied to such statements as, "All pork is meat."

• The concept of *synonyms* is also very difficult for young children. At the other end of the age range, older students with perfect scores on some subtests receive standard scores of only 11 (Grammatic Completion) and 12 (Alphabet/Word Knowledge). Perfect scores should be noted on the profile. Clearly not all subtests are sensitive at all age levels. By studying the norms tables for the ages of the students to be tested, the examiner can select the most appropriate and sensitive subtests for individual students.

• Standardization of written composition scoring is very difficult. The DAB–2 uses a combination of long words plus thematic criteria, such as use of dialogue and humor, to determine a score. Long words, as a measure of vocabulary, ignore short but unusual words. Excellent cohesive stories do not always contain humor. The Written Composition score on the DAB–2 should be interpreted with caution.

• On several subtests, additional information is needed to interpret a student's performance. For example, on Synonyms a student may not know the meaning of the stimulus word or may have word-finding problems that make it difficult for him or her to supply a synonym.

• On Math Reasoning, some of the questions are quite long; poor auditory memory or auditory comprehension, rather than lack of math skills, may cause errors,. Examiners should consider these types of possibilities when they interpret an individual student's performance.

Kaufman Test of Educational Achievement (KTEA)

Alan S. and Nadeen L. Kaufman
American Guidance Service, 1985
4201 Woodland Road, P.O. Box 99, Circle Pines, MN 55014-1796

Purpose	To measure school achievement in grades 1–12
Major Areas Tested	Reading, spelling, mathematics
Age or Grade Range	Grades 1–12
Usually Given By	Educational diagnosticians Special educational teachers Psychologists
Type of Test	Individual Standardized Norm-referenced
Scores Obtained	Age level Stanine Grade Level Standard Percentile
Student Performance Timed?	No
Testing Time	20–30 minutes (Brief Form); 60–75 minutes (Comprehensive Form)
Scoring/Interpretation Time	10–15 minutes
Normed On	Stratified random sample of 589 students in 25 cities in 15 states; sample balanced for sex, geographic region, socioeconomic status, and educational level of the parents
Alternate Forms Available?	The 2 forms, Brief and Comprehensive, may be used as alternate forms

FORMAT

The Kaufman Test of Educational Achievement (KTEA) is an individually-administered test of academic skills in reading, spelling, and math for the first through twelfth grades. Two forms are provided, Brief and Comprehensive. The Brief Form globally samples reading, spelling, and mathematics; the Comprehensive Form separates reading into decoding and comprehension and math into applications and computation. The materials for each form consist of a manual, an easel book for presentation of test items, individual forms for recording responses and profiling scores, and a parental reporting form. The subtests for the Brief Form are:

Mathematics (52 items). Assesses basic math computation skills as well as applications and reasoning. Computations are done with pencil and paper while concept and applications are read by the examiner and often have accompanying pictures.

Reading (52 items). Assesses reading of single words and reading comprehension. The comprehension items often require a gestural response.

Spelling (40 items). Assesses spelling through writing a dictated word list of increasing difficulty.

In the Comprehensive Form, mathematics is separated into a Mathematics Applications and a Mathematics Computation subtest with 60 items each. Reading is broken into Decoding (60 items) and Comprehension (50 items). The Spelling test format remains the same.

The authors recommend that the Brief Form be used unless there is a particular reason for needing the more specific information on the Comprehensive Form. On the response forms, starting points according to grade are indicated for each subtest. Items are grouped into units, and testing is discontinued whenever a student makes errors on all the items in a unit.

Raw scores for each subtest are converted into age scores, grade scores, stanines, percentiles and standard scores (mean: 100; standard deviation: 15). On the back of the response form, standard scores can be graphed to give a profile of a student's performance. Procedures are given in the manual for determining if subtest differences are significant.

STRENGTHS OF THE KTEA

• The KTEA is a well standardized reliable quick test of academic achievement. The Brief Form compares favorably with the WRAT-R, the BASIS, and the NEAT, in terms of time, content, and technical properties.

• The comprehensive form also provides criterion-referenced assessment data to analyze student errors.

• Strong internal consistency and test-retest reliability results are presented in the manual; extensive validity studies are also reported. Spring and fall norms are provided for both forms of the KTEA.

LIMITING FACTORS OF THE KTEA

• The Reading Comprehension items require silent reading and a gestural response. Many students are resistant to this task, perhaps feeling shy or foolish. When a student doesn't respond, the examiner needs to explore further to find out if he cannot read the item or doesn't want to respond.

• Although paraprofessionals may administer the KTEA, the manual suggests that trained examiners do the interpretation.

• The Report to Parents was intended to explain the results of the KTEA in non-technical terms. It is quite wordy and raises more questions than it clarifies.

Norris Educational Achievement Test (NEAT)

Janet Switzer
Western Psychological Services, 1988
12031 Wilshire Blvd., Los Angeles, CA 90025

Purpose	To provide a rapid screening measure of basic academic skills as well as a reliable measure of pupil progress
Major Areas Tested	Reading, writing, spelling, arithmetic
Age or Grade Range	Preschool–12th grade
Usually Given By	Classroom teacher Special education teacher Psychologist Administrator
Type of Test	Individual Normed Group (some subtests)
Scores Obtained	Standard Percentile Age Stanine Grade
Student Performance Timed?	Yes (some subtests)
Testing Time	30 minutes
Scoring/Interpretation Time	15 minutes
Normed On	3,000 students from 50 school districts in 19 states; sample balanced for community size, parent education level, ethnic background, age, grade, and sex
Alternate Forms Available?	Yes

FORMAT

The Norris Educational Achievement Test (NEAT) is an individual test of reading, spelling, math, and writing achievement. Norms are provided for grades 1 through 12, including 11th and 12th graders "planning to go to college."

The materials consist of an Examiner's Manual, which includes directions for administration, scoring, and interpretation, and a Master Booklet, in which either students write their answers or the examiner records student responses. Equivalent Forms A and B are provided for test–retest purposes.

The NEAT is composed of the six subtests described below:

1. *Readiness.* Given to students in second grade or younger, Readiness is composed of three tasks assessing skills prerequisite for writing, arithmetic, and reading. Fine Motor Coordination is assessed through a form-copying task. Math Concepts evaluates basic concepts such as size, shape, counting, number, writing, and adding groups. Letters includes matching, naming, and giving letter sounds. Separate scores are given for each subtest, as is a total Readiness score.

2. *Word Recognition.* Students from primer through college level read aloud single words, which increase in difficulty.

3. *Spelling.* A written spelling test is the usual classroom format. The examiner pronounces a word, uses it in a sentence, and pronounces it again. Words range from primer through high school level.

4. *Arithmetic.* This standard test of math computation includes basic operations with whole numbers and fractions. A 10-minute limit is imposed; if students are still working at the end of the ten minutes, they are given a different-colored pencil and allowed to continue.

5. *Oral Reading and Comprehension.* Students read aloud paragraphs of graded difficulty. The paragraphs are composed of words on Word Recognition. This allows a comparison of students' word reading in isolation and in context. Students begin this test with a paragraph that includes words at the level at which they have read with 90 percent accuracy on Word Recognition. Each paragraph is prefaced by an Orientation Cue from the examiner. For example, "This is a story about people wanting improvement in one of their town's roads. They tell the newspapers."

Following the oral reading, students are asked four recall questions to assess reading comprehension. A basal-ceiling procedure combining reading errors and recall questions is used to determine whether students continue with more difficult paragraphs or drop back to lower levels. Only "significant context reading errors" are scored; these include words that are significantly changed or that have altered meanings. Minor errors (boys/boy, says/said) or repetitions are not scored as errors. Recall questions are to be answered with words in the paragraph, not words in the Orientation Cue. Scores for speed, accuracy, and recall are calculated.

6. *Written Language.* Students write an original composition on the topic "On My Next Vacation" (Form A) or "On My Next Weekend" (Form B). A five-minute limit is given, and compositions are scored on a holistic basis, using one-minute "standardized" sample essays.

STRENGTHS OF THE NEAT

• The NEAT is a new test clearly designed to provide the quick screening information usually obtained through WRAT and, less frequently, the BASIS. The assessment of basic skills in reading, writing, spelling, and math in one instrument over a wide range is an obvious strength of all three tests. The NEAT offers several features not available in other tests:

Equivalent forms A and B for test–retest purposes

Measures of both reading recognition and reading comprehension

A comparison of student's word recognition skills with contextual reading skills using the same vocabulary

More complete skills assessment of Readiness level

A standardized measure of written language

• The test format and tasks presented are very familiar to students as they were selected to represent usual classroom tasks. This feature of the NEAT increases the use of administration and makes interpretation of students' scores directly applicable to classroom performance.

• The NEAT was authored by a clinician. As a result, the test procedure and the manual instructions provide many opportunities for gathering sensitive diagnostic information. One example is the "slowing point." On the Reading Recognition test, the examiner notes the point at which students "slow down," shifting from sight reading to word analysis. Another example is the way in which the spelling tests on Form A and Form B are structured. Item 33, Form A is *city*; Item 33, Form B is *cent*. By analyzing students' responses to Form A and later, in post-testing, to Form B, specific skills learned (such as the soft sound of *c*) can be documented. This procedure is followed in Arithmetic as well.

• The directions for administration are clear and sensitive to student needs. The examiner is given good instructions for scoring procedures while administering the test. For example, Word Recognition is to be scored while students are completing Arithmetic. This allows the examiner to ascertain the correct level for beginning Oral Contextual Reading.

LIMITING FACTORS OF THE NEAT

- The NEAT is a new test; Norm tables reflect a nation-wide standardization sample. Rehabilitation and validity data are currently being gathered. The value of the NEAT as a screening instrument as well as a measure of student progress cannot yet be evaluated.

- The Oral Reading Comprehension Test is a unique measure of reading skills. The directions for administering and interpreting this subtest are complex, in part due to their unfamiliarity. Extensive examples of "significant" and "minor" errors are needed to help the examiner unfamiliar with this concept. In addition, examples are needed for scoring the recall questions. It is difficult to understand the difference between "words in the paragraph" and "words in the Orientation Cue."

Peabody Individual Achievement Test–Revised
(PIAT–R)

Frederick C. Markwardt, Jr.
American Guidance Service, Inc., 1989
4201 Woodland Rd., P.O. Box 99, Circle Pines, MN 55014-1796

Purpose	To provide a wide-range screening measure of reading, spelling, mathematics, written language, and general information
Major Areas Tested	Mathematics, reading, spelling, and general information
Age or Grade Range	Grades K–12
Usually Given By	Classroom teacher Paraprofessional Special education teacher Any trained person Psychologist
Type of Test	Standardized Individual Norm-referenced
Scores Obtained	Age equivalent Grade equivalent Standard Percentile
Student Performance Timed?	No
Testing Time	30–40 minutes
Scoring/Interpretation Time	25–30 minutes
Normed On	National standardized sample of 1,738 K–12 students based on U.S. Census projections for a representative school sample for the year 1990. Sample was stratified by sex, geographic region, socio-economic status, and race or ethnic group
Alternate Forms Available?	No

FORMAT

The Peabody Individual Achievement Test (PIAT-R) is the 1989 edition of the PIAT, which was originally published in 1970. The major features of the original PIAT have been retained. However, item content and art work have been updated and many new items have been included.

The PIAT-R materials consist of four easel kits of test items, each containing the directions for subtest administration; individual test records to record student responses; and one manual which includes procedures for general administration, scoring and interpretation, the norms tables and technical information. Separate Response Booklets are needed for the Written Expression subtest. Optional materials include a cassette for the Pronunciation Guide and a carrying bag.

The PIAT-R consists of 5 subtests given in the order listed below. The test combines short answer and multiple-choice questions; no writing is required. Suggested starting points are given for each subtest, and a basal and ceiling procedure is used to reduce testing to a critical range for each student. The five subtests are:

1. *General Information.* This subtest contains 100 questions that are read to the students and answered orally. The content includes science, social studies, fine arts, and sports.

2. *Reading Recognition.* This subtest includes 100 items. It begins with letter matching and naming. The remaining items are single words that the student reads aloud. The words were selected from a basal reading series using both sight word and phonic approaches.

3. *Reading Comprehension.* This subtest includes 82 multiple-choice items. For each item, the student is presented with a page that contains one sentence to be read silently. The next page contains 4 illustrations, and the student selects the picture which best illustrates the sentence.

4. *Mathematics.* This subtest includes 100 multiple-choice items ranging from matching numbers to high school geometry and trigonometry. The questions are read to the student, who then selects the correct answer from 4 visually-presented choices. All computation must be done mentally.

5. *Spelling.* This subtest includes 100 items which assess the student's ability to recognize the correct spelling of a word. The examiner pronounces the word, and the student selects the correct spelling from 4 visually-presented choices. No written spelling is required.

While the PIAT-R was standardized on the above 5 subtests given in the prescribed order, selected subtests can be given for individual students. Age level, grade level, percentile ranks, and standard scores are provided for each subtest and for the PIAT-R total. In addition, a Total Reading Score can be obtained by combining the results for the Reading Recognition and Reading Comprehension subtests.

The test records include two profiles for graphic presen-tation of an individual student's test results. The Developmental Score Profile may be used to plot grade or age equivalents, while the Standard Score Profile is used for plotting standard scores.

In addition to the five main subtests, the PIAT-R includes an optional subtest to assess written expression at two levels: Level I, for kindergarten and first grade, tests prewriting skills such as writing one's name, copying letters and words, and writing letters and words from dictation. Level II, for grades 2–12, asks the student to write a story about a stimulus picture. Level II is scored on a three-point scale using 24 criteria that range from legibility to story completeness and use of metaphors. Grade-based stanines are used to report scores for both Levels I and II. In addition, a 15-point developmental scaled score is available for Level II. Because the psychometric characteristics of the Written Expression subtest score is not incorporated into the PIAT-R total score.

STRENGTHS OF THE PIAT–R

• The PIAT–R provides a quick rough estimate of achievement levels. The multiple-choice items allow the test taker to move quickly, and the variety of titles holds student interest. These factors make the PIAT–R especially useful for screening underachieving secondary students.

• Used in conjunction with other diagnostic tests, the subtest of the PIAT–R can provide useful information. The Mathematics subtest includes items that assess a student's problem-solving skills more effectively than a straight computation test would. The picture format of the Reading Comprehension subtest is a unique way to measure the important skill of sentence comprehension. For students who have not previously had an intelligence test, the General Information subtest can provide a quick estimate of overall functioning.

Perhaps most useful is a comparison of a student's Spelling Score in the PIAT–R (which requires only recognition of the correct spelling with written spelling performance on a test such as the Wide Range Achievement Test–3, (p. 60). For example, suppose two sixth-grade students obtained the grade scores shown here:

	WRAT3 Spelling Grade Level	PIAT–R Spelling Grade Level
Student A	4th	5.8
Student B	4th	4.7

Both students are performing significantly below grade level on written spelling. Student A, however, has the ability to recognize correct spelling, as his or her PIAT–R score indicates, thus demonstrating some visual memory skills. The remedial program for Student A would attempt to capitalize on that visual memory, and the expectations for performance in such skills as proofreading and dictionary work would be higher than would be for Student B.

• The PIAT–R is a standardized test with good technical characteristics.

Both students are performing significantly below grade level on written spelling. Student A, however, has the ability to recognize correct spelling, as his or her PIAT–R score indicates, thus demonstrating some visual memory skills. The remedial program for Student A would attempt to capitalize on that visual memory, and the expectations for performance in such skills as proofreading and dictionary work would be higher than would be for Student B.

• The PIAT–R is a standardized test with good technical characteristics.

LIMITING FACTORS OF THE PIAT-R

• The PIAT-R was not intended to be a comprehensive diagnostic instrument in any of the subtest areas. For students with academic problems, it should serve only as a guide for further, in-depth, testing.

• When interpreting a student's performance on the PIAT-R, it is necessary to keep in mind the exact task presented on each subtest. The broad general subtest names (Mathematics, Reading Recognition, Reading Comprehension, Spelling, and General Information) do not describe the tasks. For example, the examiner must be careful not to make general statements about a student's spelling based on the PIAT–R alone, because the task of recognizing correct spelling is quite different from written spelling (the more usual classroom task). Also, such a statement as, "Student C is two years below grade level in math" may be very inaccurate if based on the PIAT–R alone; the student's computation skills may be excellent.

• The multiple-choice format used on the Mathematics, Reading Comprehension, and Spelling subtests is appropriate for a screening tool but may yield very inaccurate results for individual students. For example, the impulsive student often selects an answer without thinking, whereas the student with sophisticated test-taking skills may puzzle out an answer by the process of elimination without really knowing the information.

• As with any test made up of subtests, there is a tendency to focus attention on a comparison of subtest scores; that is, to discuss Student A's performance in spelling compared to her performance in math. The PIAT–R manual discusses the problems in this type of analysis and presents guidelines for interpreting differences between raw scores on subtests. The examiner should study these guidelines carefully to avoid overinterpretation of subtest differences.

Wide Range Achievement Test–Revised (WRAT3)

Gary S. Wilkinson
Jastak Associates, A Division of Wide Range, Inc., 1993
P.O. Box 3410, Wilmington, DE 19804-0250

Purpose	To assess skills in reading, spelling, and arithmetic
Major Areas Tested	Reading, spelling, and arithmetic
Age or Grade Range	5 years–adult
Usually Given by	Classroom teacher Special education teacher Psychologist
Type of Test	Standardized Individual Norm-referenced
Scores Obtained	Standard Percentile Grade equivalent
Student Performance Timed?	Yes (Arithmetic only)
Testing Time	20–30 minutes
Scoring/Interpretation Time	15 minutes
Normed On	Nationwide sample of nearly 5,000 children and adults from 48 states; norming sample not described
Alternate Forms Available	No

FORMAT

The WRAT3 is the latest revision of the WRAT, originally published in 1937. The WRAT3 has eliminated the two levels of the WRAT-R and returned to a single test form for all individuals aged 5-75 years. Two alternate equivalent forms, Blue and Tan, are provided to allow pre- and post-testing. In addition, the Blue and Tan forms can be combined to provide a test with more items. The materials of the WRAT3 consist of the administration manual, Blue and Tan test forms for recording student responses, and a plastic reading card for each form of the test. The use of this card for the individual to read from is essential because the test form on which the examiner records responses includes the phonetic guide for each item. In addition, a Profile/Analysis Form is provided.

The administration manual includes descriptions of the subtests, directions for administration and scoring, norm tables, reliability and validity data, and interpretation guidelines.

The WRAT3 contains three subtests:

1. *Reading*. Recognizing and naming letters and pronouncing single words.

2. *Spelling*. Copying marks, writing the name, and writing single words from dictation.

3. *Arithmetic*. Counting, reading numerals, solving oral problems, and performing basic written computation skills.

"The WRAT3 was intentionally designed to eliminate, as totally as possible, the effects of comprehension." (Administration Manual, p.1) It is designed to measure the process of decoding in reading, encoding in spelling, and basic arithmetic computation.

The three subtests can be given independently. When all three are given, no particular order is required.

Each of the subtests begins with a brief assessment of pre-academic skills. In the Reading Section, the individual is asked to name 15 letters of the alphabet. The Spelling pretest includes name writing and writing single letters from dictation. The pre-arithmetic test includes counting, reading digits, showing three and eight fingers, indicating which number in a pair is larger, and solving three oral addition and subtraction problems. Older students are given the pretests only when they cannot achieve a basal level on the Reading, Spelling, or Arithmetic subtest. Level 2 students who cannot achieve a basal level are also given the pretests.

The items in each subtest are arranged in order of difficulty. The student continues working until a ceiling level is reached in Reading (10 consecutive errors) and Spelling (10 consecutive errors), or until the time limit expires in Arithmetic (15 minutes).

A raw score for each subtest represents the number of correct responses prior to reaching the ceiling. Full credit is given for the pre-academic tasks if they are not administered. Raw scores are converted into standard scores and percentiles for age as well as grade equivalents. The grade equivalents are expressed in full years (K, 1, 5, HS) and are designed to give a general indication of instructional level. Norms tables are provided for two-month intervals in the five to seven age range, six-month intervals through 11 years, one-year intervals through 16 years, and two to ten year intervals for the adult population.

STRENGTHS OF THE WRAT3

• The WRAT3 is undoubtedly the best-known and most widely used quick measure of individual achievement in basic academic skills. Students of all ages and skill levels can be tested to get an estimate of academic performance that can serve as a first step in diagnostic evaluation.

• The addition of equivalent forms enhances the value of the WRAT3 in assessing pupil progress. This feature of the test, together with its wide age range, permits the continuous measure of progress over several years of intervention.

• The WRAT3 is inexpensive in terms of materials and time. It is quick to administer and score.

• The elimination of the numerical grade score is to be applauded. Grade scores are often misused, and the reporting of standard scores and percentile is much more appropriate.

• The test forms are easy to read and student friendly.

• Providing norms for narrower age intervals in the younger age ranges increase the sensitivity of the scoring over previous versions for beginning readers.

LIMITING FACTORS OF THE WRAT3

• *In Uses and Misuses of the WRAT*, a technical report published by Jastak Associates, Inc., the limitations of the WRAT are clearly described. They apply equally to the WRAT3. This report, together with WRAT-R, Monograph 1 (Wilkinson, 1987), is issued by the publisher to avoid misuse of the test and should be "must" reading for every examiner.

• Because the WRAT3 is so easy to give and to score, it is frequently overused and misused. It must be viewed as an initial estimate of a student's basic academic skills and not as a complete diagnostic instrument. Too often, students are admitted to or excluded from special programs on the basis of their WRAT3 scores alone. An investigation of the content of WRAT3 subtests dictates that such a use of the test is not warranted.

• The Reading subtest assesses word recognition only. The student simply reads aloud a list of single words. There is no measure of sentence reading, paragraph reading, or comprehension. Some students can decode single words but cannot decode sentences and paragraphs, the more essential reading tasks. Of course, good decoders with poor comprehension are not identified on the WRAT3.

- The Arithmetic subtest suffers from the same limitations of all calculation-only tests. Student performance depends upon the curriculum that has been taught. Students instructed totally in "new math" may obtain unrealistically low scores, even though their ability to solve applied problems might be very high.

- The manual states that the WRAT3 is a valuable tool for instructional planning when the examiner analyzes the types of errors a student makes on the three subtests. No guidelines for this type of informal assessment are given. The table that follows illustrates error analysis on the spelling subtest. Information of this type should be included in the manual if the WRAT3 is to be used for instructional planning.

- The WRAT3 provides a Profile/Analysis form using the Absolute Scores and relating them to age and grade. The purpose is to track individual progress over time and to allow comparisons of skills across subtests. Although the author discusses the value of the Absolute Scale at length, he does not describe how to graph or interpret the profile in the manual. Examples are needed to make this a usable tool.

- Although the author is very specific in the manual regarding the intended use of the WRAT3, the low cost, quick administration, and easily understood scores result in overuse and misuse of the WRAT3. The information obtained which measures three specific skills should not become the primary information used in diagnosis or placement decisions.

Analysis of Spelling Errors

Word	Spelling	Error Type	Teaching Strategy
cat	ɔat	Letter reversal (kinesthetic)	Dictation, visual-motor training
boy	doy	b/d confusion (visual-kinesthetic)	Visual discrimination, visual-motor training
will	well	Vowel discrimination (auditory)	Auditory discrimination, word patterns (ill)
make	mack	Vowel error and visual recall	Silent-e rule, dictation
say	sae	Poor visual recall	Word patterns (ay), word tracing
grown explain	grone explane	Poor visual recall	Word tracing
enter advice	inter edvice	Vowel discrimination (auditory)	Auditory discrimination, dictation
surprise	suprise	Incorrect pronunciation (auditory)	Auditory-kinesthetic feedback, visual cuing, color coding
cut cook	kut kook	Poor visual recall	Word tracing
light dress watch	lite dres woch	Poor visual recall	Word tracing, color coding

Wechsler Individual Achievement Test (WIAT)

The Psychological Corporation, 1992
Harcourt Brace and Company
555 Academic Court, San Antonio, TX 78204-2498

Purpose	To create an achievement test that is relevant to curriculum trends and that would assess student's skills in eight curriculum areas. The test is directly linked with the Weschler scales to allow meaningful ability–achievement discrepancies to be derived.
Major Areas Tested	Word reading, mathematics reasoning, spelling, reading comprehension, numerical operations, listening comprehension, oral, and written expression
Age or Grade Range	K–12; (5 years through 19 years)
Usually Given By	Psychologists Educational diagnosticians
Type of Test	Individual Standardized Norm-referenced
Scores Obtained	Standard scores Grade equivalent Percentile ranks Age equivalent Stanines Normal-curve equivalent
Student Performance Timed?	No, with the exception of written expression
Testing Time	30–60 minutes; 3 subtest screener in 15–20 minutes
Scoring/Interpretation Time	30–40 minutes
Normed On	Nationwide random sample of 4,252 children, stratified by age and grade, gender, race/ethnicity, geographic region, and parent education, according to the 1988 report from the U.S. Census.
Alternate Forms Available?	No

FORMAT

The WIAT is a new individual test of academic achievement. It was developed to assess students skills in reading, writing, spelling, mathematics, listening comprehension, and oral expression. The WIAT was developed by the Psychological Corporation to accompany the WISC–III (p. 302) and to allow the measurement of ability–achievement discrepancies, the classic definition of specific learning disabilities. The materials consist of two stimulus booklets that contain the items, administration directions, and correct responses for the eight subtests. Students write their answers to math and writing subtests, which provide a comprehensive record for student responses and the WIAT Battery Manual.

The WIAT provides for the assessment of all learning disabilities specified in the federal law. Because the test is designed for students in grades K–12, each subtest assesses a wide range of skill levels. A basal-ceiling approach is used to ensure that the students are only tested over the range of their skills. Starting points and procedures for determining basal and ceiling levels are well described in both the manual and two stimulus booklets. Subtests are administered in the following order.

1. *Numerical Operations*. A 40-item math calculation test ranging from simple addition to beginning algebra. The student writes responses in the booklet provided. Generous time limits are provided for each set of problems.

2. *Listening Comprehension*. 37 items which assess a wide range of listening comprehension skills. The first 9 items require listening to a short sentence and pointing to the appropriate picture from four choices (Point to the *festive* occasion). For the remaining items, the student listens to a short story and answers one or two questions about the story read by the examiner. A picture is provided to make the task more interesting, but the answers to the questions are not in the pictures.

3. *Oral Expression*. 16 items that assess such verbal expression skills as picture naming ("Tell me a word that means *a roadway across a river*"), picture description, and giving directions.

4. *Written Expression*. This test of written expression is designed for 3rd through 12th grades. The task is to write a letter in which the student is given a choice of two topics - an ideal place to live, or a place you'd like to go for one day. A 15-minute time limit is imposed. The student's writing may be evaluated both holistically and analytically.

5. *Basic Reading*. The first seven items of this subtest assess beginning reading skills such as initial sounds, ending sounds, and single-word identifications ("Point to the word *cow*"). The remaining 48 items are single words to be read aloud by the student.

6. *Mathematics Reasoning*. 50 items that assess a student's understanding of basic math concepts and the ability to use them in problem solving. Concepts assessed include counting, telling time, word problems using all basic operations, graph reading, measurement, and others.

7. *Spelling*. 50 items that are dictated by the examiner for the student to write. Easier items include writing letters by name and sound, but 44 items list single spelling words of increasing difficulty.

8. *Reading Comprehension*. 38 items in which the student reads a sentence or a short paragraph and then orally answers questions asked by the examiner. Questions require both the recall of factual information ("How did cardamom come to Europe?") and inferential thinking ("Why is Jellinek's disease receiving more attention?").

STRENGTHS OF THE WIAT

- The primary purpose of the WIAT is to provide a test that is normed on the same population as the WISC–III (p.302) and has the same technical characteristics. Because of this, the examiner can compare directly a student's ability scores on the WISC–III with his or her WIAT achievement scores. Ability–achievement discrepancies can be derived using the procedures in the manual or the computer scoring software available. As the ability–achievement discrepancy is the hallmark characteristic of a specific learning disability and is required in many states to qualify a student for special services, it is a very desirable feature of the WIAT. The test is well standardized and normed and has good technical characteristics.

- The WIAT is a well-designed test with a very comprehensive, easy-to-read manual.

- The easel-stimulus books contain all of the information needed to administer the subtest so that the manual is not needed during administration.

- Although individual subtests can be given, the authors recommend the administration of the complete test in order to gain knowledge about a student's total skills; the child's performance on tests in the same domain can be compared and provide direction for instruction and remediation. For example, a comparison of written and oral expression skills may lead to recommendations regarding written versus oral testing procedures for a given student.

- The WIAT has some excellent subtests. The Reading Comprehension subtest has a question-and-answer format, which is more familiar to students than the often-used cloze procedure. The questions include both factual and interpretive comprehension. The Written Expression subtest can be scored by either holistic or analytic methods, which enables the examiner to obtain a good understanding of the student's writing.

- Three subtests—Word Reading, Mathematics Reasoning, and Spelling—are designed to be a screening test. Using this academic screener in conjunction with the WISC–III is a helpful assessment option.

LIMITING FACTORS OF THE WIAT

• As with any achievement test that covers a wide age range, the WIAT assesses students in the middle of the age range more accurately than younger and older students. Although the WIAT has included some items at the readiness level on several subtests, the test provides limited assessment of kindergarten and first-grade students.

• The Oral Expression test includes naming vocabulary, picture description, and giving directions. These three tasks are quite different in their skill requirements, and the total oral expression score may have little meaning for some students.

• The ability–achievement discrepancy is the central concept of the WIAT. This concept is well described in the manual, which should be read thoroughly by all examiners. It is also important to realize that many students may have specific learning disabilities who do not demonstrate a statistical discrepancy. One example is the older student who may have improved his achievement scores through the development of compensation strategies learned in tutoring. Another is the younger student who may not show the discrepancy in the early grades because this student is able to use memory skills for early reading and math. Decisions about special education eligibility should not be made on the basis of an ability-achievement discrepancy alone.

WIAT: Sample Item from Oral Expression Instructions to Students:
Look at this picture. Imagine that we have to describe the picture to someone who isn't here to see it. Look at all the things in the picture and take a few minutes to think about what to say.

Decoding Skills Test (DST)

Ellis Richardson and Barbara DiBenedetto
York Press, 1985
2712 Mt. Carmel Road, Parkton, MD 21120

Purpose	To identify reading disabled students and provide a diagnostic profile of their decoding skill development
Major Areas Tested	The decoding process of reading
Age or Grade Range	First to fifth grade reading level
Usually Given By	Reading specialist Classroom teacher Special education teacher
Type of Test	Diagnostic Criterion referenced
Scores Obtained	No scores are obtained
Student Performance Timed?	No
Testing Time	20–30 minutes
Scoring/Interpretation Time	15–20 minutes
Normed On	Not normed
Alternate Forms Available?	No

FORMAT

The Decoding Skills Test (DST) is an individually-administered criterion referenced instrument which provides a variety of types of diagnostic information about a student's decoding skills. The materials consist of the Manual of Instructions, The Presentation Book, from which the student reads, the Basal/Ceiling and Passage Scoring Key Card, Individual Scoring Booklets, and the Phonic Profile Worksheet. A stop watch is also necessary for administering the test. The Manual of Instructions includes discussion of the test design, uses of the DST, directions for administration, scoring and interpretation, as well as reliability and validity data.

The DST has three subtests:

1. *Basal Vocabulary* is composed of 11 word lists representing reading levels from preprimer through a 5.2 reader. Words were selected from high-occurrence words in 10 common basal reading series; both phonic-linguistic and conventional basal vocabulary series were used. The Basal-Finder procedure has the student read the first three words of each 10-word list until an error is made. Then the examiner begins with the Main List, starting one level lower than the list on which the error occurred and continues with successively lower paragraphs until the student reads 8 of 10 words correctly. The student continues reading the higher lists until he misses more than 5 words in a list or completes List 11.

2. *Phonic Patterns* is composed of four sections which each contain six 5-word lists. The six word lists assess the following phonic patterns; cvc, ccvc, cvce, ccvce, cvvc, ccvvc. The 4 sections are monosyllabic real words, polysyllabic real words, monosyllabic nonsense words, and polysyllabic nonsense words. Students begin with the first word in each section and continue until they make 10 consecutive errors or complete the section. The same procedure is followed for each of the 4 sections. The presentation of both real and nonsense words enables the examiner to discover not only the student's specific phonic knowledge, but also how well the student transfers phonic skills to new words.

3. *Contextual Decoding* consists of eleven passages which correspond with the 11 reading levels in Subtest 1. The 10 Subtest 1 words are embedded in the passage, as are 6 words from Subtest 2. Students begin with the passage at the same level as their basal list in Subtest 1. The basal level is the highest passage in which the student reads at least 8 of the target words from Subtest 1 correctly. A ceiling is reached when the student misses more than five target words in one passage. Thus, in the DST, target words are measured twice, once in isolation and once in context. This allows a direct comparison of the student's contextual decoding with his decoding of single words. Subtest 3 is timed to allow a measure of reading rate, and five sample recall questions test comprehension.

Following the completion of the three subtests, the examiner scores the student's performance to obtain several types of diagnostic information. This information is outlined in the table that follows.

Following the scoring of each subtest, the examiner transfers the scores to the face page of the Scoring Booklet. If the student's raw score on the 120-item Phonic Pattern Subtest is at least 10, the examiner can obtain more diagnostic information by completing the Phonic Pattern Profile. A separate worksheet is provided for this purpose. By following directions presented in the manual carefully, the examiner can gain good information about a student's consonant patterns, vowel patterns, syllabic patterns, and phonic transfer. The information is then transferred to the face sheet of the Scoring Booklet in profile form.

STRENGTHS OF THE DST

• The DST is a unique test in concept and in structure. The careful construction of the word lists, phonic tests, and passages provide the examiner with a wealth of valuable information about a student's decoding skills. The comparison of decoding in isolation and decoding in context as well as the measures of phonic transfer are two examples. The information is so designed to lead directly to instructional planning.

• The manual is complete and clearly written. Examples are given to illustrate scoring procedures. The chapter on interpretation is very helpful.

• Although the manual states that the DST is useful from first to fifth grade, it can be used very effectively with older students who continue to have decoding problems.

• The Contextual Decoding Subtest has two ceiling procedures. The standard procedure has the student read until more than 50% of the target words are read incorrectly. For those students who are clearly struggling with contextual decoding, the option is given to stop when the student reads less than 80% of the target words correctly. This is a sensitive consideration for the student for whom this process is very painful.

• The careful test construction procedures of the DST ensure its content validity. Test-retest reliability is good, and studies of good and poor readers support the criterion validity of the test.

• Despite the lack of alternate forms, the careful construction of the DST allows it to be used as a sensitive measure of progress.

LIMITING FACTORS OF THE DST

• As is noted in the manual, the DST takes time to learn to administer and score. The information obtained is different from that on most reading tests, and the scoring procedures, particularly for the phonic profile, are laborious until the examiner has given several tests.

- The cursory measure of comprehension could be discarded. Its inclusion tempts the examiner to use it in determining instructional level. The DST is strictly a decoding test and should be used that way.
- In the Interpretation Section, the author provides

guidelines for Reading Rate and Error Rate. For example, a reading rate of 50–60 words per minute at instructional level is described as average. No data are cited to support these guidelines.

Diagnostic Information Obtained From DST Subtests

Subtest	Diagnostic Information
Basal Vocabulary	1. Instructional Level. The grade equivalent of the student's basal level word list, the list on which 8 out of 10 words were read correctly.
	2. Frustration Level. The grade equivalent of the student's ceiling level word list, the list on which less than 5 out of the 10 words were read correctly.
Phonic Patterns	1. Phonic Transfer Index (PTI). A measure of the ability to transfer phonic skills to new words; obtained by dividing the number of real-word/nonsense word pairs read correctly by the total number of real words read correctly. Separate phonic transfer indices are calculated for monosyllabic and polysyllabic words.
Contextual Decoding	1. Instructional Level. The grade equivalent of the basal passage. 2. Frustration Level. The grade equivalent of the ceiling passage. 3. Reading rate. 4. Error rate. 5. Percentage of phonic words corect in context. 6. Percentage of comprehension questions correct.

Diagnostic Reading Scales–Revised (DRS–81)

George D. Spache
CTB/McGraw–Hill Division, 1963; revised editions 1972, 1981
20 Ryan Ranch Rd., Monterey, CA 93940

Purpose	To evaluate oral and silent reading abilities and auditory comprehension
Major Areas Tested	Oral and silent reading and listening comprehension
Age or Grade Range	Grades 1–7
Usually Given By	Special education teacher Diagnostician trained in reading assessment
Type of Test	Standardized Individual Criterion-referenced (supplementary phonics tests)
Scores Obtained	Grade level (supplementary phonics tests) Instructional level Independent level Potential level
Student Performance Timed?	Optional
Testing Time	45–60 minutes
Scoring/Interpretation Time	15 minutes
Normed On	534 students in grades 1–8; sample balanced for race, sex, and geographic area; poor readers and high ability students excluded from sample
Alternate Forms Available?	Yes

FORMAT

The Diagnostic Reading Scales—Revised (DRS-81) is the third revision of the Spache Diagnostic Reading Scales first published in 1963 and revised in 1972. The materials consist of an examiner's manual, an individual expendable record book for use by the examiner, and a reusable spiral-bound book for use by the students.

An examiner's cassette provides a model for administration of the DRS-81, and a technical manual provides more extensive statistical data. A stopwatch is also needed.

The battery includes 3 graded word recognition lists, 2 reading selections at each of 11 levels (ranging from grades 1.6 to 7.5 in difficulty), and 12 supplementary word analysis and phonics tests:

Initial Consonants
Final Consonants
Consonant Digraphs
Consonant Blends
Initial Consonant Substitution
Auditory Recognition of Initial Consonant Sounds
Auditory Discrimination
Short and Long Vowel Sounds
Vowels with *r*
Vowel Diphthongs and Digraphs
Common Syllables
Blending

1. *Word Recognition Lists.* These graded word lists yield a tentative level of performance and are used to determine the level of the initial passage the student should be able to read orally in the next part of the test.

2. *Oral Reading.* The student reads each paragraph aloud and answers orally questions asked by the examiner. Most of the seven or eight questions for each paragraph require factual recall, but a few interpretive questions are included. Oral reading errors, including reversals, omissions, substitutions, mispronunciations, repetitions, and hesitations are recorded by the examiner. Oral Reading stops when the student makes more accuracy errors than the maximum allowed for the paragraph or does not answer the minimum number of comprehension questions required.

3. *Silent Reading.* The student reads silently the paragraph just higher in difficulty than the last one read orally. Comprehension is assessed again by oral answers to questions asked by the examiner. Silent Reading stops when the student does not answer the minimum number of questions required on a given paragraph.

4. *Auditory Comprehension.* The examiner reads to the student the paragraph just higher than the last one read silently. Comprehension is assessed in the same manner.

5. *Supplementary Phonics Tests.* Any or all of the phonics tests (see the list above) may be administered to the student to obtain a detailed analysis of the student's word attack skills and phonics knowledge. Grade equivalent scores are provided for the phonics tests, although the author cautions using these as "norms"; the tests are essentially criterion referenced.

Two forms of the reading passages (R and S) are provided for test-retest purposes.

The scores obtained on the DRS are Instructional Level (Oral Reading), Independent Level (Silent Reading), and Potential Level (Auditory Comprehension).

Instructional Level is defined as "the level at which the student reads orally and comprehends as well as 68 percent of the standardization population at that level." The author feels that this level is likely to be found acceptable by the average classroom teacher for group reading practice.

Independent Level is the highest level the student can read silently with no less than 60 percent comprehension. It represents the upper limit for materials the student is expected to read independently.

Potential Level is the highest level to which the student can listen with at least 60 percent comprehension. It represents the level to which a student's reading level can theoretically be raised as a result of an appropriate remedial program.

STRENGTHS OF THE DRS-81

• The DRS-81 assesses word recognition and oral and silent reading in one battery. It is fairly easy to administer and takes relatively little time. Although the scores are not useful, the tests provide good information about a student's reading skills. For example, an analysis of specific errors gives clues to how the student attempts to read. Error analysis is crucial for determining the instructional needs of a student. To facilitate analysis of types of errors, the student record book contains a Work Analysis Checklist and a Checklist of Reading Difficulties.

• The Supplementary Phonics Tests are helpful in revealing the nature of word analysis skills. They include tasks involving initial and final consonants, blends, vowels, and word endings. In most cases the words used are nonsense words and for most subtests the item is correct when the element being tested is correct. For example *mat* for *man* is correct for initial consonants. These criterion-referenced tests can identify specific skills that need to be mastered.

• In addition to the standard test procedures, the manual contains useful suggestions for further informal analysis of reading difficulties. For example, the examiner may wish to present to the student words in isolation that were misread in context. Then the examiner can compare a student's success with words in context to success with them in isolation.

• Students failing in reading often feel threatened by a reading test. In the DRS-81, the passages that the student reads are not marked by grade level, an important and sensitive consideration.

• The author is sensitive to the problems of assessing

oral reading in students with nonstandard English. The manual contains an excellent section on typical pronunciations of certain words by students who speak Black dialect or are of Hispanic background. The pronunciation tendencies of Puerto Rican immigrants are carefully outlined, and an outline of procedures for testing any student with a dialect is included.

• The author's broad knowledge of reading is shared with the examiner through the excellent manual, which should be read by every examiner.

LIMITING FACTORS OF THE DRS-81

• The DRS-81 must be administered by a person with considerable clinical experience in reading diagnosis because analysis of reading performance is often a subjective evaluation. Accurate recording of oral reading errors depends heavily on the judgment of the examiner.

• The terms *Instructional, Independent* and *Potential Reading Levels* have been used consistently with informal reading inventories. They have certain meanings within that context. In the DRS-81, the terms have a different meaning. Examiners need to be aware of these differences as they interpret scores to teachers who are more familiar with the informal reading inventories. The independent level in DRS-81 suggests that a student can read independently at a level above his instructional level. This assumption is not documented and does not fit with the common view that the independent level is below the instructional level. Rather than using silent reading as a measure of the independent level as described in the manual, the examiner would do better to assess silent reading at the same levels as oral reading using the alternate form, R or S.

• The comprehension questions at all levels are short-answer questions, the majority of which are straight recall of facts. For the student with a short-term memory problem, the comprehension score can be quite misleading. An alternative way of assessing comprehension that does not depend so heavily on immediate memory would add to the test's usefulness.

Adding other fundamental types of comprehension questions would be helpful at the upper grade levels.

For example, the test does not cover such skills as the ability to grasp the main idea, the ability to weave together the ideas in a selection, or the ability to draw inferences from a short passage.

The short-answer comprehension questions pose some real concerns. Questions designed on the yes-or-no model are handicapped by a 50 percent probability of getting any question correct simply by guessing. This kind of question is all too prevalent at the upper-grade levels. For example, seventh-grade-level questions include, "Can we skim all kinds of reading?" and, "Is marble always white?"

Answers to many other questions seem quite obvious, so that any student with sufficient experience and knowledge can derive the correct answers regardless of how well he or she has read the passage. Typical questions are, "What color was his wagon?" (second grade); "How do birds help us?" (fifth grade); "What kind of flowers do poppies have?" (fifth grade). The superficial understanding required by such comprehension questions is a serious drawback.

• The measurement of reading rate as fast, average, or slow similarly presents special concern. A student may have many reading rates, depending on such factors as the difficulty of the material, the content of the passage, and the purpose for which it is being read. In view of these factors, the silent reading rate on the DRS-81 does not appear to be too meaningful.

• The examiner should keep in mind that performance on the Supplementary Phonics Tests can be directly related to the type of reading instruction a student receives. For instance, a student in a phonics-oriented program may perform much better on these tests than a student who is being taught by sight-word methods. As the manual states, the phonics tests do not possess any degree of reliability to justify grade norms. Omitting them entirely would be a better practice.

• The standardization sample for the DRS-81 is very small; the 534 students were reduced to 290 for data analysis. Validity and reliability data were adequate, but the small size of the sample limits the generalizability of the test. The DRS-81 is best used as an informal diagnostic test rather than as a norm referenced instrument.

Durrell Analysis of Reading Difficulty (DARD)

Donald D. Durrell and Jane H. Catterson
The Psychological Corporation, 1937; revised 1955, 1980
555 Academic Court, San Antonio, TX 78204-2498

Purpose	To assess strengths and weaknesses in various reading skills and subskills
Major Areas Tested	Oral and silent reading, listening comprehension, word analysis skills, spelling, and handwriting
Age or Grade Range	Grades 1–6
Usually Given By	Special education teacher
Type of Test	Standardized Individual Norm-referenced
Scores Obtained	Grade level
Student Performance Timed?	Yes (some subtests)
Testing Time	30–90 minutes (depending on number of subtests given)
Scoring/Interpretation Time	15–30 minutes
Normed On	200 students at each grade level, 1–6, from five states representing each region of the U.S.; included only children in the average range of the Metropolitan Achievement Test; consideration given to language backgrounds, socioeconomic status, ethnicity, and curriculum
Alternate Forms Available?	No

FORMAT

The materials for the Durrell Analysis of Reading Difficulty (Durrell Analysis) consist of the examiner's manual of directions, individual record booklets for recording each student's responses, a tachistoscope with word lists to accompany specific subtests, and a book containing the paragraphs for the Oral Reading, Silent Reading, and Listening Comprehension subtests. The manual includes directions for administering and scoring tests and for interpreting test results. It also includes brief information on test construction and standardization.

The Durrell Analysis contains 19 subtests designed to assess a student's performance on various types of reading tasks. The examiner selects only those subtests appropriate for each student's reading level. Subtests may be given in any order.

Following the administration of each subtest, the examiner scores the test and calculates the grade-level score according to procedures in the manual. The results of the major subtests are plotted by grade-level scores on the

Durrell Analysis Subtests

Subtest	Reading Grade Level	Task	Timed?	Normed?	Additional Information Gained?
Oral Reading	1–6	Reading aloud a series of paragraphs graded for difficulty; answering comprehension questions	Yes	Yes	Error patterns in oral reading
Silent Reading	1–6	Reading silently a series of graded paragraphs; aided and unaided recall	Yes	Yes	Eye movements per line, imagery, sequential recall
Listening Comprehension	1–6	Listening to graded paragraphs; answering comprehension questions	No	No	Comparison to silent reading
Word Recognition	1–6	Reading word lists of graded difficulty, presented by tachistoscope; time for analysis given on words not recognized	Yes	Yes	Comparison of sight-word vocabulary and word analysis skills
Listening Vocabulary	1–6	Listening to a series of words and indicating the category to which they belong by pointing to a picture (Child hears the words *glow* and *elated* and points to a picture of the sun and a smiling face, respectively.)	No	Yes	Comparison of reading vocabulary and listening vocabulary
Sounds in Isolation	1–6	Giving sounds of letters, digraphs, blends, phonograms, prefixes, suffixes	No	Yes	
Spelling Test	2–6	Writing dictated spelling words correctly from a graded list	No	Yes	Comparison of phonic and sight spelling
Phonic Spelling	4–6	Writing dictated words exactly as they sound	No	Yes	Patterns of spelling errors
Visual Memory of Words (Primary)	3 and below	Recalling words presented visually and locating them in a list of similar words	Yes	Yes	

Subtest	Reading Grade Level	Task	Timed?	Normed?	Additional Information Gained?
Visual Memory of Words (Intermediate)	3–6	Recalling words presented visually and writing them	Yes	Yes	
Identifying Sounds in Words	3 and below	Listening to a word pronounced by the examiner and finding one that begins with the same sound from three printed choices	No	Yes	Ability to perceive beginning blends and ending sounds
Prereading Phonics Abilities Inventories					
Syntax Matching	Nonreaders–1	Recognizing that a sentence is composed of single words (Child looks at the phrase *come here*. Examiner says, ''Come here,'' and asks, ''Which word is *here*?'')	No	Yes	
Identifying Letter Names in Spoken Words	Nonreaders–1	Listening to a word and giving the initial letter by name	No	Yes	
Identifying Phonemes (Letter Sounds) in Spoken Words	Nonreaders–1	Listening to a word and giving the initial sound	No	Yes	
Naming Lower-case Letters	Nonreaders–1	Naming lowercase letters in printed words	No	Yes	
Writing Letters from Dictation	Nonreaders–1	Writing letters from dictation with picture cues provided (''Write a *t* in the box next to the picture of a tree.'')	No	Yes	
Writing from Copy	Nonreaders–1	Copying four words (given only to children who are unable to write from dictation)	No	No	
Naming Uppercase Letters	Nonreaders–1	Naming uppercase letters in isolation	No	No	
Identifying Letters Named	Nonreaders–1	Pointing to letters, either lower-case or uppercase, named by the examiner (given to children who are unable to name letters)	No	No	

profile chart on the front of the individual record booklet. The profile provides a graphic representation of the student's strengths and weaknesses in reading. A checklist of instructional needs is also included in the individual record booklets, as are specific checklists of difficulties on individual subtests. These checklists, together with the profile chart, form the basis for an individualized remedial program.

STRENGTHS OF THE DURRELL ANALYSIS

• The Durrell Analysis was developed to help reading teachers understand the reading process and plan individual reading programs. To reach this goal, a wide variety of subtests are included. When used wisely, they yield a wealth of information about a student. The Durrell Analysis is one of the few tests that allow assessment of oral and silent reading, listening comprehension, word analysis skills, and spelling all in the same battery. The variety of subtests allows for testing of nonreaders as well as readers with high intermediate-grade skills.

• While maintaining the same general format, the revised Durrell Analysis includes several important changes in the third edition. The content of the reading and listening paragraphs has been updated for sex and ethnic balance. New normative data using a wider geographic sample is included. New measures of listening vocabulary allow direct comparison between reading and listening skills. New measures have been added to the prereading skills section.

• The manual is well organized and clearly written. The checklists for recording reading difficulties are helpful in bridging the gap between test scores and daily performance.

• The Durrell Analysis includes several unique subtests. Listening Vocabulary provides a measure of a student's understanding of single spoken words by assessing the student's ability to place them in categories. Phonic Spelling is a good measure of auditory analysis for intermediate students. Syntax Matching is a creative measure of the basic concept that sentences are made up of single separate words.

LIMITING FACTORS OF THE DURRELL ANALYSIS

• Although the third edition of the Durrell Analysis has been renormed, only grade scores are provided. No standard scores are included, and the grade scores themselves are of little value.

• On the Oral Reading and Silent Reading subtests, the grade scores are based on speed and vague scoring of comprehension questions. There is no rationale provided for basing instructional level on speed, and there are serious ambiguities in the directions for scoring comprehension. For example, the manual states, "Generally speaking, the scoring of the comprehension questions should be generous.... If the child...answered that the little brown dog played with 'three or four other dogs,' one might assume that knowing that there was more than one other dog was worth half-credit." (The story says "two dogs.") Such vague scoring criteria invalidate the use of the grade scores, which were questionable to begin with.

• The technical characteristics of the Durrell Analysis are very weak. The standardization sample is poorly described, no test-retest reliability studies are presented, and validity is not well substantiated. The Durrell Analysis is best thought of as an informal inventory.

• In considering the Durrell Analysis as an informal inventory, it is important to note which reading skills are poorly assessed or omitted. First, reading comprehension on both the Oral Reading and Silent Reading subtests is limited to recall of specific facts. No interpretation or generalization is required. Second, tachistoscopic presentation, such as that used on the Word Recognition subtest, is often confusing for poor readers and gives inaccurate information regarding their word recognition skills. Word lists or flashcard procedures are often more accurate. Third, no subtests assessing discrimination or recognition of vowel sounds (long or short) are included. Fourth, no pure auditory tests of discrimination or blending are included.

• The authors of the Durrell Analysis discuss the comparison of the student's raw score on Listening Vocabulary and Word Recognition. While the equivalency of lists of words is well done, the tasks are too dissimilar to compare. Word Recognition is decoding only, while Listening Vocabulary requires both comprehension of the single words and categorization skills.

Gates-MacGinitie Reading Tests (Third Edition)

Walter H. MacGinitie and Ruth K. MacGinitie
The Riverside Publishing Company, 1989
8420 Bryn Mawr Avenue, Chicago, IL 60631-3476

Purpose	To measure silent reading skills from pre-reading through high school
Major Areas Tested	Silent reading vocabulary and comprehension
Age or Grade Range	Grades 1–12
Usually Given By	Classroom teacher Special education teacher
Type of Test	Standardized Group Norm-referenced
Scores Obtained	Stanine Grade equivalent Normal curve equivalent Extended scale score Percentile rank
Student Performance Timed?	Yes
Testing Time	50–60 minutes
Scoring/Interpretation Time	15 minutes
Normed On	Nation-wide sample of 42,000 K–12 students based on the 1980 U.S. Census stratified according to geographic region, district enrollment size, and socio-economic levels
Alternate Forms Available?	Yes

FORMAT

The Third Edition of the Gates-MacGinitie Reading Tests is the latest edition in a long tradition of reading tests begun in 1926 by Arthur I. Gates. The Gates Silent Reading Test and the Gates Primary Reading Tests were the original tests. In 1965, Gates and Walter MacGinitie authored the first edition of the Gates-MacGinitie Reading Tests, following in 1978 with the second edition and in 1989, with the third edition. The basic purpose of the test series is to provide teachers and school administrators with a means of evaluating the reading levels of students throughout their school careers. The format is a group-administered test of multiple-choice questions assessing vocabulary and paragraph comprehension. In the third edition, nine levels of tests are available from the pre-reading level (late kindergarten) through twelfth grade. Alternate forms (K and L) are available from Levels 3 through 10/12 for test-retest purposes. The chart below describes the subtests available at each level.

Level	Subtest
PRE	PreReading Evaluation
	Literacy Concepts
	Reading Instruction Relational Concepts
	Oral Language Concepts (Linguistic Awareness)
	Letters and Letter-Sound Correspondence
R	Beginning Reading Skills
	Use of Letter-Sound Correspondence:
	Initial consonants and consonant clusters
	Final consonants and consonant clusters
	Vowels
	Use of Sentence Context
1, 2	Vocabulary. A test of word recognition or decoding; student matches words with pictures. Comprehension. Student chooses picture which illustrates a passage.
3, 4, 5/6 7/9, 10,12	Vocabulary. A test of word knowledge; student choses word or phrase which means most nearly the same as the test word. Comprehension. Student selects best answer to questions about prose passage or verse.

The test materials include test booklets for each student at each level. Hand scorable editions are available at each level; at the lower levels (K–3) machine scorable booklets are available, while at the higher levels (4–10/12) students may mark their answers in test booklets or on machine- or hand-scorable answer sheets. Self-scorable answer sheets are also available at the higher levels. Teacher's manuals for Directions for Administration and manuals for Scoring and Interpretation are provided for each level. The latter include directions for scoring and using the norms tables, meaning and interpretation of test scores, and comprehensive remediation strategies. Out-of-level norms are available for all forms of the test. Scoring keys and Class Summary Records are provided at each level. A Decoding Skills Analysis Form is provided for levels 1 and 2; this form allows the teacher to analyze an individual student's errors in phonic skills.

STRENGTHS OF THE GATES-MACGINITIE READING TESTS

• The Gates-MacGinitie Reading tests are well known and well normed. Because they are group tests, they are efficient and appropriate for screening purposes to determine which students are in need of diagnostic testing.

• The wide age range and alternate forms make the Gates-MacGinitie Tests excellent for test-retest purposes, that is, to determine the progress that an individual student has made in a remedial program. Many school districts use them routinely in fall and spring with both regular and special education students.

• At levels 1 through 10/12, the Vocabulary and Comprehension subtests are scored separately; a student may be given one or both parts.

• The teacher's manuals are well organized, well written, and easy to use.

• The third edition provides four different levels of tests for the end-of-kindergarten through first grade students. These tests—levels PRE, R, 1, and 2—assess skills in the child who is about to be taught to read through the first grader who is considerably above average.

• The Gates-MacGinitie Reading Tests are designed for group administration and contain many features to facilitate this process. Administration procedures are clearly presented, and there are ample practice items to acquaint students with the test format. Identical sample pages make possible testing students at several levels in the same classroom. For example, the sample items are the same for levels 4 through 10/12. A wide range of norms are available at each level; for example, for level 5/6, norms are provided for grades 4 through 9.

• In the standardization process, equating testing was done with 25,000 students so that norms for the second edition and third edition could be linked to measure progress on students given the old edition.

• Improvements have been made in the content of the comprehension test items at all levels. In addition to questions requiring specific facts, the questions require higher reading skills, such as interpretation and generalization.

• Rather than an as single words, vocabulary items are presented in short sentences or phrases which suggest their parts of speech. The authors have been careful not to give a context which suggests the meaning of the word, as a Vocabulary test would then become a Comprehension test.

- Great efforts were made during test construction to assure that the tests would be valid measures of knowledge and skills acquired in standard school reading programs.

LIMITING FACTORS OF THE GATES–MACGINITIE READING TESTS

- The Gates–MacGinitie Reading Tests measure silent-reading skills, a critical area of reading competence. In any silent-reading test, analysis of errors is difficult. For example, in Level 4, Form K, Vocabulary item 37, the test word is *soothe*, and the choices are *bathe, hold, calm, straighten*, or *call* as possible synonyms for *soothe*. If the student marks *straighten*, the examiner does not know which of the following occurred: (1) The student read the word *calm* as *clam*; (2) the student did not know the meaning of *soothe* and confused it with *smooth*; or (3) the student did not know the meaning of *calm*. Because analysis of errors on silent-reading tests is difficult, the low-scoring student should be administered an individual oral-reading test such as the Gray Oral Reading Test (p. 84).

- Factors of inattention and lack of persistence may affect a student's performance on any group test. Because special education students frequently display these problems, scores must be used with caution.

- Information on test reliability was not available for review at the time of this writing.

- The lack of a Decoding Skills Analysis form above Level 2 implies that students in third grade and higher have mastered basic phonic skills. For many special education students this is not true, and a phonic analysis process would be helpful. Such students should be given individual phonics tests such as those included in the Gates–McKillop–Horowitz Reading Diagnostic Tests (p. 81) or the Woodstock Reading Mastery Test (p. 90).

The Nelson–Denny Reading Test (NDRT)

James T. Brown, Vivian Vick Fishco, and Gerald Hanna
Riverside Publishing Company, 1993
8420 Bryn Mawr Avenue, Chicago, IL 60631

Purpose	To provide an assessment of student ability in reading comprehension, vocabulary development, and reading rate
Major Areas Tested	Silent reading rate and comprehension
Age or Grade Range	Grade 9–college
Usually Given By	Teacher Administrator Special education teacher Counselor
Type of Test	Standardized Individual or group Norm-referenced
Scores Obtained	Percentiles Grade equivalent Stanine Normal curve equivalent Scale scores
Student Performance Timed?	Yes
Testing Time	35–45 minutes
Scoring/Interpretation Time	10–15 minutes
Normed On	Three nationwide samples balanced by geographic region and socioeconomic level, age, gender, and ethnicity. High school sample: nearly 12,000 students; 2-year college: nearly 5,000 students; 4-year college: more than 5,000 students. Separate norms provided based on a sample of 531 students in law enforcement academies.
Alternate Forms Available?	Yes

FORMAT

The Nelson–Denny Reading Test (NDRT) was originally published in 1929. Content and statistical data have been periodically revised (Forms A and B, 1929; revised 1960; C and D, 1973; E and F, 1981; G and H, 1993), but the format of the test has remained the same. The materials consist of manuals for administration, scoring and interpretation, student test forms G and H, and answer sheets for computerized scoring. A Technical Report, including information on the standardization procedures is also available. The NDRT is composed of two subtests, Vocabulary and Comprehension. The Vocabulary Section includes 80 multiple-choice items, which must be completed within a 15-minute time limit. The Comprehension Section includes seven passages and a total of 38 multiple-choice questions. The time limit is 20 minutes. The questions require both factual and interpretive reading. Students may look back at the reading passage while they are answering the questions. A reading-rate score is obtained by having students mark the line they are reading in the first passage at the end of one minute. Correct responses are converted into percentile ranks, stanines, normal curve equivalents, scale scores, and grade equivalents. Separate scores are obtained for Vocabulary, Comprehension, Reading Rate, and Total Test. Norms are provided for both fall and spring administration, and alternate forms are provided to assess progress.

STRENGTHS OF THE NDRT

• Silent reading is a critical academic skill. The NDRT provides one of the few measures of silent-reading comprehension for single words and paragraphs. The authors describe the test as a screening tool that provides important information regarding the reading abilities of high school and college students.

• The provision of a measure of reading rate is a strong feature of the NDRT. Students in special education can often receive extended time on critical examinations if the examiner can document the need for additional time. The reading rate score of the NDRT can provide that documentation.

• The Comprehension subtest provides a good measure of silent paragraph reading. The seven passages are drawn from science, social studies, and humanities topics. Questions are classified as requiring either literal or interpretive reading. Analysis of an individual student's errors can be helpful in understanding reading skills.

• The NDRT provides a great deal of information about a student's reading skills in a short amount of time. In 20 minutes, an examiner can obtain a comprehension score, a one-minute reading rate, information about the student's ability to complete the test within the time limit, and information about the type of questions answered incorrectly.

• The provision of norms for two-year and four-year college populations is very helpful. The tighter sample of

college attendees is useful for assessing the skills of college students with known or suspected learning disabilities. It is also useful in helping high school students compare their skills with college students.

• The manual provides helpful guidelines for interpreting test results for students whose vocabulary development, comprehension skills, and reading rate are at differing levels. These guidelines enable a teacher to determine how to prioritize the different aspects of a secondary or postsecondary student's reading program.

• Forms G and H of the NDRT provide for an extended-time administration with separate norms. The extended-time version is recommended for students with English as a Second Language or older adult students who are returning to college. The test is given in two sessions, and no reading rate is calculated under extended-time administration. Alternatively, for students who don't fit the above description but who are slow readers due to learning disabilities, the two alternative forms G and H allow you to administer one form under the usual time limits or under extended time and the other to compare the results.

LIMITING FACTORS OF THE NDRT

• While data on the sample selection process is included in the manual, no information on reliability or validity is provided. To obtain this information, the examiner must also purchase a Technical Manual. The development of a comprehensive manual which includes administration and scoring procedures, interpretation guidelines, and technical data would greatly improve this test.

Gates–McKillop–Horowitz Reading Diagnostic Tests (Gates–McKillop–Horowitz)

Arthur Gates, Anne McKillop, and Elizabeth Horowitz
Teachers College Press, second edition 1981
Teachers College, Columbia University, 1234 Amsterdam Ave., New York, NY 10027

Purpose	To assess strengths and weaknesses in reading and related areas
Major Areas Tested	Oral reading, word analysis, and related skills
Age or Grade Range	Grades 1–6
Usually Given By	Classroom teacher Special education teacher Diagnostician trained in reading disorders
Type of Test	Standardized Individual
Scores Obtained	Grade level Age level (some subtests) Rating scale
Student Performance Timed?	No
Testing Time	40–60 minutes (depending on number of subtests given)
Scoring/Interpretation Time	15 minutes
Normed On	600 children in grades 1–6 from public and private schools, urban and rural areas, and minority groups (African Americans and Latinos)
Alternate Forms Available	No

FORMAT

The Gates-McKillop-Horowitz Reading Diagnostic Tests (Gates-McKillop-Horowitz) are a revised edition of the 1962 Gates-McKillop Tests. They are a battery of subtests designed to be used with individual students in elementary school and include tasks from the readiness level through such advanced skills as syllabication. Subtests are selected based on the student's reading level and particular reading difficulties. No specific order of administration is required.

The materials consist of a reusable booklet that contains the materials to be read by the student; a booklet in which the student and the examiner record responses; and a manual that includes the rationale for the tests, directions for administering and scoring, grade-level scores, and interpretive ratings.

The 15 subtests included in the Gates-McKillop-Horowitz are shown in the table that follows. Grade scores that may be converted into a rating of high, medium, low, or very low are given for the four general ability tests that assess oral reading, word recognition, and spelling. These grade scores allow comparison of each student with others at the same grade level. On the diagnostic tests of specific skills, such as recognition of vowel sounds, the student's raw score or number correct is compared with the norming sample and is rated average, above average, or below average.

STRENGTHS OF THE GATES-McKILLOP-HOROWITZ

• The most obvious advantage of the Gates-McKillop-Horowitz battery is that many critical skills are included. Through thoughtful selection of subtests, the skilled examiner can develop a testing battery appropriate for a beginning reader or a struggling intermediate student. Careful selection of subtests allows every student some successful reading experiences during testing, while the examiner obtains maximum diagnostic information. The variety in the format and the informal tone of the procedures hold the interest of most students.

• Comparison of students' performances on various subtest pairs also yields invaluable diagnostic information. A few examples:

1. Words: Flash Presentation and Words: Untimed allow the examiner to compare sight-word vocabulary and word analysis skills on words of equivalent difficulty.

2. Auditory Blending and Recognizing and Blending Common Word Parts offer an auditory-visual comparison, blending with auditory stimuli only, and blending skills with printed words.

This type of diagnostic information can be obtained when the Gates-McKillop-Horowitz is used by a skilled examiner. Other features, such as the checklist of difficulties for the Oral Reading subtest and the discussion of interpretation of test results in the manual, are excellent.

LIMITING FACTORS OF THE GATES-McKILLOP-HOROWITZ

• The test was normed on 600 children. Only limited information regarding the composition of the norming sample is given, and no studies of reliability or validity are reported. The lack of these critical pieces of information strongly suggests that the Gates-McKillop-Horowitz should be used as an informal battery to obtain information about a student's skills in a variety of reading tasks. The information is excellent, but the grade scores are of little value.

• The Oral Reading passages are stilted in style and content. No measure of comprehension is included. The examiner should substitute another oral reading test (Gilmore Oral Reading Test, Gray Oral Reading Tests, Spache Diagnostic Reading Scales) or devise comprehension questions for the Gates-McKillop-Horowitz in order to get some measure of oral reading comprehension.

• The first edition of these tests included three subtests that were of great diagnostic value: Recognizing the Visual Form of Sounds in Nonsense Words, in Initial Letters, and in Final Letters. The new edition has added nothing in technical soundness and is less valuable as an informal diagnostic instrument.

Gates–McKillop-Horowitz Subtests

Subtest	Task
Oral Reading	Student reads orally seven paragraphs ranging in difficulty from grades 1 to 6. Errors recorded by the examiner and classified by type. No comprehension questions included.
Reading Sentences	Student reads four sentences with phonetically regular words.
Words: Flash Presentation	Tachistoscope presents a graded list of words at half-second intervals. Tests sight recognition of single words.
Words: Untimed	Presentation of same word list as above, but student is given opportunity to use word analysis skills.
Knowledge of Word Parts: Word Attack	
Syllabication	Student is asked to read a list of nonsense words (*rivlov, kangadee*). The skill being measured is syllable blending.
Recognizing and Blending Common Word Parts	Student reads a list of nonsense words made up of common word parts (*stade, shemp, whast*). If student is unable to read the whole word, the examiner may show how to break it into an initial blend and a common ending and then blend it back together (*wh-ast—whast*).
Reading Words	Student reads 15 one-syllable nonsense words.
Letter Sounds	Student is shown printed letter and is asked to give its sound.
Naming Capital Letters	Student is shown printed uppercase letter and is asked to name it.
Naming Lowercase Letters	Student is shown printed lowercase letter and is asked to name it.
Recognizing the Visual Form (Word Equivalents) of Sounds	
Vowels	Student is shown five vowels and is asked to indicate which one is in a nonsense word pronounced by examiner (*vum, keb, hote, sate*).
Auditory Tests Auditory Blending	Student listens to word pronounced by examiner, with parts separated by quarter-second intervals; student pronounces whole word (*d-ar-k—dark*).
Auditory Discrimination	Examiner pronounces pairs of words, and student identifies them as same or different (*dim—din, weather—wetter*).
Written Expression Spelling	Words from Words: Flash Presentation and Words: Untimed are presented to the student for oral spelling.
Informal Writing	Student is encouraged to write an original paragraph on a topic of his or her choice.

Gray Oral Reading Tests–Third Edition (GORT–3)

J. Lee Wiederholt and Brian R. Bryant
PRO-ED, 1992
8700 Shoal Creek Blvd., Austin, Texas 78757-6897

Purpose	To measure growth in oral reading and to aid in the diagnosis of oral reading problems
Major Areas Tested	Oral reading
Age or Grade Range	6 1/2–18 years
Usually Given By	Special education teacher Psychologist Diagnostician trained in reading disorders
Type of Test	Standardized Individual Norm-referenced
Scores Obtained	Standard Percentile Grade equivalent
Student Performance Timed?	Yes
Testing Time	15–30 minutes
Scoring/Interpretation Time	15 minutes
Normed On	1,485 students in 18 states; sample balanced for age, sex, residence, race, ethnicity, and geographic area, and compared to the statistical abstract of the United States (U.S. Census Bureau, 1990)
Alternate Forms Available?	Yes

FORMAT

The Gray Oral Reading Tests were originally published in 1967 and authored by Dr. William S. Gray, a well-known reading educator. The revised edition, published in 1986 (GORT–R), was greatly improved both in content and technical merit. In the third edition, GORT–3, the content remains the same; however, new scoring procedures have been developed and the technical merit of the test has been improved.

The materials consist of two equivalent forms, A and B. Both A and B are included in a single spiral-bound Student Book of reading passages. There are 13 independent paragraphs of gradually increasing difficulty for each form. Each paragraph is followed by five multiple-choice questions designed to measure various types of reading comprehension. Individual Profile Examiner Record forms include reprints of each passage as well as places to record types of errors, the amount of time used to read each paragraph, and student scores. The GORT–3 Manual includes administration and scoring procedures, interpretation guidelines, norm tables, and information on test development. A stopwatch is also needed to administer the test.

Guidelines are given to help the examiner decide with which paragraph to begin the testing. Each paragraph is preceded by a "prompt" which the examiner reads to the student.

This story is about a very courageous woman. Read the story to find out what she did.

The prompt is intended to give the reader a purpose for reading. The student reads the paragraph aloud, while the examiner records errors and time. Then the examiner reads along with the student five comprehension questions, each with four possible responses, and the student selects the correct response.

In order to shorten the testing time as much as possible, basal and ceiling levels are derived. For Comprehension, the basal level is the highest paragraph on which students answer all five questions. The lowest paragraph on which students answer fewer than three of five questions is the ceiling. Separate basal and ceiling levels are obtained for passage reading, a combination of rate and accuracy.

For each paragraph read, students obtain a score for rate, accuracy, and comprehension. The rate and accuracy scores are combined into a Passage Score. The Passage and Comprehension scores for each paragraph read are summed and converted to percentiles and standard scores. The standard scores are then combined into an Oral Reading Quotient, which can also be expressed as a percentile.

In addition to providing an accuracy score, examiners are encouraged to analyze five types of oral reading errors:

1. *Meaning similarity.* Replacing a printed word with another word similar in meaning (*moment* is read *minute*).

2. *Function similarity.* Replacing a printed word with another word of similar syntactic function (*gathered* is read *gained*).

3. *Graphic–phonemic similarity.* Replacing words with words similar in appearance (*felt* is read *fell*).

4. *Multiple errors.* More than one type of error in a misread word (*struck* is read *hit*).

5. *Self-correction.* Allows analysis of student strategies.

STRENGTHS OF THE GORT–3

• The GORT–3 is one of several good reading tests that all follow the same format. Its wide age range and equivalent forms allow for both an initial measurement of oral reading proficiency and a measure of progress.

• The unique feature of the GORT–3 is that the speed of reading is an integral part of the accuracy score. In other oral reading tests, timing is optional, but the rate of reading is considered of equal importance to the number of errors. Particularly with older students, the Passage Score, which combines speed and accuracy, is more predictive of classroom performance.

• The comprehension questions on the GORT–3 differ in several ways from those found on other oral reading tests. The multiple-choice format not only allows for more standardized scoring than open-ended questions but also aids students with recall problems. The examiner reads the questions and answers aloud with students, ensuring that students read each possible response, reducing impulsive responses. The questions have been designed to measure not only literal comprehension and recall of facts, but also inferential, critical, and affective reading skills. The following questions illustrate this strong feature of the GORT–3.

What probably explains how the children got into this situation?

How do you think she feels during the ordeal?

What is the best name for the story?

How do you think the story ends?

• The "prompt" preceding each paragraph is a very useful feature. It serves to focus the student's attention and to provide a framework and reason for reading.

• The Examiner's Manual is clear and well organized and includes a great deal of information about analyzing a student's performance.

• The GORT–3 is well normed and standardized. Extensive reliability and validity data are published in the manual. They support the technical merits of this test.

LIMITING FACTORS OF THE GORT–3

• For students with reading disabilities, the time aspect of the GORT–3 causes increased pressure. Because these are the students for whom the most accurate diagnostic data is needed, another test may need to be used with students whose performance is significantly affected by the stop-watch.

• It is questionable whether speed of reading is an important criterion for beginning readers. Beginning readers who read slowly and cautiously but without errors are penalized by the GORT–3 scoring system. Also, for students with reading difficulties related to impulsiveness, reading speed may not be a desirable characteristic.

• Although the manual provides an analysis of the types of reading errors students are making, the miscue analysis is quite complex. While it may provide more information about students' uses of strategies, it takes a very skilled examiner to apply the information to remediation.

• The upper paragraphs of the GORT–3 are very difficult to read. The sentences are very complex, and the subject matter and vocabulary unfamiliar for most secondary students. These factors, combined with the timed aspect of the test, also make it very discouraging for students with significant reading or language difficulties.

• In the manual, the authors state that research findings indicate that accuracy errors, such as omissions, additions, reversals, and dialectical errors, are less important than other error types. Yet, in the scoring system they count equally. For example, an omission is counted as an error just as a substitution is. If certain errors are not as important, perhaps they should not affect students' scores in the same way.

Test of Reading Comprehension (TORC)

Virginia L. Brown, Donald D. Hammill, and J. Lee Wiedeholt
PRO-ED, 1978; revised 1986
8700 Shoal Creek Blvd., Austin, TX 78757-6897

Purpose	To provide a normed measure of silent reading comprehension
Major Areas Tested	Reading comprehension
Age or Grade Range	7–18 years
Usually Given By	Classroom teacher Special education teacher
Type of Test	Standardized Individual Group Norm-referenced
Scores Obtained	Scaled (each subtest) Standard (total test)
Student Performance Timed?	No
Testing Time	30–120 minutes
Scoring/Interpretation Time	40–90 minutes
Normed On	2,492 students in 13 states balanced for sex, age, and city and rural populations
Alternate Forms Available?	No

FORMAT

The Test of Reading Comprehension (TORC) is an instrument for measuring silent reading comprehension in students from grades 1 through 8. The 1978 edition was revised in 1986. The test may be individually or group administered. The materials consist of an examiner's manual, student booklets, answer sheets, individual student profile sheets, and separate response forms for the Reading the Directions of Schoolwork subtest.

Four subtests form the General Reading Comprehension Core:

1. *General Vocabulary* (25 items). The student reads three stimulus words that are related in some way (*teeth, nose, arm*) and selects two words from a group of four (*hair, air, legs, too*) that are related to the stimulus words. Both answers must be correct.

2. *Syntactic Similarities* (20 items). The student reads five sentences and selects the two that are most nearly alike in meaning. For example:

It was her wagon.
It was not her wagon.
It was his wagon.
The wagon was not hers.
It was not his wagon.

Both responses (in this example, the second and fourth sentences) must be correct.

3. *Paragraph Reading* (6 paragraphs). The student reads a paragraph and five questions. A multiple-choice format is used for all five questions. The student is required to select the "best" title, recall story details, draw an inference, and draw a negative inference (*Which sentence could* not *go in the story?*).

8. *Sentence Sequencing* (10 items). Each item includes five randomly ordered sentences that, when ordered properly, will create a meaningful paragraph. The student orders the sentences. Scoring is based on relational order rather than specific sequence.

Note: Sentence Sequencing was an optional test in the 1978 edition. It is now an integral part of the Reading Comprehension Core. To allow TORC users to be able to use their old forms, it has not been renumbered.

Diagnostic Supplements, which are four additional subtests, are used to gain a more comprehensive evaluation of strengths and weaknesses in a student's reading comprehension:

4. *Mathematics Vocabulary* (25 items). The student reads three stimulus items (*more than, longer, bigger*) and selects two words from a group of four (*blue, larger, food, greater*) that are related to the stimulus words. Both answers must be correct.

5. *Social Studies Vocabulary* (25 items). The student reads three stimulus items (*Congress, govern, court*) and selects two words from a group of four (*law, anarchy,*

combustion, legislature) that are related to the stimulus words. Both answers must be correct.

6. *Science Vocabulary* (25 items). The student reads three stimulus items (*tendon, ligament, muscle*) and selects two words from a group of four (*bone, medulla, carbonate, cartilage*) that are related to the stimulus words. Both answers must be correct.

7. *Reading the Directions of Schoolwork* (25 items). The student reads a common teaching instruction and carries it out. (*Number these words in alphabetical order.*) This subtest is designed to be used with younger or remedial readers (below fourth-grade level).

On all subtests, the student begins with item 1 and proceeds until a ceiling is reached. Ceiling criteria are clear in the examiner's manual. For each subtest, a raw score (number correct) is computed and converted into a scaled score and percentile using tables based on age. Scaled scores have a mean of 10 and a standard deviation of 3. The four core tests are combined into a reading comprehension quotient (RCQ) with a mean of 100 and a standard deviation of 15, allowing easy comparison of a student's TORC scores with other measures of intellectual and language functioning.

STRENGTHS OF THE TORC

• The TORC is subtitled *A Method for Assessing the Understanding of Written Language*. It is based upon the latest research on reading comprehension and psycholinguistics. Subtests are designed to assess the reader's ability to "construct meaning" from the printed word. Examiners are urged to read the manual carefully to understand the rationale for the test and avoid misinterpretation.

• Several of the subtests are unique in content and format and offer new understandings of the reading comprehension process.

• The examiner's manual is clear and complete. Directions for administration and scoring are easy to follow.

• Administrative options, such as answer sheets or booklets, one sitting or several, are included, making administration easier.

• Attention has been paid to reliability, validity, and construction of norms, all of which are clearly reported in the manual. Test-retest reliability is strong.

• No grade-equivalent scores are provided. Since the statistical problems of grade scores are overwhelming, it is to the authors' credit that they do not provide them.

• The procedures for small and large group testing are well described in the manual, including specific discussion of students who should always be tested individually.

• The TORC Summary Sheet has some interesting aspects. There is a place to indicate to whom test results have been released and/or interpreted. Quick check lists allow the examiner to indicate any special characteristics of the examiner, the environment, or the student at the time of testing. Finally, there is a brief space for summarizing inteptations and recommendations. The Summary Sheet fits with the TORC philosophy of an interactional theory and provides a model for a brief test report.

LIMITING FACTORS OF THE TORC

• The standardization sample of the 1986 TORC was changed from the 1978 standardization sample in two ways: 1) the 6 year old subjects were dropped because research indicated the TORC was not suitable for this age; 2) the sample was augmented with students from four major census areas. The 1986 sample is compared with the 1985 Statistical Abstract of the United States and is balanced for sex, geographical area of residence, rural/metropolitan residence, and age. However, there is still no description of the population regarding race, linguistic background, or reading ability. Until this is done, scores of learning disabled or minority students must be interpreted with caution.

• Several of the TORC subtests measure abilities rarely taught in classrooms. In particular, Syntactic Similarities measures the ability to recognize that two sentences mean the same thing, a very unfamiliar task. Many students need more teaching of this type of task than that provided in two examples. Because of this, scores on the subtest and, therefore, the RCQ, are suspect.

• The content area vocabulary tests are recommended to be used for students in the intermediate and upper grades to screen their readiness for reading in content areas. The vocabulary is so specific to topics previously taught that it has little value as either a screening test or a measure of progress.

• The theoretical constructs underlying the TORC are new and complex. Interpretation of scores is difficult. The TORC is best used in conjunction with other measures of reading skills.

• A major concern about the TORC is that it has attempted to cover too wide an age range with too few items (Hood, 1985). It is certainly true that the TORC is a very short test of silent reading comprehension compared with such tests as the Gates-MacGinitie.

• Whether the variety of tasks used on the TORC will compensate for the few items of each type, only time and research will tell. Validity studies using the TORC have shown low but significant correlations with other group reading comprehension tests such as the California Achievement Test and the SRA Achievement Series. The correlations are expected to be low due to the different construct of reading comprehension embodied in the TORC.

• There is no indication on the 1986 manual that the TORC has been revised. As the changes in scoring procedures and norms are significant, the 1986 manual should be labeled Revised Edition *on the cover,* or the test should be

renamed TORC-2. Many clinicians are undoubtedly unaware that they are using the older edition. Changes are outlined below.

CHANGES IN THE 1986 TORC

1. More description of the rationale for subtests.

2. Inclusion of Sequencing Sentences as one of the required tests composing the Reading Comprehension Quotient rather than an alternate or substitute subtest.

3. Augumented standardization sample with 6-year-old students dropped and population increased at upper age levels.

4. Increased age range for use of test from 6 1/2–14 1/2 years to 7–18 years.

Woodcock Reading Mastery Tests–Revised
(WRMT-R)

Richard W. Woodcock
American Guidance Service, 1987
4210 Woodland Service, P.O. Box 99, Circle Pine, MN 55014-1796

Purpose	To provide a comprehensive measure of reading ability across a wide age range
Major Areas Tested	Reading
Age or Grade Range	Grades K–college senior Adults to age 75+
Usually Given By	Special education teacher Classroom teacher Psychologist Trained paraprofessional (administration and scoring only)
Type of Test	Standardized Individual Norm-referenced
Scores Obtained	Age level Relative performance index Grade level NCE (normal curve equivalent) Percentile Standard
Student Performance Timed?	No
Testing Time	30–60 minutes
Scoring/Interpretation Time	30–45 minutes
Normed On	6,089 Subjects in 60 diverse U.S. communities; 4,201 K–12 students; 1,023 college students; 865 adults. Population balanced for geographic region, community size, sex, race, Hispanic origin, and socioeconomic status
Alternate Forms Available?	Yes

FORMAT

The Woodcock Reading Mastery Tests—Revised (WRMT-R) are a revised edition of the original Woodcock Reading Mastery Test published in 1973. It is an individually-administered comprehensive battery of subtests which assess various aspects of reading across a wide age range. The materials include a manual, an easel kit for presenting the test materials, and individual test records for recording student responses and scores. The WRMT-R has two forms, G and H. Separate easel kits and test records are needed for each form. Form G includes the complete test battery, four subtests of reading achievement, two readiness subtests, and a two-part supplementary check list. Form H includes only the four reading achievement subtests. A separate record form, G&H, may be used if both forms of the test are administered.

The subtests in Form G, the complete battery, are:

Readiness Cluster

1. *Visual-Auditory Learning.* This subtest is taken from the Woodcock-Johnson Psychoeducational Battery. The student learns a battery of unfamiliar visual symbols representing familiar words. The student then "reads" test stories composed of these 28 symbols. Visual-Auditory Learning is a 134-item paired associate learning task.

2. *Letter Identification.* The 51 items of this subtest assess the student's ability to identify by name or sound the letters of the alphabet. Upper and lower case and manuscript and cursive forms are presented.

Basic Skills Cluster

3. *Word Identification.* The student reads aloud words ranging in difficulty from the preprimer through the college level. One hundred six items are presented (*you, watch, already, urgent, cologne, carnivorous*).

4. *Word Attack.* This 45-item subtest assesses the student's ability to pronounce nonsense words (*raff, chad, yeng, cigbet, bafmotben*) using phonic and structural analysis skills.

Reading Comprehension Cluster

5. *Word Comprehension.* The Word Comprehension test is comprised of three subtests, each measuring a different level of cognitive processing:

5A. *Antonyms.* This 34-item subtest requires the student to read a word and respond orally with a word opposite in meaning (*enemy–friend, profit–loss*).

5B. *Synonyms.* The student is required to read the word and state a word similar in meaning. Thirty-three items are presented (*zero–none, nothing, zip; tint–color, shade, dye*).

5C. *Analogies.* This subtest contains 79 items that test knowledge of word meaning using an analogy format. The student reads a pair of words and ascertains their relationship. Then he reads a third word and applies the same relationship to supply a word to complete the analogy.

*foot–toes; hand–*_____
*duet–quartet; two–*_____
*famine–hunger; epidemic–*_____

The three Word Comprehension subtests are organized in such a way that it is also possible to assess a student's skills in four vocabulary areas:

General Reading Vocabulary. 30 words. (*whisper, frolic*).
Science-Mathematics Vocabulary. 40 words. (*doe, meter*).
Social Studies Vocabulary. 38 words. (*migrate, wigwam*).
Humanities Vocabulary. 38 words. (*soprano, plot*).

6. *Passage Comprehension.* This subtest includes 68 items designed to assess reading comprehension. It uses a modified cloze procedure. The student reads a two or three sentence paragraph silently; when he comes to a blank he supplies an appropriate word based upon the meaning of the paragraph. For example:

Each day Midas counted his gold. Each day, after he had _____ *it, he wished for more.*

A person can buy stocks on margin. That is, he pays only part of the price in cash, which is the margin. To pay the _____ *he borrows from his broker, paying interest on the loan.*

The WRMT-R is constructed so that students are tested only on those items within their operating range. The operating range is assumed to extend from a basal level marked by six consecutive correct reponses to a ceiling level of six consecutive incorrect responses. On two subtests, Visual-Auditory Learning and Word Attack, all students begin at the first item. For the other four subtests, a starting point table based on estimated reading grade level is provided.

The WRMT-R provides a variety of test information; error analysis, age and grade equivalent scores, a relative mastery index, instructional range, percentile ranks, and standard scores are provided separately for each subtest. Five cluster scores are also provided; Readiness, Basic Skills, and Reading Comprehension (Word Identification, Word Attack, Word Comprehension, Passage Comprehension), Total Reading-Full Scale and Total Reading-Short Scale (Word Identification, Passage Comprehension). The use of cluster scores results in higher validity.

The WRMT-R test record form provides two primary and three supplementary diagnostic profiles that offer a graphic display of a student's performance. The supplementary profiles allow the incorporation of test results from the Woodcock-Johnson Psychoeducational Battery and the Goldman-Fristoe-Woodcock Auditory Skills Test Battery.

STRENGTHS OF THE WRMT-R

• The WRMT-R maintains the basic features of the original test while incorporating several changes and additions. These changes increase the diagnostic value of the test. The major changes are:

1. The Letter Identification Test is not included in the Total Reading Score.

2. The Word Comprehension Test has been expanded to include antonyms and synonyms as well as analogies. In addition, a student's reading vocabulary in four content areas can be assessed.

3. Several tests include one or more training items to ensure that the student understands what is expected of him.

4. The norms have been extended to include college, university, and non-school-attending adults.

• The Supplementary Letter Checklist can be used in an informal manner to gain more information about a student's knowledge of letter names and sounds. This is especially useful with young children or students with very low reading levels.

• A Word-Attack Error Inventory is provided to aid the examiner in error analysis of the Word Attack Test. This inventory provides useful information for instructional program planning for a student with poor word attack skills. However, the directions for completing this inventory are poor and require a very knowledgeable examiner for useful interpretation.

• The Word Comprehension Test is designed to assess three levels of cognitive processing. Antonyms require the simplest cognitive skills as many of the responses will be at the word association level (*day-night*). Synonyms is a more difficult task as the student must supply a word that is similar in meaning as most of the words do not have another word which is exactly the same in meaning. Analogies requires the highest level of cognitive processing because it requires the understanding of relationships.

• The Total Reading-Short Scale cluster provides a quick estimate of global reading ability through the administration of just two subtests, Word Identification and Passage Comprehension. The correlation between this cluster and Total Reading-Full Scale is very high.

• A micro computer scoring program, ASSIST™ (Automized System for Scoring and Interpreting Standardized Tests) is available. For examiners using the test extensively, ASSIST™ will save time and diminish clerical scoring errors. ASSIST™ is compatible with Apple II and with IBM PCs.

• A Report to Parents is also available from the publisher. This report conveys test results and a brief interpretation of the student's performance in a form that is more understandable to parents.

• Equivalent Forms G and H allow for retesting or may be combined to increase precision and validity. Raw scores can be plotted on the diagnostic profiles. This allows the examiner to obtain information quickly; more complete analysis can be formulated later. The raw score profile can be used to give immediate feedback to the student during the actual testing process. This is especially desirable with older students.

LIMITING FACTORS OF THE WRMT-R

• The split-half reliability data for the WRMT-R included in the manual is quite strong for the grade levels reported. However, many grade levels are not reported, and no test-retest reliability data is presented.

• Limited data on validity is presented. The inclusion of data using the 1973 Woodcock Reading Mastery Test "because the psychometric characteristics of the WRMT and the WRMT-R are so similar that many generalizations are valid" is a very questionable procedure.

• No information is given as to the inclusion or exclusion of special education students in the norming population.

• The WRMT-R manual includes a lengthy discussion of how to calculate the Aptitude-Achievement Discrepancy. This calculation presumably allows the examiner to compare the student's actual achievement on the WRMT-R with aptitude measures such as the Reading Aptitude Cluster of the Woodcock-Johnson Psychoeducational Battery or the Wechsler Intelligence Scale for Children-Revised. However, the calculation is based upon *estimated* correlations between these tests and reading abilities. In addition, the final number, the percent of the population with the same size discrepancy, has little meaning in terms of diagnosis, placement, or program planning.

The Boder Test of Reading-Spelling Patterns

Elena Boder and Sylvia Jarrico
The Psychological Corporation, 1982
555 Academic Court, San Antonio, TX 78204

Purpose	To differentiate specific reading disability, or developmental dyslexia, from non-specific reading disability; to classify dyslexic readers into one of three subtypes; to provide guidelines for remediation
Major Areas Tested	Reading Spelling
Age or Grade Range	First grade through adult
Usually Given By	Teacher Speech/language clinician Reading specialist Psychologist Physician
Type of Test	Informal Individual Diagnostic
Scores Obtained	Grade level Age level
Student Performance Timed?	No
Testing Time	30 minutes
Scoring/Interpretation Time	30–45 minutes
Normed On	Not normed
Alternate Forms Available?	No

FORMAT

The Boder Test of Reading-Spelling Patterns is a unique test in concept and design. The purpose of the test is to determine whether or not an individual student is dyslexic, and if so, within which of three subtypes that student may be classified. This determination is based on a student's reading and spelling error patterns. The test materials consist of a manual, student forms for the reading and spelling tests, examiner's recording forms, and a diagnostic summary form.

The student is administered an oral reading test consisting of graded word lists. Beginning at the indicated level, the student reads a 20-word list; the odd-numbered words are phonetically regular; the even-numbered words are non-phonetic. The initial reading is a flash presentation. One second is allowed per word. If the student does not read the word on sight, he or she is given 10 seconds to decode the word before going on to the next word. The examiner records the student's reponses, checking "flash", "untimed", or "not read" appropriately.

Thirteen graded word lists are provided, pre-primer through adult. If a reading problem is suspected, the examiner begins with the pre-primer list; otherwise, the test begins two grades below the student's actual grade level, but no higher than the 5th grade list. A ceiling is reached when the student reads six or fewer words in a list correctly on sight presentation. The examiner then determines the student's reading level, which is defined as "the highest grade level at which the student reads at least 50% of the word list on sight presentation." A Reading Age is calculated by adding 5 to the Reading Grade Level. A Reading Quotient is determined by the usual formula:

$$\text{Reading Quotient} = \frac{\text{Reading Age} \times 100}{\text{Chronological Age}}$$

For each word list read, the examiner tabulates the number of words read flash and untimed and the number of words not read. Subtotals are calculated for phonetic and non-phonetic words.

Next the examiner prepares an individual spelling test by selecting 10 *known* words from the student's sight or *flash* list and 10 *unknown* words from the student's *not read* list. Five phonetic and 5 non-phonetic words comprise each list.

When the examiner administers the spelling test, the *known* words are dictated in the usual way—pronounced, used in a sentence, and pronounced again. For the *unknown* words, the student is told to "try to write the words the way they sound." The examiner pronounces the word and asks the student to repeat it aloud and then write it. *Known* words are scored for correctness only; *unknown* words are scored for their phonetic equivalence to the dictated words. For example, *flite* for *flight*, *kedl* for *kettle*, and *onrubol* for *honorable* are scored as GFE's (good phonetic equivalents).

Based upon his or her reading-spelling pattern, the student is classified as one of five reader subtypes; normal, nonspecific reading disability, dysphonetic, dyseidetic, or mixed dysphonetic-dyseidetic. The author defines the dysphonetic subtype category as one in which the student exhibits weakness in the auditory analytic function and the dyseidetic subtype category as one in which the student exhibits weakness in the visual gestalt function.

STRENGTHS OF THE BODER TEST

• The Boder, used in conjunction with other reading tests, is a very useful tool when the question being asked by the parent is, "Is my child dyslexic?" The author has defined the term and delineated several basic subtypes in a clear manner, which is helpful in understanding the disorder.

• The discussion of the subtypes in the Interpretation chapter of the manual is excellent. It not only clarifies the types of dyslexic readers, but distinguishes the dyslexic reader from the normal reader and the student with a non-specific reading disorder.

• The word lists of the Boder are carefully constructed. Not only do they include half phonetic, half non-phonetic words, they include only words which are introduced at the same grade level in both reading and spelling.

• In states in which the eligibility criteria for admission to special education require documentation of a processing disorder, the Boder is a useful test. Defects in the auditory analytical function and the visual gestalt function are clearly documented.

• Alphabet tasks are included for the student who is a non-reader or who has a sight vocabulary below the pre-primer level. Reciting the alphabet, naming the letters, giving letter sounds, and writing the alphabet test require auditory and visual memory and give important diagnostic information on the non-reading student. Other informal diagnostic tasks are described in the manual, such as syllabicating tasks and drawing a clock face from memory. These tasks provide clinical information that is helpful not only in formulating the diagnosis but also in planning remediation.

• Studies of interrater reliability, test-retest reliability, and internal consistency are reported in the manual. In addition, extensive research validating the construct validity of the Boder subtypes is reported. An extensive reference list is also provided.

• The guide to remedial intervention presented in the manual provides helpful information for classroom teachers and tutors working with students with specific reading disability.

LIMITING FACTORS OF THE BODER TEST

• The Boder test is more difficult to administer than it appears. Procedures for testing the limits of a student's sight vocabulary are difficult to understand through the complex instructions presented in the manual. Also, constructing the individual spelling test is initially very difficult and requires much practice before it can be done quickly. Examiners unfamiliar with the test should not only study the manual thoroughly but also administer the test in two sessions with the first several students tested. By giving the reading test one day and the spelling another, the examiner can prepare the spelling test between sessions.

• The Boder subtypes are not as easy to identify as the manual proclaims. There are many students who do not quite fit the criteria for dysphonetic or dyseidetic. In particular, it takes time and experience to interpret the performance of remediated students, who may not exhibit frequency as remedial programs become more widespread.

The authors recognize these problems, and a future edition of the manual will address these issues more thoroughly and empirically (Boder and Jarrico, personal communication, July, 1988).

• The high school word list is designated grades 10–12. However, no directions are given as to what grade to use to determine Reading Grade, Reading Age, and Reading Quotient. The same problem occurs with the Adult list.

• The rules for determining if a student's misspelling is a GFE (good phonetic equivalent) are ambiguous. For example, any vowel may be substituted in an unstressed syllable, making *rimembr* a GFE, but not *remimbr*. An *e* may be added to any word except when it converts the spelling or misspelling into another word; so *lisne* for *listen* is a GFE, but not *hale* for *hall*. These rules are difficult to apply. Since the Boder subtypes are all based upon the percentage of GFEs, the rules need to be much more logical and unambiguous.

• More attention should be given to the analysis of reading errors. The authors stress the analysis of spelling errors, and examples are given of typical reading error patterns for each subtype. But systematic evaluation of the reading pattern is also crucial if remedial reading programs based on test performance are to be designed.

• A single test should not be used to make any diagnosis, especially not one as complex as dyslexia. The Boder should be used as part of a battery given to students with known or suspected reading disabilities, not as an isolated diagnostic tool.

Test of Written Language–Second Edition
(TOWL–2)

Donald D. Hammill and Stephen C. Larsen
PRO-ED, 1978; 1983; 1988
8700 Shoal Creek Blvd., Austin, TX 78757-6897

Purpose	To identify students with written language disabilities, to identify strengths and weaknesses in writing, and to document progress in writing
Major Areas Tested	Written language
Age or Grade Range	Grades 2–12
Usually Given By	Classroom teacher Special education teacher Educational diagnostician Psychologist
Type of Test	Individual Group Standardized Norm-referenced
Scores Obtained	Percentile Standard
Student Performance Timed?	No
Testing Time	40–60 minutes
Scoring/Interpretation Time	15–20 minutes
Normed On	3,418 students balanced for sex, place of residence, and grade level in 14 states
Alternate Forms Available?	No

FORMAT

The TOWL–2 is the latest revision of the Test of Written Language originally published in 1978 and revised in 1983. The TOWL–2 is designed to measure three components of written expression: the conventional component (punctuation, capitalization, and spelling), the linguistic component (vocabulary and grammar), and the conceptual component (logical, coherent, and written products). The TOWL–2 contains ten subtests designed to assess these components. Five of the subtests use a contrived format; that is, they measure individual writing skills such as punctuation in isolated sentences. The other five subtests measure writing skills in a spontaneous format, a creative story written by the student. By incorporating both formats, the TOWL–2 provides a broad measure of written language.

The materials consist of a manual containing administration and scoring procedures, interpretation guidelines, and technical information. Individual student response booklets for the contrived-format subtests, and a profile/scoring form for two equivalent forms are provided. On the student response form is printed a picture that is used as the stimulus for an original story. Form A has a picture of prehistoric men killing a mammoth; Form B has a space scene. Students are asked to write a story about the picture. The scoring of that spontaneous writing sample provides five subtest scores, while five isolated contrived subtests comprise the others. Scores from the ten subtests are grouped into three composites: contrived writing, spontaneous writing, and overall written language. These composite scores, called quotients, have a mean of 100 and a standard score of 15. Percentile and standard scores are provided for each subtest and quotient. No grade scores are provided in line with the author's position that grade scores are too often misinterpreted and are less statistically reliable than standard scores.

TOWL–2 Subtests
Contrived Subtests

1. *Vocabulary* (30 items). Students are given a word and asked to write a sentence using it. Errors in spelling, capitalization, or punctuation are not scored.

2. *Spelling* and 3. *Style* (25 items). Students are asked to

TOWL–2 Form A

TOWL–2 Form B

write sentences from dictation. Written sentences are scored for spelling, capitalization, and punctuation. Students receive separate subtest scores for spelling and for style (capitalization and punctuation).

4. *Logical Sentences* (25 items). Students are given sentences that do not make logical sense and are asked to rewrite them correctly. Examples: *The cat went bow-wow; John likes baseball better than his father.*

5. *Sentence Combining* (25 items). Students are given two to five sentences and asked to write one sentence combining them.

Spontaneous Subtests

The student's story about the picture is analyzed for the following elements:

6. *Thematic Maturity.* Students receive one point for each of 30 criteria included in their story. The criteria include such elements of composition as writing in paragraphs, giving personal names to characters, and developing personalities for the characters, including past and future events. The manual is very specific in scoring directions.

7. *Contextual Vocabulary.* Students receive one point for each word in their story with seven or more letters.

8. *Syntactic Maturity.* Students receive one point for every grammatically correct word in the story.

9. *Contextual Spelling.* Students receive one point for each different correctly spelled word in the story.

10. *Contextual Style.* Students receive credit for each punctuation or capitalization rule used in the story. Each item is 1, 2, or 3 credits, depending upon the level of the punctuation used; that is, a period earns 1 point; a comma to separate words in a series, 2 points each; and capitalization of adjectives derived from proper names (Americanization) receives 3 points.

STRENGTHS OF THE TOWL–2

• The need for a standardized test to measure written expression is apparent to every diagnostician in the field. Combining subtests of isolated skills with structured analysis of spontaneous writing provides a broad measure of written language.

• The group administration format is an efficient way to assess an entire class, followed by individual analysis of strengths and weaknesses.

• The TOWL–2 manual is comprehensive and clearly written. The discussion of the rationale for each subtest is very interesting and helpful.

• *A Consumers Guide to Tests in Print* (Hammill, Bryant, & Brown, 1989) recommends the TOWL–2 for its strong norms, reliability, and validity. The TOWL–2 is a technically sound test in an area that is very difficult to standardize.

• The provision of alternate forms A and B allows the TOWL–2 to be used as a measure of progress.

LIMITING FACTORS OF THE TOWL–2

• While the TOWL–2 picture produces a reasonably good spontaneous writing sample, the assessments of that sample seem contrived and of little value in evaluating students' program needs. For example, while rating vocabulary on the length of the words used may be theoretically sound, it is not as meaningful as a system that indicates the types of words (parts of speech, common or unusual words) students are currently using and not using. It also eliminates credit for the short but unusual word.

• Also, the Thematic Maturity criteria seem very arbitrary. Students who write dialogue or stories personalizing the characters in the picture will receive a very high score that may have little to say about writers' overall thematic maturity.

• Even though the TOWL–2 reports many validity studies, impressions of clinicians are that the validity is questionable. For students in suburban communities, the subtest scores and quotients seem to overestimate students' abilities. Many students reported by their teachers to be doing very poorly in written language in school obtain average or higher scores on the TOWL–2. Such results may be due to the inherent problems of assessing such a global skill as written language with one writing sample, or they may be due to the limitations in the subtests described above. In either case, examiners should be extremely cautious about reporting students' scores without information about their writing skills in other situations.

• The three quotients of the TOWL–2 are somewhat difficult to interpret. The contrived-writing quotient reflects how well students have mastered the separate skills of writing usually taught in school, while the spontaneous-writing quotient assesses students' use of writing as communication. However, because spelling, punctuation, and capitalization are also part of the spontaneous quotient, the two scores really reflect different types of testing formats rather than different skills. An understanding of how well students are incorporating specific writing mechanics into composition is important, but comparing the two quotients is less helpful than an analysis of student performance.

• The TOWL–2 is a very long test requiring extensive writing. All of the five contrived subtests require sentence writing, after which students are asked to write a spontaneous story. Older students with writing difficulties find the TOWL–2 very demanding and difficult. As they are the students most likely to be taking this test, provisions to administer it in several sessions interspersed with other diagnostic measures is strongly recommended.

Test of Written Spelling (TWS–3)

Cohen Larsen and Donald Hammill
PRO-ED, 1976; revised 1986, 1994
700 Shoal Creek Blvd., Austin, TX 78757-6897

Purpose	To provide a standardized, reliable, and valid measure of written spelling that can be used to identify students with spelling problems, address their strengths and weaknesses, measure progress, and serve as a research tool
Major Areas Tested	Written spelling
Age or Grade Range	Grades 1–12
Usually Given By	Classroom teacher Special education teacher
Type of Test	Standardized Individual Group Norm-referenced
Scores Obtained	Percentile Standard Age equivalent Grade equivalent
Student Performance Timed?	No
Testing Time	15–25 minutes
Scoring/Interpretation Time	10 minutes
Normed On	4,760 children in 23 states; sample was balanced for race, sex, ethnicity, residence, and geographic area, and compared with statistical abstracts of the United States (U.S. Census Bureau, 1990).
Alternate Forms Available?	No

FORMAT

The Test of Writing Spelling (TWS–3) is the third revision of this test originally published in 1976. The format, a dictated written-spelling test, has remained the same. The TWS–3 covers a wide age range, grades 1–12. The materials consist of an examiner's manual and individual Summary/Response forms. The manual includes the test rationale, administration and scoring directions, interpretation suggestions, norms tables, and data on the technical aspects of the test. The Summary/Response forms provide a place for students to write the dictated words as well as a place to record TWS–3 and other test scores.

The TWS-2 includes two subtests or lists of spelling words. The first list includes 50 Predictable Words—words that follow basic spelling rules. The second list contains 50 Unpredictable Words—words that essentially have to be memorized. For example:

Predictable Words:	Unpredictable Words:
let	*eight*
stop	*fountain*
spend	*collar*
strange	*requisite*
tardy	*sure*
district	*awful*
tranquil	*campaign*

The examiner pronounces each word, uses it in a sentence, and pronounces it again. The student writes each word.

The same word lists are used with students at all grade levels. Entry levels for different grades are outlined in the manual. The testing is discontinued when the student misspells five consecutive words on each of the two lists. If the student has not spelled five consecutive words correctly on each list, the examiner returns to the entry level and tests downward until a basal is reached. Modifications of this procedure for group testing are given in the manual.

In addition to raw scores, the TWS–3 gives a percentile and standard score based on six-month age intervals for each word list. Raw scores for the two lists are summed and percentiles and standard scores provided for the total test. Age and grade equivalents are available for each subtest as well as the total test.

STRENGTHS OF THE TWS–3

• The TWS–3 is a well-constructed, well-normed, easy-to-administer test. The format of a dictated, written-spelling test is familiar to the administrator and the student. The test requires few materials and could be administered and scored by an instructional assistant.

• The assessment of written spelling through a dictation test is much more appropriate than a test that requires recognizing correctly spelled words.

• The inclusion of procedures for group administration of the TWS–3 makes it a very usable test for the regular classroom teacher.

While both students exhibit "average" spelling skill, their instructional needs are quite different. Examples of four types of spelling patterns are presented in the manual: low scores on both lists; very low scores on both lists; stronger spelling scores for predictable words; and stronger spelling scores for nonpredictable words. Brief guidelines for interpretation and planning for these patterns are included.

• The reliability and validity data presented in the manual support the technical soundness of the TWS–3.

Two Fourth Graders' Scores on the TWS–3

	Student A		Student B	
	%tile	SS	%tile	SS
Predictable Words	73	109	19	87
Unpredicable Words	26	90	68	107
Total Test	55	102	48	99

LIMITING FACTORS OF THE TWS–3

• While the Student/Response Forms have been improved, the space allowed for writing each dictated word is somewhat small. The use of regular classroom paper for younger students or for those with known visual–motor difficulties is recommended.

• Although the authors state that the TWS–3 can be used to measure progress because of its wide range, the fact is that students with learning disabilities often make very slow progress in spelling, and the TWS–3 may not provide sufficient items to assess their gains. A criterion-referenced test is also needed for such students.

Enright® Diagnostic Inventory of Basic Arithmetic Skills (Enright®)

Brian E. Enright
Curriculum Associates, Inc., 1983
5 Esquire Rd., North Billerica, MA 01862

Purpose	To assess knowledge of basic facts and computation skills in mathematics
Major Areas Tested	Math computation
Age or Grade Range	Grades 1–6 (and remedial classes in secondary school)
Usually Given By	Classroom teacher Special education teacher Educational diagnostician
Type of Test	Criterion-referenced Individual Group Standardized
Scores Obtained	None
Student Performance Timed?	No
Testing Time	Varies with skills of the student
Scoring/Interpretation Time	15–30 minutes
Normed On	Students primarily in Louisiana and in five other states
Alternate Forms Available?	Yes (some parts)

FORMAT

The Enright® Diagnostic Inventory of Basic Arithmetic Skills (Enright®) is a comprehensive instrument for assessing a student's math computation skills. The materials consist of an examiner's notebook and individual arithmetic record books. The loose-leaf examiner's notebook is designed to lie flat on the table between the examiner and the student for individual testing.

The Enright® provides three levels of information:

1. The grade level at which basic math computation skills are commonly taught.

2. Assessments of 144 basic computational skills

3. An analysis of error patterns

Each of the basic skills assessed has been referenced to five basal mathematics series selected for their nationwide use. Through tables in the examiner's notebook, it is possible to determine the grade level at which a particular skill, such as adding two-digit numbers and regrouping ones, is typically taught. This information is useful in determining sequential curriculum.

The 144 basic computational skills are assessed in a very systematic manner. First, the student is administered the Wide Range Placement Test. This 26-problem screening test establishes a starting point for assessing a student's competency in addition, subtraction, multiplication, and division of whole numbers, fractions, and decimals. For students whose area of difficulty is known, this step may be omitted.

Once it is determined which operations the student needs help with, the Skill Placement Test for that operation is given. Shown here is the Skill Placement Test for Addition of Whole Numbers. The purpose of this test is to determine the student's competency within the sequence of skills required in adding whole numbers. One problem for each critical step in the sequence is provided. The examiner's page corresponding to this Skill Test provides the grade level at which the skills are usually taught, a description of each type of problem, and an instructional objective for the skill sequence.

The student's first error on the Skill Placement Test determines which Skill Test will then be given. For example, if a student's first error is adding and regrouping two three-digit numbers from left to right, the student is given the Skill Test for that step in the operation, shown here with the corresponding examiner's page.

NAME: Rick Lowe

(Give Skill Test A-12.)

1.
$$\begin{array}{r} 4 \\ +5 \\ \hline 9 \end{array}$$

2.
$$\begin{array}{r} 6 \\ +7 \\ \hline 13 \end{array}$$

3.
$$\begin{array}{r} 3 \\ 1 \\ +5 \\ \hline 9 \end{array}$$

4.
$$\begin{array}{r} 74 \\ + 5 \\ \hline 79 \end{array}$$

5.
$$\begin{array}{r} 1 \\ 57 \\ + 5 \\ \hline 62 \end{array}$$

6.
$$\begin{array}{r} 65 \\ +22 \\ \hline 87 \end{array}$$

7.
$$\begin{array}{r} 1 \\ 37 \\ +59 \\ \hline 96 \end{array}$$

8.
$$\begin{array}{r} 1 \\ 68 \\ +74 \\ \hline 142 \end{array}$$

9.
$$\begin{array}{r} 1 \\ 28 \\ 45 \\ +14 \\ \hline 87 \end{array}$$

10.
$$\begin{array}{r} 1 \\ 35 \\ 56 \\ +64 \\ \hline 155 \end{array}$$

11.
$$\begin{array}{r} 1 \\ 637 \\ +256 \\ \hline 893 \end{array}$$

12.
$$\begin{array}{r} 2 \\ 589 \\ +345 \\ \hline 8116 \end{array}$$

Enright Skill Placement Test, Addition of Whole Numbers

This part of the process is a unique feature of the Enright®. The student computes five problems. On the examiner's page, each test item is printed with the correct response. The most common incorrect responses are also provided. By matching the student's response with one of the incorrect responses, the examiner can determine which type of error a student has made. The Enright® identifies 198 distinct error types. These have been grouped into seven error clusters. The error pattern information clarifies for teachers the approach a student is taking to arrive at an answer. This information leads directly to an individualized remedial program. Students with errors in the same error clusters may be grouped for instruction. Following remediation, the second five items on the Skill Test are administered as a posttest. A criterion of 80 percent accuracy is recommended. When all of the skills in an operation that the student had made errors on have been retaught, the alternate form of the Skill Placement Test may be given as a posttest.

A Basic Fact Test is provided for addition, subtraction, multiplication, and division. Two forms are available for each operation. Each form consists of 50 basic facts. One form of the Basic Fact Test is usually given after the Skill Placement Test. Students who do not know the basic facts may still understand the computational process and should be allowed to use manipulatives or facts tables for the Skill Placement Tests. Calculators are not permitted because they give a complete answer and do not allow error analysis. The alternate form of the Basic Facts Test may be used as a posttest.

The student's performance is recorded in the arithmetic record book. The booklet has 13 sections to correspond with the 13 operations assessed in the Enright®. The record tracks a student's progress in the acquisition of computation skills by dates and also provides information about error types. A color-coding system allows one record book for each student to be used throughout the elementary grades.

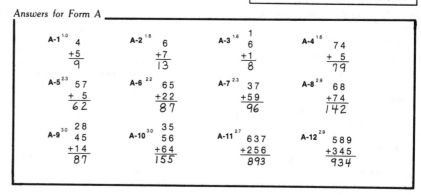

Enright Examiner's Page for Addition of Whole Numbers

(Directional 105.)   **NAME:** Rick Lowe

a.	b.	c.	d.	e.
24$\overset{2}{6}$	66$\overset{3}{8}$	43$\overset{2}{9}$	13$\overset{2}{9}$	38$\overset{4}{4}$
+386	+279	+194	+595	+468
X 5114	X 8120	X 5115	X 6116	X 7116

368	557	295	746	453
+486	+277	+439	+189	+269

Enright Skill Test A-12

ADDITION: TWO 3-DIGIT NUMBERS, REGROUPING ONES AND TENS

SKILL: Add two 3-digit numbers, regrouping ones and tens.

GRADE LEVEL TAUGHT: 2.9

STUDENT RECORD BOOK: Page 2

ASSESSMENT METHODS: Individual or group written response.

ACCURACY: At least 4/5 (80%) on the test items. When the review items are used for post testing, 4/5 (80%) is also required.

NOTES:
1. **Uses Fingers** Check to see if student adds by using his or her fingers.
2. **Addition Facts** Refer to page 2 of the *Student Record Book* if the student's error does not fit an error pattern. These kinds of random errors indicate a need for basic fact instruction and practice.

REVIEW ITEMS:

a. 368	b. 557	c. 295
+486	+277	+439
854	**834**	**734**

d. 746	e. 453
+189	+269
935	**722**

(A-12)
OBJECTIVE: By _____ (date) , when given five test items for adding two 3-digit numbers, regrouping ones and tens, _____ (student's name) will compute the numbers with at least 4/5 (80%) accuracy.

a.	b.	c.	d.	e.
246	668	439	139	384
+386	+279	+194	+595	+468
632	**947**	**633**	**734**	**852**

ERROR ANALYSIS

a.	b.	c.	d.	e.		
51212	81317	51213	61214	71412	**Regrouping 1:** Writes entire sum of each column without regrouping. *	6|8 +7|4 1 3|12
522	837	523	624	742	**Regrouping 4:** Writes ones in ones place, but does not regroup tens.	① 5 7 + 5 5 2
722	1037	723	824	942	**Regrouping 5:** Regroups tens from ones column into hundreds column. †	1 6 3 7 +2 5 6 9 8 3
5114	8120	5115	6116	7116	**Directional 105:** Adds left to right, writes tens, regroups ones, and writes sum of ones column.	A |3 B 6|8 +7|4 1|1 5

Examiner's Notes:

* If the student is adding from left to right, he or she will have the same answer shown here. Check to see if the student is adding from left to right instead of from right to left.

† These answers show that the student correctly regroups tens from tens column into hundreds column.

A class record sheet and individual progress record forms that may be used for discussions with parents are also available.

STRENGTHS OF THE ENRIGHT®

• This instrument promises to be very useful for diagnosticians and classroom teachers. There are few good math tests, and the Enright® provides not only a sequential assessment of computational skills but also an analysis of errors, which leads directly to objectives and curriculum planning.

• Although the test is designed for elementary grade students, it obviously can be used effectively with students with poor computation skills in junior or senior high school.

• The record book for tracking the progress of an individual student over the years is very helpful.

LIMITING FACTORS OF THE ENRIGHT®

• Although the Enright® can be used with first and second graders, it is of limited value until the process of regrouping in addition and subtraction has been introduced.

• The grade-level information provided on each Skill Test should be used only to identify the grade level at which the skill is commonly taught. It is not appropriate to attach grade-level scores to a student's performance.

• The Enright® is a test of computation skills only. Math concepts and applications are not assessed. A complete math curriculum would need to include many other skill areas.

• The Enright® is long and cumbersome to give. The results may not be worth the effort as there are other, informal, ways to assess a student's computational difficulties.

Enright Error Clusters

Error Cluster	Definition	Example
Regrouping	Little understanding of place value	$\begin{array}{r} 68 \\ +74 \\ \hline 1312 \end{array}$
Process Substitution	Process changed in mid problem	$\begin{array}{r} \overset{2}{\cancel{3}}27 \\ -164 \\ \hline 363 \end{array}$
Omission	Step in process or part of answer left out	$\begin{array}{r} 51 \\ 6\overline{)346} \\ \underline{30} \\ 6 \\ \underline{6} \\ 0 \end{array}$
Directional	Steps performed in wrong direction or order	$\begin{array}{r} \overset{3}{68} \\ +74 \\ \hline 115 \end{array}$
Placement	Correct computation, but numbers written in wrong place	$\begin{array}{r} 6 \\ +7 \\ \hline 31 \end{array}$
Attention to Sign	Wrong operation performed	$\begin{array}{r} 4 \\ +5 \\ \hline 20 \end{array}$
Guessing	Lack of basic understanding; random answers	$\begin{array}{r} 3 \\ 1 \\ +5 \\ \hline 315 \end{array}$

Key Math–Revised (Key Math–R)
A Diagnostic Inventory of Essential Mathematics

Austin J. Connolly
American Guidance Service, Inc., 1988
4201 Woodland Rd., P.O. Box 99, Circle Pines, MN 55014-1796

Purpose	To provide a comprehensive assessment of the understanding and applications of mathematics concepts and skills
Major Areas Tested	Mathematics
Age or Grade Range	Preschool–Grade 9
Usually Given By	Classroom teacher Special education teacher Psychologist Paraprofessional
Type of Test	Standardized Individual Criterion-referenced
Scores Obtained	Grade equivalent Standard score Age equivalent Stanine Percentile Normal Curve Equivalent
Student Performance Timed?	No
Testing Time	60–75 minutes
Scoring/Interpretation Time	30–45 minutes
Normed On	Nationwide sample of 1,798 students in grades K–9. Sample was standardized for geographic region, grade, sex, socioeconomic status, and race or ethnic group according to U.S. Census Reports of 1983 and 1986.
Alternate Forms Available?	Yes

FORMAT

The Key Math—Revised materials include a test manual, two easel kits for presentation of the test items, and individual test records for recording student responses. Colorful stimulus materials and directions for administering each item are sequentially displayed simultaneously to the examiner and the student in the easel kits. Most subtests require verbal responses to questions asked by the examiner in conjunction with the pictorial materials. The computation subtests assess written math skills. The Key Math—Revised is an individually administered test consisting of 13 subtests grouped into three mto three major areas. The following is a listing of the three areas and their subtests.

The *Basic Concepts Area* assesses the foundation knowledge upon which elementary mathematics is based.

Subtests	Numeration
	Rational Numbers
	Geometry

The *Operations Area* assesses basic computation skills.

Subtests	Addition
	Subtraction
	Multiplication
	Division
	Mental Computation

The *Applications Area* assesses the use of knowledge and computational skills.

Subtests	Measurement
	Time and Money
	Estimation
	Interpreting Data
	Problem Solving

For all of the subtests of the Key Math—Revised, students complete only those items appropriate to their range of ability. This range extends from a basal level established by three consecutive correct responses to a ceiling level marked by three consecutive errors.

A wide variety of scores are available from the test. For each subtest, raw scores are converted to percentile ranks and standard scores with a mean of 10 and a standard deviation of 3. The subtest scores within an area are combined to yield a grade or age equivalent, a percentile rank, and a standard score (mean of 100, standard deviation of 15) for each of the three areas. These scores are then combined to yield standard scores, percentiles, age and grade equivalents, stanines, and NCEs for the total test. This information can be graphically presented on the Score Profile. Standard errors of the mean are given so that confidence bands at different levels can be displayed. Information is given to allow the examiner to decide whether differences between area scores are statistically different.

STRENGTHS OF THE KEY MATH—R

• The Key Math–R has many excellent features. It is a criterion-referenced instrument based on the developmental sequence of skill acquisition and logical thinking. Extensive clinical training and experience in test administration are not required to administer the Key Math–R, making it a helpful screening and diagnostic tool.

• The Key Math–R is a highly motivating test for students because of the broad range and diversity of item content and the use of colorful and stimulating materials. The new version includes contemporary pictures and questions that hold the interest of a wide range of students—including those having difficulty with math!

• Because of its diagnostic structure and almost total lack of reading and writing requirements, the test is particularly useful for students with a wide range of intellectual abilities and for those who are learning disabled.

• The revised edition of the Key Math includes 13 instead of 14 subtests. A subtest on Rational Numbers was added to expand items from whole numbers and fractions to decimals and percents. Subtests on Estimation, Data Interpretation, and Problem Solving were added. Problem solving incorporates the old Word Problems subtest with additional problems requiring the identification of extraneous and missing information.

• The Key Math–R provides a more detailed analysis of a student's math skills than any test available. By comparing test scores among the three areas, it is possible to identify students who have excellent computation skills but do not understand concepts and, conversely, those who seem to have poor math skills when only their computation skills are weak. In addition to analysis by area, it is possible to determine each student's knowledge within the particular domain of each subtest. For example, in the Interpreting Data subtest, items are divided into Charts and Tables, Graphs, and Probability and Statistics. The test record allows you not only to do item analysis but also to identify strengths and weaknesses in that area based on the performance of the norming population with the same score in that subtest. This procedure, entitled Summary of Domain Performance, leads directly to instructional planning.

• The Key Math–R is well standardized, using a nationwide sample of students stratified according to U.S. Census figures of 1983 and 1986.

• The Key Math–R was carefully constructed to represent mathematical content in grades K–9, as well as a developmentally sequenced progression of math knowledge and skills.

• A Report to Parents form is available describing the test, the student's performance, and ways in which the results may be used to benefit students.

• A computerized scoring procedure, Key Math–R
ASSIST (Automated System for Scoring and Interpreting
Standardized Tests) is available from the publishers. ASSIST
provides a printout that summarizes and interprets data with
suggestions for future instruction.

LIMITING FACTORS OF THE KEY MATH–R

• The Key Math–R is very long to administer, score, and
interpret. The materials are motivating, and many students
are able to demonstrate great persistence using the colorful
picture materials. Despite the basal-ceiling procedure, the
test requires at least two testing sessions. For this reason, it
will probably be used only with students for whom the primary concern is math.

• Some of the subtest changes in Key Math–R eliminated
unique tests from the original Key Math. Numerical Reasoning was eliminated; Time and Money were combined
into one subtest; and Missing Elements was included in
Problem Solving. Due to their importance as skills of daily
living, more assessment of the time-and-money concept is
need than is provided in one subtest. Also, Missing Elements
was a unique test of language understanding in math that
yielded valuable information about a student; this information is not available in Key Math–R.

• Inconsistent reliability and little validity data are provided. In general, the total score is the only score suffi-
ciently reliable for diagnostic purposes. (Salvia &
Ysseldyke, 1991). The Key Math–R is most useful in
gaining a broad look at a student's math skills.

A
INDIVIDUAL TEST RECORD

KeyMath
REVISED
a diagnostic inventory of essential mathematics

AUSTIN J. CONNOLLY

Student's Name _____ Sex: M/F _____

School _____ Grade _____

Mathematics Teacher _____ Test date _____ YEAR MONTH DAY

Examiner _____ Date _____ Birth date _____

Chronological age _____

DATA FROM OTHER TESTS

Test	Date	Results
_____	_____	_____
_____	_____	_____
_____	_____	_____
_____	_____	_____

SCORE SUMMARY

Derived-score tables are in Appendix E of the *Manual*. For standard scores and scaled scores, indicate your selection of grade or age and fall or spring norms by circling the number of the appropriate table:

Standard Scores and Scaled Scores	Grade	Age
Fall norms (August–January)	Table 1	Table 2
Spring norms (February–July)	Table 3	Table 4

See Table 9 for percentile ranks, stanines, and normal curve equivalents. Obtain grade equivalents and age equivalents from Tables 10 and 11, respectively.

BASIC CONCEPTS AREA

Subtest	Raw Score	Standard Score	%ile Rank
Numeration	( )		
Rational Numbers	( )		
Geometry	( )		

BASIC CONCEPTS AREA

Raw Score → 1. ◯

Grade/Age Equivalent ▢

OPERATIONS

Subtest	Raw Score	Scaled Score	%ile Rank
Addition	( )		
Subtraction	( )		
Multiplication	( )		
Division	( )		
Mental Computation	( )		

OPERATIONS AREA

Raw Score → 2. ◯

Grade/Age Equivalent ▢

APPLICATIONS

Subtest	Raw Score	Scaled Score	%ile Rank
Measurement	( )		
Time and Money	( )		
Estimation	( )		
Interpreting Data	( )		
Problem Solving	( )		

APPLICATIONS AREA

Raw Score → 3. ◯

Grade/Age Equivalent ▢

TOTAL TEST

1. ◯ + 2. ◯ + 3. ◯ = ◯ Total Test Raw Score

	Standard Score	%ile Rank	Stanine	NCE	Grade Equivalent (optional)	Age Equivalent (optional)

KeyMath Diagnostic Profile

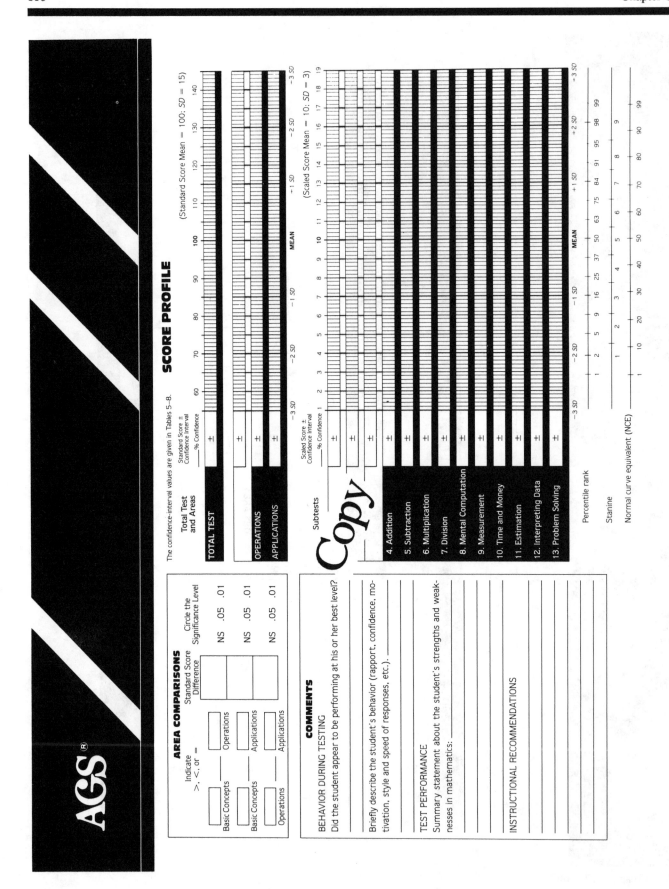

CHAPTER TWO
Perception, Memory, and Visual Motor Skills

Despite controversy over their concurrent and predictive validity, tests of perception and memory are routinely used in assessing students' academic skills. In some states, the eligibility criteria for entrance into special education programs for students with specific learning disabilities require the documentation of a processing disorder.

Although their relationship to academic skills may require further definition, perception and memory are clearly processes required for learning. As mentioned in the introduction to this book, if these process tests are used in conjunction with tests that assess basic academic skills, they can provide information that is useful in understanding a student's learning disorder.

This chapter reviews six tests of perception and memory. The first is a new test, The Wide Range Assessment of Memory and Learning (WRAML), which assesses several types of memory and learning in children and adolescents. The Lindamood Auditory Conceptualization Test (LACT) is included as one of the few single area assessments of auditory perception.

Next is a unique series of informal tests designed to identify students with dyslexia, the Malcomesius Specific Language Disability Test, the Slingerland Pre-Reading Screening Procedures, and the Slingerland Screening Tests for Identifying Children with Specific Language Disability. All include measures of auditory and visual perception and memory, as well as kinesthetic memory skills. The series now has two new tests, the Slingerland High School Level Screening and the Slingerland College Level Screening. In all, the series now serves as a screening device for students from kindergarten through adulthood who have difficulties

with prereading or reading skills. Although the Slingerland tests assess the academic area of reading and are directly related to classroom performance, they are included in this chapter due to their emphasis on the underlying perception and memory skills, rather than on actual reading and spelling tasks. The last test in this section, the Visual–Aural Digit Span (VADS), compares a student's visual and auditory memory for digits. The reader who is interested in assessing perception and memory is also referred to Chapter One, Academic Tests, Chapter Three, Speech and Language Tests, and Chapter Six, General Intelligence Tests and Developmental Scales, as many of the tests reviewed in these chapters include subtests of perception and memory.

This chapter concludes with four tests that assess visual perception and fine motor coordination. The first two are well known design-copying tasks—the Bender Visual Motor Gestalt Test (BVMGT) and the Berry–Buktenica Test of Visual Motor Integration (VMI). The Motor-Free Visual Perception Test (MVPT) assesses various areas of visual perception without the motor component.

The last test in this section is a review of The Developmental Test of Visual Perception (DTVP–2). This is the revised edition of the Marianne Frostig Test of Visual Perception discussed in Granddaddies (p. 21). The DTVP–2 is a comprehensive measure of visual perception including both visual–motor integration and nonmotor tasks. Readers who are specifically interested in the area of fine motor assessment are referred to Chapter Five, Gross and Fine Motor Skills (p. 239).

Wide Range Assessment of Memory and Learning (WRAML)

David Sheslow and Wayne Adams
Jastak Associates, Inc. 1990
P.. O. Box 3410, Wilmington, DE 19804-0250

Purpose	To develop a standardized measure of a student's ability to learn and memorize a variety of types of information
Major Areas Tested	Visual memory, verbal memory, and the ability to acquire new information over trials
Age or Grade Range	5–17 years
Usually Given By	Psychologists Speech and language pathologists Learning disability specialists Educational diagnosticians
Type of Test	Standardized Individual Norm-referenced
Scores Obtained	Scaled scores Standard scores Percentiles Age equivalents
Student Performance Timed?	No
Testing Time	45–60 minutes; 10–15 minutes for the screening tests
Scoring/Interpretation Time	25–30 minutes
Normed On	2,302 children in a national sample stratified according to data from the 1980 U.S. Census, the Rand McNally Commercial Atlas, and Marketing Guide. Age, sex, race, geography, and rural/nonrural residence were controlled.
Alternate Forms Available?	No

FORMAT

The Wide Range Assessment of Memory and Learning (WRAML) is a new test developed to assess different types of memory in children and adolescents. The WRAML grew out of the authors' need for a tool to assess memory in a pediatric-hospital setting. The testing kit contains an administration manual, examiner response forms for each student, several sets of cards and booklets needed for subtest administration, and a visual learning board with yellow foam inserts.

The WRAML consists of nine subtests, three tests of verbal memory, three tests of visual memory, and three tests of learning, that is, the acquisition of new information over repeated trials. Four additional measures of delayed recall are also provided. All subtests are administered in the order described in the manual; different starting points are used for younger and older students.

WRAML SUBTESTS

1. *Verbal Memory Scale.* Three subtests which allow a comparison of rote recall with memory for more complex information such as sentences and stories.

1A. *Number/Letter Memory.* The student is asked to repeat a series of numbers and letters spoken by the examiner; the sequences increase from two units (2-S) to 10 units (8-4-R-2-Y-Q-9-A-2-S).

1B. *Sentence Memory.* The student repeats meaningful sentences of increasing length spoken by the examiner.

1C. *Story Memory.* Two stories are read to the student, who is asked to recall as many parts of each story as he or she can.

2. *Visual Memory Scale.* Three subtests allow a comparison of simple, rote memory with memory for more complex visual information.

2A. *Finger Windows.* Using a card with nine holes, the examiner makes a spatial pattern by placing a pencil into one window and then another. The student repeats the pattern by placing a finger through each window in the same order. The pattern increases from two to nine units.

2B. *Design Memory.* The student is asked to draw from memory four designs presented by the examiner.

2C. *Picture Memory.* The student is shown a complex picture and is then asked to look at a second, similar scene. Memory is demonstrated by describing the elements that have been altered from the first picture.

3. *Learning Scale.* Three subtests assess learning over trials: one verbal, one visual, and one cross-modal task are provided.

3A. *Verbal Learning.* The student is read a list of words followed by immediate recall. The process is repeated three additional times to assess a student's ability to learn a list of unrelated words. Another subtest is administered after the fourth trial, and then a delayed-recall trial is given.

3B. *Visual Learning.* This test is given using a design board with the designs covered by yellow foam inserts. The examiner removes the cover of 12 designs for one second

each. The examiner then shows the designs one at a time on cards and asks the child to indicate the position of each design. The process is repeated three additional times to assess learning over trials. Another subtest is administered, and then a delayed-recall trial is given.

3C. *Sound Symbol.* The student is shown a series of designs that the examiner labels with a nonsense word. Then the examiner presents the designs again, and the student gives the label. The examiner corrects incorrect responses. This process is repeated three additional times. Two other tests are given, and then a delayed-recall trial is given.

Raw scores for each subtest are converted to scaled scores with a mean of 10 and a standard deviation of 3. The subtests are combined to form a verbal, visual, learning, and general-memory index with standard scores (mean equals 100, standard deviation equals 15) and percentiles. Delayed-recall scores are calculated and rated on a scale based on standard deviations from the mean (Bright Average, Average, etc.).

A short-form memory-screening index can be obtained by administering the first four subtests: Picture Memory, Design Memory, Verbal Learning, and Story Memory.

STRENGTHS OF THE WRAML

• The WRAML is the first standardized and well-normed assessment of memory in children and adolescents. Designed by authors who evaluate students in a pediatric-hospital setting, it adds to our understanding of memory and learning in children and adolescents with illness, trauma, and clinical problems. The WRAML is one of the instruments that is often a part of a neuropsychological evaluation. Previous to the publication of the WRAML, examiners needed to administer the memory subtests from a variety of instruments normed on different populations.

• The materials are interesting across the wide age-span of children and adolescents for whom the test is intended.

• The scoring processes are well described to reduce

ambiguity. Examiner judgment is required on some subtests; on those subtests the authors have provided suggestions for probes during administration and extra scoring examples.

LIMITING FACTORS OF THE WRAML

• The WRAML is a new test. The subtests measure complex memory constructs based on current memory theory. Further research is needed to ascertain its value in clinical evaluations.

• The WRAML is a complex test with difficult administration procedures. Examiners are urged to study the manual carefully and administer several practice tests before using the WRAML in a clinical evaluation.

• A student's performance on the WRAML may be lowered due to visual and auditory processing difficulties. Some of the subtests require visual perception of line drawings and geometric designs, while others require phonemic discrimination. Examiners must be alert to these compounding facts and interpret WRAML findings cautiously.

• The Delayed Recall subtest scores are based on a change score; that is, the student's score on the initial administration of the subtest is compared with his or her score on the delayed administration. The change score is then translated into a five-point scale ranging from Atypical to Bright Average. However, if the student's initial score was 1 and his or her delayed score was 1, the change would be 0, placing the student in the Bright Average category. This is clearly misleading because both the initial and delayed scores were very poor. Change scores must be viewed in relationship to the student's level of performance.

• Franzen, (1991) in his review, comments on the WRAML's lack of a developmental perspective. Subtests have not been designed with consideration for the ways in which memory functions change with age. Studies are needed of the WRAML's validity with students across the wide age-range with which it is normed to discover its usefulness with different age groups.

VISUAL LEARNING DISPLAY BOARD

8 & younger	9 & older
CHILD	*CHILD*

EXAMINER	*EXAMINER*

Lindamood Auditory Conceptualization Test, Revised Edition (LACT)

Charles Lindamood and Patricia Lindamood
1970; revised 1979
The Riverside Publishing Company
8420 Bryn Mawr Ave., Chicago, IL 60631

Purpose	To measure auditory discrimination and the ability to identify the number and order of sounds in a sequence
Major Areas Tested	Auditory perception
Age or Grade Range	Preschool–adult
Usually Given By	Special education teacher Speech/language clinician Remedial reading teacher Paraprofessional
Type of Test	Standardized Individual
Scores Obtained	Grade level
Student Performance Timed?	No
Testing Time	10–15 minutes
Scoring/Interpretation Time	10–15 minutes
Normed On	660 students in grades K–12 from a range of socioeconomic and ethnic backgrounds in a California school district; subsequently, 52 K–12 students from another California school district were added
Alternate Forms Available?	Yes

FORMAT

The materials for administering the Lindamood Auditory Conceptualization Test (LACT) include a manual, two examiner's cue sheets (one in Spanish), individual record sheets, and a set of 18 half-inch colored cubes (three each of red, yellow, blue, green, white, and black). The manual contains directions for administration and scoring, information on test construction, and suggestions for interpreting results. A tape is provided for the examiner to use as a guide for the pronunciation of individual sounds and syllable patterns.

The LACT test consists of four parts:

1. *The Precheck.* This part contains five items designed to determine whether the student can demonstrate knowledge of the following concepts: same/different, numbers to 4, left-to-right order, and first/last.

2. *Category I, Part A.* The student must identify the number of isolated sounds heard from a list of 10 items, and decide whether they are the same or different.

3. *Category I, Part B.* The student is given six items and asked to identify not only the number of isolated sounds heard and their sameness or difference, but also their order.

4. *Category II.* From a list of 12 items, the student must determine the number of sounds in a syllable and changes in the sound pattern when sounds are added, omitted, substituted, shifted, or repeated.

The Precheck is given to determine that the student understands the basic concepts necessary to obtain a valid test score. If knowledge of the Precheck concepts is not demonstrated, the test is discontinued. Categories I and II are each preceded by demonstration procedures.

In the LACT, the student manipulates colored blocks to indicate understanding of sound patterns. Each block represents a sound. There is no constant relationship between a specific color and a specific sound, so the student may select any colors. Different sounds within a pattern are represented by different colors.

As the examiner pronounces each sound pattern, the student may use visual cues (the examiner's lip movements) to aid discrimination; the examiner notes this diagnostic information. Patterns may not be repeated unless an environmental noise interferes with the student's hearing. Testing is discontinued after five consecutive errors in Category I. In Category II, the student is given an opportunity to do another similar pattern after an error. Testing is discontinued after five errors in Category II.

Points are given for each correct block pattern, and on that basis a raw score is obtained. The raw score is converted to a weighted score (one point for each correct response in Category I, Part A; three in Category I, Part B; and six in Category II). A single weighted score is obtained for the total tests; no subtest scores are provided. The examiner then compares the weighted score with a table that provides recommended minimum scores for each grade level. These minimum scores should be considered predictive of success in reading or spelling at or above that grade level.

Two equivalent forms, A and B, are available for reevaluation purposes.

STRENGTHS OF THE LACT

• The LACT provides a means of evaluating auditory perception skills related to reading and spelling without using written symbols. The student need not have knowledge of sound-symbol associations to demonstrate auditory perception skills. This makes the LACT a valuable tool for assessing auditory perception in beginning or remedial readers.

LAC Test Format

Category	Examiner Pronounces	Student's Block Pattern
Category I, Part A	Three same sounds (/b/, /b/, /b/)	Three same colors
	Two different sounds (/t/, /m/)	Two different colors
Category I, Part B	Two same sounds followed by one different sound (/s/, /s/, /p/)	Two same colors followed by one different color
Category II	Two different sounds in a syllable (/al/)	Two different colors
	New sound added at beginning of a syllable (/pal/)	New color added at beginning
	Change in last sound of a syllable (/pab/)	Change in last color

Many tests are available for assessing auditory discrimination of whole words. Other tests assess sound blending or auditory synthesis. The LACT, however, assesses the analysis of the number and order of sounds, as well as discrimination. These skills are crucial in reading and spelling.

• The Precheck section of the LACT is excellent. It allows the examiner to assess quickly the student's knowledge of the basic concepts necessary to take the test. Once it is determined that the student understands these basic concepts, errors on the test can more accurately be related to skill deficiencies in auditory perception.

• The manual provides an excellent presentation of how auditory perception, reading, and spelling relate to one another. Teachers and clinicians will find the discussion of follow-up remediation techniques and the authors' interpretation of test performances helpful.

• The LACT can be used with a wide age range of students. The alternate test forms make it a usable tool for evaluating progress in a remediation program.

• The Spanish Cue Sheet is sensitive to the language customs of Spanish-speaking children and adults. Both formal and informal verb types are presented.

LIMITING FACTORS OF THE LACT

• The LACT must be viewed as an informal test rather than a standardized instrument. *A Consumers Guide to Tests in Print* (Hammill, Bryant, and Brown, 1992) rates the LACT as unsatisfactory in every technical characteristic, including standardization sample, reliability, and validity. The LACT can provide helpful information regarding a student's auditory analysis skills for a teacher planning an intervention program, but scores should not be reported or used to make a diagnosis or qualify a student for services. administration manual is clearly written, the process of using colored blocks to illustrate sound patterns is a difficult one. Category II, in particular, requires extensive verbal explanation, and many students become confused if the examiner is not quite skilled in test administration. The order of items in Category II is particularly difficult to administer.

• Students with intellectual deficits or delays in concept development have difficulty learning the relationship between the colors and the sounds. They may continue to believe that there is a direct relationship between color and sound, such as red always equals /p/. This confusion is seen in such statements as, "There aren't enough colors." Such students may actually be able to spell the syllables in Category II (illustrating good auditory analysis) without being able to do the block patterns.

• The LACT authors have chosen to allow students to use visual cues (lip movements) to aid their auditory discrimination. It is true that visual cues are usually available in natural conversations. However, it is important for the examiner to note carefully whether or not the student uses visual cues. If the student does not, teaching him or her to do so is a good first step in remediation. If they are used extensively, it is important for the teacher to realize that, in activities where the student does not have direct contact with the speaker, auditory perception may be quite poor.

• The score obtained on the LACT is difficult to interpret. For example, suppose a third-grade student obtains a total test score of 60. According to the minimum scores table in the manual, a score of 61 is the minimum score predicting high probability of successful reading and spelling performance in high-first-grade material. Does this mean that the third-grade student's auditory perception skills are at a first-grade level? Or that the student should be instructed in first-grade material? The interpretation becomes even more confusing with an older student. A score of 93 is the minimal score for predicting reading and spelling success for the second half of fifth grade, but 99 is the minimum recommended score for 7th grade through adult. The lack of clarity in test score interpretation suggests that the LACT is better used as an informal test—a task-analysis approach to auditory perception, rather than a standardized test yielding grade-level scores.

• Throughout the manual, reading and spelling are treated as identical tasks requiring the same auditory perception skills. Validity studies should be done to separate these two processes. Although the authors feel that the reading method the student has been taught does not affect performance on the LACT, this seems questionable. Students with phonics training have clearly had more practice with auditory analysis than have sight-word readers.

• The LACT can be given to Spanish-speaking students by using the examiner's cue sheet in Spanish. The minimal grade scores recommended are the same for both English and Spanish students. It is not clear whether the Spanish form of the LACT has been tested for reliability or validity.

Malcomesius Specific Language Disability Test (MSLDT)

Neva Malcomesius
Educators Publishing Service, Inc., 1968
31 Smith Pl., Cambridge, MA 02138-1000

Purpose	To identify students with a specific language disability
Major Areas Tested	Auditory, visual, and kinesthetic skills related to reading, writing, and spelling
Age or Grade Range	Grades 6–8
Usually Given By	Classroom teacher Special education teacher
Type of Test	Informal Group
Scores Obtained	None (guidelines for evaluating test performance)
Student Performance Timed?	Yes
Testing Time	1 1/2 hours
Scoring/Interpretation Time	20–30 minutes
Normed On	Not normed
Alternate Forms Available?	No

FORMAT

The materials for the Malcomesius Specific Language Disability Test (MSLDT) consist of a teacher's manual, test booklets for the students, and a set of cards and charts used in administering the test. As in the Slingerland Tests, the MSLDT is not a test of oral language but rather a test of visual, auditory, and kinesthetic skills related to reading, spelling, and writing.

Because the Malcomesius Test was designed as an upward extension of the Slingerland Tests (junior high school level), the 10 subtests are almost identical to those in the Slingerland Tests, Forms A to D. The tests are also designed for group administration. The table below compares the Malcomesius subtests to those of the Slingerland. It is interesting that, in the Spelling—Auditory to Motor subtest, the focus is on sound-symbol association rather than correct spelling. Thus the following words would be considered correct: *dubious-doobious; exceed-excead.*

The MSLDT does not include any of the individual auditory tests that are found in the lower levels of the Slingerland Tests.

STRENGTHS OF THE MALCOMESIUS TEST

• As in the Slingerland Tests, the Malcomesius Test battery includes a series of school-related tests to aid the classroom teacher in identifying students with specific language disability. There are few tests designed for adolescents, and the Malcomesius Test provides a means of assessing the auditory, visual, and kinesthetic skills of this age group on tasks related to classroom performance.

LIMITING FACTORS OF THE MALCOMESIUS TEST

• The MSLDT is subject to the same limiting factor as the Slingerland Tests; the most serious of these is a lack of norms.

• No reliability or validity data are reported.

• The author seems to assume that the only difference between beginning readers and more mature readers is the length of the words they can process and the speed with which they can process them. This is shown by the fact that the items for sixth, seventh, and eighth graders are all the same; only time limits differentiate them. It may well be that

Comparison of the Malcomesius and Slingerland Subtests

Malcomesius Subtest	Description	Corresponding Slingerland Subtest
1. Paragraph Copying	Requires copying paragraphs from a wall chart	1
2. Near-Point Copying	Requires copying a list of words	2
3. Visual Discrimination	Requires matching visually similar words (*innuendo, inunendo, innuendo, inuennbo, innuenbo*)	4
4. Visual Perception and Recall	Requires identifying correct words and number sequences presented visually (*barbraian, barbarian, bardarian, darbraian*)	3
5. Visual Kinesthetic Recall	Requires writing phrases after a visual presentation (*Keep quite quiet.*)	5
6. Auditory Discrimination	Requires discrimination of words that sound very much alike (*trick, trek*)	None
7. Auditory Kinesthetic Memory	Requires writing phrases from dictation (*parents of the girl*)	6
8. Auditory-Visual Integration	Requires listening to a word or sequence of numbers and selecting it from four similar choices presented visually (*9,586; 6,589; 9,856; 9,589*)	8
9. Comprehension	Requires listening to a paragraph and writing it	None
10. Spelling—Auditory to Motor	Requires writing a list of 20 dictated words with focus on sound-symbol association, *not* correct spelling (*dubious-doobious, exceed-excead*)	None

an entirely different set of tasks should be used to identify these older disabled readers, rather than those used with the elementary students assessed by the Slingerland Tests.

• Subtests 9 and 10 are particularly poorly labeled. Subtest 9 is much more a measure of written language skills and sequential memory than it is of comprehension, and subtest 10 cannot be called spelling when the scoring directions specifically say, "Do not count spelling."

• The teacher's manual includes a page of "General Directions for Evaluating the Tests." This page contains a number of statements about specific language disability that are presented as fact when they really represent the author's opinion. The person using the Malcomesius Test needs to be alert to these statements and to avoid conclusions about a student's learning disability based on performance on this test alone.

Slingerland Pre-Reading Screening Procedures

Beth H. Slingerland
Educators Publishing Service, Inc., 1968; revised 1976, 1977
31 Smith Pl., Cambridge, MA 02138-1000

Purpose	To identify bright children with difficulties in the auditory, visual, and kinesthetic modalities that may indicate specific language disability
Major Areas Tested	Auditory, visual, and kinesthetic skills related to beginning reading
Age or Grade Range	Grades K–1
Usually Given By	Classroom teacher Special education teacher Psychologist Adminstrator
Type of Test	Informal Group
Scores Obtained	Rating scale (guidelines for evaluating test performance)
Student Performance Timed?	Yes
Testing Time	20–25 minutes each for three test sessions
Scoring/Interpretation Time	15–20 minutes
Normed On	Not normed
Alternate Forms Available?	No

FORMAT

The materials for the Slingerland Pre-Reading Screening Procedures consist of student booklets, cards and charts for three subtests, and a teacher's manual. Practice pages and markers are also provided. The tests are designed to be used with groups of kindergarten children who have not yet been introduced to formal reading. The recommended group size is 15 children. At least one monitor is needed to help the children locate the right page and to prohibit them from copying each other's work. The students use pencils without erasers and are taught to bracket their errors so that self-corrections can be noted.

The Slingerland Pre-Reading Screening Procedures contain 12 subtests to be given to the group and a set of individual auditory tests. The 12 subtests are:

1. *Visual Perception* requires matching single-letter and two-letter combinations.

2. *Visual Perception* requires visual matching of three-letter combinations.

3. *Visual Perception and Memory* requires visual memory of geometric and letter forms.

4. *Near-Point Copying* requires copying geometric and letter forms. Space is provided on both sides of the geometric and letter forms for left-handed and right-handed students.

5. *Auditory-Visual Perception* requires listening to a spoken direction and marking the appropriate picture. In Figure 67 the examiner says, "Mark the picture of the bird flying to its nest."

6. *Letter Recognition* requires marking the visual symbol of the letter name pronounced by the examiner. In Figure 68 the examiner says, "Mark the *f*."

7. *Visual-Kinesthetic Memory* requires visual perception and memory of geometric forms. The student draws the forms from memory after being shown a model.

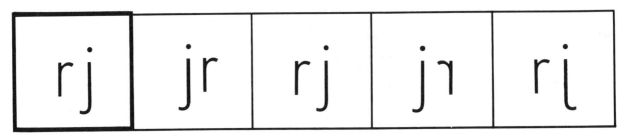

Slingerland Pre-Reading Screening Procedures, Procedure 1, Visual Perception

Slingerland Pre-Reading Screening Procedures, Procedure 2, Visual Perception

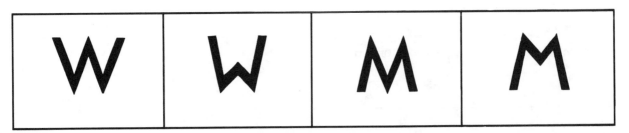

Slingerland Pre-Reading Screening Procedures, Procedure 3, Visual Perception and Memory

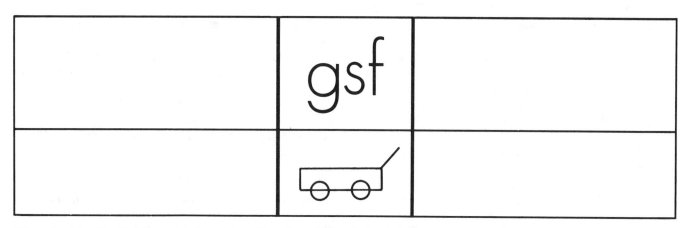

Slingerland Pre-Reading Screening Procedures, Procedure 4, Near-Point Copying

Slingerland Pre-Reading Screening Procedures, Procedure 5, Auditory-Visual Perception

**Slingerland Pre-Reading Screening
Procedures, Procedure 6, Letter Recognition**

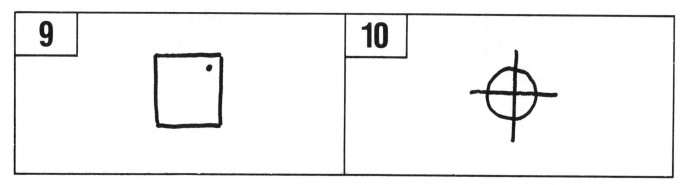

Slingerland Pre-Reading Screening Procedures, Procedure 7, Visual-Kinesthetic Memory

8. *Auditory Perception with Comprehension* requires listening to a story and indicating comprehension by marking a picture. For instance, for the illustrations shown here, the examiner would tell the following story: *Jane said to her little sister, "I wish you would go to the big table and get the little box for me. Something for you is in the little box." Mark the picture that shows where Jane wanted her sister to go.*

9. *Far-Point Copying* requires copying geometric and letter forms from a wall chart.

10. *Auditory Discrimination* requires listening to sets of three words and indicating if the words are the same or different. In Figure 72 the examiner says, "Slap, slap, slab." The student marks XX in the space between the two balloons, because the three words do not sound the same. When the words all sound the same, the student marks / / in the space.

11. *Auditory-Visual-Kinesthetic Integration* requires listening to the name of a letter, selecting it from three printed letters, and copying it. In Figure 73 the examiner says, "Copy the letter *B* in the last box in the row."

12. *Auditory-Visual Association* requires identifying pictures that begin with a specific sound pronounced by the examiner. For instance: "You see a book, a pencil, and a table. Mark the picture of the one that begins with the sound *t*."

The individual auditory tests include the following:

1. *Echolalia* requires repeating a word several times.

2. *Reproducing a Story* requires listening to and retelling a story.

The Slingerland Pre-Reading Screening Procedures are not normed for age or grade-level scores. However, a five-point rating scale (high, high-medium, medium, low-medium, and low) for evaluating student performance is given, as well as specific guidelines for scoring the tests. Alternate forms for test-retest purposes are not available.

STRENGTHS OF THE SLINGERLAND PRE-READING SCREENING PROCEDURES

• The Slingerland Pre-Reading Screening Procedures are a well-planned battery of readiness tests. They have been carefully designed to include tasks that assess a student's skills in all modalities: auditory, visual, and kinesthetic, alone and in combination. The teacher's manual is well organized, and the directions are very clear. The idea of using practice pages to train the students in the proper procedures is excellent. One part of the practice pages is a "This Is Me" picture, which yields a great deal of informa-

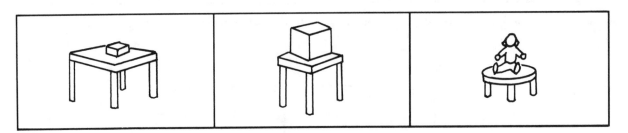

Slingerland Pre-Reading Screening Procedures, Procedure 8, Auditory Perception with Comprehension

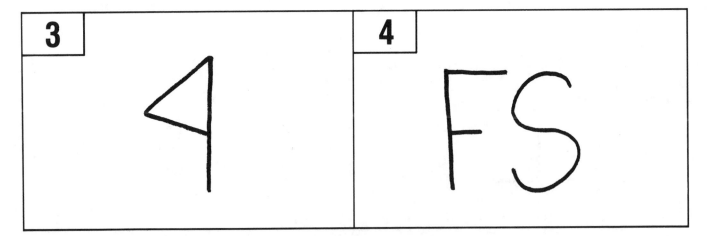

Slingerland Pre-Reading Screening Procedures, Procedure 9, Far-Point Copying

tion about the student's readiness skills. Although the subtests are timed, this is primarily to keep the group testing moving along and does not put serious constraints on the students. The teacher's manual gives excellent discussions of the subtests and the skills being measured by each. The Slingerland Pre-Reading Screening Procedures are an excellent contribution to the field when used as a group screening measure (1) to give the first-grade teacher extensive information on the modality strengths and weaknesses of a class of beginning readers and (2) to identify children who may need further individual testing.

LIMITING FACTORS OF THE SLINGERLAND PRE-READING SCREENING PROCEDURES

• The Slingerland Pre-Reading Procedures must be considered informal tests at this time. No standardized scores are presented. The five-point rating scale is based on the test results of several hundred children just entering first grade in school districts throughout the United States, but no further information about the sample is given.

• The Slingerland Pre-Reading Screening Procedures were designed to identify children who would enter first grade using the Slingerland adaptation of Orton–Gillingham (Gillingham and Stillman, 1960) techniques as a curriculum. The teacher's manual interprets test performance from the Orton–Gillingham point of view. This is not a serious problem in using the tests, but the teacher should be aware that a statement such as "The brighter the child, the more opportunities there have been for language learning" is an opinion, not a statement of fact.

• The author suggests that the Slingerland Pre-Reading Screening Procedures be used with the Pintner–Cunningham Primary Test of general intelligence (1966). This suggestion points out the need to be cautious about diagnosing any

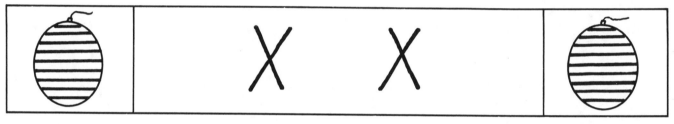

Slingerland Pre-Reading Screening Procedures, Procedure 10, Auditory Discrimination

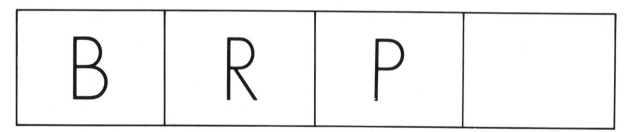

Slingerland Pre-Reading Screening Procedures, Procedure 11, Auditory-Visual-Kinesthetic Integration

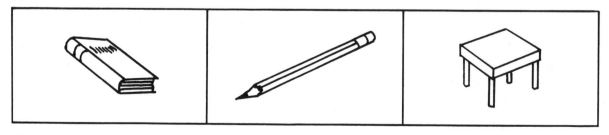

Slingerland Pre-Reading Screening Procedures, Procedure 12, Auditory-Visual Association

child's learning disabilities on the basis of one test.

• Recent factor analytic studies of the Slingerland Pre-Reading Screening Procedures identified four factors—visual motor processing (subtests 4,7,9), prereading (subtests 1 and 2), and language processing (subtests 5 and 8). The prereading factor was the best predictor of school success in first and second grades, with visual processing the next strongest. The fact that these findings were true of both reading and math suggests that the Slingerland Pre-Reading Screening Procedures assess a general readiness factor rather than skills specific to reading.

• The same studies suggest that the procedures over-identify at-risk kindergarten children, especially those from lower socioeconomic backgrounds.

Slingerland Screening Tests for Identifying Children with Specific Language Disability (SST)

Beth Slingerland
Educators Publishing Service, Inc., Forms A, B, C, 1962; revised 1970; Form D, 1974
31 Smith Pl., Cambridge, MA 02138-1000

Purpose	To identify students with a specific language disability or inadequate perceptual–motor skills, and children who compensate for inadequate perceptual-motor skills
Major Areas Tested	Visual, auditory, and kinesthetic skills related to reading and spelling
Age or Grade Range	First grade through college
Usually Given By	Classroom teacher Special education teacher Psychologist Administrator
Type of Test	Informal Group
Scores Obtained	None (guidelines for evaluating test performance)
Student Performance Timed?	Yes
Testing Time	1–1 1/2 hours
Scoring/Interpretation Time	30–40 minutes
Normed On	Not normed
Alternate Forms Available?	No

FORMAT

The Slingerland Screening Tests for Identifying Children with Specific Language Disability (SST) is a series of pencil-and-paper tests published in five forms for various grade levels.

Form	Grade Level
Pre-Reading	End of kindergarten to beginning of first grade
A	End of first grade to beginnign of second grade
B	End of second grade to beginning of third grade
C	End of third grade to beginning of fourth grade
D	Fifth and sixth grades

Despite the name, the SST are not language tests. They do not assess the typical language skills such as syntax, vocabulary, and language comprehension. Rather, they test auditory, visual, and kinesthetic abilities related to reading, writing, and spelling. Specific language disability (SLD) is another term for developmental dyslexia.

The materials for each form include the students' booklets, in which they write their answers, and a set of cards and charts for the examiner. Although the Slingerland Tests are not normed and therefore provide no age- or grade-level scores, standardized administration procedures are described in the examiner's manuals. One manual is provided for the Pre-Reading Test; a second includes the instructions for Forms A, B, and C; and a third is available for Form D. Directions for scoring and guidelines for evaluating test performance are also included in the manuals.

The Slingerland Tests (and the teaching method) are based on Orton-Gillingham techniques for teaching reading and spelling through a multisensory approach. The linkages among auditory, visual, and kinesthetic modalities are the essence of the model. The tests are designed to assess these linkages.

Forms A, B, C, and D of the Slingerland Tests include the same eight group subtests. Form D includes an additional group subtest. Forms A, B, C, and D also include a series of audityry subtests to be given individually at the conclusion of the group subtest. The eight basic subtests and the individual auditory tests are described in the table shown here. Although the number and difficulty of the items within each subtest vary in each form, the skill being measured remains the same. This format allows assessment of student progress on the same series of tasks in grades 1–6.

Because of the different format, the Slingerland Pre-Reading Screening Procedures are reviewed separately.

SLINGERLAND SCREENING FOR THE IDENTIFICATION OF LANGUAGE LEARNING STRENGTHS AND WEAKNESSES

Two new tests have been added to the Slingerland sequence. These two tests follow the format, administration procedures, scoring, and evaluation processes developed in the Slingerland and Malcomesius Tests (p.118).

Slingerland High School Level Screening
Authors: Carol Murray and Patricia Beis

This test provides a tool for assessing specific language disability (or dyslexia) in 9th through 12th grades. It may also be used with adults who have graduated from high school, but have completed less than one year of college.

Slingerland College Level Screening
Author: Carol Murray

This test is intended for college students or adults who have completed college. Both of the new tests include the following subtests:

    I. *Far Point Copying*

   II. *Near Point Copying*

  III. *Visual Perception Memory*

  IV. *Visual Discrimination*

   V. *Visual Kinesthetic Memory*

  VI. *Auditory Kinesthetic Memory*

 VII. *Initial and Final Consonant and Vowel Sounds*

VIII. *Auditory Visual Integration*

  IX. *Paragraph Comprehension.* Examiner reads a paragraph; student listens and then writes a paragraph in his or her own words.

   X. *Spelling.* Examiner dictates a list of 20 single words for the student to write.

These two extensions of the SST array provide a useful tool for the assessment of older students and adults. The Strengths and Limiting Factors of the SST apply to these new tests as well. Readers are also referred to the section on the assessment of dyslexia on page 9 of the Introduction.

Slingerland Subtests

Subtest	Description	Modality	Relationship to Classroom Skills
1. Far-Point Copying	Student copies paragraph from a chart on the wall	Visual, kinesthetic	Assesses visual-motor skills related to handwriting
2. Near-Point Copying	Student copies single words printed at top of page on lines at bottom	Visual, kinesthetic	Assesses visual-motor skills related to handwriting
3. Visual Perception Memory	Student is shown a word card for 10 seconds and then asked to find the word in a group of four visually similar words (*mnoey, mouey, woney, money*)	Visual	Assesses visual memory skills related to reading and spelling
4. Visual Discrimination	Student is asked to match words containing many easily confused letters (*lady, daly, laby, baby, lady*)	Visual	Assesses basic visual discrimination without memory component or written response
5. Visual Kinesthetic Memory	Student is shown word or design card for 10 seconds and then asked to write or draw the word or design	Visual, kinesthetic	Assesses the combination of visual memory and written response, which is necessary for written spelling
6. Auditory Kinesthetic Memory	Examiner dictates sequences of letters, numbers, and words, and then the student writes what the examiner dictated	Auditory, visual, kinesthetic	Combines auditory perception and memory with written response, skills necessary for dictation lessons
7. Initial and Final Sounds (Level D includes vowel sounds)	Examiner pronounces a word, and the student writes the initial or final sound (*shimmer—sh; clasp—p*)	Auditory, visual, kinesthetic	Assesses auditory discrimination and sequencing related to basic phonics with a written response
8. Auditory-Visual Integration	Examiner pronounces a word, and the student selects it from a group of four visually similar words (*baddy, babby, dabby, daddy*)	Auditory, visual	Assesses visual discrimination related to word recognition
9. Following Directions (Form D only)	Examiner gives a series of directions requiring a written response (*Write the alphabet. Do not use capital letters. Put a comma after each letter.*)	Auditory, kinesthetic	Assesses auditory memory and attention with a written response
Individual Auditory Tests (Forms A, B, C, and D)			
Echolalia	Examiner pronounces a word or phrase and the student repeats it four or five times aloud (*animal-animal-animal-animal*)	Auditory, kinesthetic	Assesses auditory-kinesthetic confusion related to pronunciation
Word Finding	Examiner reads a sentence with a missing word, and the student fills in the missing word (*A long yellow fruit is called a _____ .*)	Auditory	Assesses comprehension and the ability to produce a specific word on demand; word-finding problems often identify children with specific language disability
Story Telling	Examiner reads a story aloud, and the student retells it	Auditory	Assesses auditory memory and verbal expression of content material

STRENGTHS OF THE SLINGERLAND TESTS

• Beth Slingerland, the author of the tests, is an experienced teacher of students with specific language disabilities. She developed the tests for use in publis schools, and they reflect her knowledge of teaching. The subtests measure skills that are directly related to classroom performance.

• Students with specific language disabilities have deficits in auditory, visual, and kinesthetic skills and the intergration of these three systems, or modalities. Through careful analysis of a student's errors on the Slingerland Tests, a teacher can determine which modalities are the weakest and plan a remedial program accordingly. In contrast to the Illinois Test of Psycholinguistic Abilities, the Slingerland subtests measure the modalities with regular academic tasks, which makes them much more usable for the classroom teacher.

• The Slingerland Tests were designed as screening instruments. They can be administered by classroom teachers to total classroom groups. They are an economical way to identify students with difficulties in visual, auditory, or kinesthetic skills.

• As in all test batteries, some subtests are better than others. The three subtests measuring visual processing are particularly useful in determining the level of a visual perception problem. For example, the following performance on these three tests is very typical of students who have difficulty reading:

Visual Perception Memory (test 3): 80 percent correct
Visual Discrimination (test 4): 100 percent correct
Visual Kinesthetic Memory (test 5): 50 percent correct

These scores are interpreted to mean that, as the visual process becomes more complex, and when memory and a written response are required, the student's performance is poorer. In contrast is this typical performance of another student with reading difficulty:

Visual Perception Memory (test 3): 50 percent correct
Visual Discrimination (test 4): 70 percent correct
Visual Kinesthetic Memory (test 5): 95 percent correct

In this case, the kinesthetic (written) responses seem to increase the efficiency of the visual process.

LIMITING FACTORS OF THE SLINGERLAND TESTS

• At the present time, the Slingerland Tests must be viewed as informal tests. Although very specific directions for administration are given and complex scoring procedures are presented, no norms are provided. Thus, judgments about an individual student's performance are very subjective, depending on the sophistication of the examiner. The author stresses the need to develop local norms, which is probably true but not very realistic.

• One advantage of the Slingerland Tests is the fact that they use skills related to classroom tasks. But precisely because they measure classroom tasks, the tests are long and difficult for many students to take. Several subtests require extensive writing, and many students become discouraged. Because the items were selected to produce the visual and auditory sequencing and discrimination errors characteristic of studetns with specific language disability, many students become frustrated and require a great deal of emotional support to complete the test.

• There seems to be no rationale for the number or order of items within a subtest. There is no systematic increase in the difficulty of items, other than increasing vocabulary difficulty from Form A through Form D.

• Administration procedures are complex and difficult. Scoring procedures are long and also difficult, especially in view of the fact that the tests are not normed. The tests require considerable study before they can be used successfully.

• The terminology of the Slingerland Tests is very confusing. The term *specific language disability* requires explanation because it is often confused with oral language problems of other types. The titles of the subtests have no meaning to teachers or parents who have not seen the subtest items. School districts jthat choose to use this test need to devise a system of scoring, reporting scores, and describing results that are easily understood.

• Of great concern is the fact that the Slingerland Tests are frequently used as the only instrument to diagnose a student as having specific language disability. Such a practice is highly questionable for any single test and particularly for a nonstandardized, nonnormed instrument.

• A technical manual is now available that includes reliability and validity data on the SST (Forms A, B, C, D). Statistics on test-retest and interrater reliability indicate that reliability is better for Form C that for Forms A or B. The reliability data for individual subtests is below acceptable limits, while total test scores were acceptable. This would indicate that when reliable data for identification purposes is needed, the test should be given in its entirety.

• The studies of concurrent validity, reported in the technical manual, have different results depending upon ages of the students and form of the SST. When compared with Comprehensive Tests of Basic Skills (CTBS), Forms B and D appear to have grteater validity than A and C.

• Although the SST is intended to identify students with specific language disability or developmental dyslexia, there is no evidence that they are more precise in the identification of this type of learning problem than they are in identifying students with other types of specific learning disabilities.

The Visual Aural Digit Span Test (VADS)

Elizabeth M. Koppitz
Grune & Stratton, Inc., 1977
Orlando, FL 32887

Purpose	To provide a clinical tool to help diagnose specific learning problems in school children; and as a quick screening test for school beginners to identify learning problems
Major Areas Tested	Intersensory integration, sequences, and short term memory
Age or Grade Range	5 1/2–12 years
Usually Given By	Special education teacher School psychologist Educational diagnostician
Type of Test	Individual Standardized Norm-referenced
Scores Obtained	Age equivalent Percentile Grade equivalent
Student Performance Timed?	Yes
Testing Time	15–20 minutes
Scoring/Interpretation Time	15–20 minutes
Normed On	810 normal public school students; K–6th grades. Sample included a cross section of socioeconomic levels in urban and rural areas. All geographical sections of the country were included, but the majority were from New York State. The sample was balanced for age, sex, and ethnicity; no physically or mentally handicapped children were included
Alternate Forms Available?	No

FORMAT

The Visual Aural Digit Span Test (VADS) is a brief individual test which assesses sequencing and memory in a variety of modalities.

The materials needed to administer a VADS test include a set of 26 VADS stimulus cards, a VADS test scoring sheet, a pencil, and a watch. The rationale, administration and scoring procedures, norms tables, discussion of score patterns, and technical data on the test are contained in a book, *The Visual Aural Digit Span Test* (Koppitz, 1977).

The VADS consists of four subtests, each of which presents sequences of numbers for the student to recall. The mode of presentation and response varies with each subtest. The four subtests are:

I. *Aural-Oral (A-O)*. The student listens to sequences of digits pronounced by the examiner and repeats them back in correct order. This is the familiar digit span test found in several other test batteries. It requires the processing of auditory sequential material. It is a test of rote auditory memory.

II. *Visual-Oral (V-O)*. The student reads the sequences of digits and repeats them orally in the correct order. The subtest requires visual-oral integration and recall. This process is similar to that expected in reading.

III. *Aural-Written (A-W)*. In this subtest, the student listens to the digit series and responds in writing. The subtest measures auditory-visual integration with a written response. This is similar to the process required for spelling or dictation.

IV. *Visual-Written (V-W)*. This subtest requires the student to read the series of digits and write them from memory. It assesses intrasensory integration, visual input, and writing output. Similar skills are required when a student is asked to write material from memory.

The four subtests are given individually in one sitting in the order listed above. Entry points and ceiling procedures are described in Koppitz's book. In subtests I and III the examiner pronounces the digits at the rate of one per second. In subtests II and IV the student reads the digit sequences aloud and may study them for 10 seconds before the card is taken away. For subtests III and IV the student's responses are written on a single unlined piece of paper.

Each subtest is scored in the same way. The raw score is the number of digits in the longest series the student recalled correctly. Therefore the highest score obtainable on each subtest is 7.

Eleven scores are obtained from the VADS test—four for the subtests plus these seven combination scores:

Aural Input: (A-O) + (A-W)

Visual Input: (V-O) + (V-W)

Oral Expression: (A-O) + (V-O)

Written Expression: (A-W) + (V-W)

Intrasensory Integration: (A-O) + (V-W)

Intersensory Integration: (V-O) + (A-W)

Total VADS: (A-O) + (V-O) + (A-W) + (V-W)

Means and standard deviations for subtest scores are given for each age group. Six-month intervals are reported below seven years and yearly intervals thereafter. Percentile scores are presented for individual subtests and composites by age.

STRENGTHS OF THE VADS

• The VADS test is quick to administer and score. There are few materials, and the test is inexpensive. The rationale for the test is based on the experienced author's observation that students who do poorly in overcoming their learning problems have serious deficits in intersensory integration, sequencing, and recall. Digits were selected rather than letters to eliminate the anxiety produced by letter forms in poor readers. The rationale of the test is clearly explained in Koppitz's book.

• The administration procedures are clearly written and easy to follow. The author has provided good procedures for ensuring that the students can read and write the numbers on the subtest where those skills are required.

• Extensive information is provided to aid the examiner in making clinical observations of each student's performance. Observing student strategies and error patterns adds to the clinical diagnostic value of the test. Analysis of the ways the student writes his numerals on the unlined page can also be helpful. The techniques are similar to those recommended for users of the Bender Developmental Visual Gestalt Test by the same author.

LIMITING FACTORS OF THE VADS

• The VADS measures a very narrow range of behavior, short term recall of digits. Examiners should be cautious about generalizing the information into broad areas of memory. Certainly the small size and unscientific composition of the sample makes it clear that the VADS should be used as a screening device, rather than as a diagnostic tool.

• The selection of digits rather than alphabet letters for the test may have been a wise decision. However, one must be cautious about generalizing from recall of digits to recall of letters. The integration and recall processes may be quite different.

• The Koppitz book is interesting reading, providing extensive information on the test and its interpretation. However, a separate examiners manual with administration and scoring procedures and norms would facilitate administration greatly.

• The technical inadequacies of the VADS severely limit its usefulness. The one reported reliability study was poorly designed. While several studies of validity are reported, they are methodologically weak (Webster and Whitley, 1986).

There is no data presented that supports the VADS predictive validity or its concurrent validity with actual school performance. Examiners must consider the VADS a rough screening test. It does not have the technical merit to make differential diagnosis or to identify potential learning disabilities. *A Consumer's Guide to Tests in Print* (Hammill, Bryant, and Brown, 1992) rates the VADS as unsatisfactory on all technical characteristics.

The Bender Visual Motor Gestalt Test (BVMGT)

Lauretta Bender
Boyd Printing, 1946; Koppitz Developmental Scoring System, 1963, revised 1975; Pascal and Suttell Scoring System, 1951
49 Sheridan Ave., Albany, NY 12210

Purpose	To assess level of maturity in visual-motor perception and to detect emotional disturbances
Major Areas Tested	Visual-motor integration and emotional adjustment
Age or Grade Range	5–11 years (Koppitz Developmental Scoring System) 15–50 years (Pascal and Suttell Scoring System)
Usually Given By	Psychologist Special education teacher
Type of Test	Standardized Individual Group
Scores Obtained	Age level Percentile
Student Performance Timed?	No
Testing Time	10 minutes (individual administration) 15–25 minutes (group administration)
Scoring/Interpretation Time	10–20 minutes
Normed On	1,100 students from the Midwest and East, including public school children in rural, small town, suburban, and urban areas; 1974 sample included Blacks, Orientals, Mexican-Americans, and Puerto Ricans (norms refer to Koppitz standardization)
Alternate Forms Available?	No

FORMAT

The Bender Visual Motor Gestalt Test (Bender) is a series of nine abstract designs to be copied in pencil by the student. The figures illustrate certain principles of Gestalt psychology. The designs, printed on four-inch by six-inch cards, are presented one at a time. The student copies each design, with the sample before him or her. When the student finishes drawing a figure, the card is removed and the next card is placed at the top of the paper. A modification of the test requires the student to recall the designs from memory after initial performance.

The Bender is usually administered individually but can be given to a group of students. As a group test, different techniques have been devised for administration: projecting the designs onto a screen or wall, using enlarged stimulus cards, using individual decks of cards for each student, or using special copying booklets.

The standard individual administration of the Bender permits the student to erase and rework the reproductions. More than one sheet of paper may be used, and although there is no time limit on this test, data presented by Koppitz (1963) shows the average time required to complete the test along with the critical time limits. Timing the test, then, can be useful. Manipulation of the stimulus cards is allowed, but they must be replaced in the original position before the student begins copying. If the student rotates the paper while copying a design, it should be returned to its original position before the next figure is presented.

There is no basal or ceiling level on the Bender. The student copies all nine designs, which are presented in a specified order. Alternate, equivalent forms for test-retest purposes are not available.

The original Bender did not include any formal scoring system. However, as the test became more popular in clinics and schools, several scoring systems were developed. One of the most frequently used was devised by Elizabeth Koppitz, a clinical psychologist who used the test extensively with children with learning and emotional disorders. Koppitz's book, *The Bender-Gestalt Test for Young Children* (1963), describes a scoring system, age norms for children between the ages of 5 and 11 years, and reliability and validity data. Volume 2 of the same book (Koppitz, 1975) presents a revised scoring system, a norming population expanded to include minority groups, and a compilation of the research available on the test. These two books are essential for scoring and interpreting test performance.

In the Koppitz scoring system (described in detail in her books), errors are counted for distorting the shape of the design, perseverating, falsely integrating two forms, and rotating forms. The student's total error score is converted to a developmental-age score. Volume 2 provides tables for converting the total number of errors to both age-equivalent and percentile scores. Koppitz reports that these types of errors are most indicative of minimal brain dysfunction.

STRENGTHS OF THE BENDER

• The Bender is a quick, easy-to-administer test that is generally nonthreatening and appealing to students. It is popular with psychologists and is a widely used clinical instrument. The test is inexpensive and requires few materials.

• The Bender provides developmental data about a student's maturity in visual-motor integration. Of equal value is the important clinical information that can be obtained by observing a student's behavior while taking the test. For example, the experienced examiner notes such behaviors as excessive erasing and reworking of the designs, rotation of the drawing paper, time needed to complete the test, the spatial organization of the designs on the paper, and the student's attitude during testing. Two students may achieve the same score on the Bender, even producing similar-looking finished protocols, but the clinical observations of the two students may be very different. The behaviors observed during testing provide valuable diagnostic insight.

• Research has also supported the use of the Bender to detect emotional problems. Koppitz (1975) has developed two new emotional indicators (Box around Design and Spontaneous Elaboration, or Addition to Design) to add to her previous list of 10 (Confused Order, Wavy Line, Dashes Substituted for Circles, Increasing Size, Large Size, Small Size, Fine Line, Careless Overwork or Heavily Reinforced Lines, Second Attempt, and Expansion). She reports that the presence of three or more emotional indicators on a student's final product suggests the need for further psychological evaluation.

• The group adaption of the Bender is particularly economical in terms of time. Combined with other brief tests, it is moderately effective as a screening instrument, to identify high-risk students in need of further evaluation. Used in a pretest-posttest manner, the Bender can also be used as a means of evaluating the effectiveness of perceptual-motor training programs.

• The development of various scoring systems to meaningfully quantify a student's performance on the Bender has increased the test's utility. In addition to the Koppitz system for children, the Pascal and Suttel Scoring System has proven useful for adult protocols.

LIMITING FACTORS OF THE BENDER

• The Bender can be interpreted both intuitively and objectively. In either case, the examiner must be highly trained and experienced to effectively analyze the test protocols and to observe and evaluate the student's behavior while taking the test. For example, the designs may result from difficulties in immaturity in visual perception, motor coordination, or the integration of perceptual and motor skills. Less experienced examiners should definitely be cautioned against interpreting the Bender through subjective, intuitive procedures; use of an objective scoring system is more appropriate. Considerable experience is also necessary to achieve a high degree of score reliability with the Bender.

• In spite of recent improvements in the Koppitz Developmental Scoring System, the procedures still contain a high degree of subjectivity. The examiner must compare the student's reproductions with the model according to specific criteria. Scoring a Bender protocol can take considerable time because of the careful inspection required.

• Koppitz reports that the Bender can be used as a measure for detecting neurological impairment (minimal brain dysfunction). The Bender may be helpful in this regard when used in conjunction with other tests and with intellectual evaluation, medical evaluation, and social history. Such a diagnosis should *never* be made on the basis of Bender performance alone.

• Projective interpretations of the Bender should be employed with caution. The emotional indicators can discriminate between well-adjusted and emotionally disturbed groups of students but cannot be used for a definitive diagnosis of an individual child. The 12 indicators can differentiate neurotic, psychotic, and brain-damaged students only when accompanied by other tests and background data.

• The Bender is limited by age because of its developmental ceiling. The test distinguishes between students with outstanding or average visual-motor perception and those with immature perception only for students between the ages of 5 and 8. Most normal 10-year-old students can copy the Bender designs without any difficulty. Scores are meaningful for older students only if their perceptual-motor development is below the 9-year-old level.

• As a group test, the Bender has certain drawbacks. The examiner cannot observe and supervise each student individually; therefore some of the clinical value of the test is lost through group administration. For very immature and hyperactive students who cannot work independently, individual administration is more appropriate.

• A last consideration is the use of the Bender in research studies. The reported findings on using the test as a means of predicting academic achievement have often been contradictory. Further investigation might clarify these discrepant findings. More research is also needed to determine what the recall method of the Bender measures and what diagnostic implications this procedural variation holds. Another area that needs to be more fully explored and substantiated concerns the recent finding that the rate of development in visual-motor perceptual skills differs among students of various ethnic groups.

• Given the conflicting results of research using the Bender, it is best to think of this test as a measure of visual-motor integration through design copying, rather than a test of intelligence, emotional disturbance, or minimal brain damage.

• *A Consumer's Guide to Tests in Print* (Hamill, Bryant, and Brown, 1992) rates the Bender as unsatisfactory in all technical characteristics, again supporting the need to use the Bender as an informal assessment.

The Developmental Test of Visual Motor Integration Third Revision (VMI–3R)

Keith E. Beery
PRO-ED
8700 Shoal Creek Boulevard, Austin, Texas 78757-6897

Purpose	To help prevent learning and behavior problems through early screening identification
Major Areas Tested	Visual–motor integration
Age or Grade Range	Preschool through adult; norms provided ages 4–17.11
Usually Given By	Classroom teacher Special education teacher Occupational therapist Psychologist
Type of Test	Standardized Individual Group
Scores Obtained	Age level T Score Percentile Normal curve equivalent Standard
Student Performance Timed?	No
Testing Time	10–15 minutes
Scoring/Interpretation Time	10 minutes
Normed On	5,824 students between the ages of 2 years, 6 months and 19 years, balanced for ethnicity, income level, place of residence, and sex based on 1980 U.S. census figures
Alternate Forms Available?	No

FORMAT

The Developmental Test of Visual-Motor Integration (VMI–3R) was first published in 1967 and renormed in 1982. In the 1989 version, the test remains the same while scoring procedures and norms have been upgraded.

The materials for the VMI-3R consist of the manual and individual test booklets. The VMI is a pencil-and-paper test. It may be presented to groups of students, but is more often used individually. The test booklet presents 24 geometric forms for the student to copy. The forms are printed in heavy black outlines and arranged three to a page, with a space below each one for the student to copy that form. The format is clear and uncluttered, and the forms are arranged from the simplest to the most complex. The student copies the forms and may not erase or rotate the book. The test is not timed, and the student continues working until three consecutive errors are made. Although the same booklet is used for students of a wide age range, the student only copies forms within his or her ability. The raw score consists of the total number of forms copied correctly before reaching the ceiling; this score is converted to an age score, standard score, and percentile using the tables in the manual.

The VMI is published in two forms. The Long Form contains all 24 geometric forms and covers the age range of 2 to 15 years. The Short Form is somewhat less expensive, contains only the first 15 geometric forms, and is recommended for students between 2 and 8 years of age. Alternate, equivalent forms for test-retest purposes are not available.

STRENGTHS OF THE VMI

• The VMI–3R is a well-constructed test. The 24 geometric forms were chosen over letter forms because they were equally familiar to children of varying backgrounds. The forms are developmentally sequenced, with careful thought to increasing task complexity. The wide age range makes the VMI–3R a good instrument for screening purposes as well as for measurement of student progress.

• The VMI–3R is an enjoyable test for most students. The directions are clear and easy to understand. The beginning forms allow even young or seriously impaired students to experience success, whereas the more complex forms present a challenge for the adolescent student. The

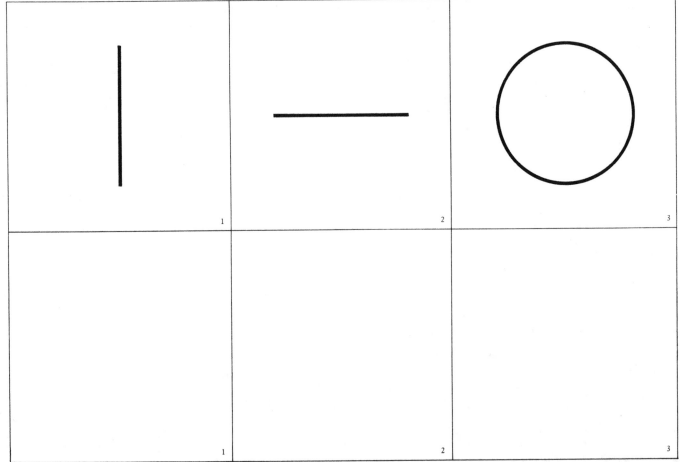

VMI, Items 1, 2, 3

test requires no verbal responses and therefore can be used with children with hearing impairments or language disabilities. It is a good test to use as a warm-up in an early part of a diagnostic battery.

• As were the older editions, the VMI–3R is a quick test to administer and score and yet yields good information about a major area of learning.

• The VMI–3R has clear directions for administration and is a good instrument for the classroom teacher to use with small groups of students. The provision of age norms for each item provides the teacher with a basis for understanding which types of geometric forms can be expected to be mastered next. This is, if a student can complete the right oblique line (/) and the left oblique line (\) successfully, we can expect that next the student will probably learn to reproduce the oblique cross (x). Extensive developmental data, including age scores for imitating forms at the younger ages, is provided in the manual.

• The VMI–3R manual is particularly helpful in describing the process of visual-motor integration and in outlining a sequence of visual-motor training activities.

• In the 1989 edition of the VMI, several important changes have been made in administration and scoring procedures which have greatly added to the value of the test.

• Instructions are given to the students in the group administration to, "Do your best on both the easy and the hard ones." Previously, students' rapid, careless approach to the easier items often resulted in lower scores. (This instruction should be given to individual students as well, although it has been omitted from the Individual Administration instructions.)

• Excellent guidelines are given to help the examiner tease out the differences between the visual perception and motor coordination aspects of a student's performance. The examiner is also encouraged to teach the young, inexperienced child how to make a few forms and then retest in two weeks. Children without deficits in this area will usually learn and retain the process.

• The scoring range of the VMI–3R has been expanded from 24 to 50 points by weighting each form according to age norms. In this manner, the more difficult forms are given four points while the simplest forms are worth one point. This expansion closes the gaps between the age groups and allows a higher

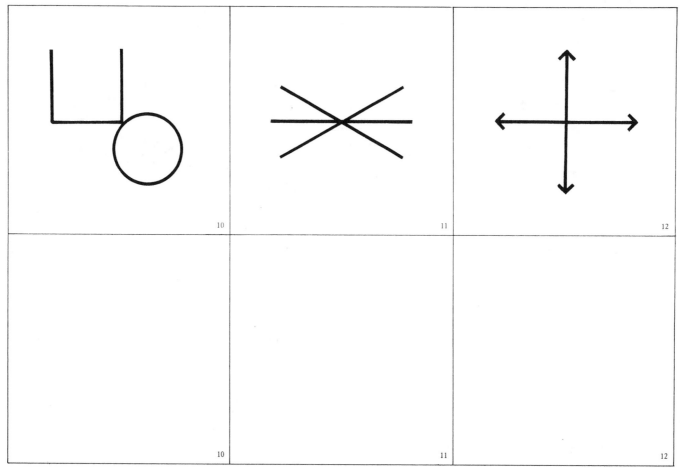

VMI, Items 10, 11, 12

DEVELOPMENTAL TEST OF VISUAL-MOTOR INTEGRATION
Copyright © 1967 by Keith E. Beery and Norman A. Buktenica

range of scores for older students.

• More specific criteria are described for scoring each form. This is important because the VMI–3R is still scored on a credit/no credit basis for each form. The two-page summary scoring provided near the end of the manual is helpful for the experienced VMI–3R examiner.

• The VMI–3R now uses standard scores with a mean of 100 and standard deviation of 15 to allow more direct comparison with other standardized tests.

LIMITING FACTORS OF THE VMI

• Although the VMI–3R has age norms for students up to 17.11 years old, it seems most useful with preschool and primary-age students. It can be used as either an individual or group test with one set of age norms. If used as a group test, monitors should be provided to keep students from rotating the book or skipping forms. The expanded forms have made the test more valid at the upper age levels. However, the norming sample has a small number of students at ages 15 and older, and scores should be used with caution. The size and composition of the standardization sample indicates that the norms are most adequate for

the 5- to 13-year old gage range.

• The VMI–3R does not measure spatial organizational skills. Each form is copied in the space provided. A student may have much more difficulty on a test like the Bender Visual Motor Gestalt Test, where nine forms are copied on a blank piece of paper. A very low score on the VMI–3R often reflects an impulsive, careless approach to the test, and this must be sorted out from true deficits in visual-motor integration.

• Despite the increased specificity for scoring forms provided, clearly the author relies upon the examiner's experience to score the test correctly. In one place he states that an inexperienced examiner will recognize when an older child has hastily copied the simplest forms which are clearly within his ability and "take such behaviors into account in scoring." (VMI–3R Manual, p. 24.) Such nebulous statements are in fact true for the experienced scorer, but research described in the manual clearly documents the need for training in scoring procedures for the not-so-experienced examiner.

• The reliability and validity studies presented in the manual provide no data but summary statements only.

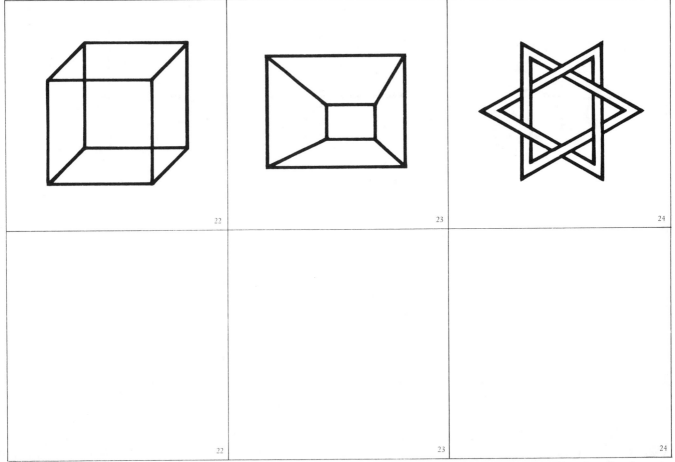

VMI, Items 22, 23, 24

Motor-Free Visual Perception Test (MVPT)
Ronald P. Colarusso and Donald D. Hammill

Academic Therapy Publications, 1972
20 Commercial Blvd., Novato, CA 94949

Purpose	To measure overall visual perceptual processing ability
Major Areas Tested	Visual perception
Age or Grade Range	4–9 years
Usually Given By	Classroom teacher Special education teacher Occupational therapist
Type of Test	Standardized Individual
Scores Obtained	Age level Perceptual quotient (PQ)
Student Performance Timed?	No
Testing Time	10–15 minutes
Scoring/Intepretation Time	15–20 minutes
Normed On	881 urban, suburban, and rural children from all races and economic levels in 22 states
Alternate Forms Available?	No

FORMAT

The materials required for administering the Motor-Free Visual Perception Test (MVPT) are the test manual, the book of test plates, and an individual scoring sheet. The test consists of 36 items arranged into five sections, each section with its own demonstration item and instructions.

Section 1. From an array of four drawings, the student selects a drawing of a geometric form that matches a stimulus drawing. The first three items in this section require matching by spatial orientation; the remaining five items require recognizing the correct form in a rival background. (See Item 6, from Section 1, shown here.)

Section 2. The student selects the geometric form that is the same shape as the model but is rotated, darker, or a different size. On some items in this section, the correct figure must also be distinguished from a rival background. (Section 2, Item 12.)

Section 3. The student is first shown a stimulus drawing and is then asked to choose it from memory from an array of four similar drawings. (Section 3, Item 15.)

Section 4. The student selects, from an array of incomplete drawings, the drawing that would, if completed, match the model. (Section 4, Item 29.)

Section 5. The student selects from four drawings the one that is different. The difference involves a change in spatial orientation of the drawing or a part of the drawing. (Section 5, Item 34.)

The examiner tallies the number of correct responses in all five sections to determine the raw score. This score can then be converted to an age equivalent, a perceptual quotient, and with some computation, a standard score. Each of these scores represents the student's performance on the total test; separate scores are not given for each section.

STRENGTHS OF THE MVPT

• The motor-free aspect of this test makes it a useful diagnostic tool, because it helps to detect which component of visual-motor integration activities may be causing an individual student's difficulty. When used as part of a test battery that includes tests of visual-motor integration and various aspects of coordination, it can make an important contribution to delineating the specific problem area and setting up an appropriate intervention program.

A   B   C   D

MVPT, Section 1, Item 6

- The MVPT is easy to administer, and although it must be given individually, it is not excessively time consuming. The scoring procedure is simple and objective. Administering the test requires no disposable materials, except for the one-page scoring sheet, making it a relatively inexpensive test to give.

- The method of reporting scores is quite useful; the availability of age scores, perceptual quotients, and standard scores makes it easy to compare a student's performance on this test to performance on other tests. In addition, the availability of scores in several forms serves as a system of checks and balances against the pitfalls of the individual scoring systems.

- The authors' use of the standard error of measurement in reporting age-equivalent scores is useful because it requires the examiner to view the student's score as a range within which the "true" score is likely to fall. The examiner is also cautioned to take into account the standard error of measurement when intepreting perceptual quotients, although this is not "built into" the reporting of these scores (unlike the age-equivalent scores).

- The test directions are, for the most part, clear and simple. However, language-impaired students sometimes have difficulty understanding what is expected on the visual closure items, and the standard procedure outlined in the manual does not permit much additional explanation.

- The MVPT's reliability is acceptable for students aged 5 years to 8 years, 11 months but is borderline for 4-year-olds. Construct validity is acceptable for students aged 5 years to 7 years, 11 months.

LIMITING FACTORS OF THE MVPT

- The authors caution that guessing, random answering, and perseveration are factors that must be considered in interpreting scores on this and most other tests. A raw score of less than 10 indicates less than chance performance and cannot be interpreted with confidence.

- The standardization sample for the norming of the MVPT is inadequate. Due to this factor, *A Consumer's Guide to Tests in Print* (Hammill, Bryant, and Brown, 1992) gives the MVPT an overall rating of not recommended.

NOTE

The MVPT–Revised will be available in spring 1995. Four new plates have been added and the norms extended to 11 years, 11 months. Remedial Checklists are also available. In addition, the MVPT–Vertical will be available in fall, 1995. It is intended to be useful with adults, particularly those receiving neuropsychological assessment.

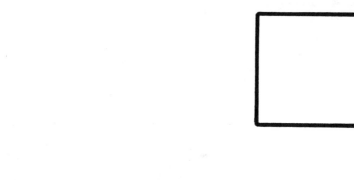

A

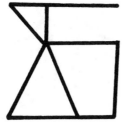

B

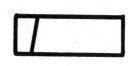

C

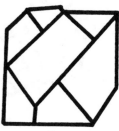

D

MVPT, Section 2, Item 12

- The high success rate on each item for 7-year-olds makes the MVPT nondiscriminatory at the upper age limits.
- The content validity of the test is open to question. The authors state that the test assesses five areas of visual perception: spatial relationships, visual discrimination, figure-ground perception, visual closure, and visual memory. For each of the five types, other researchers are cited who have measured similar aspects of visual perception. However, the authors do not establish adequately that these five areas are mutually exclusive or that they represent all aspects of visual perception.
- Some of the definitions of perceptual categories are vague and confusing. This is complicated by the division of the test into five unlabeled sections that do not seem to correspond in all cases with the perceptual categories the authors have defined. Section 1, for example, includes five figure-ground items, as well as three items that the authors would, it seems, include in their definition of spatial relations.
- The number of items in each perceptual category ranges from 5 to 11. Because the test provides only a total score, the larger percentage of items on visual closure, for example, means that a student with this difficulty may achieve an unrealistically low score.
- No information is provided about the test's construct validity for 4-year-olds and 8-year olds.
- In studying the MVPT's criterion-related validity, the authors did not correlate MVPT scores exclusively with other motor-free tests, thus introducing too many variables for accurate interpretation. This problem was further complicated by using a homogeneous sample for the interest correlations.

A   B   C   D

MVPT, Section 3, Item 15

  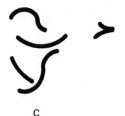 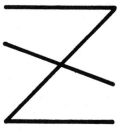

A B C D

MVPT, Section 4, Item 29

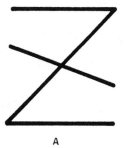  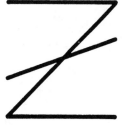

A B C D

MVPT, Section 5, Item 34

Developmental Test of Visual Perception, Second Edition (DTVP–2)

Donald D. Hammill, Nils A. Pearson, and Judith K. Voress
PRO-ED, 1993
8700 Shoal Creek Boulevard, Austin, TX 78768

Purpose	To measure different but interrelated visual–perceptual and visual–motor abilities
Major Areas Tested	Visual perception and visual–motor skills
Age or Grade Range	4–10 years
Usually Given By	Psychologist Occupational therapist Special education teacher Optometrist
Type of Test	Standardized Individual Norm-referenced
Scores Obtained	Age equivalent Standard scores Percentile
Student Performance Timed?	No
Testing Time	30–60 minutes
Scoring/Interpretation Time	20–30 minutes
Normed On	1,972 children residing in 12 states. Children were randomly selected, and the demographics of the sample were compared with Statistical Abstract of the United States, 1990
Alternate Forms Available?	No

FORMAT

The Developmental Test of Visual Perception (DTVP–2) is a completely revised and restandardized edition of the Developmental Test of Visual Perception authored by Marianne Frostig and her colleagues in the early 1960s (See Granddaddies, p. 21). The DTVP–2 is a comprehensive evaluation of visual perception in young children. The test includes assessment tasks that are exclusively visual–perceptual (requiring little motor ability) and tasks that involve visual–motor integration. The test is specifically designed to evaluate visual perception under motor-reduced and motor-enhanced conditions so that the two abilities can be compared.

The test materials consist of the Examiner's Manual, the Picture Book containing the stimulus items for many of the subtests, children's Response Booklet for the visual motor integration subtests, and the Profile/Examiner Record Form for recording responses and reporting scores.

The DTVP–2 is composed of eight subtests, which are to be administered individually in the order described below. Testing begins with Item 1 on every subtest. On several subtests there are ceiling levels, which are described in the Examiner's Manual, along with specific instructions for the administration of each subtest.

1. *Eye–Hand Coordination* (4 items). Children are asked to draw continuous lines within increasingly narrow boundaries. While the items require straight lines initially, subsequent items involve angles and curves. Detailed scoring procedures are based on children's ability to stay within the boundary.

2. *Position in Space* (25 items). Children are asked to match a stimulus picture with another in an array of visually similar pictures. All of the choices are identical in form and vary only in spatial orientation. A pointing response is used.

3. *Copying* (20 items). Children are asked to copy geometric forms directly below the stimulus. The forms progress from simple (straight lines, circles, squares) to increasingly complex. Scoring is based on a 3-point quality scale.

4. *Figure Ground* (18 items). Children are shown overlapping geometric forms and are asked to select from an array of choices the discrete forms that make up the stimulus. The more difficult items have the forms embedded in a complex background. A pointing response is used, and children must identify all of the forms correctly to receive credit for the item.

5. *Spatial Relations* (10 items). Children are asked to reproduce a design using a grid with evenly spaced dots to guide them. The score is determined by tabulating the number of dots the children connect in their drawings that were in the original design.

6. *Visual Closure* (20 items). Children are shown a design and then asked to find it in an array of incomplete figures. In order to complete the match, children must mentally supply the missing part of the drawing. The raw score is the number of correct items.

7. *Visual Motor Speed* (1 item). This is a coding task in which children are asked to copy marks within specific geometric forms (e.g., straight lines in a circle, an *x* in a square). The score is based on the number of correct marks copied within a one-minute time limit.

8. *Form Constancy* (20 items). Children are shown a stimulus form and position, shape, or background. For each

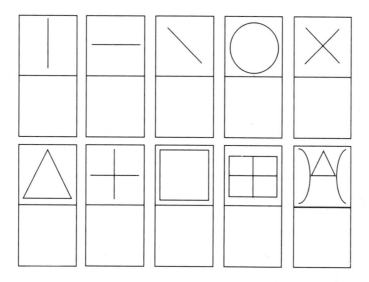

DTVP-2 Subject 3: Copying

item, two forms in the array are correct, and children must identify both in order for the response to be counted as correct.

The raw scores for each subtest are converted into age equivalents, standard scores, and percentiles using tables in the Examiner's Manual. Three composite scores are also derived. The General Visual Perception composite includes the scaled scores of all eight subtests. The Motor Reduced Visual Perception composite is composed of the four subtests that utilize a pointing response (Position in Space, Figure Ground, Visual Closure, and Form Constancy). The Visual Motor Integration composite includes the four subtests with a pencil–paper response (Eye–Hand Coordination, Copying, Spatial Relations, and Visual–Motor Speed).

Standard scores (also called quotients), percentiles, and age equivalents are also recorded for the three composites. Subtest standard scores have a mean of 10 and a standard deviation of 3, while quotients have a mean of 100 and a standard deviation of 15. The composite scores are the most reliable and valuable scores of the DTVP–2 because they are composed of several subtests and represent the theoretical construct upon which the test was developed.

STRENGTHS OF THE DTVP–2

- The DTVP–2 was designed to provide a comprehensive measure of visual perception in young children. By dividing the eight subtests into four that require minimal motor skill (motor-reduced) and four that require pencil/paper responses (motor-enhanced), the test allows the examiner to compare visual perception in its purest form with visual–motor integration. An analysis of child's performance on the two composites will allow the examiner to determine if a problem exists in visual perception alone, in visual–motor integration alone, in neither, or in both. An understanding of this difference should lead to more effective remediation strategies.

- The Examiner's Manual is clearly written. In addition to presenting a short biography of Marianne Frostig and giving her full credit for her contribution to the field, it provides an excellent description of the perceptual process and the relationship of motor skills to visual perception.

- A major criticism of the original DTVP was that it proported to measure five independent skills. The DTVP–2 discusses the interrelatedness of the subtests within each composite, discarding the independent skills theory.

- The stimulus materials in the Picture Book are of high quality and, presented in a simple uncluttered format, an important feature in a test of visual perception.

- The child's Response Booklet is also well designed for young children's use.

- Scoring procedures have been simplified (with the exception of the Eye–Hand Coordination subtest), and the Profile/Examiner Record Form is well designed and easy to use. Provisions are made for prorating scores if all eight subtests are not given or if a subtest is invalidated during administration. This is a sensitive feature in a test for young children.

- The Examiner's Manual includes extensive data on reliability and validity.

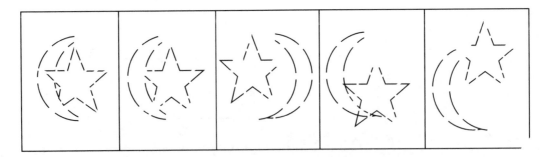

DTVP-2 Subject 6: Visual Closure

LIMITING FACTORS OF THE DTVP–2

• The DTVP–2 is not an easy test to administer and score. The examiner must move back and forth between the Picture Book and the Response Booklet. There are several different ways for obtaining ceiling levels. The scoring system for subtest 1, Eye–Hand Coordination, is quite complex. The three practice administrations advised by the authors are highly recommended.

• The Visual Motor Speed subtest seems to measure several aspects of visual perception. The child must understand the directions, have enough motor accuracy to be able to keep his or her marks within the form, and work under time constraints. The format of the page is quite complex for a child with visual perceptual difficulties, the very child who is most likely to be given the test.

• The test items on the DTVP–2 consist only of geometric forms and shapes; no letter or numbers are used. While a child may be able to distinguish a form from others that are rotated or inverted, the child may still not be able to differentiate rotated or inverted letters (b/d, p/b, or n/u). The examiner should not conclude that a student's good performance on the DTVP–2 automatically rules out difficulty in perceiving the symbols of language.

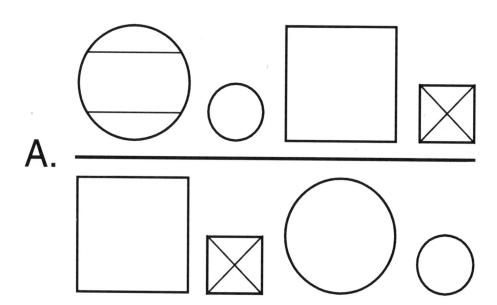

DTVP-2 Subject 7 Visual-Motor Speed

- Although the users of the DTVP–2 may purchase ProScore, a computerized system for converting raw scores into standard scores and percentiles, the print-out report generated seems of little value to parents or other professionals. It describes the test in more detail than is necessary and then draws comparisons between subtests that are of little diagnostic importance.

CHAPTER THREE
Speech and Language Tests

The primary, first-learned language system is oral. Long before children come to school, they develop skills of listening and speaking that enable them to communicate with others. The secondary language system, written language, is learned in school. Difficulties in the acquisition of reading and writing often have their basis in the student's oral language skills. This chapter deals primarily with the assessment of oral language, with its reception and expression. The tests reviewed here are usually given by speech and language therapists or clinicians. However, several of the newer tests include measures of written language, of reading and writing. These tests are more likely to be given by educational diagnosticians.

A complete speech and language evaluation includes assessment in the five major components of language:

1. *Phonology.* This is the sound system that constitutes spoken language. Phonemes such as /k/ and /f/ have no meaning in isolation, but their combination in specific sequences creates words.

2. *Morphology.* Morphemes are the smallest meaningful units of language. They are usually words like *picnic, work*, or *slow*, but they may also be grammatical markers signifying specific concepts, such as plurality (*picnics*), tense (*worked*), or shifts from adjective to adverb (*slowly*).

3. *Syntax.* This is the grammatical aspect of spoken language, the system for ordering words into meaningful sequences. Grammatical structure plays an important role in the comprehension and production of spoken language.

4. *Semantics.* This includes the meaning of words, sentences, and paragraphs. Vocabulary is a basic part of semantics.

5. *Pragmatics.* This includes the rules governing the use of language in context. Such features as conversational turn-taking and topic maintenance affect ability to communicate effectively.

A speech and language clinician assesses both the receptive and expressive processes of each of these five components. For example, in the area of syntax:

Receptive: Can the student comprehend past tense?
Expressive: Can the student express ideas in past tense?
In the area of semantics:

Receptive: What is the level of the student's listening vocabulary?
Expressive: What is the level of the student's spoken vocabulary?

The first section includes four tests of articulation and two methods for analyzing oral language samples. These types of tests and procedures require the training and expertise of a speech and language pathologist. The first procedure is the Developmental Sentence Scoring (DSS), a well-known method for analyzing a language sample. Four tests of articulation competence are included: The Fisher-Logemen Test of Articulation Competence, The Assessment of Phonological Processes, the Goldman-Fristoe Test of Articulation, and the Templin-Darley Tests of Articulation. The section ends with a review of the Tyack-Gottsleben Language Sampling, Analysis, and Training Handbook, another procedure for analyzing oral language samples.

The second section includes 16 tests of language development:

Auditory-Visual Single Word Picture Vocabulary Test. A measure of receptive vocabulary.

Chapter Three reviews 27 speech and language tests. First, there are five tests that assess phonology, primarily articulation. These tests and procedures clearly require the expertise of a speech and language pathologist. The Arizona Articulation Proficiency Scale (AAPS), the Fisher–Logemann Test of Articulation Competence, the Assessment of Phonological Processes–Revised (APP–R), the Goldman–Fristoe Test of Articulation (GFTA), and the Photo Articulation Test (PAT) are all well-known instruments for the assessment of articulation.

The remainder of the 22 tests reviewed evaluate various areas of language development from the preschool years through adolescence:

Structured Photographic Expressive Language
    Test–Revised (SPELT–II)
Assessing Semantic Skills through Everyday Themes
    (ASSET)

Speech and Language Tests Reviewed in Chapter Three Classified by Language Component and Age of Students

Language Component	Preschool	Grades K–6	Adolescent
Phonology	AAPS Fisher–Logemann AAP–R GFTA PAT PLS–3 TOLD–P–2	AAPS Fisher–Logemann AAP–R GFTA PAT TOLD–P–2	Fisher–Logemann GFTA
Morphology	SPELT–II CELF–Preschool PLS–3	SPELT–II CELF–R	CELF–R
Syntax	CELF–Preschool PLS–3 TOLD–P–2	CELF–R TOLD–P–2 TOLD–I–2 TOPS	CELF–R TOAL–3 TOPS–A
Semantics	ASSET CELF–Preschool EOWPVT–R PPVT–R CREVT BEERY–PVT PLS–3 TOLD–P–2	ASSET CELF–R EOWPVT–R PPVT–R CREVT BEERY–PVS, PVT TOWK TOLD–P–2 TOLD–I–2 WORD–R TOPS	 CELF–R EOWPVT–UE PPVT–R CREVT BEERY–PVT TOAL–3 WORD–A TOPS–A
Pragmatics			
Other	Boehm–Preschool CELF–Preschool PLS–3	Boehm–R (Concepts) CELF–R (Retrieval and Memory) TWF (Word Finding)	CELF–R TOAL–3 (Written Language)

Arizona Articulation Proficiency Scale, Second Edition (AAPS)

Janet Fudala and William Reynolds
Western Psychological Services
12031 Wilshire Blvd., Los Angeles, CA 90025-1251

Purpose	To provide a quantitative evaluation procedure for assessing articulatory competence in children that determines the need for specialized education
Major Areas Tested	Articulation
Age or Grade Range	1.6–13.11 years
Usually Given By	Speech and language clinicians
Type of Test	Individual Standardized Norm-referenced
Scores Obtained	Age equivalents Standard deviations Percentiles Standard scores
Student Performance Timed?	No
Testing Time	5–25 minutes
Scoring/Interpretation Time	30–40 minutes
Normed On	5,122 children, between the ages of 1 and 14 years, from four Western states. English was the primary language of all subjects; subjects selected with consideration of age, gender, and race based on 1980 U.S. Census data
Alternate Forms Available?	No

FORMAT

The Arizona Articulation Proficiency Scale (AAPS) was originally published in 1963 and revised in 1970. The Second Edition (1991) maintains the same items and basic format, but provides norms for a wider age range and renorms the entire test. The materials for the APPS include a spiral-bound book, which contains the visual stimuli for all test items; individual Protocol Booklets for each child tested; and the manual, which contains information on the development and technical characteristics of the test, as well as administration and scoring instructions and norms tables.

The AAPS consists of two measures of articulation: *The Picture Test* and *The Sentence Test*. The *Picture Test* includes 48 items, each represented by a single picture. The child is shown the black-and-white line drawing and asked to name the picture or answer a simple question about it. The consonants and vowels being assessed are printed on both the picture card and the protocol. The examiner records each response, indicating whether it is correct. The *Sentence Test* may be used for older students in place of, or in conjunction with, the *Picture Test*. The child is asked to read 25 sentences written at a first-grade reading level. The sentences are printed on three cards in the *Picture Test Card Booklet*, and the sounds being tested are indicated on the protocol booklet. The examiner records and scores responses. The AAPS also includes the *Story Test*, which provides a structure for obtaining a spontaneous speech sample. The child is shown two picture cards and called on to "Tell me what is happening in the picture. Tell me as much as you can." The examiner uses informal techniques to elicit a description of, or a story about, the picture (A boy with a hand in the cookie jar and a boy riding his bike), and the child's exact responses are recorded on the Protocol Booklet. The *Story Test* is not scored formally, but guidelines are given for counting the number of words.

Following the completion of the test, student responses are analyzed for types of errors. Every error is then given a weighted score. These weighted scores are based on the frequency with which that sound occurs in English. The weighted scores are totaled to obtain a consonant score, a vowel score, and a total sound score. The total sound score is a weighted error score; it is subtracted from 100 to obtain the AAPS Total Score, which represents the percentage of the child's articulation ability. Total scores can then be translated into age equivalents, standard scores, and percentiles by using the tables provided in the manual.

The AAPS also provides several other measures that are helpful to the speech clinician in planning and evaluating a remedial program.

1. *Percentage of Speech Improvement.* This score represents the gains made by an individual child, or a group of children, in an articulation therapy program.

2. *Mean Length of Response.* By using the child's spontaneous language sample elicited by the Story Pictures, the examiner can calculate mean length of utterance, a well-understood measure of linguistic competence.

3. *Severity Ratings.* These ratings can classify the child's articulation competence into four categories—normal, mild, moderate, or severe—based on age. For example, an AAPS total score of 89 would receive the following ratings:

Age	Severity Rating
6.0–6.5	Normal to mild
8.0–8.11	Moderate
10.0–10.11	Severe

Severity ratings are rough estimates of articulation proficiency based on developmental norms.

4. *Intelligibility Level.* This rating considers the global level of speech intelligibility regardless of age. The child with the total AAPS score of 89 would be described as intelligibility level 5 (on a 6-point scale). Level 5 is described as "Speech is intelligible, but noticeably in error" (Manual, p. 16).

5. *Developmental Age Scores.* These scores provide the ages at which 80 and 90 percent of children acquire each individual sound. This is useful information in planning a therapy program.

STRENGTHS OF THE AAPS

• The original AAPS has had wide usage throughout the United States and Canada. This second edition provides extended and updated norms while maintaining the basic format of the test. The elimination of examination of consonants in the medial position and the addition of a sentence test for older students are useful changes.

The AAPS has a number of features that make the test very practical in a publc school or clinic setting. These include:

1. compact, portable, and easy-to-use materials
2. one drawing on a page, which reduces distractibility in very young children
3. norms for children under 2 and over 12 years of age
4. a variety of scores that can help the clinician plan and evaluate a therapy program.

• A Survey Form is also available, which provides a quick screening of some of the most commonly misarticulated sounds.

• The provision of the *Story Test* allows the examiner to collect a sample of spontaneous language, which can be useful in assessing a child's global language competence.

• By comparing a student's total AAPS scores on *The Picture Test* and *The Sentence Test*, the examiner can compare articulation in isolated words with articulation in connected speech.

LIMITING FACTORS OF THE AAPS

- Children of diverse ethnic backgrounds were included in the standardization sample in the proportions described in the 1980 Census. However, no guidelines are provided for testing children of different language backgrounds. Other articulation tests describe typical "misarticulation" in regard to dialectical differences within the U.S. population. As the AAPS was standardized on children from Western states, this information is an important omission for examiners who test children from New York, New England, or Southern states, as well as Asian, African American, and Latino children.

- Black-and-white line drawings are less interesting and less interpretable by young children than colored pictures or photographs.

- The lack of a national sample that considers residence and socioeconomic status, as well as limited information on reliability and validity, are of concern. More extensive data on the AAPS with clinical populations, as well as more information on the technical characteristics of the test, are needed.

The Fisher-Logemann Test of Articulation Competence (Fisher-Logemann)

Hilda B. Fisher and Jerilyn A. Logemann
Riverside Publishing Company, 1971
8420 West Bryn Mawr Rd., Chicago, IL 60631

Purpose	To examine a student's phonological system in an orderly framework and to facilitate the recording and analysis of phonetic notations of articulation and the comprehensive and accurate analysis and categorization of articulation errors
Major Areas Tested	Articulation
Age or Grade Range	3 years–adult (Picture Test) 9 years–adult (Sentence Articulation Test)
Usually Given By	Speech/language clinician
Type of Test	Individual Criterion-referenced
Scores Obtained	None
Student Performance Timed?	No
Testing Time	10 minutes (screening test); 25 minutes (complete test)
Scoring/Interpretation Time	15–20 minutes
Normed On	Not reported
Alternate Forms Available?	Yes

FORMAT

The Fisher-Logemann Test of Articulation Competence (Fisher-Logemenn) is made up of two parts, the Picture Test and the Sentences Articulation Test. The materials consist of 109 picture stimuli on 35 hardboard cards in an 8 1/2- by-11-inch folio, two sets of 8 1/2- by- 11 inch record forms, and a test manual. The manual contains detailed instructions for administering each part of the test, as well as directions for recording responses and distinctive-feature analysis of the misarticulations.

The Picture Test uses spontaneous identification of colorful picture stimuli to assess the production of 25 single-consonant phonemes, 23 consonant blends, 12 single vowels, and 4 diphthongs. Single-consonant productions are evaluated in each of the syllabic positions in which they occur in the English language. This test uses only words that have the test consonant phoneme next to a vowel. Therefore, consonants may occur in "prevocalic" (*d*og), "intervocalic" (le*tt*er), and "postvocalic" (do*g*) positions. Test words were chosen on the basis of familiarity and frequency of occurrence in the vocabulary of young children.

The picture folio can be converted easily into a convenient easel for presentation of the picture stimuli. The stimulus word, test phoneme, and item number corresponding to the record form are printed on the back of each card, which faces the examiner. A suggested "prompting phrase" is printed under the test word for use if a verbal prompt is necessary to elicit the response.

The two sets of record forms provide an abundance of useful information for the examiner. Transcriptions for the Picture Test are made on both sides of a single sheet. Productions of consonant phonemes are recorded on the front of the sheet, and articulation of consonant blends and vowel phonemes are transcribed on the back. The front of the sheet is organized into a chart that highlights the nature of the articulation deficit by distinctive-feature analysis. The distinctive-feature analysis includes place of articulation, voicing, and manner of formation. Some unique features of this recording sheet include:

• A description of each single-consonant phoneme in terms of its distinctive features. For example, the *t* sound is listed as a voiceless, tip-alveolar phoneme produced as a stop consonant.

• Space for recording the specific types of misarticulation patterns, which are discussed and listed in the Phonetic Notation section of the test manual.

• International Phonetic Alphabet (IPA) symbols for each sound.

• Common spelling of each phoneme.

• The developmental age for each sound. This is the age at which 90 percent of the children are expected to have achieved mastery of the sound in all syllabic positions (Hejna, 1959). As an example, the chart indicates that 90

percent of all 7-year-olds should be able to articulate correctly the /s/ phoneme.

On the reverse of this recording form, productions of consonant blends using the phonemes /s/, /r/, and /l/ are transcribed. Spaces are provided for noting the phonemic contexts discovered to be least and most conducive to adequate productions of each. Vowel productions are also recorded on this side of the sheet and are organized in terms of place of articulation (front, central, back) and degree of constriction (high, mid, low).

The Fisher-Logemann also contains a rapid screening form of the Picture Test. This short form comprises 11 selected cards with marginal tabs for easy location. Productions of phonemes thought to be most commonly misarticulated are assessed.

The Sentence Articulation Test consists of a single card on which there are 15 sentences to be read by the student. The test evaluates production of every single-consonant sound in all three syllabic positions as well as all vowel phonemes in English. The sentences require third-grade or higher reading level. Each cognate pair of consonants (phonemes with the same place of articulation and manner of formation) is assessed in the same sentence, but consonant sounds with no cognates are grouped by similarity in the manner of production—for example, the nasal phonemes /m/ and /n/. The test phonemes are indicated by IPA symbols before each sentence, and the letters corresponding to the sounds are underlined within the utterances. (*G*eorge is at the *ch*ur*ch* wat*ch*ing a ma*g*ic show.) Spaces for recording misarticulations are provided above each test sound.

A summary of the student's sentence misarticulations may be recorded on the back of the record form. Each manner of formation and place of articulation is listed, followed by the sentence number in which the phonemes of that specific type are assessed.

STRENGTHS OF THE FISHER-LOGEMANN

• The Fisher-Logemann is available in a convenient test folio that converts easily into an easel for displaying the stimulus pictures. Its compact size makes it portable and easy to store.

• The test manual is well organized and concisely written. Detailed information on test development and administration and on recording and analyzing responses is supplemented by sample test protocols and a listing of common dialectal variations.

• This instrument is a comprehensive diagnostic tool. Articulation is assessed in both single-word productions and connected speech. Vowel sounds as well as single consonants and blends are included. Many conventional articulation tests do not contain stimulus items that specifically evaluate vowel production. Consequently, the articulation of these sounds must be assessed independently by the examiner.

• The further value of the Fisher-Logemann as a diagnostic tool lies in its adaptability to either comprehensive assessment of articulation or quick screening. It is therefore appropriate for use in public school systems where rapid measures of articulation must be made or as part of lengthier diagnostic evaluations that require in-depth testing. Because a single record form is used for both the screening and complete versions of the word test, it is possible to switch easily to the in-depth form if multiple articulation problems are revealed by the screening.

• The stimulus pictures are interesting and colorful and therefore elicit the stimulus words easily in most testing situations. Alternate pictures have been provided for students who might be affected by geographical differences in pronunciation and by dialect factors. Care was also taken to choose items for the Picture Test with which students are known to have maximum familiarity: 90 percent of the selected words are included in the Kindergarten Union Word List, a study of preschool vocabulary, and 74 percent are found in the Horn Word List of the most frequently used vocabulary items of children through age 6. The same criterion of familiarity was used in choosing the reading vocabulary for the Sentence Articulation Test.

• An excellent feature of the Fisher-Logemann is its information about the phonological variations that should be expected for several dialect groups. Common variations among standard and class dialects in different regions of the United States are presented in footnotes on both record forms. Dialect notes in the test manual list phonemic substitutions for several native dialects (general American, Eastern, New York City and environs, Southern, and Black) and describe foreign dialect influences from Spanish, Italian, French, German, and Russian and the Scandinavian, Oriental, and Eastern European languages. Such vital information broadens the use of this tool and aids the clinician in making an appropriate diagnosis of either an articulation deficit or a dialect variation.

• Perhaps the most innovative facet of the Fisher-Logemann is the organization of its record forms. They are easy to use, yet they allow the examiner to note an abundance of useful information. Particularly useful are the guidelines for distinctive-feature analysis, which describe phonemes according to the factors that govern their discrete production. The result, therefore, is not only knowledge of the phonemes a student has misarticulated, but also the specific rules of sound production that have been violated. For example, if a student consistently substitutes /p/ for /f/ and /b/ for /v/, examination of the record form immediately reveals difficulties with manner of formation and place of articulation—although the concept of voicing is intact. Furthermore, the examiner can determine that bilabial stop pho-

nemes are being substituted for labiodental fricatives. Immediate access to such information aids greatly in planning appropriate therapy.

• Many conventional articulation tests assess the production of phonemes in initial, medial, and final positions within a word. But this type of analysis does not allow for assimilation effects. Stimulus words are not selected with careful attention to the influence of surrounding phonemes on pronunciation of the test phonemes; they may be preceded or followed by either consonant or vowel sounds. But the Fisher-Logemann uses prevocalic, intervocalic, and postvocalic positioning to account for these assimilation factors. The coarticulation effects of dissimilarly produced consonant sounds are eliminated. This method of organization enables the clinician to evaluate sound production within a systematized phonology rather than as isolated occurrences.

• The judgment of whether stimulus items provide a representative sample of a student's phoneme production is essential in determining the content validity of an articulation test. The Fisher-Logemann demonstrates content validity by assessing all the consonant and vowel sounds in the English language. Furthermore, stimulus words were chosen on the basis of their frequency in the vocabulary of young children.

LIMITING FACTORS OF THE FISHER-LOGEMANN

• Inherent in the organization of a formal articulation test like the Fisher-Logemann is a limitation imposed by the environment in which articulation skill is assessed. Conversational usage of speech sounds is not evaluated. Experienced clinicians are aware that students can often produce a sound correctly in single words while making errors in less restrained conversation. The Sentence Articulation Test does provide some assessment of articulation in connected speech, but this cannot be considered a measure of spontaneous production. Furthermore, because the Sentence Articulation Test can only be used with students at a third-grade reading level, evaluation of connected speech cannot be completed with younger students, beginning readers, or students with reading disability; yet these are the groups of students who are most likely to display articulation errors.

• The developers of the Fisher-Logemann do not provide any information in the manual about the reliability of their assessment instrument. It appears that studies to determine test-retest reliability as well as inter- and intra-rater reliability have not been performed.

The Assessment of Phonological Processes— Revised (APP–R)

Barbara W. Hodson
PRO-ED, 1980, 1986
8700 Shoal Creek Blvd., Austin, TX 78757-6897

Purpose	To provide a phonological assessment instrument for highly unintelligible children
Major Areas Tested	Phonology
Age or Grade Range	No age range given. Estimated range 2 years and older
Usually Given By	Speech/language pathologist
Type of Test	Individual Criterion-referenced
Scores Obtained	Percentage of occurence Phonological deviancy score Severity interval
Student Performance Timed?	No
Testing Time	15–20 minutes
Scoring/Interpretation Time	1–2 hours
Normed On	Not normed
Alternate Forms Available?	No

FORMAT

The Assessment of Phonological Processes—Revised (APP-R) is a revision of the original APP published in 1980.

The APP-R was designed for highly unintelligible children. Results indicated not only the presence of a disorder, but also the degree of severity, and a direction for planning remediation.

The APP-R kit includes two sets of pictures, five packets of phonological forms, and a manual. The manual has general administration procedures for both the screening and full assessment modes, transcription as well as scoring, accountability and dismissal considerations, and a design for phonological remediation. All scorable categories are described with examples, including segment omissions, class deficiencies, and phonological processes. A case study, complete with pre- and post- transcription, phonological analysis, and course of remediation is provided. The test is administered using objects (boat, jump rope, etc.). These are not in the kit. Examiners are encouraged to gather these objects, supplementing with pictures when necessary.

The first step in administering the APP-R is to divide the objects into five separate groups to match the five columns on the Recording Sheet. The objects are emptied one group at a time in front of the child, who is instructed to choose a toy (or picture) and say its name. If the child does not name an object, the examiner is to say the name and ask the child to name it, preferably after some intervening time. Specific methods for eliciting responses are provided.

The author recommends that the child's responses be audiotaped for later verification. A continuous speech sample is also to be elicited to document later intelligibility gains in spontaneous conversation.

Three forms are necessary when administering the APP-R.

The child's productions are written on the recording sheet. Specific procedures, including the use of a check mark for correct production, a slash mark through omitted sounds, etc., are outlined as is the use of diacritic symbols useful in transcribing deviations. After the transcriptions of the child's utterances are verified, they are transferred to the analysis sheet. Check marks are placed in columns which correspond to the phonological processes evidenced. The first four columns are for segment omissions. Columns 5–10 are class deficiency columns. The fourteen following columns are provided for "miscellaneous error patterns," which are common phonological processes.

The summary sheet is where check marks from the analysis form are totaled and transferred to the designated lines for the 10 basic omission and class deficiency processes. A percentage of occurrence score, a phonological deviancy score, phonological processes average, and severity interval can be calculated. Two screening protocols, the Preschool and Multisyllabic, contain 12 stimulus words each. Questions are provided at the bottom of each form as guidelines to determine whether further assessment is indicated.

The authors state that the time required for completion of the screening and full assessment modes varies with the experience of the examiner and the severity of the phonological disorder. Nevertheless, estimates were four to five minutes for the preschool screening, fifteen minutes for the multisyllablic screening, and less than an hour for the full 50-item assessment.

STRENGTHS OF THE APP-R

• The choice of object stimuli makes data collection a much more natural and easy process when testing preschool, developmentally delayed, or difficult to test children.

• The time required to administer the 50-item assessment usually does not exceed the 20 minutes stated by the author. In this amount of time, the entire administration can usually be achieved in one session.

• Although most of the objects needed for the test are relatively easy to find, the addition of pictures for difficult to find objects is extremely helpful.

• Both the Preschool and Multisyllabic screening forms are very practical and useful methods for fast data collection. This is one of the few multisyllabic screening tests available for school age children. The words chosen for the Preschool form are likely to be familiar to speakers of American English. The criterion for referral for full assessment at the bottom of each screening form makes this a quick decision-making process.

• This analysis provides the clinician with excellent information to plan phonological remediation for her client. Both the manual and author's book, *Targeting Intelligible Speech*, describe in detail how to select target patterns and plan remediation cycles. (Hodson & Paden, 1983).

• Percentage of occurrence scores are useful for posttreatment accountability measures.

• This is an extremely useful measure for its intended population, the highly unintelligible child. It is based on "state of the art" research in the field of child phonology.

• This manual is a good resource for the description of 29 phonological processes.

• Both Spanish and computerized versions of the APP-R are available.

LIMITING FACTORS OF THE APP-R

• This test is not easy to use. Clinicians must have some prior knowledge of phonological processes in order to use this analysis with some degree of comfort.

• The time required to analyze the 50-item test often exceeds one hour. Although this assessment is highly useful for planning remediation, it may be too complicated and

time consuming for many clinicians to use simply as a
diagnostic tool.

•   There is no normative data in the test manual. The
author does give basic guidelines for normal 2, 3, and 4 year
olds. No detail, apart from its evolution from a retrospective
study of several hundred client's records, about how severity
ratings of age compensatory points were devised is included.

•   Re-entering the child's productions from the recording
sheet to the analysis sheet is a time consuming and cumbersome process.

•   Many of the words chosen for the Spanish APP–R are
not easily represented in object form. There are no picture
stimuli for this version. The Spanish version of the APP–R
was based on the phonological development of Mexican
American children and may not apply to other Latinos.

•   Validity and reliability data are not given to support
the severity scale. Examiners should be cautious about using
this scale to determine priority placement in remediation
programs.

The Goldman–Fristoe Test of Articulation (GFTA)

Ronald Goldman and Macalyne Fristoe
American Guidance Service, Inc., 1969; revised 1972, 1986
4201 Woodland Rd., P.O. Box 99, Circle Pines, MN 55014-1796

Purpose	To provide systematic assessment of articulation of the consonant sounds in English
Major Areas Tested	Articulation
Age or Grade Range	2–16 years
Usually Given By	Speech/language clinician Audiologist
Type of Test	Individual Criterion-referenced
Scores Obtained	Percentile
Student Performance Timed?	No
Testing Time	20 minutes
Scoring/Interpretation Time	15–20 minutes
Normed On	38,884 students in grades 1–12 throughout the United States plus an additional 852 children aged 2–5
Alternate Forms Available?	No

FORMAT

The materials for the Goldman Fristoe Test of Articulation (GFTA) include the response form, a manual, and an easel device for displaying stimulus pictures. The 8 1/2 by 11 sprial-bound easel contains 35 large and colorful pictures. Each response form provides room for recording and comparing an individual's speech responses from the three GFTA subtests:

1. *Sounds-in-Words*. Productions of single-consonant sounds and of 11 common consonant blends are elicited by identification of pictures illustrating common objects and activities. The examiner asks, "What is it?" to elicit the test phoneme and then may pose additional relevant questions to produce the desired response. Consonant phonemes are classified as occurring in initial, medial, and final positions of the stimulus words. Medial position, according to the authors, does not necessarily refer to the middle consonant in a word, but rather to some internal position within a polysyllable. Not all of the consonant phonemes are evaluated in each of three positions; a few are omitted because of the rarity of their occurrence in the English phonological system.

The stimulus words are printed on the back of the picture, facing the examiner, with the letters representing the test phonemes set off in bold type and with extra spacing around them. The numbers corresponding to the record sheet are indicated above the test phonemes.

2. *Sounds-in-Sentences*. The examiner reads two short stories aloud to the student while showing a corresponding set of pictures. In presenting each story, the examiner emphasizes the "key words" that appear in bold type on the examiner's side of the easel kit. These words contain the phonemes being evaluated in the subtest, those sounds considered by the authors most likely to be misarticulated by children. The student is then asked to retell the story in his or her own words, using the illustrations as memory aids. These pictures help provide some control over the content of the speech sample. The examiner is encouraged to prompt the student to produce any key words not elicited by the pictures.

3. *Stimulation*. This subtest evaluates the student's ability to produce previously incorrect phonemes correctly, in the context of syllables, words, and sentences, with stimulation by the examiner. The student is instructed to watch the examiner closely and to try to repeat the sound heard. Only phonemes that were misarticulated in the Sounds-in-Words subtest are evaluated and only in the word position (initial, medial, final) where the errors originally occurred. Stimulation pictures in this subtest list specific syllables, words, and sentences for testing stimulability of each phoneme. If the student is unable to imitate a sound accurately in any of the three contexts, "multiple stimulation" is used, whereby the examiner repeats the phoneme three times before the student

is asked to reproduce it again. Whenever a student is unable to articulate a phoneme correctly with multiple stimulation, testing for that sound should be discontinued. The Stimulation subtest provides valuable information concerning the sounds that may most readily be remediated by speech therapy.

The test phonemes on the response form are coded by color to designate the word positions being evaluated and also by number to designate the location of the sound on the response matrix. Blue always indicates the initial position within a word, yellow the medial position, and green the final position. Responses from the Sounds-in-Words and Stimulability subtests are recorded on one side of the form. To the left of these columns is a list of the key words as they are written on the easel. During the Sounds-in-Sentences subtest, the examiner is to place a check mark above each correctly articulated sound, or to mark the subject's subsitution or omission above the misarticulated sounds. These notations must later be transferred to the Sounds-in-Sentences matrix on the other side of the response form. Side-by-side comparison of responses on all three subtests is possible by folding over the Sounds-in-Sentences response matrix. The authors state that this test was designed to accomodate two levels of evaluation depending upon the qualifications of the tester. The first is to judge for the presence of error only for the purpose of referring a child for therapy. The second level is to judge for the type of error for therapeutic planning and determination of severity of the disorder. Standard notations to be used for each of these levels of assessment are reviewed in the manual. These range from an X-mark to signify an error to the sound substitution produced accompanied by diacritic markings. A mild distortion is marked "2," while a severe distortion is given a "3."

STRENGTHS OF THE GFTA

• The GFTA uses large and colorful pictures that are highly interesting to most students, making it relatively easy to elicit the stimulus words under usual circumstances.

• The directions for test administration are clear and concise, making this an easy test to use. The manual also contains good information on test rationale and construction.

• The pictures and word selection make this test quite useful for the preschool child. In the 1986 version, norms have been extended to include the 2 year old.

• The unique value of the GFTA is the variety of contexts in which phonemic production is evaluated. Not only is articulation performance in single-word production evaluated, but so is articulation in a controlled connected speech sample.

• Although the GFTA is designed for analysis of consonant production, articulation of vowels may also be judged. All the vowel sounds of English are present in the Sounds-in-Words subtest, and an alert examiner may obtain information on the student's production of these phonemes.

LIMITING FACTORS OF THE GFTA

• A major weakness of the GFTA is the complicated format for recording responses. Although the form is color-coded to indicate sounds occurring in initial, medial, and final positions within the words, it is often difficult to locate these phonemes rapidly on the response matrix. Even highly trained diagnosticians may have difficulty evaluating several phoneme productions within a single word and then recording these judgments in various places on the response matrix while maintaining the attention of the student. If an examiner attempts to record all the responses while administering the test, a more definitive judgment than "acceptable" or "unacceptable" production is difficult to make. In order to use this tool to make an accurate assessment of articulation, it is frequently necessary to tape record the session and to transcribe errors at a later time. This obviously extends the time needed to complete the evaluation.

• The GFTA is not available in a screening form and therefore may be too lengthy for use in public school screenings. Administration of the entire test is approximately 20 minutes, and the examiner may have difficulty maintaining the attention of young students or students who exhibit multiple articulation errors.

• Although the test manual does provide detailed information about interpreting students' responses, no consideration for dialect variations has been included. Frequently the speech and language clinician may be asked to evaluate the articulation of a non-native English speaker or an individual from a different section of the United States. Some basic information on expected articulation variations for major dialect groups—such as Americans residing in the southern, northeastern, or midwestern United States or Mexican-American students—would certainly enhance the value of this tool.

• In the organization of this test, attention was not given

to using the rules that govern production of specific speech sounds. The test provides information on which phonemes are misarticulated by the student, but it does not give information about what kind of errors occurred in terms of manner of formation or place of articulation. The examiner is not instructed to give a complete phonetic transcription of the full word even though a space is now provided for this on the response sheet for use with the Khan-Lewis Phonological Analysis. Distinctive feature theory and phonological processing have not been incorporated into the test. This limits the examiner's ability to diagnose discreetly and plan remediation.

• Information gleaned from the stimulability subtest would again be greatly enhanced if the examiner were to transcribe the entire word. In this way, movement toward adult production could be visible.

• The reliability of this articulation test may be judged by the consistency with which the same response is recorded for each phoneme in initial, medial, and final positions within the stimulus words. Test-retest reliability was obtained for the Sounds-in-Words and Sounds-in-Sentences subtests only. Measures of interrater and intrarater reliability were obtained only for the Sounds-in-Words subtest. The lack of research to determine interreliability and intrareliability for the Sounds-in-Sentences and Stimulation subtests is clearly a weakness of this tool.

• The content validity of a measure of articulation skill must involve stimulus items that provide a representative sample of a student's phoneme production. The developers of this test do not provide substantial information concerning the choice of the stimulus words, nor do they discuss the influence on articulation of such variables as word frequency and the grammatical function of a specific sound. Some measure of content validity, however, is assured by the fact that all but one of the consonants contained in the English language are assessed in the Sounds-in-Words subtest.

• *A Consumer's Guide to Tests in Print* (Hammill, Bryant, and Brown, 1992) does not recommend the GFTA because of an inadequate standardization sample and weak ratings on reliability and validity.

Photo Articulation Test (PAT)

K. Pendergast, S. Dickey, J. Selmar, and A. Soder
PRO-ED, 1984
8700 Shoal Creek Blvd., Austin, TX 78758

Purpose	To provide a measure of articulation
Major Areas Tested	Articulation
Age or Grade Range	3–12 years
Usually Given By	Speech and language pathologists
Type of Test	Individual Criterion-referenced
Scores Obtained	Means Standard deviations
Student Performance Timed?	No
Testing Time	5–15 minutes
Scoring/Interpretation Time	10–20 minutes
Normed On	684 Caucasian, middle-class children from Seattle, Washington
Alternate Forms Available?	No

FORMAT

The Photo Articulation Test (PAT), which was designed to provide a comprehensive measure of articulation, uses colored photographs as the visual stimuli for eliciting sounds. The materials for the test consist of the Manual of Instruction; 72 color photographs, printed on 8-1/2" x 11" pages in groups of nine; individual recording sheets; six articulation age overlays (AAO) for scoring purposes; and a deck of 72 individual color photograph cards. The Manual of Instructions includes directions for administration and scoring, technical information on the PAT, the eight pages of color photographs, and a Supplementary Test Words List.

The child is shown a page of nine pictures. As the examiner points to each picture, the child names the picture and the examiner records the response on the PAT recording sheet. The photos usually elicit the correct name, but if the child cannot or does not name the picture, the examiner says the word and asks the child to repeat it. Sounds are grouped into three categories (tongue, lip, and vowel), and are tested in initial, medial, and final positions. For each error, the examiner asks the child to repeat three words using the same sound from the Supplementary Words List. The examiner also may ask the child to repeat the sound in isolation. Distorted sounds are described in terms of mild, moderate, and severe distortion. All of this information is recorded on the PAT Recording Sheet.

The last three photos are designed to elicit a spontaneous speech sample. The three pictures show a boy with a bird in the cage. The boy opens the cage and the bird flies out. The child is asked to tell a story about the pictures. The examiner records the story verbatim and notes further articulation information, as well as voice, fluency, use of language, and intelligibility of connected speech.

The child receives a score for each of the three categories of sounds, as well as a total test score. The scores are in the form of means and standard deviations for age groups. For example, a boy of age 4.6 has a total error score of 20; the mean number of errors for his age is 13.8 with a standard deviation of 10.8; therefore, his score is within the average range. Separate norms are provided for boys and girls. In addition, the Articulation Age Overlay (AAO) for 4 year olds is placed over the PAT recording sheet. The outlined portion of the AAO allows a quick picture of any errors that are not "normal" for the child's age and, possibly, in need of remediation.

STRENGTHS OF THE PAT

• The colored photo cards provide interesting stimuli for eliciting sounds. The provision of two types of administration—the nine pictures on a page and the single photo cards—responds to the needs of examiners who work with very young or distractible children.

• The PAT assesses all consonants, vowels, and diphthongs, as well as nine blends. The items have been grouped for diagnostic purposes with "tongue-tip" sounds first, followed by sounds requiring lip movements. A discussion of item selection and order of administration is provided in the manual.

• The Articulation Age Overlays are a helpful feature, as they provide a visual tool for describing a child's articulation development to parents and teachers who may not understand the developmental progression of articulation.

• The Supplementary Test Words allow the examiner to explore errors that may be related to faulty pronunciation, rather than the inability to say a sound in a particular position. For example, if the child mispronounces *toothbrush*, repeating the words *nothing*, *method*, and *anything* will provide more information about the child's ability to articulate *th* in the medial position.

• The manual describes a short-form screening procedure with the PAT by using only the items that elicit initial and final sounds. A survey of 1,000 PAT protocols indicated that less than one percent of the errors would be missed if medial sounds were not tested.

LIMITING FACTORS OF THE PAT

• The PAT has technical inadequacies which seriously limit its use. These include:

1. *Inadequate norming sample.* The PAT was standardized on 500 Caucasian children in Seattle, Washington. The sample is described as "middle socioeconomic class." The PAT is neither nationally normed nor balanced for race and ethnicity, and there is no data provided on whether the children included had normally developing language.

2. *Reliability.* One study of test–retest reliability is reported with no description of the age of the children or the time interval involved.

3. *Validity of norming.* The PAT provides separate norms for boys and girls at all age levels, with no discussion of the validity of this procedure. The validity of the PAT can be compared with that of the Templin–Darley Tests of Articulation. The Templin–Darley, published in 1960, was never revised, and is no longer published.

- Until the PAT is restandardized and researched to substantiate its reliability and validity, it should only be considered as a tool for therapists planning remediation. Scores should not be used to determine eligibility for remedial services.

Structured Photographic Expressive Language Test—Revised (SPELT–II)

Ellen O'Hara Werner and Janet Dawson Krescheck
Janelle Publications, Inc., 1974, 1983
P. O. Box 15, Sandwich, IL 60548

Purpose	To identify children who perform significantly below others of their age in the production of grammatical structures; to assess individual strengths and weaknesses; to aid in planning a remedial program; and to evaluate the responses of children who speak Black English
Major Areas Tested	Expressive morphology and syntax
Age or Grade Range	4.0–9.5 years
Usually Given By	Speech and language pathologists
Type of Test	Standardized Individual Norm-referenced
Scores Obtained	Percentages Percentiles Standard scores Age ranges for each item
Student Performance Timed?	No
Testing Time	15–25 minutes
Scoring/Interpretation Time	10–15 minutes
Normed On	1,178 Caucasian children in Florida, Michigan, Georgia, Nebraska, and Ohio, between 4.0 and 9.5 years, with normally developing language; the children were primarily middle class from both rural and urban communities. Only monolingual children were included in the sample.
Alternate Forms Available?	No

FORMAT

The Structured Photographic Expressive Language Test–Revised (SPELT–II) is a standardized individual test designed to elicit a language sample for the assessment of language development in young children. The materials for the SPELT–II consist of a set of 50 photographs, response forms for recording student responses, and a manual that describes administration and scoring procedures, as well as the background and technical characteristics of the test. The child is shown a picture of a real-life situation involving children and is asked to tell the examiner about it. Each child is administered all 50 items in the order listed on the response form. For each item, the response form provides the statement used by the examiner to elicit the response, the name of the structure to be elicited (prepositional phrase, verb, etc.), and an example of the expected response with the components of the target structure underlined.

The age range at which 90 percent of the children pass the item is also provided. Additional prompting may be given according to the specific directions in the manual. The test score is the total number of correct responses expressed as a percentage of the total number of test items (50). Percentages are analyzed by comparing the child's score with the mean percents and standard deviations for his or her age. Raw scores can also be converted into age percentiles and standard scores. Further, each child's responses can be compared with the age range at which 90 percent of the children passed each item. A special discussion of Black English is included to help examiners distinguish dialect forms and true grammatical errors in speakers of Black English.

STRENGTHS OF THE SPELT–II

• The SPELT–II provides a structured approach to obtaining a language sample. Responses are elicited through visual materials, photographs, and auditory cues. In this way, the formulation of specific grammatical structures can be assessed. The structures selected include prepositions, phrases, plurals, irregular verbs, past and future tenses, copulatives, infinitives, conjunctions, participles, negatives, and various forms of questions. The formulation of these structures has been found to differentiate the language-delayed child from the child with normally developing language.

• The manual and the response forms provide very clear instructions for administration and scoring. The section on Additional Prompting is very helpful. The manual has several very important cautions about interpretation that should be studied by every examiner.

• Using photographs for the visual stimuli is more interesting for children than drawings and produces fewer errors because of misinterpretation of stimuli.

• The section of the manual that describes the procedures for scoring the test of a child who speaks Black English is very clear. This feature is a strong point of the SPELT–II. By scoring only those errors that are true errors and do not reflect dialect forms, norms for the Caucasian child, on which the test was standardized, can be used.

LIMITING FACTORS OF THE SPELT–II

• The standardization sample of the SPELT–II was well controlled for factors such as monolinguism and place of residence. However, the sample includes children from the South and Midwest. The East Coast and Western United States are notably missing from the sample. Factors such as ethnicity were not controlled, and the number of children at the 9-year-old age range is half that of the younger children.

• The SPELT–II standard scores are expressed as deviations from the mean. For example, the 54th percentile and the 46th percentile both receive standard scores of 0.10. Such notation needs explanation as this use of the term *standard scores* is not common.

• Although the SPELT–II authors state that the test may be readministered to assess progress in a remedial program, no alternate forms are provided.

• All 50 items of the SPELT–II are to be administered to every child. The authors state that "even if a child has difficulty or does not respond to some items, he may respond to items further along in the test" (Manual, p.5). However, it may be very difficult to hold the attention of young children with very delayed language through the entire test.

Assessing Semantic Skills Through Everyday Themes (ASSET)

Mark Barrett, Linda Zachman, Rosemary Huisingh
LinguiSystems, 1988
3100 4th Avenue, East Moline, IL 61244

Purpose	To assess the development of receptive, expressive, and semantic vocabulary skills
Major Areas Tested	Semantic and vocabulary skills
Age or Grade Range	3–9 years
Usually Given By	Speech and language pathologists Special education teacher Psychologist
Type of Test	Standardized Individual Norm-referenced
Scores Obtained	Age equivalents Percentiles Standard scores
Student Performance Timed?	No
Testing Time	30–40 minutes
Scoring/Interpretation Time	10–20 minutes
Normed On	1,801 children randomly selected from preschools, day-care centers, and schools in Illinois, California, Wisconsin, Nebraska, and Iowa. Race, sex, age, and type of school were considered and minority populations (Black and Latino) were included in proportion to national census data. Children who had received special education services were excluded.
Alternate Forms Available?	No

FORMAT

Assessing Semantic Skills Through Everyday Themes (ASSET) is a test of receptive and expressive vocabulary in preschool- and elementary-school children. The authors have developed a test that uses contextual, related, familiar themes, rather than isolated words, to assess vocabulary. The test uses black-and-white drawings of settings familiar to children to assess related vocabulary. For example, given a picture of a restaurant, the child is asked to identify *customer*, *dispenser*, something made of paper, and the person who takes the order. In the same picture, the child labels *menu*, *desserts*, and *the shape of a hamburger*, in addition to defining *ordering*. Materials for the ASSET include the Picture Stimuli Book of 20 line drawings of familiar scenes, individual response forms, and a teacher's manual, which includes test rationale, administration and scoring procedures, an interpretation guide, and a discussion of the technical features of the test.

The examiner shows the child the picture and asks the child to demonstrate his or her knowledge of several receptive items ("Show me the crayons. Show me something that spins. Show me the boy's elbow."). Using the same picture, the child is asked to name or describe several objects ("What does paste feel like? What is this called? What does healthy mean?"). Both the receptive and the expressive questions for each picture are given before moving to the next picture. Every child is administered the entire 20 picture test.

The ASSET is designed to measure ten receptive and expressive language skills (A–J), and the response form is designed to facilitate scoring.

Receptive Tasks	Expressive Tasks
A. Identify Labels	F. State Labels
B. Identify Categories	G. State Categories
C. Identify Attributes	H. State Attributes
D. Identify Functions	I. State Functions
E. Identify Definitions	J. State Definitions

Correct responses are given 1 point and a total score is obtained for each task A–J. The scores of tasks A–E are summed to provide a receptive score, and F–J to provide an expressive score. The receptive and expressive scores are added to form a total test score. Raw scores for each task and the three totals are converted to age-equivalent scores, percentiles, and standard scores using the tables provided in the manual.

STRENGTHS OF ASSET

• ASSET is well designed and easy to use. The picture stimuli are clearly drawn and interesting to children. The side-by-side administration creates a comfortable setting for young children. Each picture is introduced with a focusing statement that helps to gain the child's attention. Response forms provide easy recording and scoring.

• ASSET reflects the beliefs of the authors that both assessment and remediation of language skills of young children should be completed through the context of related themes. The teacher's manual provides a good discussion of the importance of each receptive and expressive task, as well as the authors' philosophy of treatment.

• ASSET allows a comparison of a child's receptive and expressive skills. This comparison, together with an analysis of the child's strengths and weaknesses across tasks, leads directly to a remediation plan.

• The study design for ASSET included:

1. an item pool study (706 subjects) to select the most discriminating and most age-progressive test items

2. a contrasted groups validity study (298 subjects) that found significant differences (.01 level) between normal- and language-disordered subjects in 25 of 26 comparisons.

• The study design for ASSET included:

1. an item pool study (706 subjects) to select the most discriminating and most age-progressive test items

2. a contrasted groups validity study (298 subjects) that found significant differences (.01 level) between normal and language-disordered subjects in 25 of 26 comparisons.

LIMITING FACTORS OF ASSET

• The technical aspects of ASSET should be carefully reviewed by the examiner. The standardization sample consists primarily of midwestern states and California. While sampling procedures were designed to reflect the most recent national census data with regard to the factors of race and ethnicity, the sample is not well described. Test–retest reliability for composite scores is adequate, but average coefficients for individual subtestes are lower. *A Consumer's Guide to Tests in Print* (Hammill, Brown, and Bryant, 1992) gives ASSET a "not recommended" rating.

• Because no basal or ceiling procedures are used, the entire 30 to 40 minute test is given to every child regardless of age. Test administration should be divided into shorter periods for young children.

Boehm Test of Basic Concepts–Revised (Boehm–R)

Ann E. Boehm
The Psychological Corporation, 1986
555 Academic Court, San Antonio, TX 78204-2498

Purpose	To assess mastery of concepts which are fundamental to understanding verbal instruction and essential for early school achievement
Major Areas Tested	Knowledge of basic relational concepts such as more–less, first–last, and same–different as well as concepts of space, quantity, and time
Age or Grade Range	Kindergarten–grade 2
Usually Given By	Classroom teacher Special education teacher Speech/language clinician
Type of Test	Standardized Individual Group
Scores Obtained	Percentile
Student Performance Timed?	No
Testing Time	30–40 minutes (Forms C and D) 15–20 minutes (Applications)
Scoring/Interpretation Time	15–20 minutes
Normed On	Nation-wide sample of over 4,600 children in each testing group; sample weighted to include percentage of large and small school districts in geographic regions representative of current population of U.S.; sample balanced by socioeconomic level, age, and grade
Alternate Forms Available?	Yes

FORMAT

The Boehm Test of Basic Concepts Revised (BTBC-R) is a revised edition of the Boehm test published in 1971. While the basic format and many of the items are the same, the content has been updated and the test completely restandardized.

The materials for the BTBC-R consist primarily of the individual student test booklets and the examiner's manual. The test has two alternate forms, C and D. In each form, the 50 concepts are divided equally into two booklets, Booklet 1 and Booklet 2. The manual includes information on test development and statistical data as well as directions for test administration, scoring, and interpretation.

The revised Boehm is designed as a group test. Instructions are read by the examiner (usually a teacher), and the students mark the correct responses directly in the individual test booklet. ("Look at the toys. Mark the toy that is next to the truck.")

The revised Boehm also includes the Application Booklet. This 26-item test booklet assesses basic concepts. ("Mark all the fish that are long and below the line.") The Applications Booklet is administered in the same way as the rest of the test. It may be used in conjuction with Form C or D or alone. It is intended for use only with first and second grade students.

Upon completion of the test, each student's responses are recorded on the Class Record Form. Each student's correct responses are totaled and converted into percentile scores using tables in the manual. These tables take into account grade level and socioeconomic level. Separate percentiles are provided for beginning and end-of-the-year testing. Separate scores are obtained for Form C, Form D, and Applications. The Class Record Form also allows the teacher to calculate the percentage of students correctly answering each item. Such information is helpful in planning a classroom program as well as in developing local norms. The authors also suggest an optional error analysis system in which the teacher records the following error types: no response, marking all pictures, choosing the opposite concept (top for bottom), and miscellaneous. Such information is helpful in understanding an individual student's performance.

STRENGTHS OF THE BOEHM-R

• The Boehm is an inexpensive way to assess the understanding of space, quantity, and time concepts in young school-aged students. Most young children find it interesting. The illustrations are clear, and the format is well organized. A gross marking response is adequate. A pointing response may also be used if the student is unable to handle a pencil or crayon and if the test is being individually administered.

• The manual is well organized. Information on test administration, scoring, and interpretation is clearly presented. Designed primarily as a group test, careful attention has been given to facilitate group administration with young children.

• The revised Boehm construction included careful attention to item selection and presentation. Items were excluded which were passed by high percentages of beginning kindergarten students. The concepts measured appear frequently in primary-grade curriculum materials. Thoughtfully employed, the test results can be used to assist teachers in recognizing the needs of individual students and classroom groups. The manual provides extensive help in instructional planning.

• The provision of two equivalent forms and separate norms for fall and spring testing make the Boehm-R a useful test for measuring progress.

• The Applications Booklet is a good addition to the test, extending its usefulness with first and second grade students.

• A preschool version of the Boehm Test of Basic Concepts (BTBC-PV) has been developed as a separate publication. This version, standardized on 3- and 4-year olds, assesses the 26 concepts that are mastered by most children entering kindergarten. It is presented in a card booklet format and is individually administered.

• Also available is a Parent-Teacher Conference Report. This form is designed to help teachers present test results to parents. It includes an explanation of the basic concepts, a brief test description, a few sample items, and suggestions for ways in which the parent can help the child learn basic concepts at home. The report can be used with both Forms C and D.

• Directions for the revised Boehm have been translated into Spanish. Spanish-speaking aides or teachers can administer the test using the same picture booklets. However, norms that are specifically for Spanish-speaking students are not provided.

LIMITING FACTORS OF THE BOEHM-R

• As is stated in the manual, the major use of this test is as a *screening* measure. Only one item is included to measure each concept, and factors such as attention and motivation may influence a child's response.

• The reliability data presented in the manual is somewhat low. This may be due to the fact that the range of scores is narrow, especially for older students, or it may reflect the unreliability of group scores with young children. In either case, the data again suggests the need to consider the Boehm-R as a screening instrument rather than as a definitive diagnostic instrument.

• Although extensive research on the original Boehm is reported in the manual, only one, poorly-reported, validity study using the Boehm–R is presented. Because this test is easily adaptable to students with various handicapping conditions, research with both normal and exceptional students is needed. *A Consumer's Guide to Tests in Print* (Hammill, Bryant, and Brown, 1992) does not recommend the Boehm–R because of a lack of reliability and validity information.

NOTE

The Boehm Test of Basic Concepts is also available in a preschool version (Boehm–Preschool Psychological Corporation, 1986). This downward extension of the BTBC–R is individually administered to children between 3 and 5 years of age or to older children with special education needs. The Boehm–Preschool assesses 26 relational concepts, including size, direction, position in space, quantity, and time. The test is best used as part of a school-readiness screening and is helpful to preschool teachers or to child-care providers in planning activities to teach basic concepts.

Clinical Evaluation of Language Fundamentals-Revised (CELF–R)

Eleanor Semel-Mintz, Elizabeth Wiig, and Wayne Secord
The Psychological Corporation, 1983, 1987
555 Academic Court, San Antonio, TX 78204-2498

Purpose	To provide a practical clinical tool for the identification, diagnosis, and follow-up evaluation of oral language skill deficits in school age children
Major Areas Tested	Word meaning; word and sentence structure; recall and retrieval
Age or Grade Range	K–12
Usually Given By	Speech/language clinician Psychologist Learning disability specialist
Type of Test	Individual Norm-referenced Standardized
Scores Obtained	Standard scores Percentile NCE's Age-equivalent
Student Performance Timed?	No (except for one subtest)
Testing Time	1–1 1/2 hours
Scoring/Interpretation Time	25–30 minutes
Normed On	2,426 students between the ages of 5 and 16; 33 school districts in 18 states were included; students in special education classes or receiving speech therapy were not included; sample was balanced for community size, geographical region, sex, age, race, and educational level of the parents
Alternate Forms Available?	No

FORMAT

The Clinical Evaluation of Language Fundamentals–Revised (CELF–R) is the revised edition of the Clinical Evaluation of Language Functions (CELF) published in 1980.

The change in name clarifies that the CELF–R is a measure of oral language skills and not language function, or pragmatics. The test is intended to measure language skills in the school-age child, grades kindergarten through 12. Subtests are designed to assess word meaning (semantics), word and sentence structure (morphology and syntax), and recall and retrieval (memory). The materials consist of an Examiner's Manual, including directions for administration, scoring, and interpretation, as well as norm tables; a Technical Manual, describing test rationale, development, standardization, and reliability and validity data; two stimulus manuals, containing the pictorial material for each subtest; and individual student record forms.

The CELF-R battery includes 11 subtests; through analysis of standardization data and predictive validity studies, the subtests that best differentiate normal and disordered language were identified by age level. The three best subtests determining a receptive Language Score and an Expressive Language Score for younger and older students are listed below.

Receptive Language

Ages 5–7	Ages 8 and Above
Linguistic Concepts	Oral Directions
Sentence Structure	Word Classes
Oral Directions	Semantic Relationships
Expressive Language	
Word Structure	Formulated Sentences
Formulated Sentences	Recalling Sentences
Recalling Sentences	Sentence Assembly

The two remaining subtests may be used as supplementary measures of the student's language, or they may be used as replacement tests if one of the above tests is invalid due to problems in administration. For example, *Listening to Paragraphs* can be an alternate receptive test.

By selecting the appropriate subtests for a student's age level, testing time is used efficiently.

Following the administration of the appropriate subtests, the raw scores are converted to standard scores and percentiles. Such derived scores can be obtained for each individual subtest. Composite scores for Receptive Language, Expressive Language, and Total Language can also be obtained. Confidence levels for each score are given. Age Equivalent scores are given for Total Language only. Information is given on interpreting whether the difference between two subtest scores or the Receptive and Expressive composites is significant. All scores are recorded on the front cover of the Individual Record Form.

The Examiner's Manual includes extensive guidelines for interpretation, including several case studies. Extension testing, the process of evaluating a student's errors, is well described for each subtest. Examples of instructional objectives and curriculum references are given.

STRENGTHS OF THE CELF-R

• The CELF-R is a comprehensive, well constructed battery of subtests to assess oral language competence over a wide age range. The new revision maintains many of the values of the CELF while introducing several subtests with improved content and administration and scoring procedures. The differences between the CELF and the CELF-R are explained in detail in the Technical Manual.

• The Examiner's Manual is extremely well organized; the directions for administration are clear and scoring procedures well explained. Guidelines for extension testing and interpretation of test performance are excellent.

• The Response Booklet is also excellent. Administration is greatly simplified by including the age range, the ceiling procedure, all items, and a place for marking the student's response so that it is immediately scorable. No transference back and forth between the manual and the record form is required. In addition, guides for error analysis are printed following every subtest.

• The format of the pictorial materials is simple and clear. Pages are uncluttered, and it is easy for the student to follow the task from item to item.

• The organization of the CELF-R is greatly improved. By providing a different battery of subtests for younger and older students, the need for a basal procedure is eliminated. Testing time is reduced as a total score can be obtained from six subtests.

• Several features have been provided to aid the examiner in eliciting the best performance from each student. These include demonstration and trial items introducing each subtest, alternating receptive and expressive tests, and providing additional tests in case one subtest is invalidated.

• The CELF-R is a flexible test to use with language and learning disabled students. The examiner is guided toward one of two subtest groupings according to the age of the student. However, if the student proves to be more or less advanced than supposed, the examiner can change levels and still calculate standard scores on the subtests given.

• Many of the tasks contained in the CELF-R battery are unique. There are few diagnostic instruments appropriate for assessing the oral language abilities of older school-age children. The CELF-R tasks and test materials are usually appealing and interesting to this age group.

• The CELF-R diagnostic battery is considered to be an intergral part of Wiig and Semel-Mintz's assessment process, which consists of Screening, Diagnosis, Extension

• *A Consumer's Guide to Tests in Print* (Hammill, Bryant, and Brown, 1992) recommends the CELF–R for its technical characteristics, including norming, reliability, and validity.

• The CELF–R authors have also published a screening test (CELF–R Screening Test), revised in 1989. The screening test covers the five to 16 year age range and provides six subtests to screen both language processing and language production. The test is standardized to identify children who need an in-depth assessment of oral language. The CELF–R Screening can be administered in approximately 10 minutes.

LIMITING FACTORS OF THE CELF–R

• Although the CELF–R is a comprehensive diagnostic tool, the authors suggest that a standardized measure of receptive vocabulary and analysis of a spontaneous speech sample be included as part of the testing process. Academic and intellectual testing may also be needed to complete an assessment of a school-age child.

• Page numbers, or tabs on the Stimulus Materials books, would increase ease of administration.

• In the Technical Manual, several studies are reported concerning the validity of the CELF–R. They appear to support the claim that the CELF–R discriminates between the learning–language-disabled student and the "normal language" student. The age of students participating in these studies is not reported. As different batteries of subtests from the CELF–R are recommended for different ages, this information is needed to assess the validity of each battery.

• Despite the good overall reliability of the CELF–R, examiners are cautioned that the Oral Directions Subtest does not have satisfactory reliability.

CELF-R Subtests

Subtest	Type	Age*	Task	Areas Measured	Comments
Linguistic Concepts (?0 items)	Receptive	5–7	Student executes oral directions requiring logical operations by pointing to a series of six colored lines. *(Before you point to the blue line, point to a red line.)*	Comprehension of concepts related to inclusion, exclusion, coordination, time, condition, and quality.	Similar to Processing Linguistic Concepts on the CELF; assesses critical linguistic concepts to discriminate language disabled from normal students.
Word Structure (36 items)	Expressive	5–7	Student looks at pictures and completes sentences spoken by the examiner. *(Here is a dog; here are two _____ . This girl jogs; she is called a _____ .)*	Knowledge of word structure rules; plurals, possessives, past tense, auxiliary + *ing*, comparatives, superlatives, etc.	New subtest on CELF-R, very similar to the Grammatical Closure on ITPA.
Sentence Structure (26 items)	Receptive	5–7	From 4 choices, student selects the picture which matches the meaning of the sentence read by the examiner.	Receptive morphology and syntax at the sentence level.	Similar to Processing Word and Sentence Structure in CELF; good visual discrimination skills are needed to process pictures.
Oral Directions (22 items)	Receptive	5+	Student executes oral commands ranging in length from 5 to 16 words by pointing to black or white circles, squares and/or triangles in two or three different sizes (Point to the smallest black square).	Comprehension, recall, and execution of oral commands of increasing length and complexity.	Same test as Processing Oral Directions on CELF.
Formulated Sentences (20 items)	Expressive	5+	Student verbally formulates a sentence using each one of 14 words given by examiner. Pictures are used to stimulate responses. In the last 6 items, the student must use two words in a sentence.	Formulation of simple, compound, and complex sentences.	Same test as Producing Formulated Sentences in CELF; extensive examples given to facilitate scoring.
Recalling Sentences (26 items)	Expressive	5+	Student repeats sentences whose length and complexity gradually increase.	Recall and reproduction as a function of syntactic complexity.	Similar to Producing Model Sentences in CELF; however, structurally incorrect sentences have been eliminated.
Word Classes (27 items)	Receptive	8+	In a group of 4 words pronounced by the examiner, the student identifies the two which are related. (before, when, under, after; cliff, hill, house, grass.)	Verbal concept development; vocabulary, association skills.	Similar to Processing Word Classes on CELF. Difficulties in auditory memory can affect performance on this task. For further diagnostic information, the examiner can ask the student why a particular word was chosen.
Sentence Assembly (22 items)	Expressive	8+	The student formulates sentences using key words and phrases. The student must give 2 sentences for each set of stimuli. (on the table, the ball, put, will you.)	Ability to assemble syntactic structures into gramatically and semantically meaningful sentences.	New test, similar to TORC; requiring two sentences is a good diagnostic feature.
Semantic Relation- ships (28 items)	Receptive	8+	From four possible responses student selects the two correct answers to a question.	Comprehension of comparatives; spatial, passive, and temporal relationships.	Modification and expansion of Processing Relationships and Ambiguities on CELF; elimination of yes-no response is a great improvement.
Word Association (3 items)	Expressive	Alternate test for either age group.	Student produces as many names of animals, transportation, and occupations as he/she can in 60 seconds.	Vocabulary; word retrieval.	Similar to Producing Word Associations on CELF; although responses are scored with respect to quantity (number of words recalled), the evaluation of quality (number of semantic subclasses represented and shifts between various subclasses) is also available.
Listening to Paragraphs (14 items)	Receptive	Alternate test for either age group.	Student listens to paragraphs read by examiner and answers four questions about each.	Auditory comprehension; recall of factual data.	New test; paragraphs increase in length, sentence and content complexity; only factual recall is required; two paragraphs at each age level is a positive feature.

*The subtest is required for the age listed; it becomes an additional diagnostic tool for the other age level.

Clinical Evaluation of Language Fundamentals–Preschool (CELF–Preschool)

Elizabeth Wiig, Wayne Secord, and Eleanor Semel
The Psychological Corporation, 1992
555 Academic Court, San Antonio, TX 78104-2498

Purpose	To provide a tool for identifying, diagnosing, and performing follow-up evaluations of language defects in preschool children
Major Areas Tested	Receptive and expressive language
Age or Grade Range	3.0–6.11 years
Usually Given By	Speech and language pathologists
Type of Test	Individual Standardized Norm-referenced
Scores Obtained	Age equivalents Percentiles Standard scores
Student Performance Timed?	No
Testing Time	30–40 minutes
Scoring/Interpretation Time	25–30 minutes
Normed On	800 children in a nationally representative sample (based on 1980 Census of Population, 1988 update); sample stratified on the basis of age, gender, race/ethnicity, parent education level, and geographic region
Alternate Forms Available?	No

FORMAT

The Clinical Evaluation of Language Fundamentals–Preschool (CELF–Preschool) is a downward extension of the CELF–R. The test assesses language form and content in both the receptive and expressive modes. As does its predecessor, the CELF–Preschool's subtests include measures of word meaning (semantics), word and sentence structure (morphology and syntax), and recall (auditory memory). The materials for the CELF–Preschool include three stimulus manuals, which contain the picture stimulus materials for all six subtests; individual record forms; and the examiner's manual. The 120-page examiner's manual includes information on administration and scoring, test development, technical characteristics of the CELF–Preschool, test interpretation, and planning a remediation program.

The subtests of the CELF–Preschool were designed to assess the same skills in preschool children that the CELF–R measures in school-age children. Subtests were created that assess relevant linguistic competencies in the three- to six-year-old age range, and an equal number of receptive and expressive subtests was included to provide balanced composite scores for both areas.

The CELF–Preschool Subtests include:

Receptive Language
Linguistic Concepts
Sentence Structure
Basic Concepts

Expressive Language
Recalling Sentences in Context
Formulating Labels
Word Structure

While the CELF–Preschool has standardized administration procedures, the authors have provided flexible guidelines for administration, including seating arrangements, breaks, and other accommodations sensitive to young children. Subtests may be given in any order. All children begin with the first item on each subtest, but a ceiling procedure is used.

1. *Linguistic Concepts.* After a process to familiarize the child with the animal pictures used in this subtest, the child is shown a picture of animals and is asked to demonstrate his or her knowledge of linguistic concepts by pointing. ("Point to one of the bears." "Point to the elephant next to the giraffe.").

2. *Recalling Sentences in Context* . The child is shown a picture in the stimulus manual. As the examiner reads the story, he or she stops periodically to ask the child to repeat verbatim a sentence in the story. ("Tell me what Jimmy said. 'We are moving.' " "What did Mom say? 'If you clean your plate, you can have dessert, too.' ").

3. *Formulating Labels.* The child is shown a series of single pictures and asked to name the object or tell what is happening in the picture. Items include such pictures as a sailboat, a flag, a boy wrapping a package, and an octopus.

4. *Basic Concepts.* The child is shown a series of pictures that illustrate basic concepts of space, size, and opposites. The child responds by pointing. Concepts assessed include inside, bottom, slow, and tall.

5. *Sentence Structure.* The child is shown a series of pictures that illustrate verb phrases, negatives, passive voice, and other morphological and syntactical forms. The child responds by pointing ("She is climbing and he is swinging." "He will eat the apple.").

6. *Word Structure.* After a process to familiarize the picture format (in which the examiner's picture is on one side of the book and the child's picture is on the facing page), the child is asked to complete a sentence based on the examiner's model. The child's use of prepositions, nouns, verbs, and pronouns is assessed ["She is waving at him. He is waving at____ (her)." "The baby eats. The baby _____ (sleeps)."].

Specific directions for scoring, and sample correct and incorrect responses for each subtest, are clearly described in the manual. Following the administration of the subtests, raw scores are converted to standard scores and percentiles for each subtest. Standard scores for the three receptive subtests are combined into a Receptive Language Score and, similarly, the three expressive subtests are combined into an Expressive Language Score. These two composite scores are added to form a Total Language Score. Subtest standard scores have a mean of 10 with a standard deviation of 3, while the three composite scores have a mean of 100 with a standard deviation of 15. An age equivalent is provided for the Total Language Score only.

STRENGTHS OF THE CELF–PRESCHOOL

• The CELF–Preschool Test is a downward extension of the CELF–R. It provides examiners of preschool children with a well standardized instrument with colorful stimuli that are interesting to young children. Flexible administration procedures allow examiners to adapt to the needs of preschoolers.

• The Behavioral Observation Check List is a useful feature. Therapists can quickly check off behaviors of the child that are important in interpreting and reporting test results.

• The CELF–Preschool Manual is complete and provides good discussions of many important aspects of the test that enhance its usefulness. These include a discussion of the interpretation of dialectical variations and out-of-range administration procedures.

• The CELF–Preschool also includes a Quick Test, which can be used for screening. For the Quick Test, only two subtests are given: Linguistic Concepts and Recalling Sentences in Context. If the child's standard scores on either or both of the subtests is 7 or lower, the authors advise the administration of the remaining tests.

LIMITING FACTORS OF THE CELF–PRESCHOOL

- The CELF–Preschool is a comprehensive and complex test. Examiners are urged to study the manual and administer several practice tests to become proficient in handling the many test materials, as well as recording responses, scoring, and interpretation.

Expressive One-Word Picture Vocabulary Test–Revised (EOWPVT–R)

Morrison F. Gardiner
Academic Therapy Publications, 1979, revised 1990
20 Commercial Blvd., Novato, CA 94949-6191

Purpose	To obtain an estimate of a child's verbal intelligence and the quality and quantity of vocabulary
Major Areas Tested	Expressive vocabulary
Age or Grade Range	2—12 years
Usually Given By	Speech/language clinician Psychologist Special education teacher Counselor
Type of Test	Individual Standardized Norm-referenced
Scores Obtained	Age equivalents Standard scores Percentiles Stanines
Student Performance Timed?	No
Testing Time	10–15 minutes
Scoring/Interpretation Time	10 minutes
Normed On	1,118 children between 2 and 12 years in the San Francisco Bay area; English was the primary language for all subjects
Alternate Forms Available?	No

FORMAT

The Expressive One-Word Picture Vocabulary Test (EOWPVT) was originally published in 1979. This revision (EOWPVT–R) has maintained the same format; a few stimulus items have been added and the test renormed on a similar group of children from the San Francisco Bay area. The test was developed to provide an estimate of the vocabulary a student has learned from the home environment and from formal education. The author felt that an expressive format provided more valuable diagnostic information than a receptive test. The materials for the EOWPVT–R include an examiner's manual, picture book, and score forms.

The EOWPVT–R is individually administered. The student names a series of individual black-and-white line drawings presented by the examiner. A table included in the manual indicates the starting point for testing, as determined by the student's age. Items are sequenced in order of difficulty, and basal and ceiling levels are provided. Two demonstration items are presented to familiarize the student with the task. All of the student's responses are recorded for analysis purposes.

Stimulus words for the EOWPVT–R were chosen based on questionnaires sent to parents of children from 18 months to 2 years of age and on vocabulary presented in educational settings in selected areas of the United States. Test items represent four language categories, including general or concrete concepts, groupings, abstract concepts, and descriptive concepts.

Raw scores are determined by the number of pictures appropriately named by the student. Scoring criteria are presented in the manual. Raw scores can be converted to mental ages, intelligence quotients, stanines, and percentiles for students between the ages of 2 years and 11 years, 11 months, at one-month intervals.

STRENGTHS OF THE EOWPVT–R

- The primary value of the EOWPVT–R lies in its uniqueness. While there are several standardized measures of receptive vocabulary available to diagnosticians, few tests assess single-word knowledge through the expressive mode. In addition to vocabulary level, examiners can quickly and easily obtain information about a student's word recall and retrieval abilities, speech articulation, and general developmental functioning.

- Because the EOWPVT–R can be administered rapidly, it is useful as a screening of expressive-language functioning. In addition, when given as part of a comprehensive test battery, the EOWPVT–R can provide information for contrasting a student's expressive and receptive vocabulary skills.

LIMITING FACTORS OF THE EOWPVT–R

- The author describes the EOWPVT–R as a "measure of how a child thinks." This implies that the test is a measure of verbal intelligence. However, verbal intelligence is much more comprehensive than the naming of pictures with one-word labels. The EOWPVT–R is a measure of expressive single-word vocabulary and should never be used as an estimate of general intellectual ability.

- The size of the sample for children between the ages of 2 years and 2 years, 11 months is very small, indicating that interpretations of performance in this age range should be viewed very cautiously.

- The standardization sample was composed entirely of children from the San Francisco Bay area. No other description of the sample is given. Because vocabulary at a young age is very much influenced by cultural and linguistic background, the racial and ethnic characteristics of the sample need to be well described. The limited geographic area and the poor sample description severely limit the generalizability of the EOWPVT–R.

- *The Consumer's Guide to Tests in Print* (Hammill, Bryant, and Brown, 1992) does not recommend the EOWPVT–R because of its inadequate norming sample and poor reliability and validity.

- Knowledge of vocabulary, perhaps more than most other acquired skills, is closely linked with cultural and educational experiences. Therefore, culturally different students can be expected to perform more poorly on such a measure as the EOWPVT–R when compared with students from the mainstream. In addition, students might have excellent funds of vocabulary but perform poorly on the EOWPVT–R because of severe word-recall and retrieval difficulties. The possibility of visual–perceptual problems should also be considered when interpreting a student's performance on this test.

- There is a Spanish version of the EOWPVT–R that utilizes the same administration and scoring procedures as the English edition. However, only one set of standardized scores is available for both languages, and it was normed on an English-speaking population. Therefore, examiners can use this Spanish version to obtain descriptive information about a student's expressive Spanish vocabulary, but the score should not be reported.

- Examiners should be aware that the EOWPVT–R does not discriminate well between certain age groups. Scores vary insignificantly between some six-month age intervals.

- The EOWPVT–R manual suggests that the test be used to determine a child's readiness for kindergarten. Such an important decision requires a reliable instrument with good predictive validity. The EOWPVT–R can best be viewed as a rough screening test to complement a more-extensive language evaluation.

Expressive One Word Picture Vocabulary Test— Upper Extension (EOWPVT-UE)

Morrison F. Gardner
Academic Therapy Publications, 1983
20 Commercial Blvd., Novato, CA 94947-6191

Purpose	To obtain a basal estimate of a child's verbal intelligence
Major Areas Tested	Expressive vocabulary
Age or Grade Range	12–16 years
Usually Given By	Classroom teacher Counselor Special education teacher Speech therapist Psychologist
Type of Test	Norm-referenced Individual or small group Standardized
Scores Obtained	Mental Age Deviation IQ Percentile rank Stanines
Student Performance Timed?	No
Testing Time	10–15 minutes
Scoring/Interpretation Time	5–10 minutes
Normed On	465 students aged 12–16 from the San Francisco Bay Area
Alternate Forms Available?	No

FORMAT

The Expressive One Word Picture Vocabulary Test—Upper Extension (EOWPVT–UE) is the upper level of the EOWPVT. It was designed to be used with students between the ages of 12 and 16 years.

The materials for the EOWPVT–UE consist of the manual, a spiral-bound book of test plates, and the individual test forms. The manual includes directions for administering and scoring the test as well as the norms tables and technical information on standardization, reliability, and validity.

The EOWPVT–UE is usually administered individually. The student looks at a line drawing illustrating a common object or group of objects, an abstract concept (time), a noun participle (flying), and letter symbols (c/o). Entry points are suggested according to chronological age, and a basal (8 consecutive correct responses) and ceiling (6 consecutive errors) process is used so that students are tested over a critical range.

Directions for group instruction are presented in the manual. Group administration requires the students to write their responses. Therefore, this method should be used only for students with adequate writing skills. The basal and ceiling rules are applied when scoring the test. Raw scores of the number of correct responses are converted into mental age, deviation IQ, stanine, and percentile ranks.

STRENGTHS OF THE EOWPVT–UE

• This test was developed to use with adolescents, for whom there are few tests of expressive vocabulary available.

• The EOWPVT–UE is easy and quick to use.

• A Spanish translation is available for use with Spanish-English bilingual students. However, only one set of norms is provided, so scores for Spanish-speaking students are not valid.

LIMITING FACTORS OF THE EOWPVT-UE

• The standardization sample is small, drawn from one geographic area, and not well described as to racial or ethnic composition. All of these are critical variables in vocabulary development.

• No test-retest reliability statistics are reported in the manual.

• Mental ages are calculated by equating a student's scores on the EOWPVT–UE with the PPVT. Therefore, the mental ages are estimates and must be used with caution. This caution is stated in the manual.

• The description of the EOWPVT–UE as a test of verbal intelligence is inaccurate. Obviously, verbal intelligence is composed of many factors, of which picture naming is only one. Use of terms such as "mental age" and "deviation IQ" are quite misleading. The test is best viewed as a rough screening of one aspect of a student's vocabulary development and may lead to a decision to do further assessment in this area.

Peabody Picture Vocabulary Test–Revised
(PPVT–R)

Lloyd M. Dunn and Leota M. Dunn
American Guidance Service, Inc., 1959; revised 1965, 1981
4201 Woodland Rd., P.O. Box 99, Circle Pines, MN 55014-1796

Purpose	To assess an individual's receptive (hearing) vocabulary for standard American English
Major Areas Tested	Receptive single-word vocabulary
Age or Grade Range	2 1/2–40 years
Usually Given By	Special education teacher Psychologist Speech/language clinician
Type of Test	Standardized Individual Norm-referenced
Scores Obtained	Age level Standard Percentile Stanine
Student Performance Timed?	No
Testing Time	10–20 minutes
Scoring/Interpretation Time	10–15 minutes
Normed On	Carefully selected nationwide sample of 5,028 persons, including 4,200 children, balanced for age, sex, geographic region, socioeconomic level, ethnicity, and community size
Alternate Forms Available?	Yes

FORMAT

The Peabody Picture Vocabulary Test—Revised (PPVT–R) consists of two equivalent forms, L and M. For each form there is an easel book of line drawings printed four on a page and individual student record forms. There is one examiner's manual including administration and scoring procedures and norms tables covering both forms. A technical supplement provides more detailed information on test construction and standardization.

To administer the test, the examiner pronounces a word, and the student selects the corresponding picture ("Show me meringue."). No verbal response is needed because the student can simply point to the correct picture. The vocabulary words gradually increase in difficulty, from such items as *arrow, furry,* and *vase* to *ascending* and *trajectory.*

Although all the items are together in one picture book, the student is tested on only the vocabulary appropriate for his or her age and language development. There are no subtests. Equivalent forms L and M may be given in alternate sessions to increase the reliability of the score, or they may be used as pretests and posttests for evaluating a student's progress. The manual includes detailed directions for administering and scoring, as well as tables for converting raw scores to age equivalents, standard scores, percentiles, and stanines.

The primary changes in the PPVT–R over the 1965 edition include the following:

1. The test was standardized nationwide and the sample was balanced for age, sex, geographic region, socioeconomic level, ethnicity, and community size.

2. The terms "mental age" and "intelligence quotient" were changed to "age equivalent" and "standard score equivalent."

3. Two-thirds of the stimulus items were replaced with new items, and 25 items were added to each form to increase the instrument's sensitivity and reliability.

4. The racial, ethnic, and sex balance in the line drawings was improved.

STRENGTHS OF THE PPVT-R

• The PPVT-R is well designed and well normed. The format of presenting a picture to elicit a pointing response makes it a nonthreatening test that even the young or seriously impaired student can take successfully. It is frequently used as the first in a battery of tests; the easy format makes it a good warm-up for more difficult material. The wide age range covered by the PPVT–R and its alternate forms make it a good instrument for test-retest purposes; it can be administered every year to assess a student's progress in specific language therapy or in general language development. The PPVT–R is relatively quick to administer and interpret. Although it is usually used as a global

measure of receptive vocabulary, analysis of a student's errors can reveal information about the specific nature of a vocabulary deficit. For example, student errors on such items as *filing, assaulting,* and *lecturing* would seem to indicate difficulty with verbs.

• The PPVT–R is available in Spanish. (See Test of Vocabulario en Imagenes Peabody (TVIP).

LIMITING FACTORS OF THE PPVT–R

• The PPVT–R is a test of single-word vocabulary only. The comprehension of spoken language in context is a different skill, and the examiner must not assume that a student's receptive language is adequate simply because he or she obtains a high PPVT–R score. Knowing the meaning of *group* when it is pronounced clearly and represented by a picture of five children is quite different from understanding the word when the teacher says, "First do the group of subtraction problems on page 10, and then do the group on page 14, starting with line 3." In addition, the PPVT–R score may not predict high verbal performance in the classroom. Understanding a word and using it correctly in spoken language are two different skills.

• The PPVT–R does not assess all parts of speech. Only nouns, verbs, and adjectives are included. The understanding of prepositions, a critical skill, is not included.

• The standardization sample of the PPVT–R is greatly improved over the original sample and includes students of various ethnic backgrounds, races, and socioeconomic levels. However, it is still important to consider the effects of different cultural backgrounds on test performance. Students from different cultures or from disadvantaged homes may not have had experience with the pictured items. For a student from a middle-class home and community, a low score may reflect a true deficit in ability to comprehend spoken language, but in a student from a culturally different or disadvantaged background, a low score may reflect lack of language stimulation or experience. The program for developing language skills in these two students would be quite different.

• As in all tests, the student's attention span is a big factor in performance. Low scores on the PPVT–R may be related to impulsive responses caused by an inability to scan four pictures. Or they may result from perseveration—continued pointing to the same position on the page. Such behavior is not unusual in low-functioning children with physical, emotional, or attention problems. A low PPVT–R score therefore may not reflect low vocabulary development but rather an inability to scan and select visual material.

• In the PPVT–R, hearing vocabulary is measured through picture stimuli. Clearly, two processes are involved in doing this: the understanding of the spoken word and the understanding of the line drawings. A low score may not necessarily reflect a problem in receptive vocabulary but possibly a problem in comprehending pictures. For example, a student may know the meaning of the word *exterior* but be unable to interpret which drawing is the *outside* of the house and which is the *inside*. Other measures of receptive vocabulary and picture comprehension are needed to confirm the results of the PPVT–R, if a specific definition of the disability is needed.

NOTE
The PPVT–R is under revision. The revised test will be published in 1996.

Comprehensive Receptive and Expressive Vocabulary Test (CREVT)

Gerald Wallace and Donald Hammill
PRO-ED, 1994
8700 Shoal Creek Blvd., Austin, TX 78757

Purpose	To identify students who are significantly below their peers in oral vocabulary, to determine discrepancies between receptive and expressive skills, to document progress in an intervention program, and to provide a research tool
Major Areas Tested	Receptive and expressive vocabulary
Age or Grade Range	Receptive vocabulary: 4.0–17.11 years Expressive vocabulary: 5.0–17.11 years
Usually Given By	Speech and language therapists Special education teachers Psychologists
Type of Test	Individual Standardized Norm-referenced
Scores Obtained	Age equivalents Percentiles Standard scores
Student Performance Timed?	No
Testing Time	20–30 minutes
Scoring/Interpretation Time	15–20 minutes
Normed On	1,920 students in 33 states; the sample was compared with the U.S. Census Data (1990) for sex, residence, race, ethnicity, and geographic area. Disabled students in the regular classroom were included in the sample.
Alternate Forms Available?	Yes

FORMAT

The Comprehensive Receptive and Expressive Vocabulary Test (CREVT) is a new test that provides for the assessment of receptive and expressive vocabulary with a single instrument normed on the same population. The materials consist of the examiner's manual, profile/ examiner record forms, and the Photo Album Picture Book. The manual includes a discussion of the development of the CREVT, administration and scoring instructions, and information on the technical characteristics of the test.

The CREVT has two subtests: The Receptive Test assesses matching spoken words to pictures; the Expressive Test requires word definitions.

1. *Receptive Vocabulary.* The Photo Album Picture Book consists of ten pages with six color photos, each of which is used in this subtest. The photos on each page represent a category of items; the categories are animals, transportation, food, clothing, tools, occupations, personal grooming, household appliances, clerical materials, and recreation. The student is shown a page with six color photos and asked to point to the picture named by the examiner. Every student begins with the first item on the page and continues until he or she completes the items on the page or has two consecutive errors. When the student completes the items or reaches the ceiling, the examiner proceeds to the next page. Each item receives one point for a correct response.

2. *Expressive Vocabulary.* The Expressive Vocabulary Subtest does not use color photos. The student is simply advised to "Tell me what this word means" for every word given by the examiner. There are two starting points, one for under-12 year olds, and one for students 12 years old and older. A ceiling is reached when a student misses three consecutive items. One point is given for each correct definition.

Correct answers are totaled for each subtest and combined to form a General Vocabulary Score. All three scores, Receptive Vocabulary, Expressive Vocabulary, and General Vocabulary, are converted into standard scores, percentiles, and age equivalent scores.

STRENGTHS OF THE CREVT

• The assessment of oral vocabulary is clearly a crucial factor in the evaluation of students with learning and language delays or disorders. The CREVT provides for the assessment of this important skill in both the receptive and expressive modes. Because both subtests are normed on the same population, receptive and expressive vocabulary skills can be compared with confidence. In addition, the words selected for both subtests are based on the same concepts.

• The color photograph stimuli are interesting and easily interpreted by students of all ages.

• The CREVT assesses vocabulary over the entire school-age range, providing an instrument for repeated testing. The provision of equivalent alternate forms A and B make the test a good choice for assessing a student's progress over time.

LIMITING FACTORS OF THE CREVT

• The CREVT is a new test that shows much promise as a useful tool for language clinicians and special education personnel. Time will provide a more comprehensive evaluation of its strengths and weaknesses. The assessment of single-word vocabulary in a format that groups words into categories is a unique approach, but it is not clear that the information gathered in this format is any more helpful in analyzing a child's vocabulary than the more typical noncategorized presentation.

• On the Receptive Vocabulary Subtest, each page contains six color photographs, yet the number of items for each page varies from four to six. Therefore, on some pages not all pictures are used, and on some pages pictures are used more than once. There are no administration instructions that explain this for the student. Because students are used to the usual format of using each picture only once, the examiner should clarify this procedure.

• Examiners need to be alert to the age range of the two subtests. While the Receptive Vocabulary Subtest has norms for the 4 year old, the Expressive Vocabulary Subtest norms begin at age 5. This is due to the fact that 4 year olds had difficulty understanding the concept of "defining" a word.

• Prior to the CREVT, clinicians typically used the Peabody Picture Vocabulary Test–Revised (p. 189) for receptive vocabulary and the Expressive One-Word Picture Vocabulary Test, Revised (p. 185) for expressive vocabulary. While the CREVT provides the assessment of both skills in a single test that allows for direct comparisons of the two skills, the CREVT uses a definition format for expressive language, rather than a naming format. The naming format provides an informal assessment of word finding difficulties that was very helpful information.

• Eighty-five percent of the items on the receptive subtest and 100 percent on the expressive subtest are nouns. The inclusion of more verbs and adjectives would add to the richness of the vocabulary sample.

Beery Picture Vocabulary Screening (BEERY PVS) and Beery Picture Vocabulary Test (BEERY PVT)

Keith Beery and Colleen Taheri
Psychological Assessment Resources, Inc., 1992
P. O. Box 998, Odessa, FL 33536

Purpose	To enhance vocabulary development by means of more relevant, efficient, and effective vocabulary evaluations of young children and "students" of all ages
Major Areas Tested	Expressive vocabulary, written and oral
Age or Grade Range	PVS: 2nd through 12th grade PVT: 2.6–40 years
Usually Given By	Psychologists Speech and language clinicians Special education teachers
Type of Test	Individual (PVT) Group (PVS) Standardized Norm-referenced
Scores Obtained	Scaled scores Percentiles Age and grade equivalents (PVT)
Student Performance Timed?	No
Testing Time	PVS: 10 minutes PVT: 10–15 minutes
Scoring/Interpretation Time	10–15 minutes
Normed On	PVS: 1,174 individuals from all 5 major geographic regions of the United States. Sample matched with 1990 U.S. Census information with respect to age, grade, and residence. PVT: 1,189 individuals, sample composed as for PVS
Alternate Forms Available?	No

FORMAT

The Beery Picture Vocabulary Screening (BEERY PVS) and the Beery Picture Vocabulary Test (BEERY PVT) form a two-step series of expressive vocabulary assessments. The PVS is a group test that may be used to assess an entire classroom, while the PVT is an in-depth evaluation of an individual student. The PVS requires a written response, while the PVT is an oral test.

Beery Picture Vocabulary Screening (BEERY PVS)

The materials for the PVS consist of 11 four-page test booklets, one for each grade from 2nd through 12th. Each booklet includes 16 black-and-white drawings of objects that have been selected as developmentally appropriate for the age range of the students in that grade. Beneath each picture is the initial letter and a line on which the child writes a response.

b _____

The teacher demonstrates two examples with the group; then students work independently, writing in all 16 items. They are given ten minutes to complete the task and told not to worry about spelling. The total number of correct responses is converted to a scaled score with a mean of 10 and a standard deviation of 3. Percentiles are also provided. It is recommended that students who score at the 10th percentile or lower be tested on the individual Beery Picture Vocabulary Test (BEERY PVT).

Beery Picture Vocabulary Test (BEERY PVT)

The materials for the PVT include the professional manual, the stimulus-card set, and individual record forms. The stimulus card set contains four training examples and 165 pictures, one to a page, which are presented to the student who is asked "What is this?" As on the PVS, the initial letter of the name of the object is printed below the picture. A basal/ceiling procedure of eight consecutive responses is used, and starting points based on chronological age are suggested. Prompts and probes are provided for the training examples but not the test items. Responses are recorded on the record form, and scores are based on one point for each correct response, until a ceiling is reached. Raw scores are then converted to standard scores, percentiles, and other normalized scores such as NCE's (normal curve equivalents), stanines, and scaled scores. Age and grade equivalents can

be estimated by plotting the total score on a graph provided on the record form.

STRENGTHS OF THE BEERY PVS AND PVT SERIES

• The PVS and the PVT Series provide a useful format of group classroom screening, followed by individual testing in the area of expressive vocabulary. The PVS was designed to be sensitive to the needs of the low-performing student. The authors are promoting yearly evaluations of vocabulary for all children, and the manual describes a procedure for using typical class achievement tests, such as the California Test of Basic Skills (CTBS), as the posttest.

• The provision of the initial letter of the object as a clue is useful in eliciting the correct response. Given a picture of a tennis game, *r* elicits *racquet* rather than *tennis*, *player*, or *court*.

• A graph is provided on the record form that allows the examiner to plot PVT raw scores on the developmental curve of the test. Age and grade scores can be estimated to aid in interpretation of test results to older students, parents, or others not familiar with standard scores. This graph provides such information in a useful way, while avoiding the focus on age scores by year and month.

• The standardization sample is well described in the manual, as are reliability and validity studies that support the technical characteristics of the test.

LIMITING FACTORS OF THE BEERY PVS AND PVT SERIES

• While the PVS provides a potentially useful tool for classroom screening, the examiner is cautioned to consider several factors that may influence a student's performance, in addition to his or her expressive vocabulary level. These include difficulty in working independently; an inability to recognize pictures, even with initial letter clues; and difficulty with spelling or writing. In many heterogeneous classrooms, more children may fall below the 10th percentile than can be tested individually. As the authors state, the PVS is a screening test and should be interpreted with caution. The PVS should not be considered an assessment of written vocabulary.

• The quality of the picture stimuli is uneven. In addition, many of the items require a knowledge of geography (map locations), or history (pictures of Presidents). Such items seem to reflect curriculum experiences rather than basic vocabulary.

• Although the initial letter is generally a helpful clue in eliciting the correct labels, sometimes the initial letter requires more sophisticated knowledge of phonics or spelling than one would expect at this grade level being tested (e.g., wrench).

- The authors recommend annual assessment, but no alternate forms are provided.

- Although the PVT has norms from ages 2-1/2 through 39 years, the authors call attention to the fact that there are significantly fewer adults included in the standardization sample, and normative data above 12th grade should be used cautiously (Manual, p. 30).

- The case examples described in the manual involve the administration of the Visual Motor Integration Test (VMI–3R, p. 137), also authored by Beery. The examples demonstrate how poor handwriting on the PVS would suggest the administration of the VMI or, conversely, how difficulty with instructions on the VMI might suggest an oral vocabulary problem. It is not clear if the VMI is part of the Beery PVS and PVT "series." Also, the Integrated Writing Test is mentioned but never discussed.

Preschool Language Scale–3 (PLS–3)

I. L. Zimmerman, V. G. Steiner and R. E. Pond
The Psychological Corporation, 1969, 1979, 1992
555 Academic Court, San Antonio, TX 78204-2498

Purpose	To assess receptive and expressive language skills in young children
Major Areas Tested	Receptive and expressive language Precursors of language
Age or Grade Range	Birth through 6 years, 11 months
Usually Given By	Speech/language clinicians Special education teachers Psychologists
Type of Test	Standardized Individual Criterion-referenced Norm-referenced
Scores Obtained	Age equivalent Percentiles Standard scores
Student Performance Timed?	No
Testing Time	15–40 minutes
Scoring/Interpretation Time	10–30 minutes
Normed On	1,200 children with normally developing language were included in the 40-state sample. Sample was stratified on the basis of mother's education, geographic region, and race, reflecting the 1980 U.S. Census
Alternate Forms Available?	No

FORMAT

The Preschool Language Scale–3 (PLS–3) is the latest edition of the popular Preschool Language Scale first published in 1969. The PLS–3, while maintaining the general format, has increased its content by adding tasks that target social interactive communication and integrative thinking skills. The test is normed on a nationwide sample and supplementary features are added to aid the examiner. The materials for the PLS–3 include an examiner's manual, a full-color picture manual, individual record forms, and the following items, supplied by the examiner:

- a 6-inch-by-9-inch square of cellophane
- a 6–12-inch teddy bear
- a tennis ball
- a shoe box
- 3 metal keys on a key ring
- 3 plastic spoons and cups
- a child's sock
- 8 one-inch cube blocks
- a watch with a second hand

The PLS–3 is a developmental inventory that contains two scales, Auditory Comprehension and Expressive Communication. Each scale consists of 12 subscales that cover 6-month periods, from birth through 4 years, and 12-month periods from 5 through 7 years. Each subscale includes 8 items, 4 receptive and 4 expressive. The items assess the following areas in both the receptive and expressive modes: vocabulary, concepts of quality, quantity, space and time, morphology, syntax, and integrative thinking skills. In addition, the early subscales assess precursors to language, including attention, vocal development, and social communication skills.

Typically, the Auditory Comprehension Scale is administered first, beginning with tasks one year below the child's chronological age. A basal is obtained when a child passes three consecutive items. Testing continues until a ceiling of five consecutive zero scores is reached. Basal and ceiling procedures are well described in the manual. The expressive Communication Scale is then administered in the same manner.

Items are quite varied. Some require observation of the child's responses, such as the one-year-old's ability to maintain attention to toys for two minutes. Some items require manipulation of blocks to show understanding of prepositions or concepts of quantity. Expressive items may require labeling, describing, or defining. All responses are recorded on the individual record form. Scores are composed by totaling the number of the correct responses for each scale, Auditory Comprehension and Expressive Communication. These two scores are summed to obtain a total test score. These raw scores are then converted to standard scores, percentiles, and age equivalents by using the tables provided in the manual.

STRENGTHS OF THE PLS–3

- The PLS–3 is a comprehensive assessment of receptive and expressive language in young children. The test is well conceptualized and well organized. The authors have provided many features that reflect their understanding of assessment of children in this age range. These features include flexibility in seating and in the order in which tests may be administered, the use of basal and ceiling procedures to shorten testing time, and the use of objects as well as pictures in administration.
- The manual includes a thoughtful section on "considerations when testing young children."
- The PLS–3 provides several optional supplemental features that enhance its usefulness. These include:

1. *Articulation Screener for ages 2.6–6.11 years.* In less than five minutes, the examiner can screen single consonants and blends in initial, final, and medial positions to determine if the child's articulation is age appropriate or needs further evaluation.

2. *Language Sample Checklist.* This checklist provides a structure that the examiner can use to note characteristics of the child's spontaneous speech during testing. Such features as pronouns, and plurals (morphology/syntax), words denoting time and quantity (semantics), and conversational skills (social language) can be noted, adding to the richness of the interpretation of test performance. In addition, the examiner can calculate a mean length of utterance and rate overall intelligibility. The information from the Language Sample Checklist is described as either "reinforcing information obtained on PLS–3," or "differing greatly from information obtained on the PLS–3," adding another dimension to the test results.

3. *Family Information and Suggestions* provide information on the family, medical history, and the family's view of the child's hearing, comprehension, and communication skills. This interview form not only provides important information about the child, but also involves the family concretely in the evaluation, thus increasing the usefulness of the assessment process.

- The PLS–3 provides important information on the assessment of hearing impaired children. While auditory trainers and signing can be used to administer the test, examiners are encouraged to be sensitive to the cautions described in the manual.
- The addition of tasks which target social interactive communication is an important feature.

LIMITING FACTORS OF THE PLS–3

- While the PLS–3 uses manipulative objects for the test items through the 2 years 5 months level, after that all items on the Auditory Comprehension Scale use only picture stimuli. Many 3 year olds and older preschoolers who are functioning at the 2–3 year level could be assessed more easily with manipulative objects. Also, on the Expressive Language Scale, six consecutive items at the 3-year-old level are only oral questions with no picture or object prompts. "Difficult-to-test" children often have difficulty maintaining attention during this portion of the test. Examiners may choose to vary the sequence, so that the child does not reach a ceiling.

- The PLS–3 total test score is simply an average of the Auditory Comprehension and Expressive Language Scales and adds no new information. It should not be reported if the scale scores vary widely.

Test of Word Knowledge (TOWK)

Elizabeth Wiig and Wayne Secord
The Psychological Corporation, 1992
555 Academic Court, San Antonio, TX 78204-2498

Purpose	To assess the semantic or meaning system of language, both receptively and expressively
Major Areas Tested	Vocabulary and word knowledge
Age or Grade Range	5–17 years (norm-referenced); 17 years + (criterion-referenced)
Usually Given By	Speech and language clinicians Psychologists Special education teachers
Type of Test	Standardized Individual Norm-referenced
Scores Obtained	Standard scores Percentiles Age equivalents Normal-curve equivalents Age equivalent
Student Performance Timed?	No
Testing Time	30–60 minutes
Scoring/Interpretation Time	25–30 minutes
Normed On	1,570 individuals in a national random sample stratified by age, parent education level, geographic region, race, and sex. Special education students in the regular classroom were included in the sample. Sample characteristics matched to the 1980 Census Report.
Alternate Forms Available?	No

FORMAT

The Test of Word Knowledge (TOWK) is a comprehensive test for assessing the semantic level of language, including receptive and expressive vocabulary, opposites, synonyms, definitions, and multiple contexts.

The materials for the TOWK consist of the Examiner's Manual, the Stimulus Manual, and individual record forms. While the Stimulus Manual includes the visual stimuli for all subtests, the Examiner's Manual includes information on test development, administration, scoring procedures, and technical characteristics of the test. The TOWK consists of eight subtests divided into two age levels: Level 1 for ages 5–8 years and Level 2 for ages 8–17 years. Each level has four core subtests, two that measure receptive skills and two that measure expressive skills. In addition, core tests for one level may be used as supplementary tests for the other level.

TOWK SUBTEST CONFIGURATION

Level 1 Referential–Relational Aspects

Core Subtests
> Expressive Vocabulary
> Receptive Vocabulary
> Word Opposites–Receptive
> Word Definitions–Expressive

Supplementary Subtest
> Synonyms (ages 6–8 only) Receptive

Level 2–Relational and Metalinguistic Aspects

Core Subtests
> Word Definitions–Expressive
> Synonyms–Receptive
> Multiple Contexts–Expressive
> Figurative Usage–Receptive

Supplementary Subtests
> Expressive Vocabulary
> Receptive Vocabulary
> Word Opposites–Receptive
> Conjunction and Transition Words–Receptive

Following the completion of the core subtests, supplementary subtests may be given. The basal/ceiling procedure is well defined both in the Examiner's Manual and on the Record Form.

TOWK SUBTESTS

1. *Expressive Vocabulary.* Student is shown a black-and-while line drawing. The examiner then asks such questions as, "What is this? (magnet), What is this place called? (gym/gymnasium)," and "What is the name of this person's job? (jeweler)." The *Expressive Vocabulary* is a core test for Level 1 and a Supplementary Test for Level 2. Over the entire 32 items, 22 nouns and 10 verbs are named.

2. *Receptive Vocabulary.* The student is shown a page with four drawings and asked to point to the word named by the examiner ("acrobat, purchasing, luminous"). *Receptive Vocabulary* is a core test for Level 1 and a Supplementary Test for Level 2. Nouns, verbs, and modifiers are assessed.

3. *Word Opposites.* The student's page includes four items: *on, around, off*, and *above*. The examiner points to the item and says, "What is the opposite of *on: around, off,* or *above?*" *Word Opposites* is a core test for Level 1 and a Supplementary Test for Level 2. Nouns, verbs, and modifiers are assessed.

4. *Word Definitions.* The student's page includes four words. The examiner points to each word and says, "Tell me what _____ means (bus, nephew, atlas, gavel). Remember to tell me what it means and some things about it." A specific cue may be given to elicit an expanded response. *Word Definitions* is a core subtest for both Levels 1 and 2. Only nouns are included.

5. *Synonyms.* The student's page includes five items: *defend, agree, protect, inspect*, and *boast*. The examiner points to an item and says, "The word at the top is *defend*. Now I will read the choices under it. Tell me the word that means the same as *defend*." *Synonyms* is a core test for Level 2 and a Supplementary Subtest for Level 1. Nouns, verbs, and modifiers are included.

6. *Multiple Contexts.* The student's page includes 4 words. The examiner reads each word and asks the student, "Tell me two things each word can mean (fish, limb, bound, shady)." *Multiple contexts* is a core subtest for Level 2.

7. *Figurative Usage.* The student's page has two items such as the following example:

Which one tells about hurting someone who has hurt you?
> a. getting over it
> b. getting yourself together
> c. getting even
> d. getting lost

The examiner says, "Now I will show you some phrases and choices. Listen to me read them and tell me which one answers the question." *Figurative Usage* is a core subtest for Level 2.

8. *Conjunctions and Transition Words.* The student's page includes two items like the one below.

My father always keeps a spare tire in the trunk of our car (   ) we have a flat tire.

even if	in case
as if	while

The examiner reads the item and the choices and asks the student which word goes in the blank space. *Conjunctions and Transitions Words* is a supplementary Test for Level 2.

Subtests are scored according to directions in the examiner's manual. Raw scores are converted into subtest standard scores and percentiles. Receptive and expressive sub-tests are combined into a Receptive Composite and an Expressive Composite, which are in turn combined into a total score. Two difference scores can be computed; a comparison of Receptive/Expressive Vocabulary and a comparison of the Receptive/Expressive Composites.

STRENGTHS OF THE TOWK

• The TOWK is a comprehensive assessment of the semantic features of oral language, both receptive and expressive. The addition of the supplementary subtests to the core battery at each age level is a very helpful feature. The authors are very knowledgeable about language development and have created a useful evaluation tool. The rationale and theoretical models for the TOWK are well described in the manual, and provide support for the use of the TOWK across the wide age range for which it is normed.

• The TOWK uses a consistent method of presentation for all subtests; the student sees the printed stimulus (pictures or words) while the examiner reads or describes the task allowed. This combined visual–verbal presentation reduces the auditory memory load and does not penalize the child with poor reading skills.

• Each subtest is carefully designed to include words that are appropriate and interesting to the age level being tested. Subtest difficulty is increased, not only by the use of more difficult words, but by increasing the number of choices on multiple-choice items.

• While student responses are simply scored right or wrong on seven subtests, on *Word Definitions*, two points are given for qualitatively better answers. Scoring procedures are clearly explained.

• Helpful guidelines for deciding whether the 8-year-old student should be given Level 1 or 2 of the TOWK are included. The examiner is asked to consider reading skills, cognitive level, and the presence or absence of an identified language disorder.

• The standardization population of the TOWK is well described in the manual and approximates the 1980 Census data. Validity and reliability studies of the TOWK are also reported and support the technical characteristics of the test.

LIMITING FACTORS OF THE TOWK

• Given the comprehensive nature of the TOWK, more guidelines for the interpretation of TOWK patterns are needed to increase the usefulness of the test for determining a student's need for language therapy and the components of that therapy program. The sharing of case examples illustrating the interpretation of a Receptive/Expressive Vocabulary discrepancy and a Receptive/ Expressive Composite score discrepancy is needed.

• The authors state that the TOWK can be used as a criterion-referenced measure of semantic skills for older individuals (Manual, p.1). However, no discussion of the use of the test with older students or young adults is provided.

• Norms are reported for yearly intervals from ages 5 to 13; however, due to "little growth" between the ages of 14 and 17, normative data were pooled for those years. More discussion of this finding would be helpful given the authors effort to design subtests that would reflect the developmental changes in adolescent language. The TOWK is a relatively new test and its use in the field will determine its validity with this age group.

Test of Adolescent and Adult Language–Third Edition (TOAL–3)

Donald D. Hammill, Virginia L. Brown, Stephen C. Larsen, and J. Lee Wiederholt
PRO-ED, 1980; revised 1987; revised 1994
8700 Shoal Creek Blvd., Austin, TX 78757-6897

Purpose	To provide a norm-referenced measure of language proficiency in adolescents and young adults
Major Areas Tested	Receptive and expressive language, spoken and written
Age or Grade Range	12–24 years
Usually Given By	Classroom teacher Special education teacher Speech/language clinician Psychologist Any trained person
Type of Test	Group Individual Standardized Norm-referenced
Scores Obtained	Scaled Percentile Standard
Student Performance Timed?	No
Testing Time	1–3 hours
Scoring/Interpretation Time	20–30 minutes
Normed On	3,056 persons residing in 26 states; sample balanced for gender, residence, race, ethnicity, geographic area, and post-secondary status, according to Statistical Abstract of the U.S. Census Bureau, 1990
Alternate Forms Available?	No

FORMAT

The original Test of Adolescent Language was developed in 1980 and revised in 1987. The newest edition (TOAL-3) is renamed The Test of Adolescent and Adult Language. In addition to strengthening the test's technical characteristics, the authors have extended the norms to include 18 through 24 years. This makes the test more useful to examiners assessing students in post-secondary settings.

The format of the TOAL-3 is identical to that of the TOAL-2. The materials consist of a manual, individual answer booklets, student booklets of test materials, and individual student profile sheets. Using a three-dimensional model, the authors have developed eight subtests to measure synaptic and semantic features of receptive and expressive language in spoken and written form.

I. *Listening/Vocabulary* (35 items). The student selects two pictures that are related to a stimulus word. (For example, both *tree* and *part of the hand* are related to *palm*). This is a variation on the Peabody Picture Vocabulary Test–Revised and the Test of Language Development-Primary that reduces guessing and taps a student's knowledge of more than one meaning for a word.

II. *Listening/Grammar* (35 items). The examiner reads three statements, and the student selects two with essentially the same meaning.

A. *Ask Jack to bring it here.*
B. *Tell Jack to bring it here*
C. *Ask Jack what to bring here.*

III. *Speaking/Vocabulary* (25 items). The student uses each vocabulary word in a meaningful sentence (*canoe, horizon, excavate*).

IV. *Speaking/Grammar* (30 sentences). The student repeats each sentence exactly as spoken by the examiner. Sentences increase in complexity and length.

He won't play with me, but I like him anyway.

Carol has a copy of their new album, which should turn platinum very soon if it proves to be as popular as their last one. (See CELF–R.)

V. *Reading/Vocabulary* (30 items). The student reads three stimulus words that are related in some way (*red, green, blue*) and then selects from a group of four (*yellow, circle, orange, light*) the two words that are related to the stimulus words. Both responses must be correct. (See Test of Reading Comprehension.)

VI. *Reading/Grammar* (25 items). The student reads five sentences and selects the two that are most nearly alike in meaning.

A. *Sam plays.*
B. *Sam will not play.*
C. *Sam played.*
D. *Sam is playing.*
E. *Sam is going to play.*

Both responses must be correct. (See Test of Reading Comprehension.)

VII. *Writing/Vocabulary* (30 words). The student uses each word in a written sentence.

VIII. *Writing/Grammar* (30 items). The student reads two or more sentences and combines them into a single written sentence.

Jack went to work every day.
He didn't like to go.
He needed the money.

Typically, all eight subtests are administered to an individual student using the basal/ceiling procedures described in the manual. Alternately, groups of students may

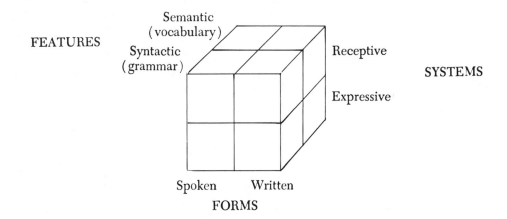

TOAL–3 Three-Dimensional Model

be given all subtests, except Speaking/Vocabulary and Speaking/Grammar, which are given individually. Upon completion of the test, raw scores for each subtest are converted to scaled scores with a mean of 10 and a standard deviation of 3. This information is plotted on the subtest profile. Subtests are then combined into composite scaled scores with a mean of 100 and a standard deviation of 15. The sum of all eight subtests represents a student's overall language proficiency. A table in the manual allows the conversion of scaled scores to percentiles, stanines, and standard scores.

No grade or age equivalents are provided, because the skills assessed on the TOAL–3 are not grade- or age-specific.

STRENGTHS OF THE TOAL–3

• The manual includes an excellent discussion of "testing the limits," that is, following-up a students's performance with probing questions to determine the nature of his or her errors or to recognize how the student would perform if the subtest was modified. The annotated bibliography of curriculum texts in language arts skills is also very helpful.

• A software scoring system is available which generates percentiles and standard scores for subtests and composites. By inputting data from cognitive tests, ability–achievement discrepancies can be determined. A lengthy report is also generated as well as a one-page summary of scores.

Section VIII. Profile of Composite Quotients and Other Test Scores

%iles	GENERAL LANGUAGE	MODES				FORMS		FEATURES		SYSTEMS		OTHER TEST SCORES:	1.	2.	3.	4.	5.	QUOTIENTS
		LISTENING	SPEAKING	READING	WRITING	SPOKEN LANGUAGE	WRITTEN LANGUAGE	VOCABULARY	GRAMMER	RECEPTIVE LANGUAGE	EXPRESSIVE LANGUAGE							
>99	•	•	•	•	•	•	•	•	•	•	•		•	•	•	•	•	150
>99	•	•	•	•	•	•	•	•	•	•	•		•	•	•	•	•	145
>99	•	•	•	•	•	•	•	•	•	•	•		•	•	•	•	•	140
99	•	•	•	•	•	•	•	•	•	•	•		•	•	•	•	•	135
98	•	•	•	•	•	•	•	•	•	•	•		•	•	•	•	•	130
95	•	•	•	•	•	•	•	•	•	•	•		•	•	•	•	•	125
91	•	•	•	•	•	•	•	•	•	•	•		•	•	•	•	•	120
84	•	•	•	•	•	•	•	•	•	•	•		•	•	•	•	•	115
75	•	•	•	•	•	•	•	•	•	•	•		•	•	•	•	•	110
63	•	•	•	•	•	•	•	•	•	•	•		•	•	•	•	•	105
50	—	—	—	—	—	—	—	—	—	—	—		—	—	—	—	—	100
37	•	•	•	•	•	•	•	•	•	•	•		•	•	•	•	•	95
25	•	•	•	•	•	•	•	•	•	•	•		•	•	•	•	•	90
16	•	•	•	•	•	•	•	•	•	•	•		•	•	•	•	•	85
9	•	•	•	•	•	•	•	•	•	•	•		•	•	•	•	•	80
5	•	•	•	•	•	•	•	•	•	•	•		•	•	•	•	•	75
2	•	•	•	•	•	•	•	•	•	•	•		•	•	•	•	•	70
1	•	•	•	•	•	•	•	•	•	•	•		•	•	•	•	•	65
<1	•	•	•	•	•	•	•	•	•	•	•		•	•	•	•	•	60
<1	•	•	•	•	•	•	•	•	•	•	•		•	•	•	•	•	55

- The Writing Vocabulary subtest may be used as a screening test. The subtest may be given to a group of students, and the remaining subtests given to those students who obtain a scaled score of 7 or lower.

- The manual contains excellent suggestions for conveying test results to secondary and post-secondary students.

- The TOAL-3 does not include age and grade scores, as the skills being assessed are not age or grade related and have little meaning when applied to adolescents and young adults.

LIMITING FACTORS OF THE TOAL–3

- While the TOAL-3 assesses many aspects of language functioning, there are several areas which are not assessed, including comprehension of paragraphs, word analogies,

and language usage (pragmatics). The authors caution examiners that the TOAL-3 should not be used as the total measure of a student's language skills.

- The TOAL-3 is described as a tool for measuring progress; however, alternate forms for this purpose are not provided.

- Little attention is given in the manual to interpretation of different subtest and composite profiles. Inclusion of several examples of student performance would be helpful.

- The TOAL-3 was designed for use with young adults in 4-year colleges, 2-year community colleges, or vocational certificate programs, and the sample for the 18–24.11 age range was gathered from that population. Results of the TOAL-3 with other young adults should be interpreted cautiously.

Test of Language Development–Primary, Second Edition (TOLD–P–2)

Phyllis L. Newcomer and Donald D. Hammill
PRO-ED, 1977, 1982, 1988
8700 Shoal Creek Blvd., Austin, TX 78757-6897

Purpose	To identify children below their peers in language proficiency, to identify specific strengths and weaknesses, to document progress, and to provide a measuring device in research
Major Areas Tested	Receptive and expressive language
Age or Grade Range	4–9 years
Usually Given By	Classroom teacher Counselor Psychologist Special education teacher Speech/language clinician
Type of Test	Standardized Individual Norm-referenced
Scores Obtained	Percentile Standard
Student Performance Timed?	No
Testing Time	30–60 minutes
Scoring/Interpretation Time	15–20 minutes
Normed On	2,436 children in 29 states aged 4–8 years; sample balanced for sex, urban/rural residence, race, ethnicity, parental occupation, and geographic region
Alternate Forms Available?	No

FORMAT

The TOLD-2-Primary (TOLD-2-P) is a revised edition of the TOLD-P. There are no substantial changes in format or content over the 1982 edition. Six hundred children were added to the norming sample.

The TOLD-2-Primary is an individually administered test for assessing language proficiency, both receptive and expressive. The age range for which the test is normed is 4.0–8.11 years. The TOLD-2-Intermediate extends the theoretical model through age 13.

The materials for the TOLD-2-P are a test manual, answer sheets, and a picture book containing picture stimuli for three subtests. The TOLD-2-P has seven subtests, all of which are identical or similar to other language tests. The tests were designed to assess three linguisitc features, Semantics, Syntax, and Phonology in both the receptive and expressive language systems.

TOLD-2-P Subtest Organization

Linguistic Features	Linguistic Systems	
	Listening Subtests	Speaking Subtests
Semantics	Picture Vocabulary	Oral Vocabulary Sentence Imitation
Syntax	Grammatic Understanding	Grammatic Completion
Phonology	Word Discrimination	Word Articulation

I. *Picture Vocabulary* (35 items). From a group of four pictures, the student selects the one picture, that best illustrates the meaning of a word pronounced by the examiner. (See Peabody Picture Vocabulary Test–Revised.)

II. *Oral Vocabulary* (30 words). The student defines each word. (See Wechsler Intelligence Scale for Children–Revised, Vocabulary subtest.)

III. *Grammatic Understanding* (25 items). From three pictures, the student selects one that represents a spoken sentence. (See Test for Auditory Comprehension of Language.)

IV. *Sentence Imitation* (30 sentences). The student repeats each sentence, which emphasizes appropriate word order and morphology. (See Detroit Tests of Learning Aptitude.)

V. *Grammatic Completion* (30 items). The examiner reads a sentence, and the student completes the sentence by supplying a grammatically correct word. Example: *The doll belongs to me. It is _____ .* (See Illinois Test of

Psycholinguistic Abilities.)

VI. *Word Discrimination* (20 word pairs). The student identifies the words in each pair pronounced by the examiner as being the same or different. (See Wepman Auditory Discrimination Test.)

VII. *Word Articulation* (20 items). The student pronounces each pictured item, which contains key sounds. (See Templin-Darley Test of Articulation.)

All seven subtests are given in the order outlined. All subtests begin with the first item and are discontinued when the student makes five consecutive errors. A raw score representing the number of correct responses on each subtest is converted into percentiles and standard scores (mean 10, standard deviation 3). In keeping with the publisher's philosophy, no language age scores are provided. Subtest scores are combined into five composites, or quotients, representing the linguistic features and systems of the TOLD-2-P. These quotients have a mean of 100 and a standard deviation of 15.

TOLD-2-P Subtests and Composite Quotients

Composite Quotient	Subtests
Spoken Language	Sum of all subtest standard scores
Listening (LiQ)	Picture Vocabulary Grammatic Understanding
Speaking (SpQ)	Oral Vocabulary Sentence Imitation Grammatic Completion
Semantics (SeQ)	Picture Vocabulary Oral Vocabulary
Syntax (SyQ)	Grammatic Understanding Sentence Imitation Grammatic Completion

STRENGTHS OF THE TOLD-2-P

• The TOLD-2-P manual is very comprehensive and well written. In addition to information on the theoretical model, administration and scoring procedures, guidelines to interpretation, and technical data, it presents excellent discussions on important topics. The definitions of linguistic features are very clearly written. Discussions of "testing the limits" of the test, establishing local norms, and meaningful differences between composite scores are particularly helpful.

• Although the age range for the TOLD-2-P is 4–9 years, older students with delayed language skills can also be assessed with the test to obtain helpful information about their language development. Of course, for students out of the age range, scores should not be reported.

• The TOLD-2-P has two other very helpful features. The abbreviated version, or short form, consists of two subtests, Picture Vocabulary and Grammatic Completion. This screening procedure yields a quotient, and norms are provided in the manual.

In the event that a subtest becomes invalidated due to environmental conditions or examiner error, norms are provided which allow a total test score to be calculated from 6 subtests. This is a helpful procedure when testing young children and is well described in the manual.

• No language ages are provided in this edition of the TOLD-2-P; however, a process for deriving a language age score, should it be required for eligibility into special education, is provided in the manual.

• Pro Score Systems is a computer program which allows examiners to score the test quickly and, by inputting cognitive test results, to determine an achievement-ability discrepancy. Pro Score Systems can be purchased for Apple or IBM Personal Computers.

• The TOLD-2-P authors recognize the necessity for assessing non-verbal abilities in students with poor language skills. The manual suggests several instruments for this assessment.

• Reliability statistics, both internal consistency and test-retest studies, are strong for all subtests (with the exception of Grammatic Understanding) and for all composite scores.

• Extensive studies in support of the TOLD–P–2's validity are reported in the manual.

• *A Consumer's Guide to Tests in Print* (Hammill, Bryant, and Brown, 1992) recommends the TOLD–P–2 for its technical characteristics.

LIMITING FACTORS OF THE TOLD-2-P

• Although the TOLD-2-P assesses many areas of language, no assessment of pragmatics or social language is included.

• There are no significant changes between the 1982 and 1988 versions of the TOLD-2-P. The subtests are identical except that additional items have been added to some subtests, and 600 subjects have been added to the norms. Grammatic Understanding, the weakest subtest in terms of reliability, has not been changed.

• One change in testing procedures is noted. The phonology subtests were optional and not recommended for children above 6 years. In the TOLD-2-P they are not described as optional; no explanation is given for this change. The rationale of including them in the total test score is questionable.

• The TOLD-2-P typically provides one item as an example at the beginning of each subtest. No provisions are given for teaching the concept or otherwise ensuring the student's understanding. The concept of Grammatic Completion can be confusing for young children, especially when no picture cues are provided.

• The directions for scoring Oral Vocabulary are different from those usually applied to vocabulary tests. Students are given one point either for a precise definition (*ice = frozen water*) or for two less descriptive characteristics (*it's cold; you skate on it; ice cubes for drinks*). Examiners need to study the procedures carefully.

• Although one purpose of the TOLD-2-P is to provide a measure of progress, the lack of alternate forms does not support this use of the test.

Test of Language Development–Intermediate, Second Edition (TOLD–I–2)

Phyllis L. Newcomer and Donald D. Hammill
PRO-ED, 1977, 1982, 1988
8700 Shoal Creek Blvd., Austin, TX 78757-6897

Purpose	To identify children below their peers in language proficiency, to specify their strengths and weaknesses, to document progress, and to provide a measuring device for research
Major Areas Tested	Receptive and expressive language
Age or Grade Range	8 1/2–13 years
Usually Given By	Classroom teacher Counselor Psychologist Special education teacher Speech/language clinician
Type of Test	Standardized Individual Norm-referenced
Scores Obtained	Percentile Standard
Student Performance Timed?	No
Testing Time	30–60 minutes
Scoring/Interpretation Time	15–20 minutes
Normed On	1,214 children in 21 states aged 8 1/2–13 years; sample balanced for sex, urban/rural residence, race, ethnicity, parental occupation, and geographic region
Alternate Forms Available?	No

FORMAT

The TOLD-2-Intermediate (TOLD-2-I) is the revised edition of the 1982 TOLD-I. Several changes in subtests have been made, and 471 subjects were added to the norms.

The intermediate form of the TOLD-2 is for students 8 years, 6 months to 12 years, 11 months. The materials consist of the manual and answer sheet. There are no picture materials. While the theoretical model for the Intermediate form is the same as for the TOLD-2-P, six different subtests have been devised to assess receptive and expressive linguistic systems. No phonology tests are included as children over six years of age have already incorporated most phonological abilities in their language.

TOLD-2-I Intermediate Subtest Organization

Linguistic Features	Linguistic Systems	
	Listening Subtests	Speaking Subtests
Semantics	Vocabulary Malapropisms	Generals
Syntax	Grammatic Com- prehension	Sentence Combining Word Ordering

I. *Sentence Combining* (25 items). The examiner reads two short sentences orally, and the student combines them into one sentence ("Bill played the game. He got 10 points."). (See TOAL–3, p. 204.)

II. *Vocabulary* (35 items). This subtest presents a unique format for assessing vocabulary. The student listens to pairs of words and decides if they mean the same, have opposite meanings, or are unrelated. For example, *peep* and *glance* are synonyms; *great* and *small* are opposites; and *calico* and *dandelion* are unrelated. A listening task, this subtest requires knowledge of word meanings and relationships.

III. *Word Ordering* (25 series of random words). The examiner reads each series, and the student reorders the words into complete and correct sentences (*spilled the Dad paint was by*). (See CELF–R, p. 178.)

IV. *Generals* (25 items). The student gives the categorical name for groups of three words (*triangle, rectangle, semicircle*).

V. *Grammatic Comprehension* (40 sentences). The examiner reads each sentence, and the student identifies it as grammatically correct or incorrect (*She ate quick.*).

VI. *Malapropisms* (30 items). The examiner reads a sentence and identifies the malapropism, or word which sounds like the appropriate word but has an absurd meaning in this context. The student must identify the incorrect word and correct it (*Father said grapes before dinner.*).

All six subtests are given in the order outlined, following the directions in the manual. A basal/ceiling format is used so that students are tested only over a critical range of items. The number of correct responses on each subtest is converted to percentiles and standard scores. The subtest standard scores are then combined into the composite quotients.

TOLD-2-1 Subtests and Composite Quotients

Composite Quotient	Subtests
Spoken Language (SLQ)	Sum of all subtest standard scores
Listening (LiQ)	Vocabulary Grammatic Comprehension Malapropisms
Speaking (SpQ)	Sentence Combining Word Ordering Generals
Semantics (SeQ)	Vocabulary Generals Malapropisms
Syntax (SyQ)	Sentence Combining Word Ordering Grammatic Comprehension

STRENGTHS OF THE TOLD-2-I

• The TOLD-2-I manual is very comprehensive and well written. It contains helpful discussions of important issues such as "testing the limits" of a test, establishing local norms, and meaningful differences between scores.

• The subtests of the TOLD-2-I can be given individually or in combinations to obtain composite scores. A short form, or language screening, composed of two subtests, Generals and Sentence Combining, is described in the manual. A standard score is provided for this short form.

• Provision is also made for computing a total test score from five subtests in case one is invalidated by examiner error.

• In keeping with the publisher's philosophy, no language age scores are provided. However, a process for deriving a language age, should it be required, is provided in the manual.

• Pro Score Systems, a computer program for scoring and calculating an achievement-ability discrepancy, is available for Apple or IBM personal computers.

• Reliability statistics, both internal consistency and test-retest stability, were high for all composites and all subtests except Oral Vocabulary

• Extensive studies in support of the TOLD–I–2's validity are reported in the manual.

• *A Consumer's Guide to Tests in Print* (Hammill, Bryant, and Brown, 1992) recommends the TOLD–2–I for its technical characteristics.

LIMITING FACTORS OF THE TOLD-2-I

• Although the TOLD-2-I assesses many areas of language, no assessment of pragmatics or the social aspects of language is included.

• Although one of the stated purposes of the test is to assess progress, alternate forms at the TOLD-2-I are not provided.

Test of Word Finding (TWF)

Diane J. Germane
The Riverside Publishing Company, 1986; revised 1989
8420 Bryn Mawr Ave., Chicago, IL 60631

Purpose	To provide a standardized, normed assessment of word finding skills in elementary school children
Major Areas Tested	Accuracy and speed of naming
Age or Grade Range	6.6 to 12.11 years
Usually Given By	Speech/language pathologist Special education teacher Psychologist Reading teacher
Type of Test	Individual Standardized Norm-referenced
Scores Obtained	Standard scores Percentiles
Student Performance Timed?	Yes
Testing Time	20–30 minutes
Scoring/Interpretation Time	20–45 minutes
Normed On	1,200 children in grades 1–6 residing in 18 states. Population was balanced for sex, ethnicity or race, geographic region, community size, and parents' educational level, based on the 1980 U.S. census; students with word finding problems were included in the standardization sample
Alternate Forms Available?	No

FORMAT

The National College of Education Test of Word Finding (TWF) is a standardized individual test of word naming skills in elementary school students. The materials consist of four components: the TWF Test Book, an easel book containing the stimulus items and the examiners' directions; the Response Booklet in which the examiner records the student's responses and scores; the TWF Technical Manual containing discussion of the theoretical model, as well as data on the norming sample, reliability, and validity; and the TWF Administration, Scoring and Interpretation Manual, which includes procedures for administering and scoring the test and interpreting the results and the norms tables. A tape recorder, blank tape, and stopwatch are also needed to administer the test.

The TWF has two forms. The primary form consists of 80 items for students in grades one and two, and the intermediate form has 90 items for grades three through six. Both forms are included in the same Test Book and recorded in the same Response Booklet. The TWF has five sections:

Section 1: *Picture Naming: Nouns*. The first section is the traditional picture naming task. The student is shown a picture which is all or partly colored and is asked to name the colored part. The examiner tape-records Section 1 in order to calculate the student's response time.

Section 2: *Sentence Completion Naming*. In this section, the examiner reads a sentence, asking the student to complete the sentence with one word. (*It's fun to watch the band march in the 4th of July _____ . The yellow part of an egg is a _____ .*)

Only accuracy, not response time, is recorded.

Section 3: *Description Naming*. The examiner reads the student a short description of an object and asks the student to name it. Each description contains three attributes. (*What floats in the sky, may be full of rain, and is gray or white? What is the name of the part of your face below your mouth that is made of bone?*)

Only accuracy of response, not time, is recorded.

Section 4: *Picture Naming: Verbs*. In this section, the student is asked to label an action shown in a picture. The question is always the same, *What is he (she) doing?* Only accuracy is scored.

Section 5: *Picture Naming Categories*. In this section, the student is asked to give the category name for a group of three pictured objects. Only accuracy is scored.

Section 6: *Comprehension Assessment*. Word finding difficulties are defined as an inability to name a word the student clearly understands. In order to assess comprehension of the words a student has made errors on, Section 6 is administered after the first five sections. The student is shown a group of four pictures, one of which is a target word or correct response to a missed item, and is asked to point to the picture named by the examiner. Only items missed by the student are presented in the Comprehension Assessment. If the student demonstrates understanding of the word by pointing to the picture, it is assumed that the error was due to a word finding problem. Section 6 is not scored; it is included to provide information about the student's receptive versus expressive vocabulary.

The TWF should be given in its entirety in the order listed above. There are no basal or ceiling procedures; the student is given all of the items in either the primary or intermediate form.

As the test is being given, the examiner records the student's response as either correct (1) or incorrect (0). For incorrect answers, the student's response is written in. In addition, the examiner notes if the student shows frustration with the naming task by gestures (snapping fingers, facial grimace, etc.) or extra verbalizations (*Uh, I know, I know; tip of my tongue,* etc.) by placing a checkmark in the appropriate column of the Response Booklet. For Section 1, the completion time of the section is also recorded. As Section 6 is being given, the examiner places a checkmark in the yes or no column of the Response Booklet as each target word in error is checked for comprehension.

Standard scores and percentiles can be obtained for each subtest as well as the total test.

In addition to recording the Completion Time for the entire section, two other response times may be calculated for Section 1. The Total Item Response Time (TRT) is obtained by playing back the tape and counting the hundredths of a second between the stimulus presentation and the student's first response on each item. All of the item response times are added to obtain the TRT for each section. The TRT is divided by the number of items to obtain an Average Response Time (ART). The TRT and total accuracy, standard score are then plotted on a grid that describes the student's performance in one of four categories:

Fast and inaccurate namer

Slow and inaccurate namer

Fast and accurate namer

Slow and accurate namer

Additional diagnostic information can be gathered from the Comprehension Assessment, the Gestures and Extra Verbalizations summary, and an analysis of substitution errors. Suggestions for integrating and interpreting all of the data on a student's word finding skills are given in the manual.

STRENGTHS OF THE TWF

• Clinicians have long described student's problems with word-finding. The TWF provides the first systematic standardized procedure for this aspect of spoken language. It fills a great void in the field.

• The Administration, Scoring, and Interpretation Manual is exceptionally well-organized and well-written. The procedures for each part of the administration and scoring processes are clearly described.

• The stimulus materials are attractive, colorful, and unambiguous, essential characteristics for a timed test of word naming.

• The author has included several features that make the test-taking process easier for young or disabled students. These include "starter items" or training items at the beginning of each subtest and the alternation of visual and auditory subtests or sections.

• The use of Section 6 to assess the student's comprehension of the words is a very strong feature of the TWF. It allows the examiner much more information about the student's receptive and expressive language difficulties.

• The author has provided norms for both the primary and the intermediate forms for students in the 8.0–8.5 age range. An examiner can use other information about the student to select the most appropriate form.

• The TWF is a well-standardized, reliable assessment tool. Concurrent and content validity studies support the validity of the test. *A Consumer's Guide to Tests in Print* (Hammill, Bryant, and Brown, 1992) recommends the TWF, based on its technical characteristics.

• The Technical Manual includes a complex description of the theoretical background of the test, its rationale, and construction. Careful procedures were used for item selection.

LIMITING FACTORS OF THE TWF

• The TWF is more difficult to administer than it appears. Examiners need to give several practice tests (the manual suggests five) to insure smooth administration, especially of the timed sections.

• The interpretation section of the manual gives appropriate cautions for not attributing cause to a student's performance; that is, a student does not have word finding problems because he is aphasic. The manual does state that when a student is unable to name a picture, object, etc., which he comprehends (can point to), that error can be assumed to be due to word finding difficulty. This assumption must be used cautiously; for example, the child may be able to "point to medicine" yet not name "medicine" because of cognitive difficulties in supplying categorical names. The inability to answer the object description may be due to poor

auditory memory for a long sentence. The ability to point to something but not name it may be the natural lag between the acquisition of receptive and expressive vocabulary.

• The TWF is a new test. It will be possible to describe its clinical usefulness in a few years.

NOTE

Two companion tests to the TWF are now available for examiners interested in assessing word-finding difficulties. The Test of Adolescent/Adult Word Finding (TAWF, Riverside Publishing Company, 1990) is identical in format to the TWF. The TAWF was normed on 1,753 individuals in a nationwide sample and provides an assessment tool for secondary students and adults, ages 12 to 80 years. The Test of Word Finding in Discourse (TWFD), 1991, provides a format for sampling a child's language using storytelling. The TWFD may be used as a standardized procedure for children, or an informal assessment of older students and adults. The TWFD includes a measure of productivity as well as word finding. In addition to the three tests (TWF, TAWF, and TWFD), a Word Finding Referral Checklist is also available for classroom teachers to use in identifying children who experience word-finding difficulties and may need assessment.

The Word Test–Revised (Elementary) (WORD–R)

Mark Barrett, Rosemary Huisingh, Linda Zachman, Carolyn Blagden, and Jane Orman
LinguiSystems, Inc., 1981; revised 1990
3100 Fourth Ave., East Moline, IL 61244

Purpose	To assess the expressive vocabulary and semantic abilities of school-age children
Major Areas Tested	Expressive vocabulary and semantics
Age or Grade Range	7–12 years
Usually Given By	Speech/language clinician Special education teacher Psychologist
Type of Test	Individual Standardized Norm-referenced
Scores Obtained	Age equivalent Percentile Standard
Student Performance Timed?	No
Testing Time	20–30 minutes
Scoring/Interpretation Time	15 minutes
Normed On	1,359 subjects from 6 states; subjects were randomly selected with consideration for ethnicity, age, gender, and school. Minority populations were included at the rate reported in the 1987 U.S. Census report. All subjects had normally developing language.
Alternate Forms Available?	No

FORMAT

The Word Test–R (Elementary) is the revised edition of the Word Test originally published in 1981. It is an individually-administered assessment of expressive language and semantics. It is designed to measure a child's ability to recognize and express critical semantic features through categorizing, defining, reasoning, and choosing appropriate words.

The materials consist of an examiner's manual and individual score forms. All tasks are administered orally and the student responds orally. The test consists of the following six subtests, each of which has 15 items. Each subtest is given in its entirety to every student regardless of age. Demonstration items are provided to ensure that the student understands the task.

1. *Associations*. The student chooses the one word that does not belong in a group of four words. The student must then explain this choice in terms of the relationship between the other three words. Credit is given separately for a correct word choice and a correct explanation.

doorbell siren light *whistle*
All the rest make noise.

2. *Synonyms*. The student expresses a one-word synonym for each stimulus word.

3. *Semantic Absurdities*. The student explains what is wrong with each stimulus sentence. (*The mother fed the lullaby to the baby.*)

4. *Antonyms*. The student expresses a one-word opposite for each stimulus word.

5. *Definitions*. The student explains the meaning of each stimulus word.

6. *Mutliple Definitions*. The student demonstrates or explains two meanings for each stimulus word. Credit is given only if both meanings are expressed.

pound: weight, English money, place (dog pound), action (hit)

The manual provides specific question probes for use when an appropriate type of response is not obtained from the student. Although the score form contains a sampling of acceptable responses, during the first few times the test is administered, the examiner should refer to the complete list of correct and incorrect or incomplete responses provided in the scoring standards section of the test manual.

Correct responses on all subtests receive one point. Raw scores can be converted to age equivalents, percentiles, and standard scores for each subtest and for the total test.

STRENGTHS OF THE WORD–R

• The Word–R is a well-organized diagnostic instrument that is quick and easy to administer. The manual is clearly written and contains all the necessary information for administration and interpretation of the test. Because the manual provides several examples of acceptable and unacceptable responses for test items, scoring judgments are usually easy to make.

• Clinicians will find The Word–R an excellent adjunct to standardized measures of receptive vocabulary, such as the Peabody Picture Vocabulary Test–Revised. When the level of a student's lexicon is known, judgments about the word recall and retrieval abilities can be aptly made with use of this test. Furthermore, it goes beyond the assessment of vocabulary by providing information about a student's ability to *use* words in the context of categorizing, reasoning, and judging appropriate word usage. These are important linguistic skills to assess, particularly with older students, and the test results can be important in planning both oral and written language-remediation programs.

• The Word–R is designed for students between the ages of 7 and 12 years; however, it can be used with older students if their functional language is within the test norms.

• The Association subtest requires not only a response but a further explanation. This is a helpful measure of a student's semantic ability.

The manual discusses the rationale of the test as well as its development and standardization in user-friendly terms. Features, such as prompting and testing minority students, are also well described. In addition, the manual includes a short but very helpful section on remedial activities for students with weaknesses in specific subtests.

LIMITING FACTORS OF THE WORD–R

• Despite the fact that the authors describe the Word Test–R standardization process as a "extensive, carefully controlled, national standardization procedure" (Manual, p. 65), the standardization sample was not balanced geographically. According to *A Consumer's Guide to Tests in Print* (Hammill, Bryant, and Brown, 1992), the internal consistency of the test is also poor and stability variable. The Definitions and Multiple Definitions are particularly weak in reliability.

The Word Test–Adolescent (WORD–A)

Linda Zachman, Rosemary Huisingh, Mark Barrett, Jane Orman, and Carolyn Blagden
LinguiSystems, Inc. 1989
3100 4th Avenue, East Moline, IL 61244

Purpose	To assess the expressive vocabulary and semantic abilities of secondary students
Major Areas Tested	Expressive vocabulary and semantics
Age or Grade Range	12–17 years
Usually Given By	Speech and language clinicians Special education teachers Psychologists
Type of Test	Individual Standardized Norm-referenced
Scores Obtained	Age equivalents Percentiles Standard scores
Student Performance Timed?	No
Testing Time	25–30 minutes
Scoring/Interpretation Time	15–20 minutes
Normed On	1,042 students from California, Utah, Wisconsin, and Maryland; subjects were randomly selected with consideration of age, gender, and race. Minority students were included in the ratio reported in the 1987 U.S. Census report. Students with language and learning disabilities were excluded from the sample.
Alternate Forms Available?	No

FORMAT

The Word Test–Adolescent (The Word–A) was designed to assess vocabulary and semantic skills in the adolescent population. While The Word–A is similar in format to its predecessor, The Word–R (Elementary), administration procedures are somewhat different, and the subtests are quite different in content. The materials for The Word–A consist of the examiner's manual and individual score forms. The manual, in addition to providing rationale, administration, and scoring procedures and the technical characteristics of the test, also includes the stimulus items for the subtests.

The Word–A is administered in its entirety to each student. The four subtests are administered verbally by the examiner and all student responses are oral. Visual stimuli are presented to accompany the examiner's verbal questions enabling the adolescent to both see and hear each item.

The Word–A Subtests

1. *Brand Names*. The student is given a brand name and is asked to explain why the descriptive name of the product or company is appropriate. (*Sunkist is the name of a juice. Why is that a good name for a juice?*)

2. *Synonyms*. The examiner shows the student a printed sentence and reads it; the student is asked to give a synonym for the stimulus word. (*Tell me another word for* crucial *in the sentence "Are vitamins crucial to your health?"*)

3. *Signs of the Times*. The student is shown a common sign and asked, "What does it mean?" and "Why is it important?" The student must answer both questions correctly to receive credit for the item.

4. *Definitions*. The student is asked to explain the meaning of words such as *legible* and *recruit*.

Demonstration items are provided for each subtest to ensure that the student understands the task. Specific directions are given regarding appropriate probes when a student's answer is incomplete. A key to acceptable responses is printed on the score form and more detailed examples are provided in the manual. Correct responses on all subtest items receive one point; raw scores are converted to age equivalents, percentiles, and standard scores for each subtest and the total test.

STRENGTHS OF THE WORD–A

• The authors of The Word–A clearly understand the clinical features of adolescent language. The vignettes of a student described in the Introduction (Manual, p. 9) and their description of the "speech and written language of these adolescents is shallow, nondescriptive, and unimaginative," is familiar to all speech and language pathologists and special education professionals. The Word–A tasks developed for each subtest provide an interesting and revealing picture of language in adolescents with language disabilities.

• The Word–A is a well-organized diagnostic instrument that is interesting to students and quick and easy to administer. The manual is clear and has been written in a manner that is easily understood by special education professionals.

• The addition of visual stimuli to accompany the oral questions for each item eliminates factors such as memory or reading ability and enables the results of The Word–A to be analyzed in terms of vocabulary and semantics, rather than auditory processing skills.

• The addition of the unique subtests *Brand Names* and *Signs of the Times* to accompany the more traditional skills of *Definitions* and *Synonyms* allows the assessment of adolescent language skills in both school-related tasks and real-life situations.

• The manual contains a brief but helpful section on remediation activities to develop the language skills of adolescents who demonstrate weaknesses on various subtests of The Word–A.

• The study design for The WORD–A included

1. an item pool study (554 subjects) to select the most discriminating and most age-progressive test items

2. a contrasted groups validity study (274 subjects) that found significant differences (.01 level) between normal and language-disordered subjects at each age level for each task and the total test.

LIMITING FACTORS OF THE WORD–A

• The standardization sample of The Word–A is limited to students from four states. There were no specific racial or economic restrictions placed on the standardization sample. However, the sampling procedures were designed to ensure adequate representation of minority populations in accordance with the most recent national census data. Although unstated in the manual, the test authors confirm that minority students were included from all sites in the study. Test–retest reliability for total test scores is good, but lower for individual subtests. *A Consumer's Guide to Tests in Print* (Hammill, Bryant, and Brown, 1992) gives The WORD–A a "not recommended rating."

Test of Problem Solving–Revised (TOPS–R)

Linda Zachman, Rosemary Huisingh, Mark Barrett, Jane Oman, Carolyn Lo Giudice
LinguiSystems, Inc., 1994
3100 4th Avenue, East Moline, IL 61244

Purpose	To assess problem solving and critical thinking for elementary students
Major Areas Tested	Critical-thinking skills including clarifying, analyzing, generating solutions, evaluating, and affective thinking
Age or Grade Range	6–11 years
Usually Given By	Speech and language pathologists Special education diagnosticians Psychologists
Type of Test	Individual Standardized Norm-referenced
Scores Obtained	Age equivalents Percentiles Standard scores
Student Performance Timed?	No
Testing Time	30–40 minutes
Scoring/Interpretation Time	10–15 minutes
Normed on	1,578 students from California, Florida, Wisconsin, Connecticut, and Texas. Students were randomly selected to match the latest census data with regard to race, sex, and age.
Alternate Forms Available?	No

FORMAT

The Test of Problem Solving–Revised (TOPS–R) is a completely revised edition of the widely used TOPS, which was first published in 1984. It is designed to assess critical thinking abilities based on a student's language strategies. The TOPS–R materials consist of a picture booklet, which uses photographs of real-life situations; response forms; and an examiner's manual, which describes the test rationale, administration and scoring procedures, and technical characteristics of the test.

The 72-item test is presented in its entirety to each student. The student is shown a photograph and asked a series of questions about it. Answers are scored according to the scoring standards presented on the response form and in the manual. Each correct response receives one point. The stimulus pictures have been selected to reflect real-life situations and to include such high-interest topics as rescue from a flood, a foot race, a hitchhiker, and a basketball game. Questions are designed to evoke several types of critical thinking. For example, for the picture of the basketball game, the questions include:

- What is teamwork?
- No one wants this boy on their team. Why?
- Why do these kids respect their coach?
- What other kinds of activities can you do on a team?

Correct responses are added to obtain a total TOPS–R score, which is then converted to an age equivalency, percentile, and standard score.

STRENGTHS OF THE TOPS–R

- The TOPS–R is an easily administered test that provides information about the level of a student's verbal reasoning and problem-solving skills. The photographs are interesting and easily interpreted by children, and they usually elicit the response desired.
- The TOPS–R was standardized on more than 1,500 students selected from five states in different parts of the country, randomly selected to match latest census data with regard to race, sex, age, and school. Reliability and validity studies are reported in the manual.
- In addition to the test itself, the TOPS–R includes a 21-item Classroom Problem Solving Scale, which is completed by the classroom teacher before or after the TOPS–R is administered. Questions such as, "Compared to classmates, the student considers other's ideas and viewpoints," or "can change his opinion, given reasons or evidence," are rated on a three-point scale. Means and standard deviations for each age group are provided in the manual.
- The TOPS–R provides a total test score rather than a series of subtests. The authors explain that individual subtests would artificially segregate critical-thinking skills, suggesting that skills such as clarification, analysis, and

prediction are separate and distinct, rather than viewing critical thinking as a holistic process (Manual, p.73).

- The manual includes an excellent discussion of the assessment and remediation of critical-thinking skills, which will be helpful in planning a remedial program.

LIMITING FACTORS OF THE TOPS–R

- While the standardization sample of the TOPS–R is greatly improved, there is no discussion of why the five states were selected and no information given on socioeconomic level or type of residence (urban or rural) of the subjects.
- The TOPS–R is a measure of verbal reasoning. It does not necessarily measure a student's ability to solve a problem. Many children (and adults) can solve problems very successfully but have little ability to verbalize the process, and there are many people who can tell you what to do in a problem situation but not do it when the problem actually occurs. The TOPS–R reflects critical-thinking skills that underlie verbal reasoning. It does not assess nonverbal problem-solving skills that are equally important. In interpreting test results to parents and teachers, this distinction should be made.

NOTE

The Test of Problem Solving–Adolescent (TOPS–Adolescent), published by LinguiSystem in 1991, provides a measure of critical thinking in 12 to 18 year olds. The format is quite different, utilizing verbal stimuli rather than pictures. The examiner reads a short problem situation along with the student, while the student reads the printed paragraph. The examiner asks two or three questions about each problem while the student answers orally. Responses are recorded and scored right or wrong. The total correct is converted into an age equivalent, percentile, and standard score. The TOPS–Adolescent was standardized on 1,004 subjects in California, Colorado, Texas, Georgia, Pennsylvania, and Michigan. Technical characteristics of the test should be carefully reviewed by the examiner. Test–retest coefficients for total test scores average .86 and range from .76 to .92 across age levels. A contrasted groups validity study (620 subjects) revealed significant differences (.01 level) between normal and language-disordered subjects at each age level for the test.

CHAPTER FOUR
Bilingual (Spanish–English) Language Tests

The assessment of students from diverse cultures and language backgrounds is a complex subject. Chapter Four serves as a brief introduction to the assessment of Spanish-speaking children. Among the factors that make this assessment difficult is language: While the availability of Spanish-speaking speech-and-language specialists, learning disability specialists, and psychologists is increasing, non-Spanish-speaking examiners must frequently complete the evaluation with interpreters and translators. There is no research-based information on working with an interpreter (Langdon, 1992), but many aspects of the process need careful attention: scheduling clinician–interpreter meetings both before and after the assessment, the clinician's presence to observe behavior, interpreter training in the field's technical vocabulary, and the interpreter's necessary neutrality throughout. There is an increasing belief that the examiner must speak the student's language fluently and also be a member of that culture.

A second factor is the limited number of standardized tests available. Some current tools are seriously limited: direct translations of English tests are often without separate normative data; Spanish versions are often not revised along with English tests; some tests are normed on a small number of students from one geographic location and have limited validity with other populations; and reliability and validity studies are frequently not conducted or not reported. In general, the technical characteristics of the Spanish-language tests are weaker than those of English-language tests. In the 1980s, there was a trend toward developing diagnostic tests that reflected the characteristics of native Spanish-speakers and were more sensitive to the sequence of language development in Spanish. To date, few such tests are available.

Chapter Four reviews six tests that are frequently used to assess language skills of Spanish-speaking students. The tests are simply a sampling and are intended to guide examiners toward other resources.

• The Bilingual Syntax Measure (BSM I and II) assesses student's oral grammatical proficiency in English and Spanish.

• The Preschool Language Scale, Third Edition (PLS–3), Spanish Edition, assesses language comprehension and production in young children.

Pruebas de Expresion Oral y Percepcion de la Lengua Espanola (PEOPLE) identifies Spanish-speaking students with language deficiencies in their native language.

• *Aprenda: La Prueba de Logros en Espanol* (APRENDA) assesses the basic academic skills of Spanish-speaking students.

• *Test de Vocabularies en Imagenes Peabody* (TVIP) measures receptive single-word vocabulary.

• Woodcock Language Proficiency Battery–Spanish (WLPS–S) assesses reading, writing, and oral language in Spanish.

TESTS THAT HAVE SPANISH TRANSLATIONS
Chapter One: Brigance Diagnostic Inventories

Chapter Two: Lindamood Auditory Conceptualization Test, Revised Edition (LACT)

Chapter Three: The Assessment of Phonological Processes–Revised (APP–R), Boehm Test of Basic Concepts–Revised (BTBC–R), Expressive One-Word Picture Vocabulary Test (EOWPVT), Expressive One-Word Picture Vocabulary Test–Upper Extension (EOWPVT–UE), Peabody Picture Vocabulary Test–Revised (PPVT–R), Pre-School Language Scale–PLS Test (Pre-School and Elementary Level)

Chapter Six: Wechsler Intelligence Scale for Children–Revised (not available for WISC–R), Woodcock-Johnson Psycho-Educational Battery (not updated for WJ–R)

The reader is also referred to *Hispanic Children and Adults With Communication Disorders* (Langdon and Cheng, 1992) for a comprehensive discussion of this topic, including lists and brief reviews of widely used language and language proficiency tests, as well as examples of achievement tests available in Spanish.

Bilingual Syntax Measure (BSM I and II)

Marina K. Burt, Heidi C. Dulay, Eduardo Hernandez Chávez
The Psychological Corporation
555 Academic Court, San Antonio, TX 78204-2498

Purpose	To measure children's oral proficiency in English and/or Spanish grammatical structures through natural speech
Major Areas Tested	Expressive syntax in English and Spanish
Age or Grade Range	BSM I: K–2nd grade BSM II: 3rd–12th grade
Usually Given By	Speech/language clinician Bilingual teacher Paraprofessional
Type of Test	Individual
Scores Obtained	Language proficiency level
Student Performance Timed?	No
Testing Time	10–15 minutes (each language version)
Scoring/Interpretation Time	5–10 minutes (each language version)
Normed On	BSM I: 1,572 children from various Spanish-speaking countries, including Mexico, Puerto Rico, and Cuba BSM II: 775 children from diverse language backgrounds, including Spanish, Korean, Japanese, and Chinese
Alternate Forms Available?	No

FORMAT

The Bilingual Syntax Measure (BSM) assesses expressive syntax in English and Spanish. BSM Level I is appropriate for children from 4 to 9 years old (grades K–2), and BSM Level II is appropriate for students from 10 to 18 years old (grades 3–12). The materials for each level consist of test manuals in English and Spanish, a picture booklet, student response booklets in English and Spanish, supplementary material (*Rationale and Technical Report*, Burt, Dulay, Chavez, 1975), and class record forms.

The purpose of the BSM is to elicit "natural speech." Simple verbal questions are used with cartoon-type pictures to provide the framework for a conversation with the student. The analysis of the student's speech yields a numerical indicator and qualitative description of the student's structural language proficiency. Therefore, the BSM can be used to determine the "degree" of bilingualism, structural proficiency in English or Spanish as a second language, and maintenance or loss of basic Spanish structures.

Administration of the BSM begins with a preliminary screening. An initial set of questions about the stimulus pictures is presented to put the student at ease. If the student is able to respond verbally to only two or fewer of these and the first five test questions, testing is discontinued. For responsive students, 25 test questions are presented while the examiner refers to the appropriate picture. The test protocols contain the stimulus questions and spaces for recording the student's responses verbatim. The examiner is reminded to try to maintain a natural flow of conversation throughout the administration of the BSM. If both the English and Spanish versions are presented to a single student, they should be administered in separate sessions.

Scoring criteria and examples of responses are provided in the test manuals. The primary criterion for scoring is grammar in conversation. Therefore, grammatically correct responses with inappropriate content, incomplete sentences considered acceptable in conversation, and colloquial conversational forms (for example, *would' a*) are credited. The correctness of a student's response is always judged in the context of the stimulus question. Thus, a response such as "He's sleeping" is considered incorrect for the question "Why do you think their eyes are closed?" Only responses verbalized in the test language are credited. Overall scoring is based on the successive evaluation of the student's responses to certain groups of test questions. Instructions provided in the student response booklet include minimal criteria for assigning the student to one of the five following proficiency levels:

Level I. No English/Spanish.

Level II. Receptive English/Spanish. The student can produce some verbal routines and repeat short sentences or questions in either English or Spanish but cannot use that language to communicate thoughts and opinions.

Level III. Survival English/Spanish. The student usually can make himself or herself understood by using a combination of simple speech, gestures, and an occasional word from his or her native language. When verbalizing in the second language, the student may omit words or word endings.

Level IV. Intermediate English/Spanish. The student has little difficulty communicating ideas in either English or Spanish and demonstrates control of a number of basic grammatical structures.

Level V. Proficient English/Spanish. The student exhibits native or near-native control in either English or Spanish.

The BSM provides instructional suggestions for each proficiency level in the areas of receptive and expressive language, reading, and other academic subjects. Also included are categories of language dominance defined by English and Spanish proficiency levels and equivalent Lau categories (*Lau vs Nichols,* 1975). The English-speaking designations consist of NES (non-English-speaking), LES (limited English-speaking), and FES (fluent English-speaking) categories, which are used for qualification for bilingual education programs in many states.

STRENGTHS OF THE BSM

• The BSM is a language proficiency instrument whose format and materials are appealing to most students. The stimulus pictures are attractive, brightly colored, and durable. The content of the pictures is interesting to students, holds their attention easily, and is familiar to many diverse cultural groups. Scoring does not rely on a student's cultural experience or knowledge, since answers contrary to fact can be credited.

• The BSM is simple to administer. Paraprofessionals who read and write in English and Spanish can be trained to administer this test. However, speech/language clinicians should judge the grammar of a student's responses.

• The BSM has several uses. It is helpful in the diagnosis of expressive language difficulties and in the placement of students in second-language instruction programs. Furthermore, gain or loss of structural proficiency in English and Spanish can be determined by administration of the BSM at the beginning and end of a specific time interval.

• The authors present detailed information in support of the content validity of the BSM. They cite psycholinguistic research indicating that students of diverse language backgrounds follow a similar pattern in acquiring a second language, and they suggest that this research has resulted in the production of the BSM scoring system. In addition, they provide evidence that the BSM proficiency classifications reflect expected relationships between the first and second languages of bilingual children.

LIMITING FACTORS OF THE BSM

• The BSM should be considered solely a measure of grammatical proficiency. It is not an appropriate instrument for identification of a language disorder because students who perform poorly on both language versions are classified as requiring special diagnosis. Students who misinterpret stimulus questions still receive credit if they produce grammatically correct responses. Furthermore, the BSM assesses only standard English syntax and is not appropriate for use with students who use Black English.

• Test–retest reliability of the BSM is low. The authors defend these figures by suggesting that they reflect characteristic changes in a student's acquisition of grammatical structures.

• Although a description of content validity is provided by the authors, formal validity studies are not reported.

Preschool Language Scales–Third Edition (PLS-3), Spanish Edition

I. L. Zimmerman, V. G. Steiner, and R. H. Pond
The Psychological Corporation, 1969, 1979, 1992
555 Academic Court, San Antonio, TX 78204-2498

Purpose	To assess receptive and expressive language skills in young children
Major Areas Tested	Receptive and expressive language Precursors of language
Age or Grade Range	Birth through 6 years, 11 months
Usually Given By	Speech and language clinician Special education teacher Psychologist
Type of Test	Standardized Individual Criterion-referenced Norm-referenced
Scores Obtained	Age equivalent Percentile Standard scores
Student Performance Timed?	No
Testing Time	15–40 minutes
Scoring/Interpretation Time	10–30 minutes
Normed On	181 Spanish-speaking children; sample balanced for age, gender, mother's educational level; sample gathered in six states and Puerto Rico
Alternate Forms Available?	No

NOTE

The Preschool Language Scales, Third Edition (PLS–3), Spanish Edition, is an adaptation of the English version. Tasks from PLS–3 were modified to include vocabulary and concepts familiar to young Spanish-speaking children. Consultants familiar with Spanish dialects reviewed the modified tasks. Bilingual examiners administered the test to 181 Hispanic children. Twenty to 32 children were tested for each year from birth through age six. All children in the standardization sample were Spanish speaking. Children with known language disorders, prematurely born, or who had "difficulties at birth" were excluded. Sampling was balanced for age, gender, and educational level of the mother. The standardization was carried out in six states (Arizona, California, Florida, Georgia, Kansas, Texas) and Puerto Rico.

See review of PLS–3 (p.198) for a description of the test format, materials, and the Auditory Comprehension and Expressive Communication Scales.

The Strengths and Limiting Factors of the PLS–3 English version also apply to the Spanish version.

STRENGTHS OF THE PLS–3, Spanish Edition

• The PLS–3 is a strong instrument in the assessment of language development in young children. The Spanish version uses the same format and style of administration. Efforts were made to adapt the items to make the test appropriate for Spanish-speaking children from a variety of populations. The sampling included children who spoke the Spanish dialects common in the southwestern United States, Mexico, Puerto Rico, Central or South America, and Cuba. Although the sampling size was small, the inclusion of children with diverse dialects was a helpful feature.

• The Articulation Screener of the PLS–3 was adapted to include Spanish phonemes not in the English version. A total of 121 children were tested, and phonemes were grouped into age levels. Criterion scores were set at the age at which 84 percent of the children articulated the phonemes correctly in the initial and final position.

LIMITING FACTORS OF THE PLS–3, Spanish Edition

• The manual for the PLS–3, Spanish Edition, includes a thoughtful section that describes cautions on interpreting the scores of Spanish-speaking children on any language test (Manual, pp. 42–44). These cautions include:

1. While the prelanguage skills assessed by the PLS–3 were mastered at the same ages for both English and Spanish-speaking children, the language skills were mastered six months later by the Spanish-speaking children. This delay in the primary language may be a natural slowdown that occurs when a second language is introduced and does not indicate disordered language.

2. The later age of mastery by the Spanish-speaking children may be due to the fact that the structures of English and Spanish may be different and may alter the sequence of acquisition.

3. Scores on the PLS–3, Spanish Edition, should be interpreted with caution (Manual, p. 43). A low score does not mean that a child's language is disordered and that he or she should be placed with children who have language delays in one language. Neither should the information be ignored. Further evaluation, including observation of the child in class and with peers, is needed. In some cases, assessment of the child's language in both Spanish and English is needed.

• Other factors may influence a child's performance on the Spanish version, including shyness and unfamiliarity with the school setting and the testing situation.

• No description of the sample of children tested to establish criteria for the Articulation Screener is given.

Pruebas de Expression Oral y Perception de la Lengua Española (PEOPLE)

Sharon Mares
Los Angeles County Office of Education, 1980
9300 East Imperial Hwy., Downey, CA 90242

Purpose	To aid in distinguishing between a language difference and a language deficit for Non-English Proficient (NEP) and Limited English Proficient (LEP) Hispanic students
Major Areas Tested	Expressive and receptive language
Age or Grade Range	6–10 years
Usually Given By	Bilingual speech and language specialists
Type of Test	Individual Standardized Norm-referenced
Scores Obtained	Standard
Student Performance Timed?	No
Testing Time	30–40 minutes
Scoring/Interpretation Time	15–20 minutes
Normed On	674 students of Mexican descent residing in 4 southern California counties. 276 students were classified as non-English speaking, 398 as limited English-speaking. Each six-month age period had fairly equal numbers of students. All students were from a low SES background and were judged by their teachers as having normal Spanish language
Alternate Forms Available?	No

FORMAT

The Prueba de Expresion Oral y Perception de la Lengua Española (PEOPLE) is an individually administered test designed to aid in identifying students of Mexican descent with a language deficit. The test was developed by the Los Angeles County School District through a state-administered grant. PEOPLE is designed to be given by bilingual speech/language specialists to non-English speaking (NES) and limited English-speaking (LES) students between the ages of 6 and 10 years.

Materials for the PEOPLE consist of a manual, individual score sheets, and a set of black and white pictures. The manual includes descriptions of the test rationale and development, instructions for administration and scoring, norms, and technical characteristics of the test.

PEOPLE consist of five subtests:

Auditory Sequential Memory. Ten items which assess a student's short-term memory for sequences of unrelated words. Ten objects or pictures of common objects are placed on a table. The examiner pronounces sequences of 3 to 7 object names and the student touches the objects in the order named. The student gets 1 point for every object identified in the order named.

Auditory Association. Thirty-five items which assess a student's knowledge of associations. The examiner reads the analogy and the student supplies the last word.

The bed is for sleeping; The chair is for _____ .

A mouse is little; an elephant is _____ .

Sentence Repetition. Thirty items which assess a student's ability to repeat sentences of increasing length and complexity read by the examiner.

Story Comprehension. Seven stories which assess the student's listening comprehension. The stories increase in length and linguistic complexity. The examiner reads the story and asks the student a series of questions about the content. The purpose of the subtest is to assess receptive skills; non-grammatical responses are scored as correct if the concept is conveyed.

Encoding. Twenty items which assess a student's ability to answer questions with common nouns. This is a word-finding skill.

What is the name of the thing you use to write your lessons in school?

Students begin each subtest with item 1 regardless of age. Each subtest is discontinued when the student makes 4 consecutive errors. Raw scores for each subtest are converted to scaled scores with a mean of 50 and a standard deviation of 10. A total test score is obtained by summing the five standardized scores, an average scaled score by dividing this total by 5. Students with one standard deviation below the mean are described as having a mild delay; two standard deviations below, a moderate delay; and three standard deviations below, a severe delay.

STRENGTHS OF THE PEOPLE

• The developers of PEOPLE are to be commended for their efforts to develop a standardized assessment procedure for NES and LES Hispanic students. The problem of identifying which children in this population have language deficits in their primary language is a significant one, and PEOPLE provides a major attempt to standardize a testing procedure.

• Extensive field testing was completed to assure that test items were appropriate for the population being assessed. The manual describes all test development stages in detail.

• Good internal consistency, test-retest, and interscorer reliability data are presented in the manual, supporting the idea that language-speech specialists can be taught to use PEOPLE with a high degree of consistency.

• Demonstration items are presented before each subtest to ensure that the student understands the vocabulary involved in the task as well as the task itself.

LIMITING FACTORS OF THE PEOPLE

• At the time of this writing, there is limited validity data on the PEOPLE. Several studies need to be done to answer such questions as, Are students identified as having moderate and severe language delays on the PEOPLE identified in the same way with more extensive clinical diagnosis? What is the correlation between performance on PEOPLE and performance on other Spanish language assessments?

• The standardization sample of PEOPLE is limited to a southern California population of Hispanic students. Generalization of the norms to other Hispanic groups should be done with great caution.

Aprenda: La Prueba de Logros en Español (APRENDA)

The Psychological Corporation, 1990
555 Academic Court, San Antonio, TX 78204-2498

Purpose	To assess the academic achievement of Spanish-speaking children
Major Areas Tested	Reading, listening, math
Age or Grade Range	K–8th grade
Usually Given By	Teachers
Type of Test	Group
Scores Obtained	Grade equivalents Scaled scores Local and nationwide percentile ranks Stanines Normal curve equivalents
Student Performance Timed?	No
Testing Time	Total test ranges from 2–4 1/2 hours
Scoring/Interpretation Time	30–45 minutes
Normed On	30,000 students in bilingual programs receiving academic instruction in Spanish; standardized in 34 districts across the nation; norms were also derived by weighting the APRENDA sample to the national standardization of the Stanford Achievement Test (Stanford 8)
Alternate Forms Available?	No

FORMAT

The *Aprenda: La Prueba de Logros en Español* (APRENDA) is a standardized achievement test for Spanish-speaking students. Patterned after the Stanford Achievement Test Series, the APRENDA was developed in Spanish, reflecting the cultural backgrounds of Spanish-speaking children. It is not a Spanish translation of an English test. The purpose of APRENDA is to provide for appropriate placement of Spanish-speaking students and to identify individual academic strengths and weaknesses. The materials consist of Directions for Administration, individual test booklets, practice tests, and scorable test booklets. Instructions to the teacher are in English, while directions to the students are in Spanish.

APRENDA provides seven levels of testing encompassing grades K–8.

Preprimer Level: Kindergarten–First Grade

1. *Sonidas y Letras*: the use of phonic andstructural analysis skills
2. *Lectura de Palabras:* word recognition
3. *Lectura de Oraciones*: oral sentence comprehension
4. *Palabras y Cuentos*: listening vocabulary and comprehension
5. *Matematicas*: basic number concepts

Primary 1 and 1 Levels: First–Third Grades

6. *Lectura de Palabras*: word reading
7. *Vocabulario:* vocabulary skills
8. *Comprehension de Lectura:* understanding of short reading passages
9. *Lenguaje*: written language skills
10. *Ortographia:* spelling
11. *Comprehension Auditiva:* listening comprehension
12. *Conceptos de Numeros*: basic number concepts
13. *Calculos Matematicos:* computation of whole numbers
14. *Aplicaciones Matematicos:* applying number concepts to problem solving

Primary 3 and Intermediate 1, 2, and 3 Levels: Third–Eighth Grades

15. *Vocabulario:* reading vocabulary
16. *Comprehension de lectura:* reading comprehension
17. *Lenguaje: Mechanica:* capitalization, punctuation, and applied grammar
18. *Lenguaje*: *Expression:* sentence structure
19. *Destre las de Estudio:* study skills
20. *Ortographia:* spelling
21. *Comprehension Auditiva:* vocabulary and listening comprehension
22. *Conceptos de Numeros:* basic number concepts
23. *Calculos Matematicos:* basic computation with whole numbers, fractions, and decimals
24. *Aplicaciones Matematicos:* applying number concepts to problem solving

Student tests can be either hand or machine scored. Individual subtest scores are computed, as are total scores for reading, language, math, and the complete battery. Scores are reported in scaled scores, national and local percentiles, stanines, and age equivalents.

STRENGTHS OF THE APRENDA

• APRENDA fills the need for a well-standardized instrument to assess the academic achievement of Spanish-speaking students. It is a comprehensive battery that provides good information on skill acquisition in basic academic areas.

• The APRENDA subtest items were developed entirely in Spanish and reviewed by Spanish-speaking educators to ensure minimal regional vocabulary and idioms. This fact, together with the nationwide standardization population, makes the APRENDA useful with diverse Hispanic populations, such as students from Cuba, Puerto Rico, and Mexico.

• The APRENDA not only provides useful information for placing Spanish-speaking students new to the school district in appropriate classes; it also provides a profile of academic strengths and weaknesses that can guide instructional planning. Information gained can also signal the need for individual assessment of some students.

LIMITING FACTORS OF THE APRENDA

• The APRENDA is a relatively new test covering many subject areas over a wide age range. Studies of its reliability and validity for measuring the skills of Spanish-speaking students will determine its usefulness in the field.

• The APRENDA suffers from the same limitations as all group tests. It is difficult to know what factors are contributing to low scores: poor attention, anxiety, motivational issues, or others. When knowledge of the prior educational experiences is also sketchy, group test scores should be interpreted cautiously.

Test de Vocabulario en Imágenes Peabody (TVIP)

Lloyd M. Dunn, Eligio R. Padilla, Delia E. Lugo, Leota M. Dunn
American Guidance Service, 1986
4201 Woodland Rd., P.O. Box 99, Circle Pines, MN 55014-1796

Purpose	To measure the extent of Spanish language acquisition; to screen verbal ability of students for whom Spanish is the language of the home and environment and the primary language of instruction at school
Major Areas Tested	Receptive, single-word vocabulary
Age or Grade Range	2 1/2–18 years
Usually Given By	Psychologist Teacher Special education teacher Speech therapist
Type of Test	Individual Standardized Norm-referenced
Scores Obtained	Age equivalent Deciles Standard score Stanines Percentile
Student Performance Timed?	No
Testing Time	15–20 minutes
Scoring/Interpretation Time	10–15 minutes
Normed On	Mexican sample: 1,219 children from Mexico City and surrounding areas. Sample balanced for sex and age. Puerto Rican sample: 1,488 children from San Juan and three small towns. Sampling plan took into account age, sex, size of community, type of school, and socioeconomic status of family
Alternate Forms Available?	No

FORMAT

The Test de Vocabulario en Imágenes Peabody (TVIP) is the Spanish version of the well known Peabody Picture Vocabulary Test–Revised. The materials consist of an examiner's manual, available in English or Spanish, a series of pictures in a spiral-bound book, and record forms, printed in Spanish with the English translation on the same page.

The procedures for the TVIP are the same as for the PPVT-R. The examiner reads a word and the student selects from four choices the picture which corresponds to the word. A basal-ceiling procedure is used to ensure that students are tested only over a critical range of items. The raw score represents the number of correct responses and is converted into an age score, percentile, standard score, stanine, or decile. Standard scores have a mean of 100 and a standard deviation of 15.

STRENGTHS OF THE TVIP

• A monograph entitled "Bilingual Hispanic Children on the U.S. Mainland: A review of research on their cognitve, linguistic, and scholastic development" (Dunn, 1986) is available from the publisher. It includes studies relevant to the TVIP, and examiners are urged to study the report before using the test.

• When the Spanish version of the TVIP is given along with the English version, the dominant language of the student may be ascertained.

• The TVIP was standardized on two Spanish-speaking populations, one in Mexico and one in Puerto Rico. While separate norms for each group are included in the manual, the authors recommend the combined norms.

LIMITING FACTORS OF TVIP

• No test–retest reliability studies are presented.

• The standardization sample includes no information on socioeconomic status. No rural students were included. The Mexican sample contained an overrepresentation of higher socioeconomic subjects in the preschool range, and the 13 to 15 year olds constituted an atypical representation of students who had remained in school past the compulsory age. These sampling problems are well described in the manual.

• TVIP assesses only receptive vocabulary, one aspect of language.

Woodcock Language Proficiency Battery–Spanish (WLPB-S)

Richard W. Woodcock
The Riverside Publishing Company, 1980
8420 Bryn Mawr Avenue, Chicago, IL 60631

Purpose	To measure proficiency in oral language, reading, and writing in Spanish
Major Areas Tested	Oral language, written language, and reading
Age or Grade Range	3 years–adult
Usually Given By	Speech/language clinician Special education teacher Bilingual teacher
Type of Test	Individual Standardized Norm-referenced Criterion-referenced
Scores Obtained	Age equivalent Grade equivalent Percentile Relative mastery Standard
Student Performance Timed?	No
Testing Time	45 minutes (all subtests)
Scoring/Interpretation Time	20–30 minutes
Normed On	802 children in grades K, 1, 3, 5, 8, and 11 from urbanized areas in Costa Rica, Mexico, Peru, Puerto Rico, and Spain and 4,732 subjects from a wide distribution of communities in the United States, balanced for sex, race, occupation, geographic location, and type of community
Alternate Forms Available?	No

FORMAT

The Woodcock Language Proficiency Battery–Spanish (WLPB–S) consists of eight subtests that assess oral language, written language, and reading in Spanish. This battery is a translation and modification of selected subtests from the English form, the Woodcock–Johnson Psycho-Educational Battery, 1977 Edition, and contains a separate set of norms. The WLPB–S materials include an examiner's manual, an easel-style test book, and a response booklet for recording responses, summarizing results, and interpreting test performance.

The subtests include:

A. *Picture Vocabulary*. The student identifies pictured objects and actions.

B. *Antonyms-Synonyms*. In part A, the student states the opposite of a stimulus word. In part B, the student states the word whose meaning approximates the stimulus word.

C. *Analogies*. The student completes verbal analogies.

D. *Letter-Word Identification*. The student identifies isolated letters and words printed in the test book. To receive credit, the student must correctly identify the letter by name or phonetic sound and must correctly read the word in 4 to 5 seconds.

E. *Word Attack*. The student reads nonsense words, which range from consonant-vowel digraphs to multisyllable items. Almost all Spanish phonemes are represented by at least one major spelling pattern.

F. *Passage Comprehension*. The student identifies key words missing from a reading passage.

G. *Dictation*. The student responds in writing to questions involving knowledge of letter forms, spelling punctuation, capitalization, and usage.

H. *Proofing*. The student identifies mistakes in typewritten passages and indicates how to correct each error. The errors include punctuation, capitalization, spelling, and inappropriate word forms.

The WLPB-S enables the examiner to combine selected items from the above subtests to obtain additional measures of performance. These three composite subtests include Punctuation and Capitalization, Spelling, and Usage.

The entire battery or an individual subtest or groups of subtests may be administered. For each subtest, items are arranged in order of difficulty, and basal and ceiling levels are provided. Although starting-point tables are included to assist the examiner in beginning subtests at an appropriate level, examiners are encouraged to use an estimate of the student's ability rather than the student's actual age or grade level.

Clusters of subtests provide the primary basis for interpretation of the WLPB-S. The Oral Language cluster consists of a combination of the Picture Vocabulary, Antonyms-Synonyms, and Analogies subtests. The Reading cluster combines the Letter-Word Identification, Word Attack, and Passage Comprehension subtests. The Written Language cluster includes Dictation and Proofing. Furthermore, a general index of overall language functioning (Broad Language Ability) can be obtained by combining these three clusters.

A broad range of scores is provided to interpret a student's performance on the WLPB–S. Raw scores can be converted to grade scores, age scores, and percentiles. Other types of scores include an extended grade scale, extended age scale, and relative performance index. Refer to the Woodcock Reading Mastery Test (p. 90) and the Woodcock–Johnson Psycho-Educational Battery (p. 312) for discussion of these scores.

STRENGTHS OF THE WLPB–S

• There are few Spanish assessment instruments that evaluate reading or written language skills. The WLPB–S makes an important contribution by providing a flexible, organized, and well-normed diagnostic tool. The examiner is able to evaluate a student's performance on clusters of subtests, a single subtest, or the entire test battery. If both the English and Spanish versions are administered to an individual student, relative language proficiency is helpful in deciding whether to provide a reading instruction program in English or Spanish for bilingual students.

• The WLPB-S is useful for identifying specific language disorders as well as for determining language proficiency. Subtests A, B, and C can provide information about a student's word recall and retrieval abilities, knowledge of vocabulary, and verbal reasoning skills. Subtest F, which consists of a cloze procedure, evaluates the student's ability to use the language context to provide an appropriate word.

• The test manual for the WLPB-S is exceptionally complete and well organized. Practice exercises are provided to acquaint the examiner with administration procedures. The clever design of the test book is also an asset.

• A student's performance on the WLPB-S can be compared with norms from two separate standardization populations. One set of norms was gathered from urbanized areas in several Spanish-speaking countries. The equated United States norms provide data for converting scores on the WLPB-S into equivalent proficiency scores on the English version. That is, these scores indicate the level of English proficiency that corresponds with the student's demonstrated Spanish proficiency. This information is quite useful for planning instructional programs for Spanish-speaking students in the United States.

LIMITING FACTORS OF THE WLPB-S

• There are several methods of analyzing a student's performance on the WLPB-S that are time-consuming and complicated. Although valuable diagnostic information can be obtained, it requires a substantial time commitment on the part of the examiner to study the test manual, practice administering the battery, and understand the scoring procedures.

• Reliability and validity information is not reported or referred to in the test materials.

• Due to the wide age range covered, there are only a few items at each level; WLPB–S is designed to assess school-related skills and is most appropriate for children of more than eight years of age.

• The WLPB–S is a translation and a modification of subtests from the 1977 edition of the Woodcock–Johnson Psycho-Educational Battery, not the revised edition. Until the WLPB–S is revised, scores must be interpreted with caution.

CHAPTER FIVE
Gross and Fine Motor Skills

Relatively few standardized tests of gross motor skills are available. More often, informal rating scales are devised by the special education teacher interested in perceptual motor training. In addition to the usual skills emphasized in physical education—running, catching, throwing, and total body coordination—basic skills such as balance and posture have often been found to be underdeveloped in children with learning and language disabilities. Special education theorists such as Newell Kephart (1960) and A. Jean Ayres (1973) have hypothesized that adequate motor development is prerequisite to developing higher-level perceptual and cognitive skills. Although research (Hallahan and Cruickshank, 1973; Cratty, 1970) has shown no direct connection between motor skills and academic performance, no one disputes the fact that many special education students have delayed motor skills for which they need specific teaching. Although training in balance, posture, rhythm, and ball skills may not improve spelling, it often leads to improvement in the equally important areas of playground activities and social skills.

For this reason, it is important to be familiar with some tests of gross motor ability. Assessment in this area is done by a variety of professionals. Some schools have a physical education teacher who works with the whole school population, while other districts have an adaptive physical education teacher who specializes in the needs of special education students. Some districts have occupational and physical therapists who do the gross motor assessments of exceptional children. But, quite often, it is the special education teacher who assesses his or her students and plans a gross motor program to meet their needs.

This chapter reviews five tests devised to assess gross motor skills. Many of them include fine motor assessment as well. The Bruininks–Oseretsky Test of Motor Proficiency assesses both fine and gross motor skills in students between 4 and 14 years of age. The Miller Assessment for Preschoolers (MAP) is designed for three to six year olds and combines sensory–motor evaluation with language and nonverbal cognitive skills. The Peabody Developmental Motor Skills (PDMS) assesses gross and fine motor skills in the infant to 7-year-old child. The Sensory Integration and Praxis Test (SIPT) is a highly technical battery administered by occupational and physical therapists to assess not only gross and fine motor skills, but also the tactile and kinesthetic perception systems. The DeGangi–Berk Test of Sensory Integration (TSI) also measures these skills in preschoolers.

Readers who are specifically interested in the assessment of gross motor skills are also referred to the McCarthy Scales of Children's Ability (MSCA) on page 283.

Bruininks–Oseretsky Test of Motor Proficiency
(Bruininks–Oseretsky Test)

Robert H. Bruininks
American Guidance Service, 1978
4201 Woodland Rd., P.O. Box 99, Circle Pines, MN 50014

Purpose	To assess motor skills, to develop and evaluate motor training programs, and to assess serious motor dysfunctions and developmental delays in children
Major Areas Tested	Motor proficiency and gross and fine motor skills
Age or Grade Range	4 1/2–14 1/2 years
Usually Given By	Special education teacher Occupational therapist Physical education teacher Motor therapist
Type of Test	Standardized Individual
Scores Obtained	Age level Standard Percentile Stanine
Student Performance Timed?	Yes (some subtests)
Testing Time	45–60 minutes (complete battery); 15–20 minutes (short form)
Scoring/Interpretation Time	15–20 minutes
Normed On	765 students from north central, southern, and western states and Canada, balanced for age, sex, race, and community size according to the 1970 census. A small sample of handicapped students was also included
Alternate Forms Available?	No

FORMAT

The materials for the Bruininks-Oseretsky Test of Motor Proficiency (Bruininks-Oseretsky Test) consist of the examiner's manual, individual record forms for recording responses and scores, student booklets that include materials for pencil-and-paper and cutting tasks, and a variety of manipulative materials for use with the various subtests. All of the materials are packaged in a specially designed metal carrying case.

The test is designed to yield three estimates of motor proficiency: a gross motor score, a fine motor score, and a battery composite score. The 46 items are divided into 8 subtests:

Gross Motor Skills

1. *Running Speed and Agility* (1 item). Running speed during a shuttle run is measured.

2. *Balance* (8 items). Static balance and walking balance on a taped line and a balance beam are assessed.

3. *Bilateral Coordination* (8 items). Simultaneous coordination of upper and lower limbs is measured by asking the student to reproduce such rhythmic patterns as tapping alternate feet and hands or jumping and clapping hands.

4. *Strength* (3 items). Shoulder and arm, abdominal, and leg strength are measured by tasks that include the broad jump, situps, and pushups.

Gross and Fine Motor Skills

5. *Upper-Limb Coordination* (9 items). Coordination of visual tracking with arm and hand movements and precise movements of the arms and hands is assessed by throwing and catching a ball, fingers-to-nose and thumb touching, and others.

Fine Motor Skills

6. *Response Speed* (1 item). Quick response to a moving visual target is measured by catching a sliding stick on the wall.

7. *Visual-Motor Control* (8 items). Coordination of precise visual and hand movements is assessed by such tasks as cutting, copying designs, and following mazes.

8. *Upper-Limb Speed and Dexterity* (8 items). Hand and finger dexterity and hand and arm speed are assessed by such tasks as placing pennies in a box, stringing beads, and rapidly drawing lines and dots.

Raw scores for individual items are converted to a point score using the conversion table printed directly below each item on the individual record form. Item scores are totaled to obtain subtest scores, which are in turn totaled to make the three composite scores:

1. Gross motor composite score (total of subtests 1 to 4)

2. Fine motor composite score (total of subtests 6 to 8)

3. Total battery composite score (total of subtests 1 to 8)

The three composite scores are converted to normalized standard scores with a mean of 50 and a standard deviation of 10. Percentile ranks and stanines are provided for the composite scores; age-equivalent scores are available for each subtest. Standard error of measurement is provided for the three composite scores.

A short form of the Bruininks-Oseretsky Test is also described in the manual. Fourteen items have been selected from the 46 items comprising the total test. Each of the 14 items was selected because of its high correlation with the subtest and total test scores, the ranges of ages for which it was useful, the short amount of time needed to administer the item, and the ease of scoring. The short-form items are clearly marked in the manual and on the individual record form. A standard score, percentile, stanine, and standard error of measurement are provided for the short form.

STRENGTHS OF THE BRUININKS–OSERETSKY TEST

• The Bruininks–Oseretsky Test is a modification of the Oseretsky motor tests developed in Russia in the 1920s. The most-used form of the Oseretsky test for children was the Lincoln–Oseretsky Development Scale. Bruinink's carefully constructed test reflects advances in content and technical quality. Validity studies indicate that the test provides a good estimate of developmental changes in motor proficiency. The assessment of motor development should be included in all comprehensive evaluations of young children.

• The wide variety of items included in the eight subtests, together with well-designed manipulative materials, makes the test interesting and challenging for students with a wide range of ages and abilities.

• The administration procedures include several good features: a pretest for determining the preferred hand and leg, more than one trial on most subtests, and demonstration of items by the examiner.

• The short form of the test is particularly helpful when large numbers of students need to be screened. Because the short form is embedded in the full test, the short form items can be used for reevaluation purposes.

• The manual is clearly written and gives not only directions for administration and scoring but also information on test construction, norming, reliability, and validity.

LIMITING FACTORS OF THE BRUININKS-OSER-ETSKY TEST

• The Bruininks-Oseretsky Test requires a skilled examiner. Many items require setting up equipment in a specific manner and timing the student's responses precisely. Several items need to be demonstrated to the student, so the examiner must also be coordinated. This test is difficult to administer and score. Inexperienced persons should not administer it without careful study of the manual and several practice tests.

• The Bruininks-Oseretsky Test requires space. A running area of 15 meters is necessary, so a playground or multipurpose room will be needed. If many students are to be tested, it is most convenient to set up the physical equipment and leave it in place for the duration of the testing.

• The scoring system for the test is complex. Each item has very specific and different scoring techniques—some record time, others number of correct responses, others pass-fail. Once each item receives a point score, the translation into standard scores, percentiles, stanines, and age-equivalent scores is a many-stepped process. The examiner is urged to doublecheck all scoring for accuracy.

• In discussing a student's scores, only three composite scores should be used; there should be no interpretation of individual subtests. The subtests contain too few items to draw conclusions, and the test–retest reliability of some subtests, especially Running Speed and Agility, Balance, Upper Limb Coordination, Response Speed, and Visual Motor Control is low.

• Although the author claims that the test can be used to determine "whether a student should enter school early" or be placed in a higher grade, such usage of a motor test is highly questionable. Although some research studies using mentally retarded and learning-disabled students are reported in the manual, it reports little data on the relationship between the disabilities and the lack of motor proficiency. In fact, limited validity information of any type is available.

• The manual does not present any information on how to use the Bruininks–Oseretsky test results to plan individual or small-group motor programs. Presumably, the eight subtests would serve as guidelines for the components of a motor-training program; more information in this area would be helpful to the user.

• *A Consumer's Guide to Tests in Print* (Hammill, Bryant, and Brown, 1992) rates the Bruininks-Oseretsky as not recommended due to an inadequate norming sample.

Miller Assessment for Preschoolers (MAP)

Lucy J. Miller
The Psychological Corporation, 1982
555 Academic Court, Allen, TX 78204

Purpose	To provide a brief screening tool for identifying preschool children in need of further evaluation, to identify children with moderate preacademic problems that may affect development, and to provide profiles of strengths and weaknesses of individual children
Major Areas Tested	Sensory and motor abilities and verbal and nonverbal cognitive abilities
Age or Grade Range	3–6 years
Usually Given By	Classroom teacher Speech/language therapist Psychologist Nurse Occupational therapist Paraprofessional
Type of Test	Standardized Individual Norm-referenced
Scores Obtained	Percentile
Student Performance Timed?	Yes (selected items)
Testing Time	30–40 minutes
Scoring/Interpretation Time	15 minutes
Normed On	1,200 preschoolers in nine U.S. Census Bureau Regions, randomly selected, stratified, and balanced by age, sex, race, urban/rural, and socioeconomic levels
Alternate Forms Available?	No

FORMAT

The materials for the Miller Assessment for Preschoolers (MAP) consist of the following:

- An examiner's manual including a description of the test, related literature, technical data, administration and scoring procedures, norms, and interpretation.
- Cue sheets for each of six age groups, including specific administration directions.
- Item score sheets for each age group for recording each child's performance and behavior.
- Record booklets for summarizing each child's performance, family history, developmental background, and supplemental observations.
- Drawing booklets for drawing and writing items.
- Scoring transparencies.
- Test kit materials, such as blocks, pennies, puzzles, and other manipulative items.

The materials are packaged in a sturdy well-designed test kit, divided notebook, and briefcase-style portfolio.

The MAP consists of 27 items grouped into five performance indices and three classifications. The entire test is usually given in the order described in the manual. The order of tests can be changed to meet an individual child's needs.

Three scoring procedures are included. Each child's performance is recorded on the four-color item score sheet appropriate for his or her age. Since the raw score on each item is recorded, the examiner can observe the child's performance in relation to other children of that age group. The performance is color-coded.

A percentile score for the total test is derived by calculating the number of reds and yellows a child obtained on the 27 items. In addition, nine areas of behavior are rated by the

Color	Performance Indication
Red	Stop—This child appears to need help (fifth percentile or below).*
Yellow	Caution—This child should be watched (fifth to twenty-fifth percentile).*
Green	Go—This child is performing within normal limits (twenty-fifth to one-hundredth percentile).*

*Percentiles vary somewhat from item to item.

examiner on a seven-point scale and recorded on the back of the item score sheet. Although behavior does not affect the child's score, the author feels that the behavioral observations are critical in determining the reliability of the test as well as in indicating areas in which the child may have difficulty.

For those clinicians who wish to use the MAP not only as a screening instrument but also to portray strengths and weaknesses of an individual child, several optional supplemental scoring procedures are outlined. Percentile scores for each performance index, as well as for each item, are included, but caution is advised in the interpretation of individual items.

A unique feature of the MAP is the supplemental observations sheet. This procedure is designed to be used by clinicians who wish to report more subjective information, such as quality of language or quality of movement. It is recommended that only examiners trained in an accredited MAP workshop utilize these assessment procedures.

MAP Organization

Classification	Performance Index	Number of Items	Functions
Sensory and Motor Abilities	Foundation	10	Kinesthesia, tactile discrimination, postural mechanisms, and motor coordination
	Coordination	7*	Gross, fine, and oral motor abilities
Cognitive Abilities	Verbal	4	Receptive and expressive language
	Non-Verbal	5	Visual-memory and sequencing
Combined Abilities	Complex Tasks	4	Combined sensory, motor, and cognitive abilities

*Three items are also in the Foundation Index.

STRENGTHS OF THE MAP

• The extensive MAP manual discusses in detail the theoretical background of the test, test construction procedures, data on the norming process, and reliability and validity studies. In addition, cautions to the examiner in terms of administration and interpretation are explicitly spelled out. All examiners should read this important information.

• Most instruments for preschool screening identify only those children with severe developmental delays; the MAP was designed to detect subtle moderate delays that often affect school performance.

• The author's experience with preschool children is demonstrated through the recognition of the need for flexible testing procedures with young children. Changes in testing order, inclusion of practice items, and positive reinforcement are part of the standardized procedures. Every effort is made to be sure that the child understands the task and to secure optional performance.

• A primary requisite of a screening test is that it be quick and reliable as well as cost efficient. Through meticulous attention to test construction, and the use of either single clinicians or trained paraprofessionals, the MAP author seems to have achieved these goals. Extensive information on test construction and standardization is included in the manual. Children with preacademic difficulties were included in the sample.

• The attention to behavioral observation and quality of performance are strong features, reflecting the author's understanding of preschool children.

• The Supplementary Observations are a strong feature of the MAP. Used by a trained, experienced examiner they help identify those children with mild or prelearning disabilities who are compensating for their difficulties. This group of children often struggle when demands increase in first grade.

• The MAP is more comprehensive than most screening instruments. It includes a broad range of skills in motor, language, and cognitive development as well as behavioral observations.

• A recently published study by the author (Miller, 1987) indicates that the MAP adequately identifies children at risk for school failure. The rate of false positives and false negatives is similar to that of other preschool measures.

• Despite the emphasis on sensory motor abilities, in a four-year follow-up study conducted by the author (Miller, 1987), a strong correlation is shown between the MAP total score and the WISC-R full scale IQ.

LIMITING FACTORS OF THE MAP

• Testing preschool children requires the examiner to know the materials and procedures well. The MAP is a complex test with many materials. The examiner must take the time necessary to become proficient in administration and interpretation.

• Several MAP subtests involve sensory and motor abilities. Since the author is an occupational therapist, she has drawn upon her background and has included tests of stereognosis, motor accuracy, finger localization, balance, imitation of postures, and others. Although extensive research is cited in the manual, other authors would feel that such tests are not predictive of later school difficulties. (See Southern California Sensory Integration Tests.)

• The MAP includes tests usually given by a teacher, a speech therapist, and an occupational therapist. Only one examiner is present so that he or she can maintain rapport with the child. This means the examiner will need to prepare especially well to administer the tests in areas that are unfamiliar.

• The MAP is a screening instrument and should not be used for diagnostic assessment or placement decisions. Although it provides more information than the typical screening instrument, especially when the Supplemental Observations are used, the items were selected for their predictive validity rather than their diagnostic features.

Peabody Developmental Motor Scales (PDMS)

M. Rhonda Folio and Rebecca R. Fewell
The Riverside Publishing Company
8420 Bryn Mawr Ave., Chicago, IL 60631

Purpose	To identify students with delayed or atypical development in gross and fine motor skills; to provide information for planning a specific intervention program when indicated; to measure progress in motor skills over time
Major Areas Tested	Gross and fine motor skills
Age or Grade Range	Birth to 83 months
Usually Given By	Occupational or physcial therapist Physical education or adaptive physical education teacher Regular or special education teacher Experienced paraprofessional
Type of Test	Standardized Individual Group (four to six year olds only)
Scores Obtained	Age level Percentile Standard Scaled
Student Performance Timed?	Yes (some items)
Testing Time	45–75 minutes
Scoring/Interpretation Time	10–30 minutes
Normed On	617 children from birth to 83 months, using stratified quota sampling procedures; rural and urban communities in 20 states were selected as geographically representative of the U.S.; sample stratified for sex, socioeconomic status, and minority (Black and Hispanic) representation
Alternate Forms Available?	No

FORMAT

The Peabody Developmental Motor Scales and Activity Cards, which are produced as a single unit, provide a comprehensive assessment and intervention program in gross and fine motor development. This review will be limited to the assessment component of the program.

The materials for the Peabody Developmental Motor Scales (PDMS) include a test manual, individual student Response/Scoring Booklets, and a variety of fine motor materials and gross motor equipment. The purchased kit is an attractive and fairly sturdy cardboard box containing most of the manipulative materials required for test administration as well as masters for reproducing the disposable materials used for the drawing and cutting of items. Additional fine motor materials and all gross motor equipment (balance beam, ball, etc.) must be provided separately. Clear specifications for the additional materials are provided in the manual.

The PDMS is comprised of a Gross Motor Scale and a Fine Motor Scale, which can be administered separately. The Gross Motor Scale is divided into 17 age levels with 10 items at each level. The earliest age levels include items such as aligning the head, turning from side to back, and bearing weight when supported; later age levels include walking a balance beam, kicking a ball, completing sit-ups, etc. The Fine Motor Scale is divided into 16 age levels with six to eight items at each level. These range from visually tracking a rattle, grasping a rattle reflexively, and releasing it involuntarily at the younger age levels to copying block patterns, buttoning buttons, and coloring and cutting with specified accuracy at the older levels. On both scales, each item is scored on a three point scale to reflect different levels of skill mastery. Through establishing basal and ceiling levels, only the items appropriate for the student's developmental level are presented. The process of determining basal and ceiling levels is clearly described in the manual.

Following administration of the scales, raw scores are tallied and converted to percentile ranks and/or age scores for each of the two scales. Charts are also provided in the manual for converting percentile ranks into three kinds of standard scores: z-scores, T-scores, and Developmental Motor Quotients. Scaled scores can also be obtained.

Although the test items are divided into age levels for the purpose of test administration, for scoring/interpretation purposes they are instead categorized by skill cluster. When scores are tallied, separate standard scores and percentile ranks are computed for each skill cluster, to allow for more specific interpretation and program planning. On the gross motor scale, these clusters include: Reflexes, Balance, Nonlocomotor, Locomotor, and Receipt and Propulsion. The four fine motor clusters are Grasping, Hand Use, Eye-Hand Coordination, and Manual Dexterity. Using the student's standard scores in these clusters, a Motor Development

Profile is plotted.

STRENGTHS OF THE PDMS

• The PDMS provides a means of quantifying development in an area that educators and medical personnel have traditionally assessed by "guesstimate." Given the sound statistical basis of this test, this is a significant contribution, both for identifying students with special needs in this area and for measuring progress over time.

• The scales include a wide variety of short appealing tasks, which is essential for assessment with this young population. The varied tasks also provide ample opportunity for clinical observation of motor skills, yielding information which supplements the test scores.

• The manual is thorough and clear, providing the essential information without excessive technical terminology. The chapter on test interpretation is particulary useful, in that the authors describe how to analyze a student's performance in various areas to find patterns of strengths and weaknesses, with case studies provided to illustrate their points. An excellent discussion of the advantages and disadvantages of various kinds of scores (standard, scaled, percentile, age) is also provided.

• The three-point scoring system is useful for distinguishing among mastered skills, emerging skills, and skills clearly beyond the student's reach. This rating system, as opposed to a pass/fail system, makes the test more sensitive to small changes in motor skills. This is a particular advantage for establishing objectives and measuring progress with severely disabled students.

• The non-motor requirements of the test are minimal, which is helpful for assessing a variety of students. For example, considerable demonstration is permitted, which helps to minimize the effects of a student's limitations in receptive language. No expressive language is required. Some conceptual and visual/spatial skills are required on the fine motor scale, but it has been kept to a minimum.

• Given the stratified quota sampling technique, the PDMS was standardized on a population of adequate size, with most age levels represented by an N of 30 to 55. A few age levels had smaller N's, however, ranging from 25 to 29. The norming population is well described in the manual. It should be noted that the final standardization data was limited to students without known impairments.

• Test/retest reliability is excellent, with correlations for total scores (including the non-administered pre-basal items) above .99. Interrater reliability is also excellent, with total score and item score correlations ranging from .94 to above .99. Both reliability measures were based on a small N of 38 and 36 students, respectively.

• Content, construct, and criterion-referenced validity are all discussed in detail in the manual. Current construct validity data suggest that the PDMS is valid as a test of motor development at most levels, with weakest data presented for birth to five-month-olds, and, in gross motor skills only, for 54–59-month-olds. Criterion-referenced validity is more difficult to establish, given the lack of comparable tests for the same age group, and the correlations presented in the manual are somewhat weak. However, as the authors note, establishing criterion-referenced validity is an ongoing process, and further studies are needed.

• The PDMS was normed on the same population for both gross and fine motor skills, and can therefore be useful for comparing a student's gross motor development with his fine motor development. The separate scores in individual skill clusters can also be useful for some students, although this interpretation requires both caution and considerable professional expertise.

• Information provided by the scales is directly applicable to developing goals and objectives, making it useful for writing IEPs.

LIMITING FACTORS OF THE PDMS

• The PDMS is a cumbersome test to administer as presented, by age levels. This is particularly true of the gross motor scale, where one might go from a jumping item to playing ball to walking the balance beam, then back to ball playing and then to another balance beam item. The frequent user will want to reorganize the test items for more efficient administration, which is permissible within the standardized procedures. The need to refer to both the response booklet and the test manual for each item is also cumbersome, especially while standing to administer the gross motor items. This is necessary even after considerable familiarity with the test because the manual, not the response booklet, has the information regarding administering and scoring each individual item. Again, the frequent user will need to provide his/her own organization system to allow for correct administration and accurate scoring while still maintaining rapport with the student and making clinical observations.

• Although administration and scoring criteria for most test items are clear, there are some exceptions, and clinical experience suggests some variation from one examiner to another in both administration and scoring of certain items. The most frequently occurring ambiguity is in distinguishing between a score of 0 (no credit) and a score of 1 (partial credit) on any given item. The manual provides general guidelines for making these distinctions, but the application of the guidelines to scoring specific test items is left to the examiner's discretion. When the test is used to measure progress, and different examiners give the pre- and post-tests, technical differences between examiners may be a limiting factor.

• "Ceiling effects" emerge in three of the skill clusters—Reflexes, Grasping, and Hand Use—indicating that all the skills assessed in these clusters have usually developed completely in children younger than the maximum ages the test covers. The authors clearly describe how to interpret scores in these three areas for older students. However, it is unlikely that the test will identify mild or moderate difficulties in any of these areas in students at the upper age ranges. The examiner will need to supplement the formal tests in these areas for older students. In borderline situations, when students are near the top ages for the skills in question, the scores can be quite misleading. For example, a 48–59 month old with an immature pencil/marker grasp but otherwise adequate grasping skills may score at the second or fourth percentile in "Grasping." One or two additional raw score points for a correct tripod grasp will give the same student a score at the 99th percentile in grasping. For older students, no scores are reported for grasping. Perhaps this policy should be applied for students at these borderline ages as well.

• The authors note that the test items are divided into skill clusters, and that "the items in each category are, in the authors' opinion, similar in the demands made on the child." It would be useful to have some statistical documentation regarding the categorization of items into these skill clusters. Two issues need to be addressed: Do all the items in one cluster measure a single area of motor development? and Are the nine clusters mutually exclusive? At times the distinctions seem arbitrary. For example, jumping forward is categorized as a locomotor skill, while jumping up is categorized as nonlocomotor, although the two clearly have something in common. The normative data indicate generally strong correlations among the different skill clusters. The authors note that this is to be expected in normal children, but in children with atypically developing motor skills, discrepancies would be expected, and they are significant when they appear. The ability to identify these discrepancies is one of the advantages of the PDMS. The examiner could interpret discrepancies with greater confidence, however, if the existence of discrete skill clusters could be documented. Until more statistical data is available, it is suggested that interpretations of discrepancies in the skill areas be presented as part of the examiner's clinical judgment, and that over-interpretation of differences between specific standard scores be avoided.

• The use of age scores is open for misinterpretation, particularly since the test was designed to be used by examiners with varied levels of sophistication. The authors provide a clear and convincing discussion of the limitations of age scores. They also include a case study of a student whose age scores were not consistent with her standard scores, and use this to illustrate the importance of relying on standard scores. Age scores are included in the manual for two purposes: some school jurisdictions require age scores to qualify students for special services, and age scores are sometimes more useful than standard scores for demonstrating small changes over time. Other uses of age scores on this test are clearly discouraged.

Sensory Integration and Praxis Tests (SIPT)

A. Jean Ayres
Western Psychological Services, 1989
12031 Wilshire Blvd., Los Angeles, CA 90025

Purpose	To assess sensory integrative functioning
Major Areas Tested	Visual, tactile, kinesthetic, and vestibular functioning; motor planning ability; postural mechanisms; bilateral integration; and coordination of gross and fine motor skills
Age or Grade Range	4–9 years
Usually Given By	Occupational therapist Physical therapist
Type of Test	Standardized Individual
Scores Obtained	Standard deviations Percentiles
Student Performance Timed?	Yes (some subtests)
Testing Time	1 1/2–2 hours
Scoring/Interpretation Time	1 1/2–2 hours
Normed On	1,997 children comprised a nationwide sample; age, geography, gender, and urban vs. rural residence reflect 1980 U.S. Census data; 133 children from Canada were included
Alternate Forms Available?	No

FORMAT

The Sensory Integration and Praxis Tests (SIPT) is the revised Southern California Sensory Integration Tests, by the same author, which was originally published in 1972. The SIPT is a diagnostic and descriptive tool designed to assess various aspects of sensory integration and motor development that underlie learning and behavior. Several subtests from the original battery have been revised, and new tests have been added to create the 17 subtests that comprise the SIPT. The materials consist of the manual, picture, and manipulative materials for the subtests, individual test answer sheets, and the forms necessary to prepare the answer sheets for computerized scoring. The SIPT must be given by a trained examiner, usually an occupational therapist or physical therapist who has taken the SIPT training course and passed the written test. All student tests are sent to the publisher for computerized scoring. The chart at the end of this review describes the subtests. The SIPT is designed to be given in its entirety in a specific order over two sessions, a total of 1 1/2 to 2 hours of testing. The examiner then prepares the answer sheets and mails them to the publisher for scoring. Individual subtest scores are reported in standard deviations as well as normal curve equivalents. The examiner receives back a multipage computer report describing each student's performance. A report for parents is also included.

STRENGTHS OF THE SIPT

• The SIPT is designed to assess the student's ability to interpret and use certain kinds of sensory information from the environment and the student's own body. Visual, tactile, kinesthetic, and vestibular functioning are assessed, as well as motor and planning skills, postural (praxis) mechanisms, bilateral integration, and coordination for basic and fine motor skills. The skills assessed are automatic rather than cognitive functions.

• The SIPT is, therefore, a comprehensive battery of tests that provides information about a broad range of motor functioning. Through the use of 17 short tests, a balance is achieved between the need to maintain student interest and the need to include sufficient numbers of test items to gain meaningful information.

• The test battery is useful not only in determining which students are experiencing difficulty in the sensorimotor areas, but also in defining the nature of those difficulties. Through the use of factor-analytic studies, several areas of sensory integrative functioning have been identified, and the SIPT provides information necessary for this differential diagnosis. For example, an apraxic student may score poorly in the tactile tests and on the motor-involved tests but may achieve average or above-average scores on tests of form and space perception that do not require precise motor responses. In this example, the SIPT would not only indicate that this student is experiencing difficulties in the sensorimotor areas, but would also identify the area of dysfunction, providing information necessary for planning an appropriate intervention program.

• The SIPT is useful in evaluating sensory motor functioning in language-impaired students. Expressive language requirements are minimal. Directions are simple and frequently accompanied by imitation. Many subtests have trial items to ensure that the child understands the task.

• The scores are presented on a color graph (The WPS Chromograph TM) that illustrates how the student's scores compare with the normative population. The graph is a helpful means of reporting scores to parents and professionals.

LIMITING FACTORS OF THE SIPT

• Although the SIPT is greatly improved over the Southern California Sensory Integration Tests in standardization procedures and population sample, the reliability and validity of the test remains highly questionable. *A Consumer's Guide to Tests in Print* (Hammill, Bryant, and Brown, 1992) gives every subtest a "not recommended" rating on every reliability and validity measure.

• The SIPT is based on the assumption that the various aspects of sensory integration and motor development form the basis for more advanced learning and behavior. There is no research to support this assumption. When a student obtains low scores on the SIPT, a course of sensory integration therapy is often recommended. Given the poor reliability of the test, the lack of data supporting its relationship to academic skills, its use should be made with great caution.

• The SIPT is a very complex test to administer and interpret, and the publishers require that all examiners take a training course and pass a test before they purchase and administer the test. The training course and SIPT materials are very expensive, limiting the use of the test to settings with large numbers of children for whom the test would be appropriate and useful.

• The computerized scoring requirement, while saving time and potentially increasing the accuracy of the complex scoring process, has significant drawbacks. The examiner must spend considerable time preparing the scoring sheets for the computer. The SIPT manual describes many cautions about this preparation and ways to insure the validity of the returned report. Such a process seems prone to error.

• The computerized test report returned to the examiner is 25–30 pages in length. The examiner must then review the report, check for validity, and translate the report into a concise, usable form. The Parent Report (three pages) attempts to explain the results of the child's assessment. But the language used is quite complex and requires extensive explanation, not only to parents but to other professionals who are unfamiliar with the SIPT, because the terminology is very technical. Terms such as *graphesthesia, kinesthesia,* and *praxis* have little meaning to other special education personnel.

• Owing to the nature of the tasks, it is often difficult to determine the student's degree of attentiveness. This is particularly true of the tactile tests.

• The tests were designed to assess automatic rather than highly cognitive functions. However, a bright, motivated student may be able to respond adequately on some tests through cognitive skills, thus obscuring some deficits in automatic functioning. A trained examiner is alert to this possibility, but this observation is subjective at best.

SIPT Tests (in order of administration)

Test	Task	Functions
Space Visualization	The student is given a simple formboard (one shape) with a peg in it and two blocks, each with a hole. Without manipulating the blocks, the student must select the block that fits onto the formboard with the hole correctly aligned over the peg. He or she then indicates the choice by placing one block onto the formboard. The item is scored for time and accuracy from the moment the student first moves (or points to) a block. Early items require only discrimination by shape, but more complex later items require mental manipulation of the blocks.	Visual perception
Figure–Ground Perception	The student is shown a test plate of several superimposed figures and a response plate of six separate figures. The student must select the three figures embedded in the test plate. Figure–ground discrimination is required. Both common objects and geometric forms are used.	Visual perception
Standing and Walking Balance	Student's balance is assessed in several tasks, including standing (feet together), standing (heel to toe), standing (one foot), walking (heel to toe), balancing on a wooden dowel. All items completed with and without vision.	Balance and postural response
Design Copying	The student copies patterns on dot grids. The responses are scored according to the ability to connect the correct dots and the precision with which the lines are drawn. On later items, the student copies designs without the aid of the grid.	Visual perception, visual motor integration, fine motor coordination
Postural Praxis	The examiner quickly assumes positions requiring specific placement of hands, arms, trunk, and legs. The student copies these postures.	Praxis, postural mechanisms, bilateral integration
Bilateral Motor Coordination	The examiner demonstrates a rhythmic pattern of light slaps against his or her thighs, and the student imitates in mirror image. The student's ability to coordinate arm movements enters into the scoring.	Bilateral integration, praxis
Praxis on Verbal Command	Examiner reads a motor command, and student must plan and execute it.	Praxis motor coordination
Constructional Praxis	In Part I, the student copies a seven-block structure built by the examiner. In Part 2, the student is given a preassembled 15-block structure to replicate.	Praxis, visual perception
Postrotary Nystagmus	The student sits on a PNT board (a board that rotates on ball bearings) and is turned in the same direction 10 times in 20 seconds. The student then stares at a blank wall, and the examiner observes his or her eyes for nystagmus. The examiner also watches for postural changes and dizziness. This procedure is repeated with turns in the opposite direction.	One component of vestibular function, namely, selected aspects of response to rotation

Mode of Presentation	Mode of Response	Significant Motor Component?	Timed?
Visual, three-dimensional	Pointing to and/or moving blocks	No	Yes—separate accuracy scores, timed and untimed
Visual, two-dimensional	Pointing to figures in a plate (multiple choice)	No	Not precisely—a time limit is set for each item
Visual with oral directions	Motor	Yes	Yes
Visual, two-dimensional	Dot-to-dot drawing with pencil	Yes	No
Visual	Motor	Yes	Not precisely; a time limit is set for each item for full and partial credit
Visual	Motor—hands and arms used in clapping pattern	Yes	No
Verbal	Motor	Yes	Yes
Visual, three-dimensional	Motor	Yes	No
Vestibular input	No voluntary response required	No	Yes

Test	Task	Functions
Motor Accuracy	With one hand and then the other, the student traces a curved line about 51 inches long, printed on paper 17 by 11 inches. This requires fine finger movements, as well as shoulder-girdle and elbow adjustments on a horizontal surface. In scoring, the examiner measures the length of the line the student traced inaccurately and the distance strayed from the correct line. The scores achieved with the more-accurate hand and the less-accurate hand are compared with those of the normative sample.	Praxis, other aspects of upper-extremity coordination
Sequencing Praxis	Student repeats a series of hand- or finger-tapping movements, series increase in difficulty.	Praxis, sequential memory, bilateral integration
Oral Praxis	Student is asked to imitate a series of movements and positions of fingers, lips, and mouth; both rhythm and sequencing are scored.	Praxis, fine motor sequencing
Manual Form Perception	With a shield occluding the student's vision, the examiner places a geometric form in the student's hand. The student feels the form and then points to the picture that he or she thinks shows that form.	Tactile discrimination, form and space perception
Kinesthesia	A shield occludes the student's vision throughout. The examiner places the student's index finger at a spot on the kinesthesia chart and then says that it is the student's "pretend house" from which he or she will visit a "pretend friend's house." The examiner moves the student's finger to a second spot ("Bob's house") and then back to the original spot. The student attempts to return to "Bob's house" without guidance, and the examiner measures the distance from it to the student's finger. The process is repeated for each "friend's house."	Perception of joint position and movement
Finger Identification	With a shield occluding the student's vision, the examiner touches one or two of the student's fingers, and the student attempts to point to the designated finger(s) on a paper chart.	Tactile discrimination
Graphesthesia	With a shield occluding the student's vision, the examiner traces a simple design with a pencil eraser on the back of the student's hand. The examiner then removes the shield, and the student attempts to retrace the design with a fingertip on his or her own hand.	Tactile discrimination, form and space perception, fine motor coordination
Localization of Tactile Stimuli	A shield occludes the student's vision throughout the test. First, the examiner touches a spot on the student's hand or arm with the tip of a pen; then the student attempts to touch the spot with a fingertip. The examiner measures the distance from the spot to the student's finger.	Tactile discrimination

Mode of Presentation	Mode of Response	Significant Motor Component?	Timed?
Visual	Tracing with pencil	Yes	Yes—separate accuracy scores, timed and untimed
Visual	Motor	Yes	No
Visual, three-dimensional	Motor	Yes	No
Tactile, vision occluded	Pointing to pictures, vision permitted	No	Yes
Kinesthetic, vision occluded (examiner moves student's arm)	Moving arm, vision occluded	Yes	No
Tactile, vision occluded	Pointing to fingers, vision permitted	No	No
Tactile, vision occluded	Retracing designs with a fingertip, vision permitted	Yes	No
Tactile, vision occluded	Touching designated spots on hands and arms, vision occluded	No	No

Test of Sensory Integration (TSI)

Georgia DeGangi and Ronald Berk
Western Psychological Services, 1983
12031 Wilshire Blvd., Los Angeles, CA 90025

Purpose	To provide an overall measure of sensory integration for preschool children
Major Areas Tested	Postural control, bilateral motor integration, and reflex integration
Age or Grade Range	3–5 years
Usually Given By	Occupational therapists Physical therapists
Type of Test	Criterion-referenced Individual
Scores Obtained	Ratings
Student Performance Timed?	Yes
Testing Time	30 minutes
Scoring/Interpretation Time	10–15 minutes
Normed On	Norming population not described
Alternate Forms Available?	No

FORMAT

The DeGangi–Berk Test of Sensory Integration (TSI) is a 26-item screening test designed to assess sensory integration in preschool children. The test includes visual and manipulative materials needed for test administration, protocol booklets, an examiner's manual that presents the theoretical background of the TSI, directions for administration and scoring, and reliability and validity studies. Several items must be supplied by the examiner, including a 3-foot wooden dowel, a rolling pin, a hula hoop, and a scooter board.

The TSI assesses three areas of sensory integration because of their clinical significance in the motor development of the preschool child:

1. Postural Control includes postures that require stabilization of the neck, trunk, and upper extremities

2. Bilateral Motor Coordination emphasizes bilateral coordination, as well as laterality, including trunk rotation, crossing the midline, and bilateral symmetrical postures

3. Reflex Integration includes symmetrical and asymmetrical neck reflexes.

The TSI is designed to be given in its entirety in a prescribed order because the items are sequenced so that the child can move easily from one position to the next. Thirteen tasks are given to allow the examiner to score 36 items.

1. Monkey Task: Ability to assume a position requiring hanging from the dowel by hands and feet. Scored for ability to hold the position while dowel is lifted and for number of seconds held.

2. Side-Sit Cocontraction: Ability to side-sit and keep hands on floor while examiner pushes on shoulder. Scored for ability to take resistance and number of seconds position is held.

3. Rolling-Pin Activity: Ability to sit cross-legged and hit a ball on a string with a rolling pin. Scored for maintaining grasp of pin, for rotating the body past the midpoint, and for number of rotations.

4. Prone on Elbows: Ability to maintain neck cocontraction while in the prone position.

5. Wheelbarrow Walk: Assesses stability of trunk, neck, and upper extremities. Scored for elbow position and distance walked.

6. Airplane: Ability to assume and maintain an antigravity posture of extension. Scored for amount of support needed, arm position, number of seconds held, and degree of extension.

7. Jump and Turn: Ability to jump and turn body orientation. Scored for amount of trunk rotation to left and right and for landing position.

8. Scooter-Board Contraction: Ability to move scooter board back and forth by cocontracting upper extremities. Scored for number of push–pull repetitions.

9. Asymmetrical Tonic Neck Reflex: Assesses integration of tonic neck reflex in quadruped position. Scored for degree of head resistance and flexion of arm on each side.

10. Symmetrical Tonic Neck Reflex Integration: Assesses integration of symmetrical tonic neck reflex in quadruped position. Scored for elbow and trunk extension.

11. Diadokokinesis: Ability to rotate palm up and over. Scored for number of rotations for each hand, both hands, and overflow movements in arms and resting hand.

12. Drumming: Ability to imitate drumming pattern using hands on thighs. Scored for number of repetitions.

13. Upper Extremity Control: Ability to trace around a five-point star shape within a prescribed border. Scored for time of completion, stability of trunk and arm, and crossing the midline for each hand.

Each item is on a 2–5 point scale, and the points for each of the three areas of sensory integration are totaled. The student performance is compared with the normative sample based on Interpretive Range Tables in the manual. Ranges are provided for three to four and five year olds. For example, a four year old's scores might result in this description.

Area	Functioning Level
Postural Control	Normal
Bilateral Motor Integration	Deficient
Total Test Score	At Risk

No interpretive rating is given for Reflex Integration because the authors felt that the reliability data were not strong enough to allow a separate interpretation of those items. They are included in the Total Test Score.

STRENGTHS OF THE TSI

• The TSI is a brief test that identifies sensory integration problems in the preschool child. No other tests in this area are specifically designed for three to five year olds. The tasks are appropriate for and interesting to preschoolers.

• Although designed for use by occupational and physical therapists who are trained and experienced in assessments in the motor area, the TSI can also be given by other special education personnel or by trained paraprofessionals. The authors recommend that in such situations, occupational and physical therapists be involved in the interpretation of test results.

• The TSI manual contains clear and thorough discussions of the theoretical background of the TSI. It is useful reading for special educators who are not familiar with sensory integration terminology and theory.

• The manual is direct and easy to read. Photographs of a child performing each task add to the clarity of administration directions. Scoring instructions are well stated, and examples are given to objectify scoring. The protocol booklet is well designed and easy to use.

LIMITING FACTORS OF THE TSI

- No information is given describing the TSI standardization sample other than two qualifying statements: "However, the difficulties encountered in obtaining the samples for the predetermined testing schedule resulted in nonrepresentative distributions for the variables of interest" (Manual, p. 31) and "It was also intended that each sample be composed of an equal number of males and females from diverse ethnic and socioeconomic backgrounds. However, not all the criteria were met." (Manual, p. 31). No description of how many or what kind of children were included is provided. Reliability and validity studies are reported in the manual and indicate variable item validity for distinguishing between normal and delayed children, and inconsistent reliability data. The authors state that there is an "urgent need for cross validation studies." At this time, the TSI can be best thought of as a rough screening tool providing qualitative information about a child's performance, but it should not be used to make a diagnosis or to determine eligibility for therapy services.

CHAPTER SIX
General Intelligence Tests and Developmental Scales

No area of assessment has caused as much controversy as intelligence testing. Debates rage over such topics as the meaning of intelligence, the use of IQ tests as predictors of school achievement, the cultural biases of standard IQ tests, and the interpretation (or misinterpretation) of IQ scores. There may never be any widespread agreement about whether IQ tests should be given, what they measure, or what they mean, but they continue to be used regularly in the field of special education.

Seventeen tests are included in this chapter. Some are well-known scales of general intellectual ability, while others are measures of specific types of cognitive skills or aptitudes. Some have been used for many years, and others are new. They are listed below in alphabetical order.

• Coloured Progressive Matrices (CPM). A test of nonverbal intelligence, useful with language-disabled, physically handicapped, and non-English-speaking students.

• Denver II. A brief screening instrument used for detecting developmental delays in infants and young children.

• Detroit Tests of Learning Aptitudes 3 (DTLA–3). A revised edition of the original Detroit Aptitude Test; assesses a broad range of abilities.

• Detroit Tests of Learning Aptitude–Primary (DTLA–P:2). A special edition of the DTLA–2 for young children.

• Goodenough Harris Drawing Test. A scoring system for the original Draw-A-Man Test.

• Kaufman Assessment Battery for Children (K–ABC). A relatively new test that combines the assessment of cognitive abilities and achievement.

• Leiter International Performance Scale. An assessment of nonverbal intelligence for special populations of exceptional children.

• McCarthy Scales of Children's Abilities (MSCA). A test of general intellectual ability for young children.

• Slosson Intelligence Test for Children and Adults (SIT–R). A brief test of mental ability.

• Stanford Binet Intelligence Scale (SB). The oldest and best-known test of general intelligence.

• Test of Nonverbal Intelligence (TONI). A test of nonverbal abilities for hard-to-test populations that requires minimal motor responses.

• Wechsler Intelligence Scale for Children–III (WISC–III). The most commonly used test of general intelligence in special education; the Wechsler Pre-School Primary Intelligence Scale (WPPSI–R) and the Wechsler Adult Intelligence Scale (WAIS–R) are also discussed.

• Woodcock–Johnson Psycho-Educational Battery (WJR). Widely used in special education, this test includes cognitive and achievement scales. The Mini-Battery of Achievement (MBA) is also described.

Coloured Progressive Matrices (CPM)

J. C. Raven
A. P. Watt and Son, 1947; revised 1956, 1984
The Psychological Corporation
555 Academic Ct., San Antonio, TX 78204-2498

Purpose	To provide a quick assessment of mental development in children under the age of 11 years
Major Areas Tested	Visual perception and analogous reasoning
Age or Grade Range	5 1/2–11 years
Usually Given By	Psychologist Speech/language clinician Educational diagnostician
Type of Test	Standardized Individual Norm-referenced
Scores Obtained	Percentile
Student Performance Timed?	No
Testing Time	10–40 minutes
Scoring/Interpretation Time	10 minutes
Normed On	627 children in the Burgh of Dumfries, Scotland, whose names began with letters E through L
Alternate Forms Available?	No

FORMAT

The Coloured Progressive Matrices (CPM) is a test of nonverbal intelligence designed for use with children and older people. The materials consist of an examiner's manual, a book of colored illustrations, a set of puzzle boards and moveable pieces, and scoring forms. The test may be administered as either a series of form boards or in book form.

The CPM is composed of three sets of matrices, each with 12 items. In book form, the designs are printed on a brightly colored background. Each item consists of a pattern with a missing piece. The student selects from six visual patterns the one that completes the puzzle. At early levels, visual matching is used. At higher levels, the student must perceive changes in two or three pattern variables. Each student begins with the first item and continues through the 12 items of Set A. By working through the items in standard order, the student learns to solve the progressively more difficult puzzles. Set AB also contains 12 items beginning with the least difficult and progressing through the more difficult items. A third set of 12 items, Set B, allows the student a third opportunity to work through the progression. The board form of the test allows the student to select from six puzzle pieces the one necessary to complete the pattern. In either format, one point is given for each correct response, and the total score is converted into a percentile rank using the tables in the examiner's manual.

If the student does very well on Sets A, AB, and B, the examiner should continue with the Standard Progressive Matrices, which provide norms from 6 years to adult.

STRENGTHS OF THE CPM

• The major strength of the CPM is its usefulness with difficult to assess populations.

• The CPM has minimal verbal instructions and requires no verbal response. It can be used satisfactorily with students who exhibit severe language disorders, physical disabilities, deafness, or limited English.

• The CPM is designed to assess analogous reasoning. Students are allowed ample instruction and demonstration to learn the task. The sets of items are arranged to facilitate learning during the test.

• The book and the board form of the test give practically the same results in children over 6 years of age.

• The colorful format and self-paced nature of the CPM make it very interesting to students.

• American norms are now available, including local and ethnic norms for a variety of populations. These populations include African Americans, Latinos, and Navajos. The norms are published in a research supplement, *A Compendium of North American Normative and Validity Studies* (Raven, 1986).

LIMITING FACTORS OF THE CPM

• While the CPM is a test of mental development or nonverbal intelligence, the author cautions against using it as a general test of mental deficiency. Inadequate norms for United States populations make it inappropriate for use in placement decisions.

• Although norms are provided for children between the ages of three and six years, the author demonstrates no evidence for their prognostic value.

• The CPM is a multiple-choice test; students must be cautioned and monitored to discourage impulsive selection of the answers. Although the manual states that "bright children" or those over eight years old can work on their own and record their own answers, it is not recommended for students suspected of learning disabilities or other handicapping conditions.

• The inadequate technical characteristics of the CPM significantly limit its usefulness. The standardization sample for the 1986 norms is not described nor compared with U.S. census data. There is little usable information provided regarding reliability and validity. Reynolds and Kamphaus, in the *Handbook of Psychological and Educational Assessment of Children* (1990), comment, "Given that other tests with known psychometric qualities and representative U.S. norms are available, neither the Raven's Standard or Coloured Progressive Matrices can be recommended as the instrument of choice to examine nonverbal cognitive functioning" (p. 359).

Denver Developmental Screening Test–Revised
(Denver II)

William Frankenburg, M.D., et al.
1970, 1971, 1975, 1976, 1981; complete revision and restandardization May 1990
Denver Developmental Materials, 1990   P. O. Box 6919   Denver, CO 80206

Purpose	To detect developmental delays
Major Areas Tested	Personal–social, fine motor–adaptive, language, and gross motor skills
Age or Grade Range	Birth–6 years
Usually Given By	Special education teacher Speech/language clinician Occupational therapist Doctor/nurse Psychologist
Type of Test	Standardized Individual
Scores Obtained	Age level
Student Performance Timed?	No
Testing Time	10–20 minutes
Scoring/Interpretation Time	10 minutes
Normed On	2,096 children from Colorado; sample paralleled distribution of Colorado population on the following variables: maternal education, ethnicity, gender, and place of residence.
Alternate Forms Available?	No

FORMAT

The Denver II is the latest version of the Denver Developmental Screening Test that was first published in 1923 and revised several times. Originally developed for doctors to use as a screening tool for detecting developmental delays, the Denver II is used worldwide by physicians, educators, and psychologists as a screening tool. The Denver II materials consist of a screening manual, a technical manual, and individual scoring sheets. A few simple materials, such as red yarn, one-inch colored cubes, and a tennis ball, are included in the kit. The screening manual includes instructions for administration, scoring, interpretation, and follow-up. The technical manual contains information on the standardization procedures and other technical characteristics.

The Denver II is arranged in four sections: personal–social, fine motor–adaptive, language, and gross motor.

Every effort is made to make the young child comfortable with the testing situation. A parent or other familiar person is always present, and the child often sits on that person's lap. Items in the personal–social sector are administered first because many of these items can be reported by the parent. In other sectors, the examiner begins with items slightly below the child's chronological age and continues downward until three items are passed; then the examiner proceeds to items at the child's age level or above until three items are

Denver II

Sector	Description of Tasks	Age	Sample Tasks	
			Task Name	Task
Personal-Social	Tasks that indicate the child's ability to get along with people and to take care of himself or herself	5½ mo.	Resists Toy Pull	Resists having toy taken away
		2½ yr.	Dresses with Supervision	Puts on T-shirt
Fine Motor-Adaptive	Tasks that indicate the child's ability to see, to use hands to pick up objects, and to draw	3½ mo.	Reaches for Object	Grasps rattle when it touches hand
		2 yr.	Tower of Six Cubes	Balances six cubes on top of each other
Language	Tasks that indicate the child's ability to hear, to carry out commands, and to speak	1 yr.	Three Words Other Than Ma-ma, Da-da	Uses at least three specific words for three objects
		4½ yr.	Defines Words	Defines six out of nine words by use, shape, composition, or category (words are *ball, lake, desk, house, banana, curtain, ceiling, hedge, pavement*)
Gross Motor	Tasks that indicate the child's ability to sit, walk, and jump	11 mo.	Stoops and Recovers	Bends over, picks up a toy, and stands up again without holding on or touching the floor
		2½ yr.	Broad Jump	Jumps with both feet together over an 8½-inch paper placed flat on the floor

failed. Items are scored as Pass, Fail, Refusal, or No Opportunity. If a child refuses to try an item, the examiner instructs the parent on how to administer it. The examiner records the child's performance on the individual scoring sheets, which are arranged with age scales across the top and bottom. Ages are given in monthly intervals from one to 24 months and in three-month intervals from ages two to six years. Each of the 125 items is represented on the form by a bar that indicates at what age 25, 50, 75, and 90 percent of the children in the standardization sample passed the item.

A *delay* is defined as any failed item that is completely below the chronological age line; that is, the child fails an item that 90 percent of the children pass at a younger age. Test results are considered "questionable" if the child has one delay and/or two or more cautions. Cautions are defined as failing an item which is passed by 75 to 90 percent of age peers. A rating of "abnormal" is given if a child has two or more delays. Children whose tests are determined abnormal or questionable should be retested in two or three weeks. If test results are still abnormal, the child should be referred to a doctor.

STRENGTHS OF THE DENVER II

• The Denver II is clearly designed to give quick but reliable and valid information on children's performance in the major areas of early development. It is concise, clear, and relatively simple to administer and interpret.

• The Denver II was developed to upgrade the norms and eliminate questionable items from the Denver Developmental Screening Test (DDST–R), 1981 revision. This 1990 revision has several major differences including:

    1. a larger, more-controlled norming population;
    2. 86 percent more language items, including two speech-intelligibility items;
    3. 20 percent fewer parent-report items;
    4. the elimination of difficult-to-administer and-interpret items;
    5. the addition of 20 items without increasing the administration time.

• The manual is well written and gives explicit directions for each test item as well as for such basic procedures as what to tell parents and how to calculate chronological age.

• The scoring sheet is well designed, and the scoring procedures are explicit.

• The author's knowledge of early child development is reflected in the standardization sample that controls for factors such as socioeconomic status reflected by maternal education, ethnicity, urban versus rural residence, and gender, all of which relate to different areas of development. In addition, the norming sample included larger numbers of children at the younger ages to assure better validity of test items.

• The Denver II includes subjective ratings of the child's behavior during testing, such as compliance, alertness, fearfulness, and attention span. The individual scoring sheet provides a place to rate these variables on a three-point scale.

• The Denver II is designed to reflect a child's development on a broad range of skills. It is similar to a growth chart, a familiar tool for medical personnel. As the Denver II covers a six-year age span, it can be used to monitor a child's ongoing development. It specifically does *not* include a total test score that could be interpreted as an intelligence or developmental quotient.

• The Denver II was constructed with care to improve the test–retest and interrater reliability. Studies on both reliability and validity are reported in the technical manual and in supplementary articles in *Pediatrics* (Frankenberg et al., 1992).

• The Denver II is available in Spanish, and the Latino population of Colorado is well represented in the norming sample.

• Complete training materials are available in both English and Spanish for the trainer of paraprofessionals in the administration of the Denver II.

LIMITING FACTORS OF THE DENVER II

• The Denver II was developed primarily by doctors for use in medical settings, suggesting physical causes for developmental delays. The term *abnormal* also reflects the medical model. However, as a screening tool the Denver II is useful in both infant and preschool educational programs.

• Although the examiner's manual states that the test may be given by persons unfamiliar with psychological testing, the authors strongly recommend that the test be administered only by those trained in its use. Research has also demonstrated that periodic retraining is needed as the examiner makes critical judgments beyond the scope of test administration.

• The authors stress that the criteria for *Normal, Questionable*, and *Abnormal* test results were determined arbitrarily and are not the same as referral criteria. Referral criteria need to reflect variation in developmental areas (language, motor, etc.) as well as state guidelines for degree of delay necessary for eligibility for services.

• The authors also emphasize that Denver II results need to be placed in the context of knowledge about the total child—family, educational and cultural experiences, and any medical factors. The developmental status of a child at any one point in time must be interpreted with caution.

• While the Denver II doubles the size of the norming sample, the sample includes only children in Colorado. Results with different populations, such as inner city children in the eastern United States, must be interpreted cautiously.

• Although the Denver II can be administered by trained paraprofessionals, interpretation and reporting to parents should be done by professionals. Information on clinically significant differences among subgroups is included only in the Technical Manual, but paraprofessionals must be cautioned about drawing conclusions on the cause of a delay.

• The examiner's ratings of test behavior are completely subjective and must not be given equal weight with the child's performance on normed test items. The same is true for the two speech intelligibility ratings.

Detroit Tests of Learning Aptitude, Third Edition (DTLA-3)

Donald D. Hammill
PRO-ED, 1991
8700 Shoal Creek Blvd., Austin TX 78757

Purpose	To determine strengths and weaknesses among mental abilities; to identify students significantly below their peers in aptitude; to serve as a research tool in studies of aptitude, intelligence, and cognitive behavior.
Major Areas Tested	Vocabulary, visual discrimination, memory, reasoning, storytelling
Age or Grade Range	6–17 years
Usually Given By	Psychologist Special education diagnostician Speech/language pathologist
Type of Test	Standardized Individual Norm-referenced
Scores Obtained	Percentiles Standard scores Age equivalent
Student Performance Timed?	No
Testing Time	50–120 minutes
Scoring/Interpretation Time	20–30 minutes
Normed On	2,587 students in 36 states; sample balanced for sex, age, race, ethnicity, geographical area, urban/rural residence, parents' education; special education students included in sample, which is representative of national statistics reported in Statistical Abstract of the U.S. (1990)
Alternate Forms Available?	No

FORMAT

The Detroit Test of Learning Aptitude, Third Edition (DTLA–3) is the latest edition of the Detroit Test, which was originally published in 1935 and revised in 1967 and 1985. It is an individual test of aptitude for students between 6 and 17 years. The Detroit Test has retained popularity over the years because it allows the assessment of individual strengths and weaknesses in mental abilities and does not need to be administered by a psychologist. The DTLA–3 materials consist of the examiner's manual, two Picture Books containing the stimulus materials for the visual subtests, student response forms, an examiner's record booklet for recording responses, and a Profile/Summary Form. The comprehensive manual includes a discussion of aptitude testing, the DTLA–3 rationale, administration and scoring procedures, a guide to interpretation, and technical information on the test.

The DTLA–3 is composed of 11 subtests. In most instances, all of the subtests are given in the order listed, which is the order used during the standardization process. In some subtests, starting points according to age are given on the Examiner's Record Form, and a basal-ceiling procedure described in the manual is followed. For others, the subtest is given in its entirety. Administration procedure and scoring criteria for each subtest are clearly described in the manual. Raw scores are calculated for each subtest and are converted into percentiles and standard scores with a mean of 10 and a standard deviation of 3. The eleven DTLA–3 subtests can be combined to form four sets of composite scores:

1. *General Mental Ability Composite*: formed by adding standard scores of all subtests; the best measure of general intelligence.

2. *Optimal Level Composite*: formed by adding standard scores of the individual's four highest subtests; an estimate of what is sometimes called "potential."

3. *Domain Composites*: six composites that reflect linguistic, attentional, and motor abilities.

Linguistic:	Verbal, Nonverbal
Attentional:	Attention Enhanced
	Attention Reduced
Motoric:	Motor Enhanced
	Motor Reduced

4. *Theoretical Composite*: eight composites, which reflect the four major theoretical constructs of intelligence.

Cattell and Horn: Fluid/Crystallized

Das: Simultaneous/Successive

Jensen: Associative/Cognitive

Wechsler: Verbal/ Performance

The sum of the standard scores for each subtest in a composite score is summed into a quotient that has a mean of 100 and a standard deviation of 15. These composite scores are the most reliable and useful scores of the DTLA–3 because they include several subtests and represent the basic concepts of the test. The constructs and their interpretation are well described in the examiner's manual.

DTLA Composite Scores
General Motor Ability: all 11 tests
Optimal Level: 4 highest subtest scores
Domain Composites

Linguistic Domain

Verbal Aptitude
Word Opposites
Sentence Imitation
Reversed Letters
Story Construction
Basic Information
Word Sequences
Picture Fragments

Nonverbal Aptitude
Design Sequences
Design Reproduction
Symbolic Relations
Story Sequence

Attention Domain

Attention Enhanced
Design Sequences
Sentence Imitation
Reversed Letter
Design Reproduction
Word Sequences
Story Sequence

Attention Reduced
Word Opposites
Story Construction
Basic Information
Symbolic Relations
Picture Fragments

Motoric Domain

Motor Enhanced
Design Sequences
Revised Letters
Design Reproduction
Story Sequence

Motor Reduced
Word Opposites
Sentence Imitation
Story Construction
Basic Information
Symbolic Relations
Word Sequences
Picture Fragments

Theoretical Composites

Cattell and Horn

Fluid
Design Sequences
Design Reproduction
Symbolic Relations

Crystallized
Word Opposites
Sentence Imitation
Reversed Letters
Story Construction
Basic Information
Word Sequences
Story Sequence
Picture Fragments

Das

Simultaneous
Word Opposites
Sentence Imitation
Story Construction
Design Reproduction
Basic Information
Symbolic Relations
Picture Fragments

Successive
Design Sequences
Reversed Letters
Word Sequences
Story Sequences

Jensen

Associative
Design Sequences
Sentence Imitation
Reversed Letters
Design Reproduction
Word Sequences
Picture Fragments

Cognitive
Word Opposites
Story Construction
Basic Information
Symbolic Relations
Story Sequence

Wechsler

Verbal
Word Opposites
Sentence Imitation
Reversed Letters
Story Construction
Basic Information
Word Sequences
Picture Fragments

Performance
Design Sequences
Design Reproduction
Symbolic Relations

DTLA–3 Subtest	Title in DTLA–2	Task
Word Opposites	Word Opposites	Student gives antonyms for words pronounced by examiner.
Design Sequence	Object Sequences	Student demonstrates visual attention and memory by reproducing a design sequence using cubes.
Sentence Imitation	Sentence Imitation	Student repeats sentences of increasing length and complexity pronounced by the examiner.
Reversed Letters	Letter Sequences	Student writes in reversed order a sequence of letter names pronounced by the examiner.
Story Construction	Story Construction	Student is shown three pictures and asked to tell a story about each. Stories are scored on sequence of events, naming characters, attempts at humor, etc.
Design Reproduction	Design Reproduction	Student draws complex geometric forms from memory.
Basic Information	New	Student answers a series of questions about commonly known facts acquired from everyday life rather than formal schooling. For example: ("What is the greenhouse effect?")
Symbolic Relations	Symbolic Relations	Student completes a pattern by selecting the correct design from four choices.
Word Sequences	Word Sequences	Student repeats series of unrelated words pronounced by the examiner.
Story Sequences	New	Student orders a series of cartoonlike pictures into a meaningful, humorous story.
Picture Fragments	New	Students are shown pictures with varying elements missing and asked to identify the familiar object, a gestalt closure task.

STRENGTHS OF DTLA–3

• The DTLA–3 is a thoughtfully constructed test of general intelligence or aptitude. The test is well standardized and normed. The technical merits of the test are fully described in the comprehensive manual. *A Consumer's Guide to Tests in Print* (Hammill, Bryant, and Brown, 1992) gives the DTLA–3 an overall Recommended rating, with many of the technical characteristics Highly Recommended. This is particularly important in a test of general ability.

• While most tests of general intelligence are reserved for administration by psychologists, the DTLA–3 can be given by special education teachers or speech and language therapists. This is a very helpful feature of the test.

LIMITING FACTORS OF THE DTLA–3

• The DTLA–3 is a lengthy test to administer, score, and interpret. It is not clear at this time whether the information it yields is more useful than that obtained by the Wechsler Intelligence Scale for Children–Revised (WISC–R). Although individual subtests can technically be given, that is clearly not the intent of the author.

• The DTLA–3 replaces the DTLA–2, which was published in 1985. While the test revision is definitely an improvement, it will be helpful if this edition continues to be current. The DTLA–3 is complex and examiners will need to administer the test to many students of varying ages and difficulties before they will generate the familiarity and expertise necessary for thorough interpretation.

• Several of the subtests of the DTLA–3 are very complex and require the integration of several skills. Reversed Letters, for example, requires the student to memorize the spoken letter sequence and write it in reversed order. Errors may be due to weaknesses in short-term memory or an inability to write letter forms. The additional requirement that the letters be written in small boxes without extending beyond the box adds the element of visual motor coordination. The most efficient strategies would seem to be to write the sequence quickly before it is forgotten. The added dimension of neatness seems unnecessary. Design Sequences uses cubes with five complex geometric designs printed on the sides. Having to locate the design on the cube adds to the memory load, making the already complex task much more difficult. Presumably this is done to make the test difficult enough to test the limit of students at the top of the age range.

• Despite overall strong technical characteristics, *A Consumer's Guide to Tests in Print* (Hammill, Bryant, and Brown, 1992) reports that Design Sequences, Story Sequences, and Picture Fragments have unacceptable stability.

• DTLA–3 users may purchase scoring software, which also generates two reports. The long form is very thorough and contains much of the information available in the manuals; it appears to be much too detailed to be valuable for teachers and parents. The short form is easily generated by hand.

• The DTLA–3 manual provides an excellent discussion of the theoretical models of intelligence most used in test construction. As the manual states, the scores obtained in the theoretical domains have little clinical value.

Detroit Tests of Learning Aptitude–Primary, Second Edition (DTLA–P:2)

Donald Hammill and Brian R. Bryant
PRO-ED, 1986–1991
8700 Shoal Creek Blvd., Austin, TX 78757-6897

Purpose	To determine strengths and weaknesses in developed mental abilities, to identify students significantly below their peers, to make predictions about future performance, to be used as a research tool in cognitive behavior.
Major Areas Tested	Language, attention, and fine motor abilities
Age or Grade Range	3–9 years
Usually Given By	Psychologist Special education diagnostician Speech/language pathologist
Type of Test	Standardized Individual Norm-referenced
Scores Obtained	Percentile Standard Age equivalent Ratings
Student Performance Timed?	No
Testing Time	15–45 minutes
Scoring/Interpretation Time	15–20 minutes
Normed On	2,095 children in 36 states; sample compared with national population on the following factors: race, ethnicity, gender, residence, and geographical area, based on U.S. Census data, 1990
Alternate Form Available?	No

FORMAT

The Detroit Tests of Learning Aptitude–Primary, Second Edition (DTLA–P:2) is the revised edition of the DTLA–P that was published in 1986. The materials include a picture book, individual response forms, and profile/examiner record forms for each student. The manual includes test development theory, instructions for administration and scoring, and information on standardization and other technical characteristics. Changes from the DTLA–P include fewer items, updated norms, and easier administration.

The 100 items of the test are arranged in order of difficulty. An entry point is determined by the student's age. Each item is administered until a ceiling of eight consecutive items is reached. The examiner records 1 (correct) or 0 (incorrect) for each item on the record form. After the test is completed, the examiner tabulates the correct responses for each subtest. The test items represent three domains, each with two subtests:

Linguistic Domain: Verbal Behavior, Nonverbal Behavior
Attentional Domain: Attention Enhanced, Attention Reduced
Motoric Domain: Motor Enhanced, Motor Reduced

Sixteen cognitive behaviors are assessed: Articulation, Conceptual Matching, Design Reproduction, Digit Sequences, Draw a Person, Letter Sequences, Motor Directions, Object Sequences, Oral Directions, Picture Fragments, Picture Identification, Sentence Imitation, Symbolic Relations, Visual Discrimination, Word Opposites, and Word Sequences. Standard scores, percentiles, age equivalents, and ratings (Very Superior, Superior, etc.) are calculated for the total DTLA–P:2 (General Mental Ability Quotient) and each of the six subtests. Differences between domains and subtests within a domain give a picture of a student's strengths and weaknesses in cognitive behaviors.

STRENGTHS OF THE DTLA–P:2

• The authors of the DTLA–P:2 have simplified the administration procedure. Directions for each item are printed on the Profile/Examiner Record Form, eliminating the need for the manual during administration. The manual is clear, thorough, and easy to read.

• The technical characteristics of the DTLA–P:2 are strong. *A Consumer's Guide to Tests in Print* (Hammill, Bryant, and Brown, 1992) recommends the test and gives it "highly recommended" ratings in many areas.

• A software scoring and report system are available.

LIMITING FACTS OF THE DTLA–P:2

• The DTLA–P:2 assesses important developed behaviors; using such data to predict future performance should be done cautiously, taking into consideration past cultural and educational experiences and medical histories.

• The manual lists the 16 cognitive behaviors assessed across the six subtests, identifying them by item number; yet, the student's performance on these items is never analyzed. Knowing the student's strengths and weaknesses on various cognitive tasks is as relevant to teachers as the child's performance on the six arbitrarily named subtests.

• On the DTLA–P:2, the Motor Enhanced score represents a student's ability with pencil, writing, drawing, etc. It assesses neither gross motor skills nor the full range of fine motor abilities. All of the Attention Enhanced subtest items have a memory component, but attention tasks that do not require memory are not included. DTLA–P:2 reports that only refer to a child's performance on each subtest will have little meaning to parents or other professionals without reference to the cognitive behaviors assessed.

• Although the manual describes the point spread necessary to determine a significant difference between subtests, the information is near the end of the manual and may well be missed by many examiners. Given the importance of this information, it should be highlighted in the Scoring Section.

• Studies have shown a decided bias in the DTLA–P:2 for English-speaking subjects (Manual, p. 48); scores should be interpreted with caution with limited-English-proficient subjects.

Goodenough-Harris Drawing Test (Goodenough-Harris)

Dale B. Harris
Harcourt Brace Jovanovich, Inc., 1963 (revised extension of the Goodenough Draw-A-Man Test by Florence Goodenough, 1926)
The Psychological Corporation
555 Academic Court, San Antonio, TX 78204

Purpose	To assess cognitive development and intellectual maturity
Major Areas Tested	Conceptual and intellectual maturity and personality characteristics
Age or Grade Range	3–15 years
Usually Given By	Special education teacher Psychologist
Type of Test	Standardized Individual Group
Scores Obtained	Standard Percentile Quality scale
Student Performance Timed?	No
Testing Time	10–15 minutes
Scoring/Interpretation Time	10–15 minutes
Normed On	275 urban and rural children from the South, West Coast, Upper Midwest, Middle Atlantic, and New England; sample representative of 1950 United States population in regard to father's occupation
Alternate Forms Available?	No

FORMAT

Materials needed for the Goodenough-Harris Drawing Test (Goodenough-Harris) consist of a test booklet, with separate pages for three drawings, and a pencil. Plain white typing paper may be used in lieu of a test booklet, but crayons should not be substituted for a pencil. Very simple oral instructions are required. The student instructions read, "Make a picture of a man. Make the very best picture that you can. Be sure to make the whole man, not just his head and shoulders." After drawing a picture of a man, the student is instructed in a similar fashion to draw a picture of a woman. The student's final drawing is a self-portrait.

The Goodenough-Harris is administered with no time limit, but most students rarely take more than 15 minutes to complete all three drawings. The test can be given individually or in groups. Individual administration is necessary for preschool children and for students being examined clinically. Group administration requires an assistant to help proctor the tests. Erasing, redrawing some features of a figure, or starting completely over again is allowed on the Goodenough-Harris. If given individually, the examiner may question the student about any unclear apsects of the drawings. Responses are recorded on the drawing itself. The examiner may encourage the students with praise. However, the examiner must refrain from offering any suggestions that might influence the nature of the drawing.

No alternate, equivalent forms of the test are available. However, because the correlation of the man and woman scoring scales is about as high as the split-half reliability of the man scale, Harris suggests that the two drawings be considered alternate forms.

The test manual for the Goodenough-Harris contains detailed, exact scoring instructions, with examples of items marked for credit or no credit. Illustrative scored drawings are also provided. There is a total of 73 scorable items, chosen on the basis of age differentiation, relation to total scores on the test, and relation to group intelligence scores. Credit is given for such features as the inclusion of individual body parts, clothing detail, proportion, and perspective.

After carefully studying the instructions, scoring may be accomplished by teachers or paraprofessionals. Separate sections for scoring the man and woman scales are provided. In addition, separate norms for boys and girls and for the man and woman scales are given.

A short scoring guide for both the man and woman point scales is contained in the manual. This guide should only be used by experienced scorers, however.

The total raw score for each drawing is obtained first. The raw score, representing the total points earned, is then converted into a standard score with a mean score of 100 and a standard deviation of 15. The standard score is particularly useful because it expresses a student's relative standing on the test in relation to the student's own age and sex group.

Thus a standard score of 130 indicates that the student's performance is two standard deviations above the average of his or her age and sex group.

Another advantage of standard scores is that they can be averaged. Averaging the standard scores on the man and woman drawings results in a more reliable estimate of maturity than is found when using the scores on either test alone. To score the self-drawing, the examiner uses the point scale of the appropriate sex.

An alternative method of evaluating performance on the Goodenough-Harris is the use of the quality scale. The examiner selects one of 12 sample drawings that most closely resemble the student's drawing and then assigns the scale value of that sample to the drawing. The quality scale value is converted into a standard score, which can ultimately be converted into a percentile score. The quality scale is advantageous for school psychologists who wish to screen large groups of students efficiently. Separate quality scales are provided for man and woman drawings.

STRENGTHS OF THE GOODENOUGH-HARRIS

• The Goodenough-Harris is an easy-to-administer test that is generally nonthreatening and appealing to students. It is valuable as a measure of intellectual maturity, providing indications of development in the areas of self-perception and body concept.

• The results of extensive reliability studies with the original Goodenough Draw-A-Man Test have been encouraging. Both interscorer and same-scorer correlations were found to be high. The effect of art instruction on test scores was found to be negligible, as was examiner effect. The majority of correlations with other intelligence tests are adequate. In addition, the Goodenough-Harris has been used in many studies of different cultures and ethnic groups.

• The results of the Goodenough-Harris give the classroom teacher some information about the intellectual maturity of students. The psychologist may use the test as a screening device to gain a quick impression of a student's general ability level. The test identifies students needing further clinical evaluation.

• If administered individually by an experienced examiner, the Goodenough-Harris may provide valuable clinical information from observations of the student's behavior. For example, spontaneous comments made while drawing, excessive erasing, the sequence of drawing the figure, or using the examiner or self as a model are all important diagnostic indicators. Although the test is not designed to be a measure of visual-motor integration per se, comparisons of the drawings with other tests measuring visual-motor skills is often useful.

• Helpful to the examiner who uses the Goodenough-Harris is Harris's *Children's Drawings as Measures of Intellectual Maturity* (1963). It contains a comprehensive survey of literature dealing with the psychology of children's drawings, as well as a wealth of other information.

LIMITING FACTORS OF THE GOODENOUGH-HARRIS

• Any adult can learn to reliably score the Goodenough-Harris, but psychological training is necessary to adequately interpret the test results. Clinical observations of the student, together with the score, lead to valuable diagnostic insights.

• Although the author does not recommend using the Goodenough-Harris as a personality or projective test, it is often used in this way by psychologists. The student's self-portrait is used for projective purposes. Harris includes an experimental qualitative checklist for evaluating the self-drawing by comparing it with the other two drawings. The self-drawing is not standardized and is therefore regarded as a tentative measure of intellectual maturity. To date, the projective uses of the self-drawing have been disappointing. Thus, one should be cautious in making generalizations about the usefulness of drawings in personality assessment.

• Neither the 1926 nor the 1963 version of the Goodenough-Harris reports any correlation studies with academic achievement.

• The Goodenough-Harris is most useful for assessing the conceptual maturity of the elementary-age student. Beyond grade school, the test has only limited applicability. The mean raw scores increase sharply between the ages of 5 and 14. Above 14 years, however, the scores level off for both sexes on both the man and woman scales. For older students, the point scale is a better scoring method than the quality scale, because the latter shows less age differentiation at the upper ages. The test can also be given to 3- and 4-year-olds. Harris provides tentative guides for interpretation.

• The manual, which is Part 2 of Harris's book, is reproduced in its entirety and published separately. It contains, however, only the instructions for administration and scoring. For specific information on constructions and technical properties of the Goodenough-Harris, the examiner must consult the book.

Kaufman Assessment Battery for Children (K–ABC)

Alan S. Kaufman and Nadeen L. Kaufman
American Guidance Service, Inc., 1983; revised 1985
4201 Woodland Rd., P.O. Box 99, Circle Pines, MN 55014-1796

Purpose	Psychological, clinical, and psychoeducational assessment of learning-disabled and other exceptional children, including minority groups and preschoolers
Major Areas Tested	Cognitive ability and achievement
Age or Grade Range	2 1/2–12 1/2 years
Usually Given By	Psychologist Reading diagnostician Educational diagnostician Counselor Learning disability specialist Any trained person
Type of Test	Individual Standardized Norm-referenced
Scores Obtained	Age level Scaled Standard Grade level Percentile
Student Performance Timed?	Yes (some subtests)
Testing Time	45–90 minutes depending upon age of child
Scoring/Interpretation Time	30–45 minutes
Normed On	2,000 children, 100 at each half-year age interval between 2 years, 6 months and 12 years, 5 months, stratified for sex, parent education, race or ethnic group, geographical region, community size, and grade level; additional sample of 496 Black and 119 low-socioeconomic-status children; 7% of sample from special education classes
Alternate Forms Available?	No

FORMAT

The Kaufman Assessment Battery for Children (K-ABC) is an individually administered test of mental processes and achievement. The materials consist of three easel kits of test items, an administration and scoring manual, an interpretive manual, individual test records, and manipulative materials for four subtests. All of the materials are included in one materials box or plastic carrying case.

Cognitive functioning is defined as problem solving ability, that is, the ability to be flexible and adaptable when faced with unfamiliar problems. The K-ABC divides cognitive functioning into two types of information processing. Sequential processing requires the person to manipulate stimuli presented one at a time, while simultaneous processing requires manipulation of stimuli presented all at once. Sequential processing focuses on serial or temporal order, while simultaneous processing requires spatial integration or a gestalt approach. In contrast to these problem-solving skills, academic achievement is a set of acquired skills or knowledge of facts. These three dimensions—sequential processing, simultaneous processing, and academic achievement—are assessed through 16 subtests on the K-ABC.

Sequential Processing Scale

1. *Hand Movements.* Performing a series of hand movements in the same sequence as the examiner.

2. *Number Recall.* Repeating a series of digits in the same sequential order as given by the examiner.

3. *Word Order.* Touching a series of pictures in the same order as named by the examiner.

Simultaneous Processing Scale

4. *Magic Window.* Identifying a picture exposed slowly behind a narrow window.

5. *Face Recognition.* Selecting from a group photograph one or two faces previously seen. (The photograph shown here is similar but not identical to that which appears in the K-ABC.)

6. *Gestalt Closure.* Naming a partially completed pictured object. (The illustration shown here is similar but not identical to that which appears in the K-ABC.)

7. *Triangles.* Arranging several identical triangles into an abstract pattern to match a model.

8. *Matrix Analogies.* Selecting a picture or geometric form to complete a visual analogy.

9. *Spatial Memory.* Recalling the placement of pictures on a page after brief exposure.

10. *Photo Series.* Placing photographs of an event in chronological order.

Achievement Scale

11. *Expressive Vocabulary.* Naming pictured objects.

12. *Faces and Places.* Naming the well-known person, fictional character, or place pictured.

13. *Arithmetic.* Demonstrating knowledge of numbers and math concepts, counting and computation.

14. *Riddles.* Inferring the name of a concept, given a list of its characteristics.

15. *Reading/Decoding.* Identifying letters and reading words.

K-ABC Face Recognition

K-ABC Gestalt Closure

16. *Reading/Understanding*. Following commands printed in sentences.

The student's scores on each of the three sequential processing subtests and the seven simultaneous processing subtests are converted to a scaled score with a mean of 10 and a standard deviation of 3; the six achievement subtests each convert to a standard score with a mean of 100 and a standard deviation of 15.

Four global scales are computed:

• Sequential processing scale, emphasizing temporal order.

• Simultaneous processing scale, using a gestalt or holistic approach.

• Mental processing composite; a combination of sequential and simultaneous processing, yielding a global estimate of cognitive functioning.

• Achievement scale, assessing knowledge of facts, language concepts, and school-related skills.

A special Nonverbal Scale is also provided. It includes six subtests that may be administered totally in pantomime and that require nonverbal responses. Each of these five scales has a mean of 100 and a standard deviation of 15. Scores are recorded on the individual test record, which is designed to highlight a comparison of the global scales.

STRENGTHS OF THE K-ABC

• The K-ABC subtests are presented through colorful, attractive, unique visual materials that are helpful in maintaining the interest of young children.

• Despite the complexity of the test, the K-ABC is relatively easy to administer and objective to score. The manual is clear, well-organized, and extremely comprehensive.

• The K-ABC was designed to provide a clinical assessment of three hard-to-assess groups of students: handicapped students, minority students, and pre-schoolers. The standardization sample includes a good representation of each group.

• The K-ABC makes extensive use of visual stimuli and motoric responses requiring a minimum of verbal response. In addition, the nonverbal scale provides a means of assessing hearing impaired, speech and language disordered, and non-English speaking children.

• Each subtest includes three teaching items that permit the examiner to use alternative wording, gestures, and other methods to ensure that the student understands the nature of the task. This is especially important, given the uniqueness of the K-ABC subtests and the student population for which it was intended.

• The development and standardization of the K-ABC were extensive and thorough. The test is well normed. Not only does the standardization sample include exceptional and minority students, but the standard errors of measurement are provided for all scales at all ages. A variety of significance levels are also included. In each case, the limitations on the norms provided are carefully delineated in the manual.

• The uniqueness in theory and presentation of the K-ABC has led to extensive studies assessing its reliability and validity. In addition to many studies reported in the manual, an extensive literature of research is developing, reported in both psychology and special education journals. In addition, a new book, *Clinical and Research Applications of the K-ABC* (Kamphaus and Reynolds, 1987), provides a compilation of the research, a discussion of key issues, and supplementary norms for a Verbal Scale, a Total Battery, and a Reading Composite Score.

• The Interpretive Manual includes over 100 pages devoted to helping the examiner interpret an individual student's performance. Teaching techniques for students with strengths in simultaneous or sequential processing are presented.

• A computer program titled ASSIST for the K-ABC is available from the publisher to enter and analyze data. The ASSIST Manual is well written and usable by persons relatively inexperienced with computers. For clinicians administering large numbers of K-ABC's, ASSIST is a useful tool.

• A Spanish version of the Mental Processing Scales is available. However, the authors strongly recommend that bilingual Spanish-speaking children in the United States be tested with the English version as the English norms are more appropriate.

• A 33-minute video cassette is available to aid examiners in becoming proficient in K–ABC administration.

LIMITING FACTORS OF THE K–ABC

• The K–ABC draws extensively upon the theories of cognitive psychologists and neuropsychologists. It incorporates research on brain specialization and hemispheric functioning. These features make the K–ABC very useful in the clinical assessment of children who have known or suspected brain dysfunction. However, the authors' focus on sequential and simultaneous processing seems to have less value in predicting academic performance for children with more generic learning disabilities.

• While the K–ABC is a well-normed and standardized test, the four global scales and the nonverbal scale are the most reliable scores. *A Consumer's Guide to Tests in Print* (Hammill, Bryant, and Brown, 1992) recommends the global scales but reports poor reliability on several subtests, including Hand Movements, Magic Window, and Face Recognition.

- Remedial suggestions presented in the Interpretive Manual are aimed at differential teaching approaches for students strong in sequential or simultaneous processing. These remind us of the remedial programs designed on the basis of the Illinois Test of Psycholinguistic Abilities that later proved faulty. Caution must be taken to view these suggestions as simply interesting ideas to be explored, rather than as recipes for designing remedial programs.

- The K-ABC model purports to separate the measurement of mental processes and achievement, a useful distinction for clinical populations. However, "aptitude" and "achievement" differentiation is extremely difficult to make. The authors discuss the complexity of this problem, urging careful analysis of each individual's performance. However, this aspect of the K-ABC is prone to misuse by untrained or unsophisticated examiners.

Kaufman Adolescent and Adult Intelligence Test
(KAIT)

Alan S. Kaufman and Nadeen L. Kaufman
American Guidance Service, Inc., 1992
4201 Woodland Road, Circle Pines, MN 55014-1796

Purpose	To provide a comprehensive measure of intelligence in adolescents and adults that yields rich clinical and neuropsychological information.
Major Areas Tested	Vocabulary, memory, logical reasoning, auditory comprehension, and abstract reasoning
Age or Grade Range	11–85 years
Usually Given By	Psychologist Neurologist Others with professional training in individual cognitive assessment
Type of Test	Individual Standardized Norm-referenced
Scores Obtained	Standard scores Percentile
Student Performance Timed?	Yes (selected subtests)
Testing Time	Core Battery: 1 hour Extended Battery: 1 1/2 hours
Scoring/Interpretative Time	20–30 minutes
Normed On	A nationwide sample of 2,000 subjects ranging from 1–94 years; stratified random sample based on 1988 U.S. Census controlled for gender, geographic region, socioeconomic status, race, and ethnic group
Alternate Form Available?	No

FORMAT

The Kaufman Adolescent and Adult Intelligence Test (KAIT) is an individually administered test of general intelligence that draws its theoretical basis from Horne and Cattell's (1966) theory of fluid and crystallized intelligence. The materials consist of a manual, two easel books for administration of the subtests, and the Individual Test Record, as well as a set of blocks, an auditory tape, and an item booklet that is needed for specific subtests. The single manual includes the information about the development of the test and the statistical studies, as well as the information needed for scoring and interpretation.

The KAIT is composed of ten subtests, six of which comprise the Core Battery and an additional four subtests that, together with the Core Battery, make up the Extended Scale. The same subtests are used across the entire adolescent to adult age-range. The subtests are evenly divided between tests that measure Crystallized Intelligence, which is dependent upon formal schooling, cultural experiences, and verbal development, and Fluid Intelligence, which measures a person's adaptability and flexibility in problem solving for both verbal and nonverbal tasks.

Crystallized Subtests

Subtest 1. Definitions: The examinee is given a word with missing letters and a clue to its meaning, and is asked to figure out the word.

Example: It's awfully old.

$$\_\_ \text{nt} \_\_ \text{q} \_\_ \_\_ \_\_ \_\_ \_\_$$

Answer: antiquated

Subtest 4. Auditory Comprehension: The examinee listens to a recorded news story and answers literal and inferential questions about its content.

Subtest 6. Double Meanings: The examinee studies two pairs of words and then thinks of a word with two meanings that relates to both parts.

Example: animal   baseball
                        —
                     vampire   stick

Answer: bat

Subtest 10. Famous Faces: The examinee names well-known people from sports, entertainment, or history based on their photographs and a verbal clue.

Fluid Subtests

Subtest 2. Rebus Learning: The examinee learns to "read" phrases and sentences composed of rebuses.

Subtest 3. Logical Steps: The examinee listens to and reads logical premises and then answers questions based on those premises.

Subtest 5. Mystery Codes: The examinee studies pictorial codes and then figures out the code for a novel pictorial stimulus.

Subtest 6. Memory for Block Designs: The examinee studies a block design exposed for five seconds and then reproduces the design from memory, using six yellow-and-black blocks.

Subtest 7. Rebus Delayed Recall: The examinee "reads" rebus "sentences" administered earlier.

Subtest 8. Auditory Delayed Recall: The examinee answers questions about the new story presented earlier.

Following the administration of the KAIT, raw scores are converted to subtest-scaled scores, which are then summed to obtain the three major scores: the Crystallized Scale, the Fluid Scale, and the Composite Intelligence Scale. Subtest scaled scores are based on a mean of 10 with a standard deviation of 3, while the three intelligence scales have a mean of 100 and a standard deviation of 15. A supplementary Mental Status subtest, composed of ten items that assess attention and orientation, is included for examinees of any age who are too low-functioning to be evaluated by the complete KAIT.

STRENGTHS OF THE KAIT

• The authors are clearly knowledgeable about the characteristics of the examinees for which the KAIT is designed. In the manual, they give specific suggestions for using subtests from the Extended Battery in place of core subtests for clients with dyslexia, expressive or receptive language deficits, or motor problems.

• The KAIT subtests are varied and hold the interest of individuals across a wide age range.

• As stated in the manual, examiner qualifications permit the KAIT to be given by examiners with professional training in individual assessment. This allows the test to be given by experienced special education professionals, a very helpful feature of the KAIT.

• The four subtests in the Expanded Battery are very useful in the assessment of persons with cognitive and neuropsychological deficits. The manual provides research data on the use of the KAIT with clinical populations.

• The Profile Analysis section of the KAIT Test Record gives information about how to determine if a difference between two subtests is significant. Extensive information on test performance interpretation is included in the manual.

• The KAIT is a new test, and its clinical usefulness is still to be determined. The reliability and validity studies report in the manual are promising, in terms of technical characteristics of the KAIT.

• KAIT ASSIST C, a computer scoring program, is available. It flags subtests that are significant strengths and weaknesses and provides hypotheses to explore. Three port formats are generated: score summary, profile analysis, and narrative report.

- A KAIT training video is also available for frequent users.

LIMITING FACTORS OF THE KAIT

- The KAIT does not include many of the traditional measures of intelligence, including visual motor skills and vocabulary. The Definitions subtest of the KAIT is more a measure of visual analysis than of word meanings.
- Persons with reading disabilities may have difficulty with Definitions or Double Meanings, and an alternate test from the expanded Battery should be used. Similarly, subjects with significant difficulties in hand use may find the Block Design subtest too difficult.

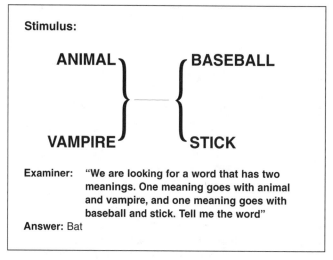

KAIT Double Meanings

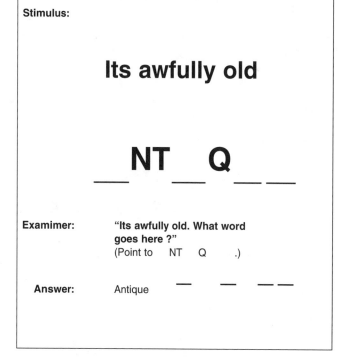

KAIT Logical Steps

KAIT Definitions

Stimulus:

Stimulus:

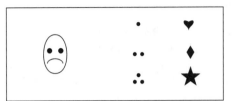

Examiner: "Here are three faces. Each has its own code. This face (point to the first face) has the code single-dot, diamond."

"This face (point to second face) has the code double-dot, diamond."

"And this face (point to the third face) has the code single-dot, heart."

Examiner: "What code goes with this face?"

Answer: ● ● ♥

KAIT Rebus Learning

McCarthy Scales of Children's Abilities (MSCA)

Dorothea McCarthy
The Psychological Corporation, 1972; revised 1978
555 Academic Ct., San Antonio, TX 78204-2498

Purpose	To measure intelligence and to identify children with possible learning disabilities
Major Areas Tested	General intellectual ability
Age or Grade Range	2 1/2–8 1/2 years
Usually Given By	Special education teacher Psychologist
Type of Test	Standardized Individual Norm-referenced
Scores Obtained	Mental age Standard Percentile
Student Performance Timed?	Yes (some subtests)
Testing Time	1 hour
Scoring/Interpretation Time	30 minutes
Normed On	1,032 urban and rural children stratified by age, sex, race, father's occupation, and geographic region; sample included children with "mild" or suspected handicaps
Alternate Forms Available?	No

FORMAT

The materials for the McCarthy Scales of Children's Abilities (MSCA) consist of an examiner's manual, individual scoring sheets, and a kit of attractive manipulative materials (ball, blocks, puzzles, xylophone, and others).

The MSCA consists of 18 subtests grouped into six scales. (See chart.) The sequence of subtests has been carefully organized to facilitate and maintain the interest and attention of the young child. The test begins with two manipulative tests and then gradually increases the demand for a verbal response. The three motor tests are grouped in the middle of the sequence to provide a natural activity break. The drawing tests come next to refocus attention. The battery ends with three tests requiring minimal verbal response. Examples are given on most subtests, and in many cases "second chances" secure the child's best performance.

Using an eight-step process clearly outlined in the manual, the following scores are obtained and recorded on the individual scoring sheet.

• The general cognitive scale raw score is converted into a standard score with a mean of 100 and a standard deviation of 16. This score is called the general cognitive index and is the equivalent of an IQ score.

• Separate scale indexes on each of the other five scales have a mean of 50 and a standard deviation of 10.

• Percentile ranks for each of the scaled scores.

• An estimated mental-age score for the general cognitive index.

STRENGTHS OF THE MSCA

• The MSCA is a well-designed, theoretically based instrument to assess the intellectual functioning of preschool and primary-age children. The tasks include a variety of different activities of interest to young children, and the colorful and interesting materials naturally engage the children in the tasks. Particular attention has been given to the sequence of the subtests and to procedures for providing feedback and support to the child during the testing situation. The well-written manual explains the test administration and scoring procedures very clearly.

• The MSCA includes a number of subtests particularly appropriate for children with suspected learning disabilities. The Motor Scale includes an assessment of gross motor ability, which is not included on any other individual IQ test. The subtests that measure verbal and nonverbal short-term memory are also good.

• The MSCA was normed on a representative standardization sample stratified by age, sex, race, father's occupation, and urban or rural residence. Good test-retest reliability is reported, and although more validity studies are needed, those reported by Kaufman and Kaufman in *Clinical Evaluation of Young Children with the McCarthy Scales* (1977) and in a research summary by Kaufman (1982),

demonstrate good concurrent and construct ability. The Kaufman and Kaufman book contains an excellent critique of the MSCA as well as helpful information on administration, scoring, and interpretation.

• The field of assessment is greatly in need of valid instruments for assessing Black children. The MSCA was constructed with this in mind, and the items were selected to avoid cultural bias. Kaufman and Kaufman report studies of good construct validity of the MSCA for both racial groups. Kaufman also reports that the Black preschool children did not differ significantly from white children on the mean general cognitive index; but for school-age children, Black children obtained a lower mean general cognitive index.

• The MSCA Manual is exceptionally comprehensive. In addition to clear instructions for administration and scoring, extensive research data is provided. The frequent user should also have Kaufman and Kaufman (1977), a very helpful textbook on interpretation.

• Kaufman (1982) in his summary of research states that it is legitimate to use the GCI as an estimate of mental functioning; however, if the student is learning-disabled, examiners need to be cautious, as IQ's of learning-disabled students on the MSCA tend to be lower than on the WISC-R.

LIMITING FACTORS OF THE MSCA

• The MSCA should be administered by examiners experienced in the clinical assessment of young children. The test may only be given by psychologists, learning-disabilities specialists, or other professionals well trained in individual testing. The test requires a fair amount of time to administer, score, and interpret. The computational process for scoring is long and offers many opportunities for error.

• The MSCA covers a very limited age range. The tasks and materials are clearly designed for young children; there is no test form for older children. This presents some problems for using the test with children who require periodic reevaluations. The ceiling is too low for most children older than 7 years.

• The MSCA is lacking in items that assess social and practical judgment as well as abstract problem-solving skills. This is another reason why the McCarthy Scales are more appropriate for preschool children.

• Research reported by Kaufman and Kaufman (1974) indicated that learning-disabled children obtained general cognitive index scores about 15 points lower than their IQ scores on the Wechsler Preschool and Primary Scale of Intelligence and the Stanford-Binet Intelligence Scale. Given the rigid criteria for qualifying a child for a learning disability program in some schools, the MSCA may need to be supplemented with another IQ test or an adaptive-behavior scale to document a significant discrepancy between ability and achievement.

• The MSCA does not provide an alternative subtest or a means of prorating for a subtest that is invalidated in its administration. As this often occurs when testing preschool children, the provision of an alternate test or prorating system would be very helpful.

• The MSCA has too low a ceiling for testing older students or those with gifted abilities.

• The MSCA was normed in the 1970s and needs to be revised to reflect changes in the population in the last 20 years.

McCarthy Scales Subtests

Scale	Content/ Process	Response	Subtests	Task
Verbal	Words	Verbal	3. Pictorial Memory	Recalling pictured objects
			4. Word Knowledge	Identifying and naming objects; defining words
			7. Verbal Memory	Repeating words, sentences, and story
			15. Verbal Fluency	Naming things within four categories
			17. Opposite Analogies	Completing verbal analogies
Perceptual-Performance	Concrete materials	Nonverbal	1. Block Building	Copying block structures
			2. Puzzle Solving	Assembling two- to six-piece puzzles
			6. Tapping Sequence	Repeating sequences of three to six notes on xylophone
			8. Right-Left Orientation	Recognizing right and left on self and on picture
			12. Draw-a-Design	Copying geometric designs
			13. Draw-a-Child	Drawing a child of the same sex
			18. Conceptual Grouping	Demonstrating concepts of size, color, and shape; discovering rules
Quantitative	Digits	Verbal and Nonverbal	5. Number Questions	Answering questions about number facts and quantitative concepts
			14. Numerical Memory	Recalling sequences of digits, forward and backward
			16. Counting and Sorting	Counting and sorting blocks into groups using concepts such as *equal*
Motor	Motor coordination	Nonverbal	9. Leg Coordination	Walking, tiptoeing, and hopping
			10. Arm Coordination	Bouncing, catching, and throwing
			11. Imitative Action	Performing three tasks of eye and hand preference
			Subtests 12 and 13	
Memory	Short-term memory	Verbal and nonverbal	Composite of subtests 3, 6, 7, and 14	
General Cognitive			Composite of Verbal, Perceptual-Performance, and Quantitative scales	

McCARTHY SCREENING TEST (MST)

The MST is an adaptation of the MSCA designed to identify children in the 4–6 year old range who are "at risk" for learning disabilities and may require additional educational assistance in their early years.

The MST is comprised of 6 scales taken directly from the MSCA:

Right-Left Orientation
Verbal Memory, Part I
Draw-A-Design
Numerical Memory, Parts I and II
Conceptual Grouping
Leg Coordination

The test is individually administered in about 20 minutes. The student receives a "score" of either "satisfactory development" or "need for further assessment."

STRENGTHS OF THE MST

• Categories of "At Risk" and "Not At Risk" based on sound normative data.

• Clear manual.

• Interesting tasks.

• Less racially biased than other preschool cognitive measures (Kaufman, 1982).

LIMITING FACTORS OF THE MST

• Choice of subtests selected unclear on either a theoretical or statistical basis.

• Poor predictive validity studies.

• No exceptional children in standardization sample.

• No standardization of MST as a separate instrument.

MCCARTHY SCALES OF CHILDREN'S ABILITIES—SHORT FORM

The short form of the MSCA was developed by A.S. Kaufman (1977). The short form consists of six subtests which were selected to give proportional representation to Verbal, Performance, and Quantitative Scales; to show no sex or racial bias; and to be especially useful with children from 3–6. The average short form correlation with the full scale test across the age range is .92 (Kaufman 1977). The subtests of the short form are:

Puzzle Solving
Word Knowledge
Numerical Memory
Verbal Fluency
Counting and Sorting
Conceptual Grouping

Slosson Intelligence Test–Revised (SIT–R)

Charles Nicholson and Terry Hibpschman
Slosson Educational Publications, 1990
Box 280, East Aurora, NY 14052

Purpose	To provide a quick index of verbal intelligence
Major Areas Tested	General verbal cognitive ability
Age or Grade Range	4–65 years
Usually Given By	Classroom teacher Special education teacher Psychologist Counselor Principal Nurse
Type of Test	Individual Standardized Norm-referenced
Scores Obtained	Standard scores Percentile Mean age-equivalent Stanine
Student Performance Timed?	No
Testing Time	15–30 minutes
Scoring/Interpretative Time	10 minutes
Normed On	1,800 individuals in 31 states; sample designed to match current U.S. Census Report on variables, including geography, occupation, educational level, gender, and race
Alternate Form Available?	No

FORMAT

The Slosson Intelligence Test–Revised (SIT–R) is the latest version of the Slosson Intelligence Test, which was originally published in 1961. The purpose of the SIT–R is to provide a quick screening measure of verbal intelligence. This revised edition includes a broader standardization sample, new norms, and updated content in six categories, including General Information, Similarities and Differences, Vocabulary, Comprehension, Digit Span, and Visual Motor and Auditory Memory for Sentences. The test's 187 oral questions and tasks are arranged in order of difficulty.

The materials consist of the examiner's manual, which contains the test questions; directions for administration and scoring; and SIT–R score sheets. The SIT–R technical manual includes information on test construction and norming reliability and validity. No other materials, except a pencil, are needed to administer the test with preschool students through adults.

The SIT–R is a question-and-answer test; no reading or writing is required. The examiner asks the student a series of short-answer questions. The following questions illustrate the types of content areas assessed. (These questions are similar but not identical to test items.)

Math Reasoning: "A boy was carrying a box of four dozen eggs. He dropped the box and broke a third of them. How many eggs did he break?"

Vocabulary: "If you heard that the old man was frugal, what would that mean?"

Auditory Memory: "Say these letters backwards to me. For example, if I should say, '"a, b, c,"' you would say, '"c, b, a."' Say these letters backwards: '"m, r, b, v, t."'"

Information: "Name the three months of the summer season."

The testing usually begins with a question at the student's chronological age and continues forward until the student answers 10 consecutive questions correctly. This constitutes the basal age. If necessary, the examiner goes backward, asking easier questions, until the basal age is obtained. Testing continues until a ceiling level of 10 consecutive errors in a row is achieved.

The answers to each item are printed immediately following the item. Scoring is completed as the test is administered. Each correct item receives one point; raw scores are converted to a Total Standard Score with a mean of 100 and a standard deviation of 16. This total score is converted to a variety of standard scores, percentiles, and stanines. A mean age-equivalent (MAE) can also be obtained by using the tables in the manual.

STRENGTHS OF THE SIT

• The SIT is a brief individual test of intellectual ability. It was designed as a screening test to be used by professionals relatively untrained in individual testing. It can be administered and scored in 30 minutes. As a quick screening device, it can provide useful information about a student's probable level of mental ability and can identify students in need of more intensive intellectual assessment.

• Specific instructions are given for administering the SIT–R to persons with handicaps, including the visually handicapped, learning disabled, mentally handicapped, and behavior disordered.

• A computer scoring program for the SIT–R is available.

LIMITING FACTORS OF THE SIT–R

• Although the size and national distribution of the standardization sample of the SIT–R is greatly improved over previous versions, the standardization sample is not well described. There is little information on test–retest reliability, and validity studies utilized very small samples at each age group.

• The SIT–R has limited use for preschoolers; the items are too verbal for children with language delays or language differences because of cultural or physical factors.

• The SIT–R is primarily a measure of crystallized intelligence, that is, information that is learned through educational or cultural experiences. It is less relevant and useful for individuals who have limited mainstream education backgrounds. In addition, the content of the SIT–R is limited to items that can be presented in a question-and-answer format. No performance tasks are included, other than a few design-copying items. Thus, students who have excellent visual–spatial skills have no opportunity to demonstrate them, and students who have deficits in these areas will go unidentified.

- Examiners are reminded that the SIT–R is a screening device, and "it is not intended for use in final placement decisions (Jones and Van Leirsburg, 1994).

- Examiners are urged to use the Total Standard Score, rather than the Mental Age Equivalent (MAE), because of frequent misinterpretations of mental age scores. The authors state that these scores are provided only because "some educational systems use them (Nicholson and Hibpshman, 1990).

Stanford-Binet Intelligence Scale, Fourth Edition (SB)

R. L. Thorndyke, E. Hagen, and J. Sattler
The Riverside Publishing Company, 1985
8420 Bryn Mawr Ave., Chicago, IL 60631

Purpose	To differentiate between students who are mentally retarded and those who have specific learning disabilities; to aid in understanding why a student is having difficulty learning in school; to identify gifted students; to serve as a research instrument in cognitive skill development
Major Areas Tested	Verbal reasoning, quantitative reasoning, abstract/visual reasoning, short-term memory
Age or Grade Range	2–23 years
Usually Given By	Psychologist
Type of Test	Standardized Individual Norm-referenced
Scores Obtained	Standard score
Student Performance Timed?	Some subtests
Testing Time	60–90 minutes
Scoring/Interpretation Time	35–40 minutes
Normed On	A nationwide sample of over 5,000 subjects in 160 testing centers in 47 states; sample balanced according to the U.S. census figures of 1980 for geographic region, community size, ethnic group, age, gender, and SES
Alternate Forms Available?	No

FORMAT

The fourth edition of the Stanford-Binet Intelligence Scale (SB) is a major revision of this well-known test of intellectual ability. The materials for the Stanford-Binet Intelligence Scale consist of an examiner's manual, individual record booklets, and a variety of pictures and manipulative materials necessary for administration of the individual test items. All of the materials are packaged in a suitcase-style carrying case.

The format of the new SB is very different from its predecessors. While many of the items from the 1960 version have been retained, they have been organized into 15 subtests which are grouped into areas. (See chart at end of review.)

The SB is designed for multistage testing, which allows the examiner to gain precise information in a short amount of time. The Vocabulary Test is given to all students, beginning with a specific item according to chronological age. Then the highest pair of items administered on the Vocabulary Test together with chronological age determines the entry level for all remaining subtests. This entry level determines which subtests are given to an individual student. Various batteries of tests are recommended for different age groups. These batteries and their prescribed order are well described in the manual. The complete battery consists of 8–13 subtests, depending upon entry level and age of student.

Abbreviated test batteries are recommended for specific testing purposes, such as quick screening, a cognitive abilities pattern, identification of gifted children, and identification of children with school learning problems.

Raw scores for each subtest are converted to Standard Age Scores with a mean of 50 and a standard deviation of 8. Subtest scores are then combined into Area Scores and the 4 area scores are combined into a Total test score with a mean of 100 and standard deviation of 16.

STRENGTHS OF THE SB

• The revised edition of the SB is now similar in format to the other individual intelligence scores; that is, with individual subtests that are organized into composites and a total test score. This format allows a more detailed analysis of the student's strengths and weaknesses.

• The subtests of the SB are interesting and challenging to young children and older students. The mixture of manipulative items, oral items, and pencil-paper tasks allows a variety of response formats that aid in maintaining attention and motivation.

• The technical characteristics of the SB, standardization, reliability, and validity are all strong. *A Consumer's Guide to Tests in Print* (Hammill, Bryant, and Brown, 1992) recommends the SB, cautioning only that the reliability of the Memory for Objects subtest is poor.

• Several supplementary tools are available for the SB. These include the *Examiner's Handbook—Expanded Guide for Fourth Edition Users*, a guide to interpretation and reporting, and *Four Score*, the Computer Scoring Program. Also available is *A Century of Ability Testing* (Thorndike and Lohman, 1990), which discusses the history of intelligence testing and possible future trends in ability testing.

LIMITING FACTORS OF THE SB

• The fourth edition of the SB is a major revision over previous editions and requires a commitment on the part of examiners to learn administration, scoring, and interpretation procedures.

• Eight studies reported in the manual were with already identified exceptional children (gifted, learning disabled, and retarded). It is not clear whether the SB would have classified these children in the same way as the Wechsler Tests originally used.

• The new SB takes significantly longer to administer and interpret than other individual intelligence tests. As it becomes more widely used and researched, it will become clear to what extent the value of the information obtained outweighs the time disadvantage.

SB Subtests

Area	Subtest
Verbal Reasoning	*Vocabulary*. Includes both picture vocabulary and oral definitions.
	Comprehension. Requires answers to "why" questions. (Why do people have umbrellas?)
	Absurdities. Asks why pictures presented are absurd.
	Verbal Relations. Requires listening to four words and identifying why three are alike and one is different.
Quantitative Reasoning	*Quantitative*. Includes both manipulative and pencil and paper computational skills.
	Number Series. Requires completion of numerical series by recognizing the rule. (1, 4, 9, 16, 25, _____)
	Equation Building. Requires formulating correct equations from numbers and symbols.

Abstract Visual
Reasoning

Pattern Analysis. Includes a form-
board for younger students and block
design tasks for older ones.

Copying. Includes copying designs
with blocks or pencil, depending upon
age.

Matrices. Includes both multiple
choice materials as well as written
responses for older students.

Paper Folding and Cutting. Consists
of a multiple choice in which the responses represent how a sheet of
paper might look after it is cut and un-
folded.

Short-Term
Memory

Bead Memory. Requires matching or
reproducing bead chains of different
colors and shapes.

Memory for Sentences. Requires
repeating sentences of increasing
length and complexity.

Memory for Digits. Includes digit
sequences to be repeated both forward
and backward.

Memory for Objects. Assesses visual
sequential memory by requiring the
student to point to pictures in some
order previously shown.

System of Multicultural Pluristic Assessment (SOMPA)

Jane R. Mercer and June F. Lewis
The Psychological Corporation, 1977, 1979
555 Academic Court, San Antonio, TX 78204

Purpose	To provide schools and agencies with a basis for reaching educational decisions that take sociocultural differences into account
Major Areas Tested	Cognitive abilities, sensory-motor skils, and adaptive behavior
Age or Grade Range	5–11 years
Usually Given By	Psychologist (student assessment) Educational diagnostician (parent interview) Counselor (parent interview) Paraprofessional (parent interview)
Type of Test	Standardized Individual Norm-referenced
Scores Obtained	Percentile Scaled
Student Performance Timed?	Yes (some items)
Testing Time	1 1/2–2 hours (student assessment) 1 hour (parent interview)
Scoring/Interpretation Time	1 hour
Normed On	2,085 public school children in California, aged 5 to 11 years, carefully selected for equal proportions of Black, Anglo, and Hispanic students
Alternate Forms Available?	No

FORMAT

The System of Multicultural Pluristic Assessment (SOMPA) is a unique instrument in the field of educational assessment. The purpose of the SOMPA is to assess the whole child, including medical status, sociocultural environment, and functioning in academic and social situations. The SOMPA incorporates three assessment models: the medical model, the social system model, and the pluristic model. Concepts of abnormality are treated differently in the three models. The medical model looks for organic abnormality. The social system model looks at role performance, while the pluristic model compares students of the same age from a similar sociocultural background.

The SOMPA is composed of nine instruments, divided into the student assessment instruments and the parent interview instruments. While the student assessment instruments are intended for individual examination of the student, the parent interview instruments are designed to obtain information about the student and the student's environment. All of the parent interview instruments may be administered in Spanish, as may most of the student assessment instruments.

The SOMPA includes many materials for administration and recording results. These include:
- Student assessment manual
- Parent interview manual
- Technical manual
- Student assessment record forms
- Parent interview record forms in English
- Parent interview record forms in Spanish
- SOMPA profile folders
- Adaptive Behavior Inventory for Children (ABIC)–Spanish Edition
- ABIC transparencies for scoring

In addition to the materials provided in the SOMPA kit, examiners will need the administration and scoring materials for The Bender Visual Motor Gestalt Test (BVMGT) and the Wechsler Intelligence Scale for Children–Revised (WISC-R). After completing the student assessment and parent interview forms, all of the information is transferred to the SOMPA profile folder for a permanent record. The profile folder is printed in two colors; scores that fall in the red areas indicate students "at risk" in the skills or information assessed in that scale. "At risk" means that the student is in

SOMPA Student Assessment Instruments

Instrument	Tasks	Time	Language of Directions
Physical Dexterity Tests	29 tasks divided into six scales: Ambulation Equilibrium Placement Fine Motor Sequencing Finger Tongue Dexterity Involuntary Movement	20 minutes	English or Spanish
The Bender Visual Motor Gestalt Test (see p. 130)	9 design-copying tasks	10–15 minutes	English or Spanish
Weight by Height Visual Acuity Auditory Acuity	Measurement of height and weight Snellen eye test Audiometric screening	10–15 minutes	English or Spanish
Wechsler Intelligence Scale for Children—Revised (see p. 265)	Verbal Scale (see Table 30, pp. 268–269) Performance Scale (see Table 30, pp. 270–271)	50–75 minutes	English only

need of special or immediate attention by the school authorities.

Extensive information is provided in the SOMPA manuals to interpret the student assessment and parent interview data. A unique aspect of the SOMPA is a comparison of the student's school functioning level (SFL) and his or her estimated learning potential (ELP). The SFL is the student's WISC-R score, since the WISC-R is an instrument useful in identifying children at risk for school failure. However, the WISC-R is best at predicting the success of students with similar learning experiences, encouragement, reward systems, and test-taking opportunities. The ELP score combines the raw scores on the SOMPA Sociocultural Scales instrument with raw scores from the WISC-R for each of the three ethnic groups—Anglo, Black, and Hispanic. ELP represents the degree to which a child is likely to progress in an educational program that takes into account the child's sociocultural background. It does not predict the child's success in a mainstreamed program.

STRENGTHS OF THE SOMPA

• The SOMPA is the most recent attempt in a series of efforts over the years to produce a nondiscriminatory assessment procedure. The comprehensive nature of the test, developed to view the total child, is a definite strength and supports the need for multicultural educational programs. The use of previously normed instruments (the WISC-R and the Bender) is commendable. The development of parent interview scales of family situations, behavior, and health history is an excellent feature of the test.

• The materials, interview forms, and manuals of the SOMPA are clear and easily followed. Recording of data is systematically done, and the profile folder provides a convenient, easily read, permanent record. Important cautions are made to assessment personnel regarding interpretation. For example, it is a serious error to overlook a problem in the medical model; in the social system mode, it is serious to overinterpret behavior.

• The SOMPA recognizes the need to use paraprofessionals in parent interviewing procedures. Among the strengths of the test are the techniques described for training interviewers. Suggestions regarding style and communication, as well as specific information gathering, are provided.

• The ABIC is an excellent behavioral rating scale, with uses beyond the population usually assessed by the SOMPA. The veracity score, which provides information on the validity of the interview, and the wide range of behaviors covered increase the ABIC's utility in many special education settings.

Materials	Scoring	Comments
Stopwatch Student assessment manual Record form	Error score is obtained for each of the six scales and transformed into a scaled score and percentile rank. The six scales are then averaged to obtain a physical dexterity average scaled score and percentile.	Includes measures of balance, reflexes, and other measures usually included in a neurodevelopmental examination
Bender cards Paper and pencil Student assessment manual Record form *The Bender-Gestalt Test for Young Children* (Koppitz 1963)	Total error score is calculated using the Koppitz scoring criteria and is transformed into a SOMPA scaled score and percentile rank.	A standard, familiar measure of visual-motor integration in children
Physicians' scale with height bar Snellen chart Audiometer Record form	Using charts by sex, a scaled score is derived representing a height-by-weight ratio. No conversion necessary for visual or auditory acuity.	Weight of the child, controlled for height and sex, is an overall indicator of health.
WISC-R materials Record forms Stopwatch	WISC-R standard scoring procedures	Must be given by a trained psychologist in the standard manner

SOMPA Parent Interview Instruments

Instrument	Areas Measured	Description
Sociocultural Scales	Four scales: Family Size Family Structure Socioeconomic Status Urban Acculturation	11 questions covering the four scales; a rating of the respondent's use of standard English is included.
Adaptive Behavior Inventory for Children (ABIC)	Six scales of social adaptation: Family Community Peer Relations Nonacademic School Roles Earner/Consumer Self-Maintenance	242 questions; the first 35 are asked of all respondents; of the remaining 207, only those for the appropriate age range are asked.
Health History Inventories	Health History	45 questions grouped into prenatal/postnatal, trauma, disease and illness, and vision and hearing inventories

Test of Nonverbal Intelligence, Second Edition
(TONI–2)

Linda Brown, Rita Sherbenou, and Susan Johnsen
PRO-ED, 1990
8700 Shoal Creek Blvd., Austin TX 78757

Purpose	To provide a standardized, norm-referenced test of nonverbal intelligence with reduced motoric requirements and reduced cultural factors for hard-to-test subjects.
Major Areas Tested	Abstract figural problem solving
Age or Grade Range	5–85 years
Usually Given By	Teachers Psychologists Speech/language therapists Other qualified professionals
Type of Test	Standardized Individual or group Norm-referenced
Scores Obtained	Standard scores Percentiles
Student Performance Timed?	No
Testing Time	10–20 minutes
Scoring/Interpretation Time	10–15 minutes
Normed On	2,764 subjects in 30 states; age, gender, race, ethnicity, geographic location, and residence match U.S. Census data (1985); subjects with disabilities are included in the sample
Alternate Forms Available?	Yes

FORMAT

The Test of Nonverbal Intelligence, Second Edition (TONI–2) was designed to assess intelligence in hard-to-test subjects, that is, individuals with severe language disorders, hearing and motor impairments, brain injury, or diverse language and cultural backgrounds. It is a language free measure of abstract, figural problem solving. Two equivalent forms of the test, A and B, are provided. The materials include an easel-style picture book containing the 55 items for each form of the test, answer booklets and response forms (A and B), and an examiner's manual, including test rationale, instructions for administration and scoring, and technical characteristics of the TONI–2.

The TONI–2 assesses nonverbal intelligence through a series of items that require the subject to identify the relationships between abstract figures, such as size, shape, and position, and then solve problems involving these relationships. The format for each item is the same. The subject sees a stimulus pattern in which one or more of the pieces of the pattern is missing. The subject then selects from four to six choices the pieces to complete the pattern. As items increase in difficulty, the number of relationships and the rules for determining the solution increase in number and complexity. Some items require simple matching, while others require analogous thinking, classification, intersection, or progressions. Examples of each type of item are presented at the end of this review.

The test begins with six training items. The examiner pantomimes the problem-solving process, gesturing to the stimulus item and then to each of the multiple choices. Subject indicates response by pointing to his choice. Subjects are encouraged to participate in this training process and are then allowed to complete the training items without coaching. If the examiner feels that the subject does not understand the task after two trials on each training item, testing is discontinued. Otherwise, the examiner proceeds with the test items. Starting points are selected according to the age of the subject, and a basal/ceiling approach is used. While the TONI–2 was designed as an individual test, groups (less than five subjects) can be tested, depending upon the types of subjects being assessed.

Items are scored right or wrong, and the number of correct items below the ceiling are tallied to obtain a total test score. This score is converted into a percentile ranking and a standard score (quotient) with a mean of 100 and a standard score of 15.

STRENGTHS OF THE TONI–2

• The TONI–2 is well designed for its target population. Directions are pantomimed and no verbal response is required, making the test appropriate for subjects with language delays, disorders, or primary languages other than English. In contrast to many nonverbal tests, the only motor requirement is a pointing response. No listening, speaking, reading, or writing are required. The presentation of one item per page reduces confusion, as does the fact that every item follows the same format.

• The TONI–2 is easy to administer and score. The materials are inexpensive, and the test can be completed in a brief amount of time. The TONI–2 provides a cost- and time-efficient alternative to initial testing for subjects who often require extensive time for both testing and interpreting results. When appropriate, group testing may be a time-saving option.

• The TONI–2 has strong technical characteristics. Good descriptions of the standardization sample are provided in the manual, as well as reliability and validity data. The results of eight studies correlating the TONI–2 with achievement tests, and 15 studies correlating the TONI–2 with other measures of ability, are reported. *A Consumer's Guide to Tests in Print* (Hammill, Bryant, and Brown, 1992) recommends the TONI–2 on the strength of its technical features.

• Alternate equivalent forms A and B are useful in several circumstances. For example, if the examiner feels the subject's performance was compromised by environmental distractibility or emotional factors, the alternative form may be administered a few days or weeks later. Alternate forms can be used to assess functioning with and without medication. Alternate forms might also be used to assess the progress of a brain-injured subject over time.

LIMITING FACTORS OF THE TONI–2

• As is well stated in the manual (p. 5), the TONI–2 assesses only one type of intelligence, that of abstract, figural problem-solving. It is not a comprehensive measure of intellectual ability and should only be used for difficult-to-test subjects for whom scores are hard to interpret on broad-based tests or in conjunction with measures of other intellectual abilities.

• Despite the fact that only one item is on a page, many of the items are quite complex in their visual presentation. Subjects with visual perceptual problems may find the task overwhelming, despite good figural problem-solving skills in other formats.

• Although the TONI–2 is not difficult to administer, the pantomime format may be unfamiliar to many examiners. In such instances, examiners are urged to practice the test several times before using the test with difficult-to-test subjects.

• The manual states that group administration is acceptable with groups of five or fewer individuals. Specific instructions for group administration are provided in the manual. However, given the types of subjects for whom the TONI–2 is most appropriate, in most cases individual testing seems warranted. In the group-testing format, each subject needs a picture book and the examiner must move from person to person demonstrating items, ensuring understanding, and scoring correctly to obtain basal and ceiling levels. Even for an examiner well practiced in the TONI–2 groups of subjects, some of whom are likely to be low-functioning, distractible, or motorically impaired, group testing would be difficult and individual performances might well be compromised.

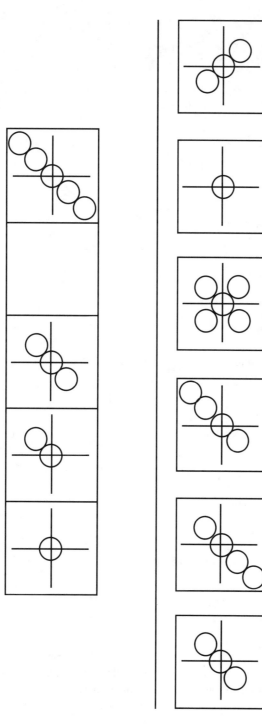

TONI-2: Item B-27

Wechsler Intelligence Scale for Children, Third Edition (WISC–III)

David Wechsler
The Psychological Corporation, 1991
555 Academic Court, San Antonio, TX 78204-2498

Purpose	To measure specific mental abilities that together reflect a child's general intelligence
Major Areas Tested	General intelligence
Age or Grade Range	6–17 years
Usually Given By	Psychologist
Type of Test	Standardized Individual Norm-referenced
Scores Obtained	Verbal IQ Performance IQ Full-scale IQ
Student Performance Timed?	Yes (7 subtests)
Testing Time	50–75 minutes (10 subtests)
Scoring/Interpretation Time	30–40 minutes
Normed On	2,200 children using a stratified random sample to match U.S. Census data (1988) on gender, race, ethnicity, geographic region, and parent education
Alternate Forms Available?	No

FORMAT

The Wechsler Intelligence Scale for Children, Third Edition (WISC–III) is the latest edition of the most widely used individual test of children's intelligence. The WISC–III is a complete revision of the WISC–R. It continues the basic format of all the Wechsler tests, while providing new items, an additional subtest, and new standardization.

Test materials for the WISC–III are packaged in a brief-case-sized kit. They include the manual, individual record forms, and the cards, blocks, puzzles, and booklets necessary for the various subtests. The examiner must supply a stopwatch.

The WISC–III is comprised of 13 subtests that assess different types of cognitive abilities. The test is divided into two main parts—a verbal scale and a performance scale—each having five mandatory subtests. Three supplemental or optional subtests are also provided. Subtests are administered in the prescribed order indicated below.

Verbal Scale	Performance Scale
2. Information	1. Picture Completion
4. Similarities	3. Coding
6. Arithmetic	5. Picture Arrangement
8. Vocabulary	7. Block Design
10. Comprehension	9. Object Assembly
12. Digit Span*	11. Symbol Search**
	13. Mazes*

*Supplementary Test
** Supplementary Test that can be substituted only for Coding.

The specific items within each subtest on the WISC–III are arranged in order of increasing difficulty. Starting points are determined by the student's age, and a basal/ceiling process is used on each subtest. A general idea of the kinds of abilities assessed by each subtest and other descriptive information are given in the table that follows. The examples given in the table are similar, but not identical, to those found on the WISC–III.

In scoring the WISC–III, raw scores on each subtest are first transmitted into scaled scores within the student's age group. Tables of such scores are given for every four-month interval between the ages of 6 years and 16 years, 11 months. The subtest scaled scores are expressed in terms of a distribution with a mean of 10 and a standard deviation of 3.

After obtaining the subtest scaled scores, the next step is to add these scores together to produce an overall verbal score, an overall performance score, and a full-scale score. Finally, using the norm tables, the scores are converted into verbal, performance, and full-scale IQs; each IQ has a mean of 100 and a standard deviation of 15. Thus, an IQ of 100 on any of the scales defines the performance of the average student of a given age on that scale. An IQ of 130 on any of the scales defines the performance of the very superior student, falling two standard deviations above the mean for that age group. With equal standard deviations, IQs are directly comparable for various ages.

The three supplemental subtests may be used in a variety of ways. Digit Span, Symbol Search, and Mazes may be administered, in addition to the ten required subtests, to give a more comprehensive picture of the student's intellectual abilities. Digit Span and Mazes may instead be used as a substitute for a subtest that was invalidated or not given for some reason. Symbol Search may only be substituted for Mazes.

In addition to the three IQ scores—Verbal, Performance, and Full Scale—the WISC–III yields four factor-based composite scores to increase the comprehension of test interpretation. The four factor-based composite scores and the subtests that comprise them are listed below. Note that the supplementary tests Digit Span and Symbol Search must be given to use the composite scores in analysis. The four factor composites have a mean of 100 and a standard deviation of 15.

Factor I: Verbal Comprehension

Information, Similarities, Vocabulary, Comprehension

Factor II: Perceptual Organization

Picture Completion, Picture Arrangement, Block Design, Object Assembly

Factor III: Freedom from Distractibility

Arithmetic, Digit Span

Factor IV: Processing Speed

Coding, Symbol Search

STRENGTHS OF THE WISC–III

• The WISC–III is the most widely used individually administered test of intellectual ability in children. The standardization sample is composed to represent the current U.S. population. The technical characteristics of the test, reliability, and validity are very strong.

• The division of the test into verbal and performance scales allows a picture of an individual student's strengths and weaknesses, making it an excellent instrument for assessing school-age children with special needs.

• The WISC–III profile presents a graphic profile of a student's performance on each subtest, providing a good tool for interpreting test results to parents and others working with the student.

• The administration procedure of alternating between

verbal and performance subtest is an excellent feature. The change from one type of task to another helps maintain student interest and keeps the student who may have a decided weakness in one type of ability from becoming discouraged. Also, the WISC–III Picture Completion, the least demanding subtest for most students, is given first, a sensitive feature to help students with test anxiety.

• Allowing the examiner to demonstrate the solution to a problem or to provide the correct answer to a question when a student fails the first item of any test is also helpful.

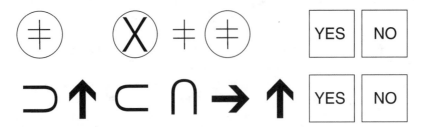

WISC-III Coding Symbol Search

WISC-III Profile

Subtests	Raw Scores	Scaled Scores					
Picture Completion			13		13		
Information		6		6			
Coding			7				7
Similarities		7		7			
Picture Arrangement			17		17		
Arithmetic		7				7	
Block Design			9		9		
Vocabulary		6		6			
Object Assembly			14		14		
Comprehension		9		9			
(Symbol Search)			(12)				12
(Digit Span)		(6)				6	
(Mazes)			(14)				
Sum of Scaled Scores		35	60	28	53	13	19
		Verbal	Perfor.	VC	PO	FD	PS

Full Scale Score
95

OPTIONAL

	Score	IQ/Index	%ile	95% Confidence Interval
Verbal	35	83	13	78 – 90
Performance	60	113	81	104 – 120
Full Scale	95	97	42	91 – 103
VC	28	84	14	78 – 92
PO	53	120	91	110 –126
FD	13	81	10	74 – 93
PS	19	99	47	89 – 109

IQ Scores   **Index Scores (Optional)**

VIQ	PIQ	FSIQ	VCI	POI	FDI	PSI
83	113	97	84	120	81	99

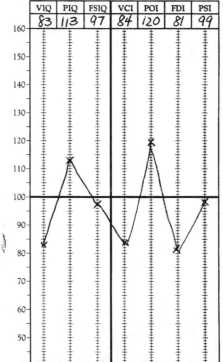

Subtest Scores

Given the correct response to at least the first item helps ensure that the student understands the nature of each test. This is especially important for young students and for those who are mentally deficient.

• One of the primary strengths of the WISC-III is the wealth of diagnostic information it provides. For example, analysis of the size of the difference between the verbal IQ and the performance IQ may be of clinical significance. Wechsler claims that a discrepancy of 15 points or more is important and warrants further investigation. Generally, a student's verbal and performance IQs do not differ significantly. A large difference bewteen them suggests a true difference in ability, which may need further diagnosis.

It is important for an examiner to know how large a difference there must be between a student's scaled scores on two separate subtests for that difference to be considered meaningful. As a general rule, Wechsler states that a difference of three or more scaled-score points between any pair of tests may be considered significant at the 15-percent level of confidence. It is thus possible to analyze intersubtest scatter to determine a student's strengths and weaknesses and to help answer such questions as, "What particular educational deficits are handicapping Mary?" In the WISC-III profile shown here, one can readily see a significant imbalance between verbal and performance skills and the great degree of intersubtest scatter suggestive of specific disabilities. The low Coding score, for example, may indicate poor visual–motor coordination; the depressed verbal scores may indicate a language disability. On the plus side are the near-average Comprehension score and the superior Picture Arrangement score; these scores reflect strengths in common-sense knowledge and social competence.

• In addition to analyzing scores and subtest patterns of the WISC-III, the examiner can consider the quality of a student's responses. By observing the student's behavior in the test situation, the examiner may gain valuable insights that may explain the student's difficulty. Why are some items passed and others failed? If, for example, a student fails questions dealing with temporal-sequential and spatial relationships on the Information subtest, the examiner will want to investigate more thoroughly the student's mastery of such concepts. If a student begins a story in Picture Arrangement at the right instead of at the left, other tasks requiring left-to-right progression should be investigated. If a student performs poorly on Mazes, the reason may be extremely slow working speed or perhaps a lack of foresight and planning ability.

The examiner will also need to assess a whole range of behavioral factors during testing. What is the student's relationship with the examiner: cooperative? self-reliant? confident? fearful? negative? What is the student's reaction to tasks: motivated? persistent? attentive? impulsive? reliant on trial and error? The testing situation can provide the exam-

iner with clinical observations that may be more significant in many cases than the actual test scores.

• Finally, particular mention should be made regarding the usefulness of the WISC-III for the evaluation of the student suspected of having a learning disability. The dichotomy between verbal and performance skills is only one of the several ways the tests could be grouped. Other groups have included:

1. *Meaningfulness versus Nonmeaningfulness of the Subtests*. In this grouping, all the verbal subtests, with the exception of Digit Span, are considered meaningful tasks. The meaningful nonverbal tests are: Object Assembly, Picture Arrangement, and Picture Completion. The performance tests considered nonmeaningful (Block Design, Coding, and Mazes) are categorized as such because they deal with material that is not generally within the typical experience of the student. Analyzing WISC-III subtests within this framework may show a student's ability to process meaningful information successfully and an inability to deal with nonmeaningful material (or vice versa).

2. *Social versus Nonsocial Tasks*. The verbal subtests all involve social perception, with the exception of Digit Span and Similarities. Only the Picture Arrangement subtest of the performance tests entails this ability. The division into social versus nonsocial may be another useful way of viewing a student's WISC-III patterns in relation to learning disabilities.

3. *Spatial versus Conceptual versus Sequential Tasks*. Bannatyne (1968) has offered another way to analyze WISC-III subtest patterns, by categorizing them as follows:

Conceptual Score. Sum of scaled scores of Comprehension, Similarities, and Vocabulary. Language ability is required by these subtests.

Spatial Score. Sum of scaled scores of Block Design, Picture Completion, and Object Assembly. These subtests require the ability to manipulate objects in multidimensional space, either directly or symbolically.

Sequential Score. Sum of scaled scores of Digit Span, Coding, and Picture Arrangement. These subtests demand short-term memory of visual and auditory sequences.

The composite scaled score for each of these three groupings should average 30. Bannatyne compares a student's scores in the three areas to obtain information about particular strengths and weaknesses. In 1974, Bannatyne added a fourth category, Acquired Knowledge, composed of Information, Arithmetic, and Vocabulary.

In summary, the WISC-III is a high-quality general-purpose intelligence test that compares favorably with other individual scales and will likely remain the most commonly used measure of intelligence within the school system. It is a reliable and well-known instrument that usually provides scores correlating highly with school achievement.

• The addition of the four factor composite scores—

Verbal Comprehension, Perceptual Organization, Freedom from Distractibility, and Processing Speed—adds significant information that may be helpful in understanding an individual's test performance and learning style. This analysis is especially helpful in planning instructional strategies for the student with specific learning disabilities.

• The WISC–III is the middle test of the three Wechsler Scales. Its age range overlaps with the Wechsler Preschool and Primary Scale of Intelligence (WPPSI–R) at the six-year-old level and with the Wechsler Adult Intelligence Scale (WAIS–R) at the 16-year-old level. Thus, the examiner of students at these two ages can select the test that best fits the estimated intellectual level of the student. For example, the very bright six year old is probably better assessed by the WISC–III, and the very bright 16 year old by the WAIS–R.

LIMITING FACTORS OF THE WISC–III

• It is common practice for students in special education to be assessed frequently. The examiner must be aware that frequent exposure to the WISC–III may result in higher scores due to practice effects, particularly on the performance items (Manual, p.7). Therefore, examiners should allow as much time between tests as possible to ensure valid results. Common practice is not to readminister the WISC–III within 12 months.

• Caution must be exercised in interpreting WISC-III scores. The level of intellectual ability achieved on the test indicates only a small sample of the student's performance at one moment in time. An IQ is not immutable; it reflects the present capacity of the student and shows what can be expected if current conditions remain the same. Furthermore, the test may or may not be an adequate sample of a student's potential intellectual abilities. All tests give only a limited measure of a student's assets. The significance of an IQ score for a particualr student can accurately be assessed only when it is compared to other data: the student's social–emotional maturity level, the amount of schooling, achievement levels, and cultural or language background. The testing situation itself is important because emotional reactions, such as anxiety, can significantly diminish a student's performance. Thus, the examiner must weigh a number of factors and check for discrepancies and congruencies in order to better understand the meaning of the IQ results and test scatter obtained.

• It is clear that the verbal scale is more closely related to academic achievement than the performance scale. The verbal score also predicts much more accurately than the performance score how successful an individual is likely to be in future school situations. This fact should be borne in mind when evaluating the protocols of students showing high nonverbal scores but poor verbal facility. Although the performance score may reflect average intellectual func-

tioning, this score alone cannot be taken at face value when assessing a student's chances for future school success.

• While student performance on a general intelligence test such as the WISC–III is a crucial factor in diagnosing mental retardation, a low score on the test alone is not sufficient to establish the diagnosis. Multiple sources of information about a child's functioning at home and school, such as information obtained on an adaptive behavior scale, is a necessary part of the assessment process.

• Normative data on the four-factor composites is not included in the WISC–III manual. Until additional research is completed supporting these scales, scores should be interpreted with caution. Barkley (1991) states that the Freedom from Distractibility Scale should not be used as evidence for an attention defect because the scale does not discriminate between students with attention deficit disorders and students with learning disabilities.

WECHSLER PRESCHOOL AND PRIMARY SCALE OF INTELLIGENCE (WPPSI–R), 1989

The WPPSI–R is a fully revised edition of the WPPSI, originally published in 1967. It is a downward extension of the WISC–R intended for the assessment of children between the ages of three and seven years. There are 12 subtests, five mandatory and one optional on the Verbal Scale and five mandatory and one optional on the Performance Scale. Verbal and Performance subtests are alternated during administration to provide variety. The subtests are listed below in order of administration.

Performance Scale	Verbal Scale
1. Object Assembly	2. Information
3. Geometric Design	4. Comprehension
5. Block Design	6. Arithmetic
7. Mazes	8. Vocabulary
9. Picture Completion	10. Similarities
11. Animal Pegs*	12. Sentences*

*Optional

The subtests of the Verbal Scale are essentially the same as those of the WISC–III. Sentences is a test of auditory memory. The child is asked to repeat sentences of increasing length and complexity. Repeating sentences is felt to be a more appropriate measure of memory in young children than Digit Span because it is less abstract. Sentences is used as an additional test to provide more information or as a replacement for a verbal test that was not given or invalidated.

The Performance Scale of the WPPSI–R includes three of the WISC–III subtests: Object Assembly, Block Design, and Picture Completion. Mazes, an optional test on the WISC–III, is a required subtest on the WPPSI–R. Two new subtests were designed for the assessment of young children.

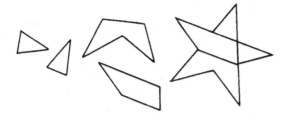

WISC-III Object Assembly

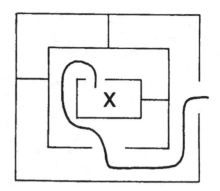

WISC-III Mazes

WISC-III Picture Completion

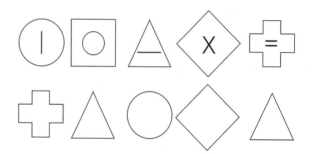

WISC-III Coding A

WISC-III Coding Block Design

Performance Scale

Presented visually; requires motor, nonverbal output. Although brief verbal directions for each task are given by the examiner, the student receives the information visually and nonverbally, and the motor response demands no verbalization.

Subtest	Description	Sample Test Items
Picture Completion	26 line drawings on cards (15 objects, 7 human figures, 4 animals) each requiring the student, after a 20-second exposure, to identify verbally or by pointing to a missing element	"What is missing in this picture?" (see Figure 75 on p. 272)
Picture Arrangement	12 comic-strip picture sequences of three to five pictures requiring logical rearrangement	"Put these pictures in the right order." (see Figure 76 on p. 272)
Block Design	11 two-color block designs requiring reproduction either from an actual block model or from a picture	"Make a block design like this one." (see Figure 77 on p. 273)
Object Assembly	5 puzzle pictures of four to eight pieces depicting familiar objects; the name of the object is given on the first two pictures only	"Put these pieces together to make a star." (see Figure 78 on p. 273)
Coding Coding A (under 8 years)	45 symbols in the test booklet requiring the student to match shapes and write the proper symbols inside	"Put the right mark inside each of these shapes." (see Figure 79 on p. 273)
Coding B (8 years and above)	93 symbols with numerals in the test booklet requiring the student to match numerals and write the symbols below	"Put the right mark in the box below each number." (see Figure 80 on p. 273)
Mazes	9 mazes to be followed by the student without lifting the pencil	"Draw a line from the circle to the X without lifting your pencil." (see Figure 81 on p. 273)
Symbol Search Symbol Search A (under 8 years) Symbol Search B (8 years and older)	45 items, each including 2 groups of symbols; the student indicates whether the target group is included in the search group by marking the appropriate box	"Look at these shapes. One of these shapes is in the group here, so mark the YES box. If the shape is not in this group, mark the NO box."

Timed?	Areas Measured	Notes
Yes	Visual alertness to surroundings, remote visual memory, attention to detail, visual perception (closure ability), ability to isolate essential from nonessential detail, perceptual and conceptual skills	This subtest may indicate word recall problems or inadequate vocabulary if the student points to the missing part but is unable to give the word.
Yes	Visual perception, comprehension, and synthesis of environmental experiences used to anticipate and size up a total situation; logical sequencing of events; attention to detail; ability to see cause-effect relationships	This is considered a test of social intelligence. Compare with Comprehension subtest.
Yes (bonus points given for quick perfect performance at the higher levels)	Ability to perceive, analyze, synthesize, and reproduce abstract forms; visual perception; nonverbal concept formation; capacity for sustained concentration; visual-motor coordination; abstract and concrete reasoning applied to spatial relationships; general ability to plan and organize	This is considered the best single non-verbal measure of general intelligence in the battery, because it is little influenced by cultural factors.
Yes (bonus points given for quick perfect performance)	Immediate perception of a total configuration; understanding the relationship of individual parts; visual perception and anticipation of part-whole relationships; visual synthesis abilities; visual-motor-spatial coordination; simple assembly skills; ability to work flexibly toward a goal	This subtest does not correlate highly with general intelligence.
Yes (bonus points given for perfect score)	Ability to associate meaning with symbol, visual-motor dexterity (pencil manipulation), flexibility and speed in learning tasks when stimuli are visual and kinesthetic, ability to memorize rapidly	This subtest does not correlate highly with general intelligence.
Yes	Ability to shift attention and visual focus quickly and accurately, ability to use left-right progression	
Yes	Ability to formulate and execute a visual-motor plan, pencil control and visual-motor coordination, speed and accuracy, planning capability, foresight	
Yes	Ability to match abstract symbols rapidly.	This subtest does not correlate highly with general intelligence.

WISC-III Picture Arrangement

Geometric Design, a test of visual perception and coordination, requires matching geometric designs and, on the higher items, copying them. Animal Pegs (called Animal House in the WPPSI) requires the child to place a colored peg under the picture of one of four animals. For example, the child places a black peg under each dog, white under each chicken, and so forth. Attention and concentration are enhanced by the game-like quality of this test, which is more appropriate for preschoolers than the pencil–paper task of Coding on the WISC–III.

As on all Wechsler Scales, verbal, performance, and full-scale IQs are obtained with a mean of 100 and a standard deviation of 15. There are no factor-composite scores such as are found on the WISC–III and the WPPSI.

STRENGTHS OF THE WPPSI–R

- Nationwide standardization sample of 1,700 children selected to match U.S. Census Data (1986) for gender, geographic region, ethnicity, and parent education.
  - Strong reliability and validity.
  - Highly interesting materials for most young children.
  - Alternation of verbal and performance tasks is a useful format for holding the attention of young children.
- The first items on all subtests can be used for demonstration and teaching.
- Provides profile that highlights child's cognitive strengths and weaknesses. This information is very helpful in the assessment of children with special needs.
- Constructed on the same format and reflecting the same theories of intelligence of the WISC–III, allowing continuity of cognitive testing on comparable instruments as the student grows older.

LIMITING FACTORS OF THE WPPSI–R

- Takes time to administer (approximately 1 1/2 hours). For younger or difficult-to-test children, the WPPSI–R may require two sessions.
- Should be supplemented with observations and measures of adaptive behavior for children suspected of mental retardation.
- The WPPSI–R has been found to yield lower scores than the Stanford Binet for children in the gifted range. The WPPSI–R should be used in conjunction with other tests and measures of creativity in the assessment of children being considered for gifted programs.

WECHSLER ADULT INTELLIGENCE SCALE— REVISED (WAIS-R), 1981

The revision of the WAIS began with a total restandardization in 1976 and was published as the WAIS-R in 1981. The standardization sample is excellent, and reliability and stability are very high for Verbal, Performance, and Full Scale IQ's and most subtests. Picture Arrangement and Object Assembly are weak. Although 80% of the WAIS-R items are the same, new items show sensitivity to minority groups and eliminate obsolete items. The 11 subtests, listed below, are the same. However, administration procedures have changed to conform to the WISC-R and the WPPSI. That is, Verbal and Performance Subtests are alternated.

Verbal Scale	Performance Scale
1. Information	2. Picture Completion
3. Digit Span	4. Picture Arrangement
5. Vocabulary	6. Block Design
7. Arithmetic	8. Object Assembly
9. Comprehension	10. Digit Symbol
11. Similarities	

Verbal, Performance, and Full Scale IQ's with a mean of 100 and a standard deviation of 15 are obtained as on the other Wechsler Scales.

Woodcock–Johnson Psycho-Educational Battery–Revised (WJ–R)

Richard W. Woodcock and M. Bonner Johnson
The Riverside Publishing Company, 1990
8420 Bryn Mawr Ave., Chicago, IL 60631

Purpose	To provide a comprehensive instrument to assess cognitive abilities and academic achievement over a wide age range
Major Areas Tested	Cognitive ability and academic skills in reading, writing, mathematics, and general knowledge
Age or Grade Range	2 years through 90 years
Usually Given By	Psychologist Educational diagnostician
Type of Test	Individual Standardized Norm-referenced
Scores Obtained	Grade level Age level Percentile Standard Score
Student Performance Timed?	Yes (only on some subtests)
Testing Time	1 1/2–2 hours for complete battery
Scoring/Interpretation Time	30–45 minutes
Normed On	6,359 subjects ranging in age from 18 months to 90 years; nationwide sample based on the latest U.S. Census figures and balanced for size of community, socio-economic status, age, sex, and ethnicity
Alternate Forms Available?	Cognitive Scales–No Achievement Scales–Yes

FORMAT

The Woodcock–Johnson Psycho-Educational Battery–Revised (WJ–R) is the new edition of the original Woodcock–Johnson Psycho-Educational Battery (WJPEB) published in 1977. The battery has been expanded into an even more comprehensive collection of tests designed to assess cognitive abilities and academic skills over a wide age range. While the easel-book format has remained the same, the structure of the test battery is quite different.

The WJ–R consists of 35 subtests, which are organized into four batteries (Standard and Supplemental Batteries of Tests of Cognitive Ability and Standard and Supplemental Batteries of Tests of Achievement). The table below outlines the test organization. The materials include four easel books (one for each battery), individual student record forms (one Cognitive and one Achievement), auditory cassettes for administering some subtests, student response forms (for written language and math computation subtests), four examiner's manuals (two for Cognitive and two for Achievement), a technical manual, and a carrying case. In addition, Alternate Form B is available to allow for pre- and posttesting in both the Standard and Supplemental Batteries Tests of Achievement.

The authors view the WJ–R as a "chest of assessment tools"; it is not intended that the four complete batteries be given to any subject, but rather that subtests be selected appropriate to the student's age and the diagnostic questions being asked. The Standard Battery in each area, Cognitive and Achievement, yield a broad overview of the student's skills, while the supplemental batteries provide more comprehensive information about selected skills. As in the 1977 edition, a Selective Testing chart is printed on the student record form to aid the examiner in selecting appropriate subtests.

Each subtest is given according to the explicit directions printed on the examiner's pages of the easel book. Basal and Ceiling procedures are used to limit testing to items appropriate for the students's age and abilities.

The WJ-R yields a wide range of scores. Age and grade equivalents, percentiles, and standard scores are available for individual subtests, as are "clusters" of subtests that assess the same cognitive factor or content/curriculum area. The types of scores available are listed in the table below. A variety of graphic profiles may be completed by the examainer to illustrate the student's performance. These include a profile of age or grade subtest scores, a profile of cluster percentile scores, and an instructional implications profile that provides useful information for curriculum planning.

STRENGTHS OF THE WJ–R

• The WJ–R is a comprehensive assessment of cognitive abilities and academic achievement. The unique feature of the test is that these two components are available in the same instrument, normed on the same population. This allows the examiner a direct comparison of ability and achievement.

• The WJ–R is a well-standardized instrument; the nationwide sample reflects the U.S. Census data on factors including age, gender, ethnicity, size of community, and socioeconomic status. *A Consumer's Guide to Tests in Print* (Hammill, Bryant, and Brown, 1992) gives the WJ–R a "highly recommended" rating for the standardization sample.

• The division of both the Tests of Cognitive Ability and the Tests of Achievement into two batteries, Standard and Supplemental, allows the examiner to use the Standard Batteries for a quick screening and the Supplemental Batteries to provide more in-depth information in certain areas.

• Alternate forms A and B are provided for the achievement test, allowing the WJ–R to be given more frequently to assess progress.

• Age and grade equivalents, standard scores, and percentiles are provided for individual subtests as well as clusters.

• The Early Development Scale (five cognitive and six achievement tests) allows the assessment of children as young as two years of age.

• The WJ–R contains several useful measures of written language. These include sentence writing (Writing Samples) and writing speed (Writing Fluency). Handwriting, punctuation, spelling, usage, and proofreading are also assessed, giving a broad assessment of written-language skills.

• CompuScore, a computer scoring program, is available for all four batteries. The printout produces a full range of scores for each subtest and cluster as well as an analysis of discrepancies between ability and achievement.

• The WJ–R is the most widely used comprehensive assessment battery. There are many supplementary materials available for the frequent user. These include:

Use and Interpretation of the WJ–R (Hessler, 1992), a handbook on the administration of the WJ–R and interpretation of both scales using case studies

Report Writer for the WJ–R (Schrank and Woodcock, 1993), a software program to assist in writing narrative reports

Journal of Psychoeducational Assessment (1993), a special issue on recent research and clinical uses of the WJ–R

Woodcock–Johnson Psycho-Educational Battery–Revised Recommendations and Reports (Mather and Jaffee, 1992), a guide to translating WJ–R results into behavioral objectives

Instructional Guide to the WJ–R (Mather, 1992), a comprehensive guide for translating WJ–R into instructional planning

• The Spanish edition of the WJ–R is currently in production and is expected to be available in late 1995.

LIMITING FACTORS OF THE WJ–R

• The reliability of the WJ–R cluster and subtest scores is somewhat variable. On the Cognitive Scales, Incomplete Words, Visual Closure, and Cross Out are not stable, while Writing Fluency and Handwriting, on the Achievement Scales, have questionable reliability. Validity studies support the use of the broad cluster score on both the achievement and cognitive scales. Individual subtests of the cognitive scale raise questions about their validity. The WJ–R is a relatively new test and, given its complexity, more studies with clinical populations are needed.

• As with any multiple subtest battery, the 35 subtests of the WJ–R are of variable value in the assessment of an individual student. Several subtests include features that require cautious interpretation.

Memory for Names is mislabeled. It is actually a visually presented, paired associate learning task. For many students, it is a very difficult task and should not be given first in a testing session.

Picture Vocabulary assesses several skills, including picture interpretation, naming vocabulary, and word-finding difficulties. An item analysis of errors will help the examiner interpret a low score.

Incomplete Words is more valid with young children; older students often visualize the sound pattern and fill in the missing letters visually.

Letter/Word Identification, Word Attach, Visual Matching, and Picture Vocabulary (the word-finding aspect) are helpful subtests in the assessment of older students with reading problems.

WJ-R Organization

Cognitive Factors	Standard Battery	Supplemental Battery
Tests of Cognitive Ability		
Long-Term Retrieval	1. Memory for Names	8. Visual-Auditory Learning 15. Delayed Recall-Memory for Names 16. Delayed Recall–V-A Learning
Short Term Memory	2. Memory for Sentences	9. Memory for Words 17. Numbers Reversed
Processing Speed	3. Visual Matching	10. Cross Out
Auditory Processing	4. Incomplete Words	11. Sound Blending 18. Sound Patterns
Visual Processing	5. Visual Closure	12. Picture Recognition 19. Spatial Relations
Comprehension-Knowledge	6. Picture Vocabulary	13. Oral Vocabulary 20. Listening Comprehension 21. Verbal Analogies
Fluid Reasoning	7. Analysis-Synthesis	14. Concept Formation 19. Spatial Relations 21. Verbal Analogies

Curriculum Area	Standard Battery	Supplemental Battery
Tests of Achievement		
Reading	22. Letter-Word Identification 23. Passage Comprehension	31. Word Attack 32. Reading Vocabulary
Mathematics	24. Calculation 25. Applied Problems	33. Quantitative Concepts
Written Language	26. Dictation 27. Writing Samples	34. Proofing 35. Writing Fluency
Knowledge	28. Science 29. Social Studies 30. Humanities	

Note: Underlined tests are taken from the 1977 WJPEB. Those tests marked with an asterisk are from the Early Development Scale and have additional items and norms making them appropriate for subjects down to 24 months of age.

WJ-R Interpretive Options

	Clusters	Subtest Included
Tests of Cognitive Ability		
Broad Cognitive	Standard	1–7
	Supplemental	1–21
Early Development	Standard	1, 2, 3, 5, 6
Cognitive Factors	Long Term Retrieval	1, 8, 15, 16
	Short Term Memory	2, 9, 17
	Processing Speed	3, 10
	Auditory Processing	4, 11, 18
	Visual Processing	5, 12, 19
	Comprehension/ Knowledge	6, 13, 20, 21
	Fluid Reasoning	7, 14, 20, 21
Achievement Aptitudes	Oral Language	
	Reading	
	Mathematics	
	Written Language	
	Knowledge	
Tests of Achievement		
Reading	Broad Reading	22, 23, 31, 32
	Basic Skills	22, 31
	Comprehension	23, 32
Mathematics	Broad Mathematics	24, 25, 33
	Basic Skills	24
	Reasoning	25, 33
Written Language	Broad Written Language	26, 27, 34, 35
	Basic Skills	26, 34
	Expression	27, 35
Knowledge	Broad Knowledge	28, 29, 30
	Early Development	28, 29, 30

Woodcock–McGrew–Werder Mini Battery of Achievement (MBA)

Richard Woodcock, Kevin McGrew, and Judy Werder
Riverside Publishing Company, 1994
8420 Bryn Mawr Ave., Chicago, IL 60631

NOTE: This test is a short form of the WJ–R.
The MBA is an individually administered brief test of basic skills designed to be used with children and adults from 4 to 90 years of age. The MBA assesses four areas of achievement: reading, writing, mathematics, and factual knowledge. The organization of the eight subtests, which can be given separately or in any combination, is shown below. A basal/ceiling procedure is used to determine stopping and starting points on each subtest.

1. **Reading**
   A. *Identification*: reading letters or single words
   B. *Vocabulary*: giving opposites for words read
   C. *Comprehension*: reading a short passage and supplying the missing word (cloze procedure)

2. **Writing**
   A. *Dictation*: spelling, punctuation, capitalization, and word usage
   B. *Proofreading*: identifying mistakes in written passages

3. **Mathematics**
   A. *Calculation*: computation of problems ranging from basic operations through algebra and geometry
   B. *Reasoning and Concepts*: applied problems using visual clues and examiner-read "stories"

4. **Factual Knowledge**
   General information about social studies, science, and humanities

Cluster scores are provided for Reading, Writing, and Mathematics by combining the subtest scores in each area. These three areas can then be combined into a Basic Skills composite. Factual Knowledge is a single subtest score. Age-equivalent scores, percentiles, and standard scores are available for individual subtests and clusters. Standard scores are based on a mean age of 100 and a standard deviation of 15.

STRENGTHS OF THE MBA

• Provides a screening of a number of academic skills in a brief period of time, approximately 30 minutes. The MBA can be used in a variety of situations, including:

the initial screening of new students in an educational setting

the initial assessment to determine the need for in-depth evaluation in specific areas

the screening of post-secondary students entering college, vocational, or occupational training programs

a quick screen to determine the literacy skills of job applicants

• The MBA was normed on a nationwide sample, which was controlled for sex, race, geographical region, community size, and educational factors for the adults.
• The MBA is easy to administer and can be given by paraprofessionals.
• A computerized scoring and reporting program is available that generates a brief interpretive report.

LIMITING FACTORS FOR THE MBA

• Although the norms for the MBA include four and five year olds, with the exception of the Mathematics subtest and Factual Knowledge, the skills assessed are typically not learned before first grade. The MBA is not appropriate for use as a kindergarten-readiness assessment tool. No data is available on its predictive validity.

• The MBA is a screening test; scores obtained should not be used to determine eligibility for special education services or placement. Its primary value is to provide general information about a student's or adult's competency or to serve as the initial step in a more comprehensive evaluation.

• The MBA can only be scored by computer, limiting its usefulness in some settings.

CHAPTER SEVEN

Attention-Deficit/Hyperactivity Disorders (ADHD)

One of the most common reasons for a student to be referred for assessment to the school study team is the perceived problem with the student's attention and activity level. Teachers describe the children as inattentive, impulsive, "spacey," and hyperactive. Parents call pediatricians and mental health clinics with questions about attention-deficit disorder. Children describe themselves as "hyper." The assessment of children and adolescents with attention problems has moved from the doctor's office to the school, where the symptoms are easily observed in the classroom and on the playground. Students diagnosed with "attention-deficit/hyperactive disorder" are eligible for special education services, sometimes under the label *learning disabled*, and sometimes under a more medical heading, such as *other health impaired*. New assessment, teaching, and behavioral management approaches appear on the market daily.

The purpose of this chapter is to discuss the evaluation process for a student with behavior patterns that suggest an attention-deficit/hyperactivity disorder. An overview of the process will be given, as well as reviews of specific evaluation tools. At the end of the chapter is a list of suggested readings for school personnel.

ATTENTION-DEFICIT/HYPERACTIVITY DISORDER (ADHD)

Attention-Deficit/Hyperactivity Disorder (ADHD) is the current label for children and adolescents with significant problems with attention, impulse control, and over activity (Barkley, 1990). In much of the literature, the term ADD, Attention-Deficit Disorder, and ADHD are used interchange-

ably. The label has changed from time to time, reflecting the characteristic of the disorder believed to be the most important. The *Diagnostic and Statistical Manual IV*, 1993, lists the disorder as Attention-Deficit/Hyperactivity Disorder (ADHD). That is the term which will be used throughout this chapter.

ADHD, according to DSM–IV, has five essential features (p. 78):

1. A persistent pattern of inattention and/or hyperactivity–impulsivity that is more frequent and severe than is observed in individuals at a comparable level of development.

2. Some of the hyperactive–impulsive or inattentive symptoms must have been present before age seven.

3. The impairment must be present in at least two settings (home, school, work).

4. There must be clear evidence of the impairment interfering with social, academic, or occupational functioning.

5. The impairment is not better accounted for by another mental disorder.

The behavioral manifestations of ADHD are easily identified by teachers. Poor attention to detail, careless work, lack of persistence, difficulty following directions, and incomplete work are common complaints, as are disorganization and avoidance of tasks that require sustained attention, such as homework. Attention problems not only interfere with academic learning, but with social skills as well.

The hyperactivity part of ADHD may be seen in fidgeting, inability to play quietly, and excessive talking. Young children are frequently described as "on the go" or "driven by a motor." Impulsivity in the classroom takes the form of blurting out answers, an inability to wait one's turn, interruptions, and clowning around. Obviously, these characteristics are present in most students (and adults!) from time to time. It is the pervasiveness and severity of these behavioral patterns that make the diagnosis of ADHD.

Although most students with ADHD have both inattention and hyperactivity–impulsivity, some have a predominance of one type of symptom. DSM–IV provides for three diagnostic categories for ADHD:

1. *ADHD, Combined Type* requires six or more symptoms of both inattention and hyperactivity/impulsivity

2. *ADHD, Predominantly Inattention Type* requires six or more symptoms of inattention

3. *ADHD, Predominantly Hyperactivity–Impulsivity Type* requires six or more symptoms of hyperactivity–impulsivity.

DIAGNOSTIC CRITERIA FOR ATTENTION-DEFICIT HYPERACTIVITY DISORDER (DSM–IV)

A. Either *1* or *2* below:

1. Six or more of the following symptoms of inattention have persisted for at least six months to a degree that is maladaptive and inconsistent with developmental level:

Inattention

a. often fails to give close attention to details, or makes careless mistakes in schoolwork, work, or other activities

b. often has difficulty sustaining attention in tasks or play activities

c. often does not seem to listen when spoken to directly

d. often does not follow through on instructions and fails to finish schoolwork, chores, or duties in the workplace (not due to oppositional behavior or failure to understand instructions)

e. often has difficulty organizing tasks and activities

f. often avoids, dislikes, or is reluctant to engage in tasks that require sustained mental effort (such as schoolwork or homework)

g. often loses things necessary for tasks or activities (e.g., toys, school assignments, pencils, books, or tools)

h. is often easily distracted by extraneous stimuli

i. is often forgetful in daily activities

2. Six or more of the following symptoms of hyperactivity–impulsivity have persisted for at least six months to a degree that is maladaptive and inconsistent with developmental level:

Hyperactivity

a. often fidgets with hands or feet or squirms in seat

b. often leaves seat in classroom or in other situations in which remaining seated is expected

c. often runs about or climbs excessively in situations in which it is inappropriate (in adolescents or adults, may be limited to subjective feelings of restlessness)

d. often has difficulty playing or engaging in leisure activities quietly

e. is often "on the go" or often acts as if "driven by a motor"

f. often talks excessively

Impulsivity

g. often blurts out answers before questions have been completed

h. often has difficulty awaiting turn

i. often interrupts or intrudes on others (e.g., butts into conversations or games)

B. Some hyperactive–impulsive or inattentive symptoms that caused impairment were present before age 7 years.

C. Some impairment from the symptoms is present in two or more settings (e.g., at school or work and at home).

D. There must be clear evidence of clinically significant impairment in social, academic, or occupational functioning.

E. The symptoms do not occur exclusively during the course of a pervasive Development Disorder, Schizophrenia, or other Psychotic Disorder and are not better accounted for by another mental disorder (e.g., Mood Disorder, Anxiety Disorder, Dissociative Disorder, or a Personality Disorder).

The subtype is determined by predominant behaviors *over the past six months*. Most children and adolescents have the combined type.

While the diagnostic criteria for ADHD are clear, it is not easy to sort out the reasons for a student's inattention. Inattention may be related to hearing loss, language difficulties, or an inability to do the classroom work because of cognitive deficits or learning disabilities. Hyperactivity–impulsivity may be related to anxiety, lack of sleep, a behavioral disorder, or lack of opportunity to learn social skills. The behaviors associated with ADHD are also seen in many other childhood and adolescent conditions. Between 19 and 26 percent of children with learning disabilities have ADHD, and children with ADHD are more likely to have disorders of expressive language (Barkley, 1990). For these reasons, the assessment of ADHD, a life-long serious condition affecting many areas of functioning, deserves a complete evaluation process.

THE DIAGNOSTIC PROCESS

The diagnostic criteria for ADHD define the diagnostic process. Classroom observations of students are needed to verify reports of parents and teachers. Behavior-rating scales incorporate information on behaviors that may not be observable but that occur in more than one setting. A parent interview to determine early development history is a critical part of the process. Assessment of learning and behavior to determine the relationship of ADHD to these areas of development is also crucial. While many evaluations of students with special needs are often primarily conducted between the examiner and the student, the assessment of ADHD must include parents and teachers at every step of the process.

Russell Barkley, in his book *Attention Deficit Hyperactivity Disorder: A Handbook for Diagnosis and Treatment* (1990), states that a comprehensive evaluation of a student for ADHD includes the following essential components:

1. The clinical interview with the parents

2. The medical examination

3. The completion of behavioral rating scales. In addition, the use of standardized tests and direct observations of the child in natural settings are important components for some students. A diagnosis of ADHD should never be made on the basis of one type of information alone.

While a complete discussion of the processes of assessing a student with attention problems is beyond the scope of *100 Tests*, this chapter will present an overview of the process, a review of six behavioral rating scales, and a description of several tests that are frequently used in the assessment of students with ADHD.

THE PARENT INTERVIEW

When a student has been referred to the school assessment team, a mental health practitioner, or a pediatrician, the first step in the process is the parent interview. This interview not only provides essential information about a student's behavior from the persons who know him or her best, it also enables the evaluator and the parent to develop the rapport that is necessary to conduct an effective comprehensive evaluation. It is crucial for the evaluator to gain an understanding of the parents' perception of the child, the degree to which they see the behavior as a problem, and other concerns they may have about their child. While many evaluations of children's special needs involve primarily individual testing with the student, the assessment of ADHD requires not only parent permission, but also parent participation. If a diagnosis of ADHD is given, parent counseling regarding behavior management is likely to be a major component of the intervention. Enough time must be allowed for the initial parent interview to enable the evaluator to gather the developmental history, discuss the current situation at home, and explain the evaluation process. The behavioral rating scales should be given to the parents with clear instructions for completing and discussion of how the rating scales are to be used. School districts need to develop a structured parent interview to ensure the gathering of information significantly related to the ADHD diagnosis. The ADHD Clinic Parent Interview (Barkley, 1990) provides a useful guide to the type of questions that should be included.

A MEDICAL EXAMINATION

At some time during the evaluation of attention disorders, the student should be referred for a complete physical examination. A detailed medical interview may yield information critical to the diagnostic process. The examination will also indicate related conditions, such as allergies or asthma, that may need medical management. In addition, the medical examination will determine if any conditions exist that preclude the use of ADHD medications. Because pediatricians will most likely prescribe and monitor any medications, it is important to involve them in the evaluation process.

BEHAVIOR RATING SCALES

In the assessment of attention span and concentration, behavior rating scales play an important role. Rating scales are means of objectifying parents' and teachers' views of a student's behavior and, with older students, their view of their own behavior. As with all assessment instruments, group behavior-rating scales have strengths and limitations, and each individual scale has its own merits and limiting factors.

Behavior-rating scales have many advantages, including gathering information from informants who have known the child for years in a variety of situations, collecting data on infrequent but important behaviors that may not occur during an observation, and incorporating the opinions of several significant people in the student's life. In addition, behavior-rating scales are brief and inexpensive. However, behavior-rating scales are essentially ratings of someone's opinion and are affected by many factors, including each person's views and values concerning behavior. "Talking back" may be viewed by one teacher as a *mild* problem and another teacher as *severe*; a weekly temper tantrum may be seen by one parent as *frequent* and another as *rare*. For this reason and others, behavioral rating scales should be seen as only one part of the evaluation.

In the area of ADHD, effective behavior rating scales have the following characteristics:

1. Items on the questionnaire are clearly worded and easily observed.

2. The rating scale has a range (*mild* to *severe*, *not at all* to *frequently*) rather than a yes–no response.

3. The scale has research to support that it discriminates between students with ADHD and students with other behavioral difficulties or learning problems.

4. Scales have acceptable reliability over time and across raters.

5. Scales are sensitive to changes in behavior and can thus evaluate the effects of medication and other interventions.

Pediatricians, psychiatrists, psychologists, and other mental health professionals frequently use behavior-rating scales as an initial source of information in the clinical assessment of ADHD. Typically, questionnaires are given to parents to complete either together or separately and to the student's primary teacher or teachers. In the assessment of adolescents, a self-rating scale is often completed by the student as well. The data from the scales is then compiled and added to information from parent and child interviews, observations, and formal testing. The diagnosis of ADHD should never be made from scores on behavior-rating scales alone. Even the best ADHD rating scales correlate only moderately with actual observations of ADHD symptoms taken in home or classroom settings (Barkley, 1990).

The brevity, availability, and convenience of behavioral-rating scales make them popular in the schools for students with attention problems. While they are an essential tool, school personnel need to be experienced in their usage. Parents and teachers need full explanations of the purpose for which the scale is being completed, directions for completing and returning the form, and the information on the way the information will be used. Forms should not be sent in the mail for parents to complete without this full explanation. As with any other assessment tool, the process of completing the forms and the data gathered is confidential.

The diagnosis of ADHD has important implications for the student and his parents. When the results of behavior-rating scales, together with other evaluations, suggest ADHD, the parent should be referred to the pediatrician, psychiatrist, or other mental-health personnel to complete the evaluation process and discuss intervention options.

At the conclusion of this chapter, several of the most commonly used behavior-rating scales are described.

OTHER DIAGNOSTIC TOOLS

Barkley (1990) feels that the most promising laboratory measure of ADHD is the continuous performance task, a computerized assessment of vigilance and sustained attention.

1. *The Gordon Diagnostic System* is a continuous performance test that has been developed for use in the clinical assessment of ADHD. The computerized test requires the student to look at a small screen on which a sequence of numbers appears in random order. Each time the student sees a 1 followed by a 9, he or she pushes a button. The test continues for nine minutes. Correct responses, omitted responses, and incorrect responses are totaled and compared with a norming sample of more than 1,000 children between the ages of three and 16 years. The Gordon Diagnostic System has been found to discriminate ADHD and normal children and to reflect changes in medication (Barkley et al., 1988). It has been shown to have a false positive rate (normal children being classified as ADHD) of 2 percent and a false negative rate (ADHD children missed) of 15 to

33 percent (Gordon et al., 1989), again demonstrating that a diagnosis of ADHD cannot be made by one test or one type of information alone.

2. *The Test of Variable Attention (TOVA) Continuous Performance Test* is also a computerized assessment of ADHD. On the TOVA, the student must discriminate between two stimuli, responding each time the target stimulus appears. The 22-minute test is designed to measure attention and impulsivity/disinhibition. Errors of omission are defined as inattention; errors of commission are interpreted as a measure of impulsivity. Response time is also recorded. The TOVA has been standardized on 2,000 children and adults and has norms for ages four to 80 years. The test has been found useful in the diagnosis of ADHD and in measuring changes in attention and impulsivity with medication.

Several software programs similar to the Gordon and TOVA are available for use on personal computers. These programs show promise but currently do not have the research data to determine their validity and usefulness.

In addition to the continuous performance tests of vigilance and sustained attention, several pencil/paper tasks have been used to assess ADHD.

3. *The Wisconsin Card Sort Test (WCST)* (Grant and Berg, 1981) was developed to assess brain dysfunction in adults and is primarily used by neuropsychologists. The WCST assesses an individual's ability to recognize abstract principles and to "shift sets" from one principle to another within a card-sorting test. Individuals are given a deck of 128 cards, each of which has a combination of one to four figures (plus sign, star, circle, triangle) in one of four colors. They are asked to sort the cards by placing them in piles to match stimuli cards. Students are told if they are correct so that they can discover the sorting rule. Once they reach criterion, the rule changes and they must "shift sets" and discover a new rule. Performance is scored in several ways including total correct, total errors, perseverative responses, nonperseverative errors, perseverative errors, and number of set shifts. The perseveration score is felt to be the most important in identifying persons with focal frontal lobe lesions (Egeland, 1985). The WCST is intended for individuals 12 years of age and older. Adequate norms for younger children are not yet available, although research reports are beginning to report findings with these children (Chelune and Baer, 1986). Because current views hold that ADHD is likely to involve some impairment of the frontal lobe (Barkley, 1990), tests of frontal-lobe dysfunction may be useful in assessing ADHD. Chelune and others (1986) have reported differences between children with ADHD and children without ADHD on the WCST. But this finding has not been replicated, and Barkley does not recommend the WCST for use in the diagnosing of ADHD.

4. *The WISC–III Freedom from Distractibility Factor* is comprised of three subtests, Arithmetic, Digit Span, and Coding, and is frequently used as an "indicator" of ADHD. While scores on this factor show a correlation with other measures of attention (Klee and Garfinkle, 1983), further research has not shown that the Freedom from Distractibility Factor discriminates between ADHD children and normal or learning-disabled children. For these reasons, examiners are cautioned about using the WISC–III factor score as evidence for ADHD. (See page 302.)

In summary, while continuous performance tests and other psychological measures appeal to our need for standardized results (numbers!), the ADHD diagnostic process must include less-standardized procedures of interview, rating scales, and observation.

Conners Parent and Teacher Rating Scales (CPRS/CTRS)

C. Keith Conners
Multi-Health Systems, 1990
908 Niagara Falls Blvd., N. Tonawanda, N.Y. 14120-2060

Purpose:	Developed to screen problem behaviors, evaluate the effect of interventions, and study factors associated with child psychopathology
Form 1	**Conners Teacher Rating Scales (CTRS)** **CTRS–R (28 items) 1978** Informants: Teachers Time to Complete: 5–10 minutes Age Range: 3–17 years Scales: Conduct Problem Hyperactivity Hyperactivity Index Inattentive–Passive
Form 2	**CTRS–30 (39 items) 1982** Informants: Teachers Time to Complete: 5–10 minutes Age Range: 4–12 years Scales: Anxious–passive Asocial Conduct Problems Daydream–Attention Problems Emotional–Overindulgent Hyperactivity Hyperactivity Index
Form 3	**Conners Parent Rating Scales (CPRS) CPRS–93** **(93 items) 1970** Informants: Teachers Time to Complete: 10–15 minutes Age Range: 6–14 years Scales: Antisocial Anxious–shy Conduct Disorder Hyperactive–Immature Learning Problem Obsessive–Compulsive Psychosomatic Restless – Disorganized

Form 4	**CPRS–48 (48 items) 1978**
	Informants: Teachers
	Time to Complete: 5–10 minutes
	Age Range: 3–17 years
	Scales: Anxiety
	          Conduct Disorder
	          Hyperactivity Index
	          Impulsive–Hyperactive
	          Learning Problem
	          Psychosomatic

FORMAT

All four versions of the Conners Scales provide four rating options for each item. Informants rate each item by marking how much the student has been bothered by the problem in the last month (not at all, a little, pretty much, very much). Materials consist of the questionnaire, triplicate response forms, and the manual. Raw scores are transferred to the profile sheet, which convert the informants' ratings to standard scores and enable the examiner to compare the student's score on each scale with the norming populations. Computer scoring software is also available.

STRENGTHS OF THE CPRS/CTRS

• Well-known scales that have been used in research on hyperactivity and other childhood problems for more than 20 years.

• Abbreviated Symptom Questionnaire (ASQ) is also available for teachers and parents; each contains 10 items.

• Often used to evaluate the effect of medication, therapy, and other interventions.

LIMITING FACTORS OF THE CPRS/CTRS

• Only the CTRS–39 has a standardization sample of adequate size, and it is not well described; Conners Scales are not recommended by *A Consumers Guide to Tests in Print* (Hammill, Bryant, and Brown, 1992) due to poor technical characteristics.

• Many samples were studied more than 15 years ago, and definitions of *Attention-Deficit Disorder* and *Hyperactivity* have since changed.

Child Behavior Check List (CBCL)

Thomas Achenbach and Craig Edelbrook
Department of Psychiatry, 1982, 1988, 1991
University of Vermont, VT 05401

Purpose	To provide a standardized format for recording children's and adolescents' competencies and problems as reported by their parents, teachers, and themselves

Form 1	**Child Behavior Check List (CBCL/4–18)**
	Informants: Parents
	Time to Complete: 15–20 minutes
	Age Range: 4–18 years
	Scales: Social Competence
	             Withdrawn
	             Somatic Complaints
	             Anxious–Depressed
	             Social Problems
	             Thought Problems
	             Attention Problems
	             Delinquent Behavior
	             Aggressive Behavior

Form 2	**Child Behavior Check List–Teacher Report Form (CBCL–TRF) 1984, 1991**
	Informants: Teachers
	Time to Complete: 10–15 minutes
	Age Range: 5–18 years
	Scales: Academic Performance
	             4 Adaptive: Working Hard, Behaving Appropriately, Learning, Happy
	             8 Scales from CBCL/4–18

Form 3	**Child Behavior Check List – Youth Self-Report Form (CBCL–YSR) 1987, 1991**
	Informants: Children and adolescents
	Time to Complete: 10–15 minutes
	Age Range: 11–18 years
	Scales: Social Competence
	             Academic Performance
	             8 Scales from CBCL/4–18
	             Self-Destructive/Identify Problems (boys only)

FORMAT

The CBCL is a series of forms that allows the systematic rating of childhood and adolescent behavior by their parents and teacher. The 1991 Edition is a revision of the original scales, which were published in 1983. Informants rate items about competence and problem behaviors on a three-point rating scale. Points for each item are tallied and plotted on a profile according to the child's age and sex. Age groups are four to 11 and 12 to 18. Percentile scores are given for each syndrome assessed by the CBCL. The profile also designates which scores are high enough to be considered "clinical" problems. The scales are grouped into internalizing behaviors (withdrawal, somatic complaints, anxious–depressed) and externalizing behaviors (delinquency, aggression). Rating forms from parents (CBCL/4–18), teachers (TRF), and the student, if appropriate, (YSR), are integrated with cognitive assessments, physical assessments, clinical interviews, and observations to form a multiaxial, broad-based picture of a student's behavior.

STRENGTHS OF THE CBCL

• The CBCL "is the most well-developed empirically derived behavior-rating scale currently available for assessing psychopathology and social competence in children" (Barkley, 1990). The standardization sample included more than 2,300 "normal" children who were well stratified regarding socioeconomic class and ethnic composition. Reliability and validity information published in the manual supports the technical characteristics of the forms.

• The 1991 Profiles extend the age range to 18 and focus on Syndrome Scales that affect both boys and girls across a wide age range.

• The Social Competence Scale of the CBCL rates a child's social skills on three dimensions: Activities, Social, and School. A profile is plotted based on the child's age and sex. The CBCL is one of the few rating forms that includes information on this aspect of the child's development and provides a more comprehensive picture of the child's behavior.

• Research studies on the CBCL show that the rating-scale discriminates between hyperactive and nonhyperactive children (Barkley, 1981; Edelbrock, 1984). It has also been used to assess changes in conduct problems following a parent-training program in child management skills (Webster-Stratton, 1984).

• The CBCL–TRF includes an Adaptive Functioning Scale that reflects the student's work habits, academic performance, and general happiness, in addition to the Behavior Problems Scale. In general, the reliability of the externalizing (acting out) behaviors is higher than that of the internalizing (withdrawn) behavior.

• Validity studies using the CBCL–TRF indicate that the checklist discriminates children with ADHD from children with other behavior disorders.

• The Youth Self-Report (CBCL–YSR) is quite similar in content to the parent and teacher questionnaires, providing a more comprehensive picture of the child. Research has shown that the CBCL–YSR "may be more useful as a screening measure for symptomatology frequently associated with ADHD (e.g., aggression, depression) than for ADHD itself (Barkley, 1990).

• In addition to comprehensive manuals for the CBCL/4–18, TRF, and YRF, examiners will find essential information helpful in integrating information in "Integrative Guide for the 1991 CBCL/4–18, YSR, and TRF Profiles (Auchenback, 1991).

• The CBCL/2–3 is a two-page form for gathering parent information about young children's behavior.

• The Direct Observation Form (DOF) is designed for recording observed behaviors, both problems and on-task, in the classroom, or at recess. The authors recommend that three to six 10-minute observations be recorded on the DOF. A second child in the group serves as a "control" against which the observed child's scores can be compared.

• The semistructured Clinical Interview for Children (SCIC) is available for interviewing 6-11 year olds and the Young Adult Behavior Check List (YABCL) is designed to gather parent reports about young adult "children."

• In order to assess the effect of medication or other interventions, a Parent's Follow-Up Report form is also available.

LIMITING FACTORS OF THE CBCL

• With a rating scale of problem behavior using teachers as informants, children tend to show improvement even without intervention. This finding was noted on the CBCL–TRF. It may reflect the natural need of teachers to see children improve.

• The authors of the CBCL note that many of the items use complex language and suggest that parents completing the forms have at least a fifth-grade reading level. Instructions are given for administering the CBCL to parents by reading them the questionnaire while they read along and mark the items on their copies.

• The CBCL provides "standardized descriptions of behavior rather than diagnostic inferences" (Manual, p. iii). Students should not be "labeled" on the basis of a rating scale alone.

Home and School Situations Questionnaire (HSQ/SSQ)

Russell A. Barkley
Department of Psychiatry, 1987
U. of Massachusetts Medical Center
55 Lake Ave. North, Worchester, MA 01655

Purpose	To evaluate where children and adolescents may be exhibiting problem behaviors
Form 1	**Home Situations Questionnaire (HSQ, 1987)** Informants: Parents Time to Complete: Less than 5 minutes Age Range: 4–18 years Scales: Social Interaction, Oppositional–Unfocused, Oppositional–Focused, Self-Engaged Situations
Form 2	**Home Situations Questionnaire–Revised (HSQ–R, 1990)** Informants: Parents Time to Complete: Less than 5 minutes Age Range: 6–12 years Scales: Self-Care/Public Setting Chore/Social Settings

Form 3	**School Situations Questionnaire (SSQ, 1987)**
	Informants: Teachers
	Time to Complete: Less than 5 minutes
	Age Range: 4–11 years
	Scales: Social Interaction
	                 Focused Attention
	                 Novel Activities Situations

Form 4	**School Situations Questionnaire–Revised (SSQ–R, 1990)** Informants: Teachers Time to Complete: Less than 5 minutes Age Range: 6–12 years Scales: Not yet determined

FORMAT

The format of these four questionnaires is the same. On the original questionnaires, parents or teachers answer the question, "Does the child (student) present any problems with compliance to instructions, commands, or rules for you in any of these situations?" The HSQ uses situations such as meal times, watching television, and bedtime, while the SSQ asks about school arrival, individual desk work, small-group instruction, recess, and other school activities. If there is a problem, the informant rates its severity on a 9-point scale. The revised questionnaires, HSQ–R and SSQ–R are designed to assess specific problems with attention and concentration. The question asked is, "Does this child (student) have problems paying attention or concentrating in any of these situations?" On all four forms, two scores are obtained: the number of problem situations and the average severity score.

STRENGTHS OF THE HSQ/SSQ

• The HSQ, HSQ–R, SSQ, and SSQ–R all assess *where* students exhibit problem behaviors or difficulty with attention and concentration. By using both the parent and teacher forms, a profile of the student's behavior at home and school can be derived. The situational profile developed is very helpful in planning interventions for parents and teachers.

• The questionnaires have also proven useful in documenting changes due to medication or other types of intervention (Barkley, 1990).

LIMITING FACTORS OF THE HSQ/SSQ

• The original questionnaires do not discriminate between conduct disorders and attention problems. For the assessment of attention-deficit disorder (ADD), the revised questionnaire should be used.

• The 9-point scale of severity, ranging from mild to severe, is more difficult to use than other rating scales that ask, "How often does this behavior occur—monthly, weekly, hourly, daily?"

• Data is currently being collected on the reliability and validity of the revised scales.

Academic Performance Rating Scale (APRS)

George J. DuPaul
Department of Psychiatry, 1990
U. of Massachusetts Medical Center
55 Lake Ave. North, Worchester, MA 01655

Purpose	To complement other teacher rating scales by providing information on a student's academic productivity and accuracy in the classroom
Informants	Teachers
Time to Complete	Less than 5 minutes
Age Range	Grades 1–6
Scales	Learning Ability Academic Performance Impulse Control Social Withdrawal

FORMAT

Teachers rate children's classroom behaviors on a five-point scale. Examples of items include:

- How quickly does the child learn new material?
- How consistent has the quality of the child's academic work been over the past week?
- .• Estimate the percentage of written math work completed (regardless of accuracy) relative to classmates.

Normative data is provided by grade level and gender.

STRENGTHS OF THE APRS

- APRS provides a quick measure of gathering teacher input about a child's classroom behavior. The items tap information well known by a teacher.
- While many teacher rating scales assess problem behaviors and social skills, few assess learning ability and academic performance.

- The APRS can be used to assess the effects of medication on academic performance.

LIMITING FACTORS OF THE APRS

- Information on the norming sample of the APRS is not available. The APRS is clearly intended to be used in conjunction with more-comprehensive rating scales.

ADHD Rating Scale

George J. DuPaul
Department of Psychiatry, 1990
U. of Massachusetts Medical Center
55 Lake Ave. North, Worchester, MA 01655

Purpose	To assess the 14 symptoms of ADHD described in the DSM–III–R (1987)
Informants	Parent or teacher
Time to Complete	Less than 5 minutes
Age Range	6–12 years
Scales	Inattention/Restlessness Impulsivity/Hyperactivity

FORMAT

A four-point scale is used to rate the student on 14 behaviors that reflect the DSM–III–R diagnosis of ADHD. Items include:

- often does not seem to listen
- often blurts out answers to questions.

Scores of 2 or higher on the scale are considered inappropriate for the student's developmental level. Examiners can quickly count the items with scores 2 or higher and determine if the 8 out of 14 criteria recommended by DSM–III–R are met. Three scores are determined for each student: Inattention/Restlessness, Impulsivity/Hyperactivity, and total score. Norms are available for both boys and girls, 6–12 years, by parents and teachers.

STRENGTHS OF THE ADHD

- Provides direct ratings of the essential characteristics of ADHD under DSM–III–R.
- Good norming sample.

- Research indicates scale discriminates between students with ADHD from normal students and students with learning disabilities.
- Scale is sensitive to effects of medication.

LIMITING FACTORS OF THE ADHD

- DSM–III–R has been replaced by DSM–IV, and diagnostic criteria have changed.

Attention Deficit Disorders Evaluation Scale
(ADDES)

Stephen B. McCarney
Hawthorne Educational Services, 1989
P. O. Box 7570 Columbia, MO 65205

Purpose	To provide educators, school psychologists, pediatricians, and other medical personnel with an evaluation tool for ADD with input from parents and teachers
Informants	Parents and teachers
Time to Complete	15 minutes
Age Range	4–18 years
Scales	Inattention Impulsivity Hyperactivity

FORMAT

The ADDES provides a five-point scale for parents and teachers to rate ADD. The Home Version has 46 items assessing behaviors in the home environment, while the School Version includes 60 items easily observed by teachers. Scores are obtained for each subscale and the total test for each version. Norms for both boys and girls are provided.

STRENGTHS OF THE ADDES

• The ADDES has the largest normative sample of any ADD rating scale. The national sample is balanced for parent's educational level, rural and urban residence, and ethnicity.

• The ADDES provides the largest number of items for assessing ADD in school-age children.

• Studies demonstrate strong reliability, both over time and across raters.

• The ADDES was designed primarily for use in schools. Recommendations are easily incorporated into individual education plans (IEP's).

• Many materials are available to help the frequent user of the ADDES. These include:

1. The PreReferral Attention Deficit Checklist provides early intervention before assessment.

2. The Attention Deficit Disorders Handbook provides IEP goals, objectives, and interventions by item (also available in computerized form).

3. Computerized scoring is available for both versions.

4. A Parent Guide to ADD provides useful suggestions to parents.

• ADDES is now available in Spanish.

LIMITING FACTORS OF THE ADDES

• The ADDES is a relatively new assessment tool. As research studies are conducted on its ability to discriminate students with ADD from other groups of students with special needs, its value to the field will be determined.

• The ADDES Spanish form is a translation. It has not been normed on a Latino population.

Professional Materials on ADHD

1. *Attention-Deficit/Hyperactivity Disorder*
Russell A. Barkley
The Guilford Press, 1990 (747 pp.)
New York, NY
Comprehensive analysis of ADHD includes symptoms, theoretical background, assessment, research on intervention with student and family.

2. *Attention-Deficit/Hyperactivity Disorder, A Clinical Handbook*
Russell A. Barkley, (1990)
(see above)
Contains master set of blank interview forms and rating scales for children with ADHD. Scales are easily photocopied, and norms and scoring instructions are provided. Forms for monitoring school behavior and a handout for parents regarding medications is also provided.

3. *Managing Attention Disorders in Children*
Sam Goldstein and Michael Goldstein
John Wiley & Sons, 1990 (451 pp.)
New York, NY
A practical guide for the clinical diagnosis and treatment of children with attention problems includes descriptions of several pencil/paper tests.

4. *The Hyperactive Child & Family*
John F. Taylor
Everest House, 1980 (251 pp.)
New York, NY
A guide for parents, teachers, and counselors for the management of children with attention problems including nutrition management.

5. *Raising a Hyperactive Child*
Mark Stewart, Sally Wendkos Olds
Harper & Row, 1973 (299 pp.)
New York, NY
Written primarily for parents, *Raising a Hyperactive Child* provides practical tools for managing daily activities at home within the context of understanding the condition of hyperactivity.

CHAPTER EIGHT
Neuropsychological Assessment

Neuropsychology is the study of the neurological bases for behavior. Neurology is a familiar topic in special education, where terms such as *minimal brain dysfunction*, *attention deficits*, *seizure disorders*, and *brain injury* are frequently seen in written reports and often included in discussions of children. Language disorders, cognitive deficits, and specific learning disabilities are recognized as resulting from neurological dysfunction. However, for special educators in the field, the acknowledgment of the relationship between brain dysfunction, learning, and behavior has led to little practical value because the results of neurological examinations and neuropsychological assessments have rarely yielded specific recommendations for placement, teaching strategies, or behavior management.

However, the convergence of two factors is making neuropsychological assessment more relevant to education. First, the number of children with known or highly probable brain dysfunction in regular classrooms is increasing. These children are the survivors of serious accidents, near drownings, very premature births, and childhood cancers. Medical advances have saved their lives, and educators must learn to address their neurological differences. Second, as in all the fields of assessment, the measures of neuropsychological functioning are improving in theory, technical characteristics, and usability.

While a full discussion of neuropsychological assessment is beyond the scope of this book, the purpose of this chapter is to present an overview of the assessment process and reviews of the two most widely used neuropsychological batteries: the Halstead–Reiten Neuropsychological Test Battery and the Luria–Nebraska Neuropsychological Battery–Children's Revision.

NEUROPSYCHOLOGICAL ASSESSMENT

Neuropsychological assessment is a clinical attempt to relate an individual's behavior to brain functioning and to provide information that can be useful in diagnosis, planning, and implementing treatment and providing after-care and follow-up. Children and adolescents referred for neuropsychological testing often have medically related issues in their development. They may be exhibiting learning and language delays secondary to premature birth. They may be childhood accident victims in which law suits are pending. They may be children with difficult-to-control seizure disorders. They may be children who are being or have been treated with radiation and chemotherapy for leukemia and other forms of childhood cancer. In all cases, the results of neuropsychological assessment are used to guide physicians, therapists, and teachers by assessing damage, determining strengths, and developing and monitoring intervention.

Neuropsychologists are psychologists who are intensely trained not only in developmental psychology, but also in the neurological bases of behavior and learning. Graduate programs have been developed in this field, and the training and experience of the neuropsychologist is a critical factor in the validity of the assessment. Although many of the assessment tools used in neuropsychology are the same as those used by psychologists in schools and clinical practice, the administration procedures may vary somewhat and the interpretation of the results may differ dramatically.

The interpretation of neuropsychological assessment data relies upon four inferential techniques (Dean, 1990):

1. The student's scores on each test are compared with normative standards, and "cut off" scores that have been found to be predictive of neurological dysfunction are used.

2. Inferences regarding hemispheric functioning are made, based on research on cerebral lateralization.

3. Pathogenic signs (constellations of behaviors that hold significance as indicators of neuropathology) are considered.

4. Pattern analysis is used to integrate the information from test performance, hemispheric functioning, and pathogenic signs.

The interpretation of neuropsychological assessment data is more difficult in children than in adults because the developmental stage of the child and many environmental factors must be considered. Injuries to developing brains appear to have more global effects than the same injuries to adult brains (Dean, 1990).

APPROACHES TO ASSESSMENT

There is general agreement in the field that the goal of neuropsychological assessment is to ensure that all important areas of functioning are assessed. While the selection of instruments is widely debated, in general the assessment process includes measures of language, cognition, sensory motor skills, and emotional functioning. Wainright, Fein, and Waterhouse (1991) recommend that evaluations include eight broad functional areas:

1. Language
2. Memory functions
3. Visual spatial skills
4. Motor function
5. Abstract reasoning
6. Attention and executive functioning
7. Academic skills
8. Social cognition

Wainright, Fein, and Waterhouse agree with others that the complete neuropsychological assessment includes the administration of a standardized measure of cognition (usually the age-appropriate Wechsler Scale), parent interview, and behavioral observations in both a structured setting, such as school, and in a play environment. A neuropsychological assessment can be accomplished completely by a neuropsychologist or by a team of specialists in which the assessment plan is developed by the neuropsychologist and test results are interpreted from that perspective.

ASSESSMENT BATTERIES

There are two major neuropsychological assessment batteries used with children and adolescents. The first, the Halstead–Reitan Neuropsychological Test Battery (HRNB) is a battery of subtests that have been empirically shown to link behavioral functioning with brain structure. The second, the Luria–Nebraska Neuropsychological Battery–Children's Revision is a series of subtests that focuses on functional systems that Luria believed underlie the processes of learning

and behavior. The broad-band approach offered by these batteries is the most common model for neuropsychological assessment, and both of these batteries are reviewed on the following pages. Rather than use one battery, many neuropsychologists select tests of cognition, language, and motor and academic skills to encompass the areas listed above. This chapter concludes with tests that might be selected for such an assessment process.

Neuropsychological assessment of children and adolescents is a rapidly expanding field. Those who advocate for assessment that relates directly to teaching, such as curriculum-based assessment and "authentic" assessment, will find the process orientation of neuropsychological assessment to be on the opposite side of the continuum. Developing recommendations for remediation and teaching strategies is clearly a challenge for neuropsychologists, but one that, if conquered, will provide special education with another important source of information about individual differences.

Halstead–Reitan Neuropsychological Test Battery (HRNB)

Halstead Neuropsychological Test Battery for Children (HRNB–C)

Ralph M. Reitan
Reitan Neuropsychology Laboratories, 1970–1981
2920 S. Fourth Ave., Tucson, AZ 85713

DESCRIPTION

The Halstead–Reitan Neuropsychological Test Battery consists of three batteries for different age ranges: five to eight years, nine to 14 years, and 15 years and older. The HRNB was developed primarily for adults, with downward extensions for children. Each battery includes 10–12 subtests designed to assess different aspects of brain functioning. The HRNB subtests are given to each student and a total score for the battery is obtained. While data on each subtest is available in accompanying research reports, the Halstead Impairment Index is the summary score discussed in the manual that is the most sensitive to the general prediction of brain damage. The HRNB and HNTB–C are always given in conjunction with the Wechsler Intelligence Scale for the appropriate age level.

Subtests

Subtest	Format	Construct Assessed	Comments
Category Test	Variety of concepts, including matching Arabic and Roman numerals, counting sets of objects and matching to numerals, identifying proportions of figures drawn in solid versus dotted lines; can be administered by slides, computer, or pencil/paper	Concept formation abstraction, integration	Most widely known of HRNB subtests, sensitive to deficits in nonverbal reasoning
Tactual	Placing shapes in a form board with and without vision	Tactile discrimination, manual dexterity, kinesthesia, spatial memory	Test is timed
Speech Sounds Perception	Auditorially presented speech sounds are selected from several visual representations	Auditory discrimination of verbal stimuli, phonetic skills, auditory–visual integration	May relate to reading disability
Rhythm Test	Identification of 30 pairs of rhythmic beats as same or different	Nonverbal auditory discrimination	
Trail Marking A & B	A: Connecting 25 dots in numeric order B: Connecting 25 dots that alternate between alphabetic and numeric order (A–1, B–2, C–3, etc.)	A: Motor speed, visual scanning B: Integration of alphabetic and numeric systems	Timed test
Finger Tapping	Number of taps of each index finger in 10 seconds	Motor speed, dexterity	Mean score, 5 trials for each hand

Subtest	Format	Construct Assessed	Comments
Aphasia Screening Test	Naming, spelling, reading, writing, computation, enunciation, pantomime, drawing	Wide band of language education, nonverbal functions	22–52 items, total error score
Sensory Perceptual Examinations	Simultaneous touch, finger localization, tactile recognition of shapes	Lateralized sensory perception	Common neurological measures
Strength of Grip Test	Strength of grip in preferred and nonpreferred hands	Motor strength	Common neurological measure

STRENGTHS OF THE HRNB

• The HRNB is the most widely used and researched measure of neuropsychological functioning. Since its development began in 1947, subtests have been altered, added, and omitted. The subtests that remain in the battery have been shown to best discriminate between normally functioning individuals and those with documented brain damage (Dean, 1985).

LIMITING FACTORS OF THE HRNB

• The revision of the original Halstead battery by Reitan in 1974 increased the battery's sensitivity to cortical dysfunction but decreased the utility of the HRNB as a measure of individual functions such as memory (Dean, 1985).

• The HRNB consists of a set of expensive, large, non-portable equipment; this factor limits its reliability and validity. The examiner relies on a body of research data for the interpretation of individual subtest scores, as well as the battery as a whole. Cut-off scores that separate impaired and normal populations are available in the research and are frequently used in interpretation. This approach to differential diagnosis is common in the medical field. Overall test preparation is more dependent on the individual examiner's training and expertise than on the technical characteristics of the test (Dean, 1985).

• The HRNB is a long and expensive battery to administer. It is not clear that the diagnostic findings "improve upon the conclusions" based on a more "sensory behavioral neurological assessment" or a "well-conducted neurological exam" (Meier, 1985).

• The HRNB does not contribute substantially to planning rehabilitation, remediation, or retraining activities (Meier, 1985).

Luria–Nebraska Neuropsychological Battery–Children's Revision (LNNB–C)

Charles Golden, 1987
Western Psychological Services
12031 Wilshire Blvd., Los Angeles, CA 90025-1251

DESCRIPTION

The Luria–Nebraska Neuropsychological Battery–Children's Revision (LNNB–C) is a comprehensive battery designed to identify brain dysfunction in children 8 to 12 years of age. Utilizing the research of Luria, a Russian physician, the LNNB–C is based on a theory of functional systems. The LNNB–C has 149 items grouped into four categories: clinical, optional, summary, and factor. Each item receives a score of 0 (normal), 1 (weak evidence of brain disorder), or 2 (strong evidence of brain disorder). Item scores are summed and converted to T scores with a mean of 50 and a standard deviation of 10.

In addition, each child's age is used to determine a critical level. Scores falling above the criticial level are considered indicative of cognitive impairment. The higher the score is above the clinical level, the more suggestive the score is of brain damage.

STRENGTHS OF THE LNNB–C

• The detailed instructions, carefully prepared manual, and objective scoring system are very helpful features in the administration of this very complex battery.

• The quantitative scoring aspects of the LNNB–C provide a standardized score for each Clinical scale. The Optional, Summary, and Factor Scales can then be calculated for more in-depth interpretation. A profile of the child's performance can then be plotted facilitating pattern analysis.

• The LNNB–C can be interpreted on several levels: (1) the existence or nonexistence of brain dysfunction, (2) a description of what the child can and cannot do, (3) indication of probable etiology of the deficits, and (4) an integration of all the data into a description and theory of how the child's brain is functioning.

• The LNNB–C is designed to allow the examiner to adapt the administration to meet the needs of the child; subtests may be given in any order and combination. This flexibility is helpful in assessing children suspected of brain damage.

• The examiner may hand score the LNNB–C, utilize computerized scoring, or fax protocols to the publisher for scoring. Protocols scored by the publisher will be returned with a computer-generated report and a full-color profile of test scores.

• A screening test is available for the LNNB–C. The screening test is comprised of 15 items that can be administered and scored by a technician or trained paraprofessional. Testing is discontinued when the critical level is reached, significantly reducing testing time.

LIMITING FACTORS OF THE LNNB–C

• The technical characteristics of the LNNB–C are weak. The standardization was completed on a sample of 719 protocols collected in hospitals and clinics across the country. The sample included children with normal development, brain injuries, learning disabilities, and psychiatric disorders. The sample is not described on variables such as race, geography, ethnicity, or education. Inconsistent internal reliability and validity caused *A Consumer's Guide to Tests in Print* (Hammill, Bryant, and Brown, 1990) to give the LNNB–C a not-recommended rating.

• The LNNB–C requires extensive training and experience on the part of the examiner and takes well over two hours to administer. Its usefulness is limited to the clinical populations for which it was developed.

Scales of the LNNB–C			
Clinical Scales	**No. of Items**	**Function**	**Tasks**
C1	34	Motor Functions	Fine and gross motor skills, speed, (longest scale to administer) kinesthetic movement, visual–spatial organization, oral–motor, pencil–paper tasks
C2	08	Rhythm	Auditory perception, pitch and melody, acoustic signals
C3	16	Tactile Functions (the most complex and difficult scale to administer)	Stereognosis, astereognosis, sensation, tactile discrimination

Scales of the LNNB–C			
Clinical Scales	**No. of Items**	**Function**	**Tasks**
C4	07	Visual Functions	Spatial orientation, perceptual reasoning
C5	18	Receptive Speech	Spoken word, phonemic patterns, definitions, phrases, grammar
C6	21	Expressive Speech	Verbal statements, reading, letter–number recognition, pronunciation, word naming, fluency
C7	07	Writing	Phonetic analysis, copying, spelling and writing
C8	07	Reading	Phonetic synthesis, reading letters, words, and phrases
C9	09	Arithmetic (the scale most highly related to brain dysfunction)	Visual and verbal mathematical reasoning
C10	08	Memory	Verbal and nonverbal
C11	14	Intellectual Process	Complex reasoning and problem-solving skills
Optional Scales (used when errors occur on C7)	**No. of Items**	**Function**	**Tasks**
01	07	Spelling	Written and oral
02	05	Motor Writing	Slowness, motor impairment, such as tremor
Summary Scales	**No. of Items**	**Function**	**Tasks**
S1	13	Pathognomonic	Items that are significant for brain dysfunction
S2	09	Left Sensory Motor	Left-hand sensory and motor impairments
S3	09	Right Sensory Motor	Right-hand sensory and motor impairments
Factor Scales (composed of items from individual clinical scales)	**No. of Items**	**Function**	**Tasks**
F1	17	Academic Achievement	Basic academic skills
F2	06	Integrative Functions	Spatial organization, lateralization, directionality, complex arithmetic
F3	06	Spatial-Based Movement	Spatial movement by verbal instructions
F4	06	Motor Speed, Accuracy	Timed repetitive hand movements
F5	06	Drawing Quality	Visual spatial analysis, line–motor coordination, constructional praxis
F6	06	Drawing Speed	Grapho-motor speed
F7	04	Rhythm Perception and Production	Auditory perception, pitch discrimination, auditory attention
F8	08	Tactile Sensations	Gnostic perception: sharp, dull, up, down
F9	05	Receptive Language	Ability to discriminate letters and words presented verbally
F10	08	Expressive Language	Repetition of phonemes, words, phrases; reading, counting, naming
F11	04	Word and Phrase Repetition	Comparison, classification, and verbal abstract reasoning

Neuropsycholgical Assessment: Tools for Assessing Specific Areas of Functioning

LANGUAGE

Expressive One-Word Picture Vocabulary Test

McCarthy Scales: Opposite Analogies, Verbal Fluency, Word Knowledge

Peabody Picture Vocabulary Test

Rapid Automatized Naming (Denkla & Rudel, Cortex, 1973)

Test of Language Development

Token Test for Children (The Psychological Corporation)

WISC–III Vocabulary and Comprehension

Woodcock–Johnson: Picture Vocabulary, Antonyms/Synonyms

Luria–Nebraska: Receptive and Expressive Speech

MEMORY FUNCTIONS

California Verbal Learning Task (The Psychological Corporation)

K–ABC: Spatial Memory, Number Recall, Word Order

McCarthy Scales: Verbal Memory, Tapping Sequence, Numerical Memory, Tactical Performance Task, Picture Memory

Wide Range Assessment of Memory and Learning

WISC–III: Digit Span

Woodcock–Johnson: Memory for Names, Memory for Sentences, Memory for Words

VISUAL–SPATIAL FUNCTIONS

Developmental Test of Visual Motor Integration

KABC: Gestalt Closure, Magic Window, Triangles, Photo Series

McCarthy Scales: Draw a Design, Draw a Child, Block Building, Puzzle Solving, Right/Left Orientation

Ravens Progressive Matrices

Halstead–Reitan: Tactual Performance Task, Trail Making

WISC–III: Picture Completion, Object Assembly, Coding, Block Design

Woodcock–Johnson: Visual Matching, Analysis–Synthesis, Visual Closure, Cross-Out, Picture Identification

Luria–Nebraska: Visual Functions

MOTOR FUNCTIONS

Developmental Test of Visual Motor Integration

Halstead–Reitan: Finger Tapping, Strength of Grip

K–ABC: Hand Movements

McCarthy Scales: Leg and Arm Coordination

Luria–Nebraska: Motor Functions

ABSTRACT REASONING, PROBLEM SOLVING, CONCEPTUAL SKILLS

K–ABC: Matrix Analogies, Photo Series

McCarthy Scales: Counting and Sorting, Conceptual Grouping, Number Questions

Woodcock–Johnson: Analysis–Synthesis, Concept Formation

WISC–III: Arithmetic, Picture Arrangement, Similarities

Wisconsin Card Sort

Halstead–Reitan: Category Test

Luria–Nebraska: Intellectual Processes

ATTENTION AND EXECUTIVE FUNCTIONING

Continuous Performance Tasks

Rapid Automatized Naming

Halstead–Reitan Trail-Making Test

WISC–III: Freedom from Distractibility Factor

Wisconsin Card Sort

ACADEMIC SKILLS

KABC: Achievement Tests

Key Math Diagnostic Arithmetic Test

Test of Written Spelling

WISC–III: Information, Arithmetic

Wide-Range Achievement Test

Woodcock–Johnson Achievement Test

Peabody Individual Achievement Test

Wechsler Individual Achievement Test

SOCIAL COGNITION

KABC: Photo Series, Face Recognition

WISC–III: Picture Arrangement, Comprehension, Test of Problem Solving

BEHAVIORAL OBSERVATION CHECKLISTS

Child Behavior Check List

Conners Parent and Teacher Questionnaires

Vineland Adaptive Behavior Scales (American Guidance Service)

References

Ackerman, Peggy T.; Paul, Nicholas P.; Holloway, Carol; and Dykman, Roscoe A. 1992. Test Selection Efficacy in the Diagnostic Confirmation and Subtyping of Children with Dyslexia, *Learning Disabilities Research and Practice* vol. 7.

Anatasi, Anne, 1985. Mental Measurement: Some Emerging Trends. *The Ninth Mental Measurements Yearbook* vol. 1, edited by J. V. Mitchell, Jr. The Buros Institute of Mental Measurement. Lincoln, NE: The University of Nebraska Press.

Anastasiow, Nicholas J., et al. 1973. *Educational Psychology: A Contemporary View*. Del Mar, CA: CRM Books.

Arter, J. A., and Jenkins, J. R. 1978. Differenital Diagnosis—Prescriptive Teaching: A Critical Appraisal. Center for the Study of Reading, Univ. of Illinois: Technical Report no. 80.

Auchenbach, Thomas M. 1991. *Manual for the Child Behavior Checklist/4–18 and 1991 Profile*. Burlington, VT: University of Vermont, Department of Psychiatry.

————. 1991. *Manual for the Youth Self-Report and 1991 Profile*. Burlington, VT: University of Vermont, Department of Psychiatry.

————. 1991. *Manual for the Teacher's Report Form and the 1991 Profile*. Burlington, VT: University of Vermont, Department of Psychiatry.

————. 1991. *Integrative Guide for the 1991 CBCL/4–18, YSR, and TRF Profiles*. Burlington, VT: University of Vermont, Department of Psychiatry.

Ayres, A. Jean. 1973. *Sensory Integration and Learning Disorders* (2nd ed.). Los Angeles, CA: Western Psychological Services.

Ayres, Michael, and Burns, Lisa. 1991. Luria–Nebraska Neuropsychological Battery–Children's Revision. In *Tests Critiques* vol. 8, edited by Daniel J. Keyser and Richard C. Sweetland. Austin, TX: PRO-ED.

Bannatyne, Alex. 1968. Diagnosing Learning Disabilities and Writing Remedial Prescriptions. *Journal of Learning Disabilites* vol. 1.

————. 1974. Diagnosis: A Note on the Recategorizations of the WISC Scaled Scores. *Journal of Learning Disabilities* vol. 7.

Bayley, Nancy. 1969. *Bayley Scales of Infant Development*. New York: The Psychological Corporation.

Betts, Emmett A. 1946. *Foundations of Reading Instruction*. New York: American Book Co.

Blank, Marion. 1968. Cognitive Processes in Auditory Discrimination in Normal and Retarded Readers. *Child Development* vol. 39.

Bloom, L. 1970. *Language Development: Form and Function in Emerging Grammars*. Cambridge, MA: MIT Press.

Bolt, Deborah A. 1990. Managing Curriculum-Based Assessment in the Classroom. In *Curriculum-Based Assessment: Testing What Is Taught*? ed. by John Salvia

and Charles Hughes. New York: Macmillian Publishing.

Brown, Roger. 1973. *A First Language: The Early Stages*. Cambridge, MA: Harvard University Press.

Brown, Virginia L.; Hammill, Donald D.; and Widedernolt, J. Lee. 1978. *Test of Reading Comprehension Examiner's Manual*. Austin, TX: PRO-ED.

Burgemeister, B. B.; Blum, L. H.; and Lorge, I. 1972. *Columbia Mental Maturity Scale* (3rd ed.). New York: Harcourt Brace Jovanovich.

Burkhart, Jennifer E.; Fox, Robert A.; and Rotatori, Anthony R. 1987. Neuropsychological Assessment of Exceptional Children: Impact on Special Education. In *Issues in Special Education*, edited by Anthony R. Rotatori, Mary M. Banbury, and Robert A. Fox. Mountain View, CA: Mayfield Publishing.

Ceci, Stephen J.; Ringstorm, Maureen; and Lea, Stephen E. G. 1981. Do Language–Learning Disabled Children (L/LD's) Have Impaired Memories? In Search of Underlying Processes. *Journal of Learning Disabilites* vol.14, no. 3.

Chelune, G. J., and Baer, R.A. 1986. Developmental Norms for the Wisconsin Card Sort. *Journal of Clinical and Experimental Neuropsychology* vol. 8.

Chelune, G. J.; Ferguson, W.; Koon, R.; and Dickey, T. O. 1986. Frontal Lobe Dysfunctions in Attention-Deficit Disorder. *Child Psychiatry and Human Development* vol. 16.

Chesboro, Patricia A. Basic Achievement Skills Individual Screener. *Test Critiques* vol. 2, edited by Daniel J. Keyser and Richard C. Sweetland. Kansas City, MO: Test Corporation of America.

Chomsky, Noam. 1957. *Syntactic Structures*. The Hague: Mouton.

————. 1965. *Aspects of the Theory of Syntax*. Cambridge, MA: MIT Press.

Comprehensive Testing Program, Educational Record Bureau. 1992. Princeton, NJ: Educational Testing Service.

Cratty, Bryant J. 1970. *Perceptual and Motor Development in Infants and Children*. New York: Macmillan.

Das, J. P. 1948. Planning: Theoretical Considerations and Empirical Evidence. *Psychological Research* vol. 41.

Dean, Raymond S. 1985. Halstead–Reitan Neuropsychological Test Battery. In *The Ninth Mental Measurements Yearbook*, edited by James V. Mitchell. Lincoln, NE: University of Nebraska Press.

Dean, Raymond S., and Gray, Jeffrey W. 1990. Traditional Approaches to Neuropsychological Assessment. In *Handbook of Psychological and Educational Assessment of Children: Intelligence and Achievement*, edited by Cecil R. Reynolds and Randy W. Kamphaus. New York: The Guilford Press.

de Hirsch, Katrina; Jansky, Jeanette J.; and Langford, William

S. 1966. *Predicting Reading Failure*. NY: Harper & Row.

Dembinski, Raymond J., and Mauser, August J. 1977. What Parents of the Learning Disabled Really Want from Professionals. *Journal of Learning Disabilites* vol.10.

Deno, S. L. 1985. Curriculum-Based Assessment: The Emerging Alternative. *Exceptional Children* vol. 52.

Egeland, Byron. 1985. Wisconsin Card Sort. In *The Ninth Mental Measurements Yearbook*, ed. by James V. Mitchell. Lincoln, NE: University of Nebraska Press.

Esquivel, Giselle B. 1983. Colour Progressive Matrices. *Test Critiques* vol. 1, edited by Daniel J. Keyser and Richard C. Sweetland. Kansas City, MO: Test Corp. of America.

Essex-Sorlie, Diane. 1984. Test of Written Language, *Test Critiques* vol. 1, edited by Daniel J. Keyser and Richard C. Sweetland. Kansas City, MO: Test Corp. of America.

Evans, Patricia R., and Peham, Mary Ann Sachs. 1981. Testing and Measurement in Occupational Therapy: A Review of Current Practice with Special Emphasis on the Southern California Sensory Integration Tests. Monograph No. 15. University of Minnesota: Institute for the Research of Learning Disabilities.

Executive Committee of the Council for Children With Behavioral Disorders. 1989. Best Assessment Practices for Students With Behavioral Disorders: Accommodation to Cultural Diversity and Individual Differences. *Behavioral Disorders* vol. 14.

Farr, Roger. 1969. *Reading: What Can Be Measured?* Newark, DE: International Reading Association Research Fund.

Ferrier, E. E. 1966. An Investigation of the ITPA Performance of Children with Functional Defects of Articulation. *Exceptional Children* vol. 32.

Fillmore, Charles. 1968. The Case for Case. In *Universals in Linguistic Theory*, edited by Emmon Bach and Robert T. Harms. New York: Holt, Rinehart and Winston.

Fisher, Wyman E. 1987. Halstead Category Test. In *Test Critiques* vol. 6, edited by Daniel J. Keyser and Richard C. Sweetland. Austin, TX: PRO-ED.

Flavell, J. H., and Wellman, H. M. 1977. Metamemory. *Perspectives on the Development of Memory and Cognition*, edited by R. V. Kail and J. W. Hagen. Hillsdale, NJ: Lawrence Erlbaum.

Floden, Rober E. 1985. Basic Achievement Skills Individual Screener. *The Ninth Mental Measurements Yearbook* vol. 1, ed. by J. V. Mitchell, Jr. The Buros Institute of Mental Measurement, Lincoln, NE: University of Nebraska Press.

Foster, S. 1963. Language Skills for Children with Persistent Articulation Disorders. Ph.D. dissertation, Texas Women's University.

Frankenburg, William K.; Dodds, Josiah; Archer, Philip; Shapiro, Howard; and Breonick, Beverly. 1992. The Denver II: A Major Revision and Restandardization of the Denver Developmental Screening Test. *Pediatrics* vol. 89.

Frazen, Michael D. 1991. Wide Range Assessment of Memory and Learning. *Test Critiques* vol. 9, ed. by Daniel

J Keyser and Richard C. Sweetland. Austin, TX: PRO-ED.

Fuchs, Lynn S., and Deno, Stanley L. 1994. Must Instructionally Useful Performance Assessment Be Based in the Curriculum? *Exceptional Children* vol. 61.

Fulmer, S. P. 1980. *Pre-Reading Screening Procedures and Slingerland Screening Tests for Identifying Children with Specific Language Disability: Technical Manual*. Cambridge, MA: Educators Publishing Service.

Gaines, R. 1972. Review of Southern California Figure–Ground Visual Perceptions Test. In *Buros' Seventh Mental Measurements Yearbook*, edited by Oscar K. Buros. Highland Park, NJ: Gryphon Press.

Germann, G., and Tindal, G. 1985. An Application of Curriculum-Based Asssesment: The Use of Direct and Frequent Measurement. *Exceptional Children* vol. 52.

Gessell, Arnold, and Amatruda, Catherine S. 1949. *Gesell Developmental Schedules*. New York: The Psychological Corporation.

Gillingham, Anna, and Stillman, Bessie W. 1960. *Remedial Training for Children with Specific Language Disability in Reading, Spelling, and Penmanship* (6th ed.). Cambridge, MA: Educators Publishing Service.

Greenwood, Charles R., and Rieth, Herbert J. 1994. Current Dimensions of Technology-Based Assessment in Special Education. *Exceptional Children* vol. 61.

Hallahan, Daniel P., and Cruickshank, William M. 1973. *Psychoeducational Foundations of Learning Disabilites*. Englewood Cliffs, NJ: Prentice Hall.

Hammill, D. D. 1985. *Detroit Test of Learning Aptitude–2*. Austin, TX: PRO-ED.

Hammill, Donald D., and Weiderholt, J. L. 1972. Review of the Frostig Visual Perceptions Test and the Related Training Program. In *The First Review of Special Education* vol.1, edited by L. Mann and D. Sabatino. Philadelphia, PA: JSE Press, Grune & Stratton.

Hanley, Tom V. 1995. The Need for Technological Advances in Assessment Related to National Education Reform. *Exceptional Children* vol. 61.

Harris, Dale B. 1963. *Children's Drawings as Measures of Intellectual Maturity*. NY: Harcourt Brace Jovanovich.

Hessler, Gary, 1982. *Use and Interpretation of the Woodcock–Johnson Psycho-Educational Battery*. Hingham, MA: Teaching Resources.

Hutton, Jerry B. Conner's Parent and Teacher Rating Scales. 1994. In *Test Critiques* vol. 10, ed. by Daniel J. Keyser and Richard C. Sweetland, Austin, TX: PRO-ED.

Jensen, R. 1980. *Bias in Mental Testing*. NY: The Free Press.

Johns, Jerry L., and Van Leirsburg, Peggy. 1994. Slosson Intelligence Test–Revised. In *Test Critiques* vol. 10, edited by Daniel J. Keyser and Richard C. Sweetland, Austin, TX: PRO-ED.

Johnson, Wendell; Darlye, Frederick L.; and Spriestersbach, D. D. 1963. *Diagnostic Methods in Speech Pathology*. New York: Harper & Row.

Jongsma, Eugene A. March, 1987. Test Review: Test of Reading Comprehension (TORC). *The Reading Teacher*.

Kahn, Linda, and Lewis, Nancy. 1986. *Kahn–Lewis Phonological Analysis*. Circle Pines, MN: American Guidance Service.

Kaufman, A. S. 1982. An Integrated Review of Almost a Decade of Research on the McCarthy Scales. *Advances in School Psychology* vol. 2, edited by T. R. Kratoch. Hillsdale, NJ: Lawrence Erlbaum.

Kaufman, Nadeen L., and Kaufman, Alan S. 1974. Comparison of Normal and Minimally Brain-Dysfunctioned Children on the McCarthy Scales of Children's Abilities. *Journal of Clinical Psychology* vol. 30.

———. 1977. Clinical Evaluation of Young Children with the McCarthy Scales. New York: Grune & Stratton.

Keogh, Barbara, and Becker, Laurence D. 1973. Early Detection of Learning Problems: Questions, Cautions and Guidelines. *Exceptional Children* vol. 40.

Kephart, Newell C. 1960. *The Slow Learner in the Classroom*. Columbus, OH: Charles E. Merrill.

Keyser, Daniel J., and Sweetland, Richard C. 1985. *Test Critiques* vol. 4. Kansas City, MO: Test Corp.of America.

———. 1986. vol. 5.

———. 1987. vol. 6.

———. 1988. vol. 7.

———. 1991. vol. 8. Austin, TX: PRO-ED

———. 1992. vol. 9. Austin, TX: PRO-ED

———. 1994. vol. 10. Austin, TX: PRO-ED

King-Thomas, Linda, and Hacker, Bennie J. 1987. *A Therapist's Guide to Pediatric Assessment*. NY: Little, Brown, and Co.

Kirk, Samuel A., and Kirk, Winifred D. 1971. *Psycholinguistic Learning Disabilities*. Urbana: University of Illinois.

———. 1978. Uses and Abuses of the ITPA. *Journal of Speech and Hearing Disorders* vol. 43.

Koppitz, Elizabeth M. 1963. *The Bender–Gestalt Test for Young Children* vol. 1. New York: Grune & Stratton.

Koppitz, Elizabeth M. 1977. *The Visual–Aural Digit Span Test*. New York: Grune & Stratton.

———. 1975. *The Bender–Gestalt Test for Young Children* vol. 2. New York: Grune & Stratton.

Landis, D. 1972. Review of Southern California Perceptual Motor Tests. In *Buros' Seventh Mental Measurements Yearbook*, edited by Oscar K. Buros. Highland Park, NJ: Gryphon Press.

Langdon, Henriette W., with Cheng, Li-Rong Lilly, 1992. *Hispanic Children and Adults with Communications Disorders*. Gaithersburg, MD: Aspen Publications.

Lau vs. Nichols. 1975. Washington, DC: Department of Health, Education, and Welfare, Office for Civil Rights.

Lesiak, Judi, and Bradley-Johnson, Sharon. 1983. *Reading Assessment for Placement and Programming*. Springfield, IL: Charles C. Thomas.

Lorge–Thornedike Teacher's Word Book of 30,000 Words. 1944. NY: Teacher's College of Columbia University.

MacDonald, J. D.; Blott, J. P.; Gordon, K.; Speigel, G.; and Hartmann, M.C. 1974. An Experimental Parent-Assisted Treatment Program for Preschool Language-Delayed Children. *Journal of Speech and Hearing Disorders* vol. 39.

Markley, Robert P. 1985. Wisconsin Card Sort. In *The Ninth Mental Measurements Yearbook*, edited by James V. Mitchell. Lincoln, NE: University of Nebraska Press.

Marston, D., and Magnussen, D. 1985. Implementing Curriculum-Based Measurement in Special and Regular Education Settings. *Exceptional Children* vol. 52.

Marston, D., and Ysseldyke, James. 1980. *Derived Subtest Scores from the Woodcock–Johnson Psycho-Educational Battery*. Hingham, MA: Teaching Resources Corporation.

Meeker, M. 1969. *The Structure of Intellect*. Columbus, OH: Charles E. Merrill.

Meier, M. J. 1985. Halstead–Reitan Neuropsychological Test Battery. In *The Ninth Mental Measurements Yearbook*, ed. by James V. Mitchell. Lincoln, NE: Univ. of Nebraska.

Menyuk, P. 1969. *Sentences Children Use*. Cambridge, MA: MIT Press.

Merz, William R. 1984. K–ABC. *Test Critiques* vol. 1, edited by Daniel J. Keyser and Richard C. Sweetland. Kansas City, MO: Test Corporation of America.

Miller, J., and Yoder, D. 1974. An Ontogenetic Language Teaching Strategy for Retarded Children. *Language Perspectives: Acquisition, Retardation and Intervention*, edited by R. Schiefelbusch and L. Lloyd. Baltimore, MD: University Park Press.

Miller, Lucy Jane. 1987. Longitudinal Validity of the Miller Assessment for Preschoolers, Study 1. *Perceptual and Motor Skills* vol. 65.

Miller, Ted L. 1984. Special Issue: The K–ABC. *Journal of Special Education* vol. 18, no. 3.

Mitchell, James V., Jr. 1985. *The Ninth Mental Measurements Yearbook* vol. 1. The Buros Institute of Mental Measurement. Lincoln, NE: University of Nebraska Press.

———. 1985. vol. 2.

Morehead, D., and Ingram, D. 1973. The Development of Base Syntax in Normal and Linguistically Deviant Children. *Journal of Speech and Hearing Research* vol. 16.

Morrissey, Patricia. 1979. Pre-Academic Predictors of Success in a Multisensory Reading Program. Ed.D. dissertation, University of San Francisco.

Mullis, I. V. S. 1984. Scoring Direct Writing Assessments: What are the Alternatives? *Educational Measurement Issues and Practice* vol. 3, no. 1, edited by F. B. Womer.

Myers, P. I., and Hammill, D. D. 1976. *Methods for Learning Disorders*. New York: Wiley.

Myklebust, Helmer R. 1973. *Development and Disorders of Written Language, Volume Two: Studies of Normal and Exceptional Children*. New York: Grune & Stratton.

Osgood, Charles E. 1957. A Behavioristic Analysis. In *Contemporary Approaches to Cognition* Cambridge, MA: Havard University Press.

Osgood, Charles E., and Sebeok, T. A., eds. 1965. *Psycholinguistics*. Bloomington, IN: Indiana Univ. Press.

Paraskevopoulous, John, and Kirk, Samuel. 1969. *The Development and Psychometric Characteristics of the Revised Illinois Test of Psycholinguistic Abilities*. Urbana, IL: University of Illinois Press.

Pascal, G. R., and Suttrell, B. J. 1964. *The Bender–Gestalt Test: Quantification and Validity for Adults*. NY: Grune & Stratton.

Pintner, Rudolf; Cunningham, Bess V.; and Durost, Walter N. 1966. *Pintner–Cunningham Primary Test*. New York: Harcourt Brace Jovanovich.

Puente, Antonio E. 1985. Wisconsin Card Sort Test. In *Test Critiques* vol. 4 , edited by Daniel J. Keyser and Richard C. Sweetland. Kansas City, MO: Test Corp. of America.

Raven, J. C. 1986. *A Compendium of North American Normature and Validity Studies*. San Antonio, TX: Psychological Corporation.

Rockowitz, Ruth J., and Davidson, Phillip W. 1979. Discussing Diagnostic Findings with Parents. *Journal of Learning Disabilites* vol. 12.

Salvia, John, and Ysseldyke, James E. 1978. *Assessment in Special and Remedial Education*. Boston, MA: Houghton Mifflin Company.

Salvia, John, and Ysseldyke, James E. 1991. *Assessment in Special and Remedial Education* (5th ed.). Boston, MA: Houghton Mifflin Company.

Satz, Paul; Friel, Janette; and Goebel, Ron A. 1975. Some Predictive Antecedents of Specific Reading Disability: A Three-Year Follow-Up. *Bulletin of the Orton Society* vol. 25.

Sawyer, Diane J. 1987. Special Feature: The Decoding Skills Test, A Review. *Topics in Language Disorders* vol. 7, no. 3. Frederick, MD: Aspen Publishers.

Schultz, Richard E. 1985. Basic Achievement Skills Individual Screener. *The Ninth Mental Measurements Yearbook* vol. 1, edited by J. V. Mitchell, Jr. The Buros Institute of Mental Measurement. Lincoln, NE: Univ. of Nebraska Press.

Sequential Test of Basic Skills. 1958. Palo Alto, CA: Educational Testing Service.

Shaftel, F., and Shaftel, G. 1970. *People in Action: Role Playing and Discussion Photographs for Elementary Social Studies*. New York: Holt, Rinehart and Winston.

Shepard, Lorrie. 1991. Interview on Assessment Issues with Lorrie Shepard. *Educational Researcher* vol. 20.

Smith, Judith M.; Smith, Donald.; and Brink, James R. 1977. *A Technology of Reading and Writing* vol. 2. New York: Academic Press.

State of California. *Assessing Pupils Suspected of Having a Specific Learning Disability*. 1982. State of California Education Code Sections 56320–56329.

Sternberg, R. J. 1984. What Cognitive Psychology Can (and Cannot) Do For Test Development. *Social and Technical Issues in Testing: Implications for Test Construction and Usage*, ed. by B. S. Plake. Hillsdale, NJ: Lawerence Erlbaum.

Stoddard, Ann H. 1994. Detroit Test of Learning Aptitude–Primary (2nd ed.). In *Test Critiques* vol. 10, ed. by Daniel J. Keyser and Richard C. Sweetland. Austin, TX: PRO-ED.

Swicegood, Philip. 1994. Portfolio-Based Assessment Practices. *Intervention in School and Clinic* vol. 30.

Thorndyke, R. L.; Hagen, E.; and Sattler, J. 1986. *Technical Manual: The Stanford–Binet Intelligence Scale* (4th ed.). Chicago: Riverside Publishing Co.

Tiegs, E. W., and Clark, W. W. 1970. *California Achievement Tests*. New York: CTB/McGraw-Hill.

Van Leirsburg, Peggy. 1994. Detroit Tests of Learning Aptitude–3. In *Test Critiques* vol. 10, edited by Daniel J. Keyser and Richard C. Sweetland. Austin, TX: PRO-ED.

Vellutino, Frank R., and Scanlon, D. M. 1987. Phonological Coding, Phonological Awareness, and Reading Disability: Evidence from a Longitudinal and Experimental Study. *Merrill–Palmer Quarterly* vol. 33.

Wainright, Laurel; Fein, Deborah; and Waterhouse, Lynn. 1991. Neuropsychological Assessment of Children with Developmental Disabilites. In *Neurology: Behavior and Cognition of the Child with Brain Dysfunction*, edited by Amir, N.; Rapin, J.; and Branski, D. Basel, Switzerland: Karger Publishing Company.

Webster, Raymond E., and Whitley, Theodore W. 1985. The Visual–Aural Digit Span Test. In *Test Critiques* vol. 2, edited by Daniel J. Keyser and Richard C. Sweetland. Kansas City, MO: Test Corporation of America.

Wechsler, David. 1947. *Wechsler–Bellvue Intelligence Scale*. New York: The Psychological Corporation.

Welch, Marshall. 1994. Ecological Assessment: A Collaborative Approach to Planning Instructional Interventions. *Interventions in School and Clinic* vol. 29.

Wesson, C.; King, R.; and Deno, S. L. 1984. Direct and Frequent Measurement of Student Performance: If It's Good for Us, Why Don't We Do It? *Learning Disabilities Quarterly* vol. 7.

Whitworth, Randolph H. 1984. Bender Visual Motor Gestalt Test. *Test Critiques* vol. 1, ed. by Daniel J. Keyser and Richard C. Sweetland. Kansas City, MO: Test Corp. of America.

Wiig, E. H., and Semel-Mintz, E. M. 1974, Logico-Grammatical Sentence Comprehension by Learning-Disabled Adolescents. *Perceptual and Motor Skills* vol. 38.

———. 1975. Productive Language Abilities in Learning-Disabled Adolescents. *Journal of Learning Disabilites* vol. 8.

———. 1976. *Language Disabilities in Children and Adolescents*. Columbus, OH: Charles E. Merrill.

———. 1980. *Language Assessment and Intervention for the Learning Disabled*. Columbus, OH: Charles E. Merrill.

Wilkinson, Gary S. 1987. *WRAT–R, Monograph 1*. Wilmington, DE: Vastak Assessment Systems.

Woodcock, Richard. 1975. *Development and Standardization of the Woodcock–Johnson Psycho-Educational Battery*. Hingham, MA: Teaching Resources Corporation.

Glossary of Testing Terms

Words set in italics are defined elsewhere in the glossary. The glossary contains six sections: General Terms, Diagnostic Categories, Academic Terms, Visual and Visual-Perceptual Motor Processing, Oral Language and Auditory Processing, and Fine and Gross Motor Skills.

GENERAL TERMS

AGE NORM. (Age score). A score indicating average performance for students classified according to *chronological age*. Generally expressed in terms of *central tendency, standard score, percentile rank,* or *stanine*. In an *achievement test,* the age equivalent for grades.

AGE SCORE. See *age norm*.

ALTERNATE FORMS. See *equivalent forms*.

BASAL LEVEL. The level at which all items of a test are passed, just preceding the level where the first failure occurs. All items below the basal point are assumed correct. Contrast with *ceiling level*.

BATTERY. A group of carefully selected tests administered to a student, the results of which are of value individually, in combination, and/or totally.

CEILING LEVEL. The maximal level of a test. The highest item of a sequence in which a certain number of items has been failed. All items above the ceiling item are assumed incorrect. Contrast with *basal level*.

CENTRAL TENDENCY. A statistical measure used to describe typical values in a set or distribution of scores. The most common such measures used in educational testing are the *mean, median,* and *mode*.

CHRONOLOGICAL AGE (CA). Age from birth expressed in years and months; for example, 7 years, 6 months.

CORRELATION COEFFICIENT (r). A statistical index that measures the degree of relationship between any two variables (for example, sets of scores). It ranges in value from -1.00 (a perfect negative correlation) to +1.00 (a perfect positive correlation). An example is the high positive correlation between vocabulary and *intelligence*.

DERIVED SCORE. Any score that has been converted from a qualitative or quantitative unit on one scale into the units of another scale, thereby allowing a direct comparison of the student's performance on different tests or a comparison of his or her performance to the performance of others. Examples of derived scores are *percentile rank, age norm, standard score, T-score, Z-score,* and *normal curve equivalent score*.

DIAGNOSTIC TESTING. An intensive, in-depth evaluation process using formal, *standardized tests* and *informal tests* designed to determine the nature and severity of specific learning problems. Generally provided by an interdisciplinary team of specialists.

EQUIVALENCY METHOD. One method of standardizing a new test. Each raw score on the new test is matched with the same raw score on a test with established norms. In this way, the raw scores of the new test can be directly associated with the standard scores of the anchor test. The advantage of the equivalency method is that a smaller standardization sample is needed. A major assumption is that the new test measures the same process as the anchor test. The equivalency method was used in standardizing the Diagnostic Spelling Potential Test (using the Wide Range Achievement Test as the anchor test) and the Slosson Intelligence Test for Children and Adults (using the Stanford-Binet Intelligence Scale as the anchor test).

EQUIVALENT FORMS (Alternate forms). Two comparable or parallel forms of a test that measure the same skill or trait to the same degree and are standardized on the same population. Useful for *pretest* and *posttest* measurement.

EXTRAPOLATION. A process of estimating the scores of a test beyond the range of available data.

FREQUENCY DISTRIBUTION. A tabulation of scores from low to high that indicates the number of individuals who obtain each score.

FUNCTIONAL ASSESSMENT. Techniques developed by classroom teachers to assess individual pupil progress in the classroom curriculum. Is the student learning what is being taught? An alternative to norm-based tests.

> ECOLOGICAL ASSESSMENT. Uses checklists and rating scales to assess the classroom environment.
>
> CURRICULUM BASED ASSESSMENT (CBA). Measurement tools taken directly from classroom curriculum.
>
> PORTFOLIO ASSESSMENT. Systematic collection of student work and other documents that reflect change and growth.

INTELLIGENCE. A global construct or entity composed of several functions. The abilities constituting intelligence are such factors as cognitive skills or processes, abstract verbal and numerical aptitudes, comprehension and memory functions, and the abilities to learn, reason, and solve problems.

INTELLIGENCE QUOTIENT (IQ). An index of mental ability, expressing a student's performance on an intelligence test. If a student's *mental age* and *chronological age* are equal, his or her IQ is 100 (which represents average performance). Thus IQ is a *standard score* with a *mean* fixed statistically at 100 and the *standard deviation* fixed according to the test author's discretion.

DEVIATION IQ. Indicates the amount by which a student's performance on an IQ test is above or below the average performance of students of his or her age group.

RATIO IQ. A *derived score* that expresses the student's *mental age* in relation to *chronological age*, according to the formula:

$$IQ = \frac{MA}{CA} \times 100$$

INTERPOLATION. A process of estimating an intermediate value between two known points. In the example, a *raw score* value of 55, by interpolation, would be assigned a *grade norm* of 4.9.

Raw Score	Grade Norm
52	4.5
54	4.8
56	5.0
58	5.2

MEAN (M). The sum of a set of scores divided by the number of scores. The value of the mean can be strongly influenced by a few extreme scores.

MEDIAN (MD). The middle point in a set of ranked scores. The value that has the same number of scores above it and below it in the distribution. For example, the median in the following set of scores is 10: 17, 13, 11, 10, 9, 9, 8. In a distribution of scores such as 9, 8, 6, 5, the median, by *interpolation*, would be 7.

MENTAL AGE (MA). A measure of a child's level of mental development, based on performance on a test of mental ability and determined by the level of difficulty of the test items passed. If a child, no matter what age, can pass only those items passed by the average 8-year-old, the child will be assigned a mental-age score of 8.

MODE (MO). The score that occurs most frequently in a distribution. In the distribution 18, 14, 12, 11, 10, 10, 7, the mode is 10. Its value is entirely independent of extreme scores.

NEUROPSYCHOLOGY. The study of the neuropsychological bases for behavior. This science explores the relationship between brain dysfunction, learning, and behavior.

NEUROPSYCHOLOGICAL ASSESSMENT. A battery of psychological, educational, language, and motor tests that attempt to relate a child's behavior to brain functioning. In children with known brain trauma, neuropsychological assessment assesses damage, determines strengths, and can be useful in planning interventions.

NONVERBAL TEST. See *performance test*.

NORMAL CURVE EQUIVALENT SCORES (NCE). A scale designed to transform percentile rankings into equal units. The NCE scale is designed so that NCEs of 150 and 99 coincide with percentile rankings of 150 and 99. However, a difference of

5 NCE units represents the same difference in achievement at any point on the NCE scale; therefore, NCEs are suitable for computing averages. The NCE that corresponds to any raw score is lower at the end of the year than at the beginning, since students learn to read better during the year. Therefore, different NCE charts are needed for different intervals of the year.

PERCENTILE RANK. A type of converted score that expresses a student's score relative to his or her group in percentile points. Indicates the percentage of students tested who made scores equal to or lower than the specified score. If a score of 82 has a percentile rank of 65, this means that 65 percent of the students who took the test had a score of 82 or lower than 82.

PERFORMANCE TEST (Nonverbal test). Designed to evaluate the general intelligence or specialized aptitudes of students. Consists primarily of motor test items or perceptual items in which verbal abilities play a minimal role. Contrast with *verbal test*.

PROJECTIVE TECHNIQUE. A test situation in which the student reponds to ambiguous stimulus materials, such as pictures, inkblots, or incomplete sentences, thereby projecting personality characteristics.

PROTOCOL. The original record of the test results.

RANK ORDERING. The arrangement of scores form highest to lowest.

RAW SCORE. The basic score initially obtained by scoring a test according to the directions in the manual. Generally equal to the number of right answers—but may be the number of incorrect responses, the time required for a task, or some other criterion.

RELIABILITY. The degree to which a student would obtain the same score if the test were readministered (assuming no further learning, practice effects, or other change). Stability or consistency of scores.

ALTERNATE-FORM RELIABILITY. A method of estimating test reliability by the *correlation coefficient* between two equivalent or comparable forms of the test. The student is tested with one form on the first occasion and with another parallel form on the second.

INTERSCORER RELIABILITY. A method that requires a sample of tests to be scored independently by two examiners. The two scores are correlated, and the resulting *correlation coefficient* is an estimate of interscorer reliability.

SPLIT-HALF RELIABILITY. A method for determining the reliability coefficient for a test by obtaining the *correlation coefficient* for two halves of the same test. Usually items are split odd-even to provide the two comparable halves.

TEST-RETEST RELIABILITY. A method of establishing reliability that involves readministering the same test to the same sample of students and then determining the degree of correlation between the two sets of test scores.

SCATTER. The extent of variation among a student's scores on all subtests of a single test or on several different tests.

May indicate whether all aspects of a student's ability are developing evenly or whether the student has an unusual facility or handicap in a certain area. Wide discrepancies in a student's profile of abilities do not necessarily suggest underlying pathology.

STANDARD DEVIATION (SD). The most commonly used measure of variation. A statistic used to express the extent of the distribution's deviations from the *mean*. In the normal distribution, about 68 percent of the scores lie within one SD above or below the mean.

STANDARD ERROR OF MEASUREMENT (SEM, Standard error, Test error). A statistic that indicates how chance errors may cause variation in the scores that a given student might obtain if he or she were to take the same test an infinite number of times. If the SEM is 3, the chances are 2 to 1 that any given student's score will fall within a range of three points of the obtained score. For example, if Jerry gets a score of 160, his "true" score lies somewhere between 157 and 163.

STANDARDIZATION. In test construction, refers to the process of trying the test out on a group of students to determine uniform or standard scoring procedures and methods of interpretation.

STANDARDIZATION SAMPLE. Refers to the section of the reference population that is chosen for use in establishing test norms. Should be representative of the reference population in main characteristics, such as sex, race, age, grade, geographical location, socioeconomic status, and other factors.

STANDARDIZED TEST. Contains empirically selected materials, with specific directions for administration, scoring, and interpretation. Provides data on *validity* and *reliability,* and has adequately derived norms.

STANDARD SCORE. *Derived score* that transforms a *raw score* in such a manner that it has the same *mean* and the same *standard deviation*. The standard score scale is an equal-interval scale; that is, a difference of, say, five points has the same meaning throughout the scale.

STANINE. A weighted scale divided into nine equal units that represent nine levels of performance on any particular test. The stanine is a *standard score.* Thus the intervals between different points on the scale (for example, the difference between 8 and 5 and between 4 and 1 on the scale) are equal in terms of the number of correct test responses they represent. The *mean* is at stanine 5 in the example.

Stanine	1	2	3	4	5	6	7	8	9
Percent in Stanine	4	7	12	17	20	17	12	7	4

TEST ERROR. See *standard error of measurement.*

T-SCORE. A standard score with a mean of 50 and a standard deviation of 10.

VALIDITY. The extent to which a test measures what it is designed to measure. A test valid for one use may have negligible validity for another.

CONCURRENT VALIDITY. How well scores on a test correspond to performance on some criterion data available at the time of testing. For example, comparing end-of-course achievement test scores with school grades.

CONSTRUCT VALIDITY. Reports the extent to which the test measures a theoretical construct or trait. *Intelligence,* verbal fluency, and mechanical comprehension represent theoretical constructs.

CONTENT VALIDITY. How well the content of the test samples the behavior domain or subject matter about which conclusions are to be made. This concept is used principally with *achievement tests.*

FACE VALIDITY. The idea that the test appears as if it should be valid. That is, a test is assumed to be valid simply by definition. For example, a scale is a valid instrument of weight, by definition of what consitutes weight.

PREDICTIVE VALIDITY. How effectively predictions made from the test are substantiated by data obtained at a later time. An example is the correlation of intelligence test scores with school grades.

VERBAL TEST. Designed to evaluate the general *intelligence* or specialized aptitudes of students. Consists primarily of items requiring the use of language. Contrast with *performance test.*

Z-SCORE. A standard score with a mean of 0 and a standard deviation of 1.

DIAGNOSTIC CATEGORIES

A-, AN-. A prefix equivalent to un- or in- that signifies absence, lack, -less, not. Contrast with *dys-*.

ACALCULIA. See *dyscalculia.*

AGNOSIA. Lost or impaired ability to identify familiar objects or events in the absence of a defective sense organ.

AUDITORY AGNOSIA. Impairment of the ability to recognize sounds or sound combinations (for example, nonrecognition of the ring of an alarm clock).

TACTILE AGNOSIA (Astereognosis). Impaired ability to recognize objects through the sense of touch.

VISUAL AGNOSIA. Inability to recognize objects, persons, or places by sight.

AGRAPHIA. See *dysgraphia.*

ALEXIA. See *dyslexia.*

APHASIA. See *dysphasia.*

APRAXIA. See *dyspraxia.*

BRAIN DAMAGE. Any structural damage or insult to the brain, whether by accident or disease.

DYS-. In medicine, a prefix denoting difficult or painful, faulty or impaired, abnormal or morbid.

DYSCALCULIA. Disturbed or impaired ability to calculate, to manipulate number symbols, or to perform simple arithmetic.

DYSFUNCTION. Abnormal or impaired behavior of any organ.

DYSGRAPHIA. A type of *dyspraxia* affecting the visual-motor system. Results in the inability to remember the kinesthetic patterns that go into writing. That is, an inability to relate the mental image of words or symbols to the motor movements necessary for writing them.

DYSLEXIA. Partial inability to read. Generally thought to be associated with neurological dysfunction.

DYSNOMIA. (Word-finding difficulty). Weakness in the ability to name objects or to recall and retrieve words. Generally the individual knows the word, recognizes it when spoken, but cannot retrieve it at will.

DYSPRAXIA. Impairment of the ability to recall and perform purposeful, skilled movements. Contrast with *praxis*.

> MOTOR DYSPRAXIA. Weakness in the ability to plan and execute unfamiliar motor tasks, even though coordination may be adequate for familiar tasks.

> ORAL DYSPRAXIA. Severe impairment in the ability to perform voluntary movements involving the speech musculature, even though automatic movements of the same musculature appear to be intact.

MINIMAL BRAIN DAMAGE. See *miminal brain dysfunction*.

MINIMAL BRAIN DYSFUNCTION. (Minimal brain damage, Minimal cerebral dysfunction). A mild neurological abnormality that causes learning difficulties in the child with near-average or even above-average intellectual potential. Common behavioral characteristics may include hyperactivity, distractibility, impulsivity, and poor motor functioning.

MINIMAL CEREBRAL DYSFUNCTION. See *minimal brain dysfunction*.

NEUROSIS. Behavior disturbance characterized by emotional conflict and anxiety but not a loss of contact with reality. Represents the milder forms of mental illness. Contrast with *psychosis*.

PERSEVERATION. The tendency to continue a specific act of behavior after it is no longer appropriate (for example, repeating a word over and over again, continuing a movement such as letter writing, prolonging laughter). Related to difficulty in shifting from one activity to another.

PSYCHOSIS. The class of the more severe mental disorders, in which there is a departure from normal patterns of thinking, feeling, or acting. Commonly characterized by loss of contact with reality, distortion of perception, disruptions of cognitive and emotional processes, and abnormal mental content, including hallucinations and delusions. Contrast with *neurosis*.

SPECIFIC LANGUAGE DISABILITY (SLD). Refers to those who have great difficulty learning to read and spell but who are otherwise intelligent. Generally applies to any language deficit impeding learning (oral, visual, or auditory). Sometimes used interchangeably with *dyslexia*.

WORD-FINDING DIFFICULTY. See *dysnomia*.

ACADEMIC TERMS

ACHIEVEMENT TEST. An objective test that measures how much a student has learned or knows about a specific subject.

ACTUAL GRADE PLACEMENT. The student's grade and month-in-grade at the date of testing. A tenth of a grade-placement unit is added for every month of school finished. For example, a first-grade student tested in late October has an actual grade placement of 1.2.

CHANNEL. The sensorimotor route through which language flows (for example, visual-motor, visual-vocal, auditory-motor). Theoretically, many combinations are possible.

CLOZE FORMAT. A procedure used in teaching and testing reading comprehension in which certain words are deleted from the text, leaving blank spaces. Measurement is made by rating the number of blanks that the student can accurately fill.

CRITERION-REFERENCED TEST (CR). Objective test yielding a *ratio score* and designed to assess a student's development of certain skills in terms of absolute levels of mastery. CR devices are made up of a specified set of sequential skills, (criterion behaviors) arranged in a hierarchial order. These tests provide answers to specific questions such as, "Can Billy identify the topic sentence in at least three out of four paragraphs?" Contrast with *norm-referenced test*.

DECODING. In reading, refers to the ability to translate the printed symbol into language. Entails visual perception and discrimination, preceded by auditory perception and discrimination.

DISCRIMINATION. The process of detecting differences among stimuli.

> AUDITORY DISCRIMINATION. Ability to determine whether two acoustic stimuli (either speech sounds or nonspeech sounds) are the same or different.

> TACTILE DISCRIMINATION. Central response to stimuli presented only to the tactile sense. The ability to recognize differences and similarities in shape and pattern by touch alone.

> VISUAL DISCRIMINATION. Ability to distinguish between different objects, forms, and letter symbols presented visually.

ENCODING. In writing, refers to the ability to translate verbal language into graphic symbols. The act of committing one's thoughts to the written form encompasses the ideational use of language, as well as visual, auditory, and visual-motor abilities.

FRUSTRATION READING LEVEL. The level at which a student reads orally with less than 93 percent accuracy or 70 percent comprehension. Frequent errors, repetitions, and omissions occur at this level, indicating that the material is too difficult for instruction. See *independent reading level and instructional reading level*.

GESTALT PSYCHOLOGY. A German school of psychology that places emphasis on a whole perceptual configuration and the interrelations of its component parts.

GRADE EQUIVALENT. See *grade norm.*

GRADE NORM (Grade equivalent, Grade score). The average test score obtained by students classified at a given grade placement. For example, a grade score of 3.4 indicates that the student performed as well on the test as an average student who has been in the third grade for four months.

GRADE SCORE. See *grade norm.*

HOLISTIC IMPRESSION. A method for overall assessment of written language. The holistic impression method requires looking at a piece of writing as a whole, not as having a series of separate, specific characteristics.

INDEPENDENT READING LEVEL. The level at which a student reads orally with 98 percent accuracy and 90 percent comprehension. Reading is fluent and expressive. Library reading, recreational reading, and homework should be assigned at the independent reading level. See *instructional reading level* and *frustration reading level.*

INFORMAL TEST. Nonstandardized test, often teacher-constructed, useful in analyzing a student's learning style and thinking processes. Indicates what the student does and how he or she does it.

INSTRUCTIONAL READING LEVEL. The level at which a student reads orally with 94 percent accuracy and 70 percent comprehension. Material is challenging and not too difficult. Classroom learning under teacher direction should be assigned at the instructional level. See *independent reading level* and *frustration reading level.*

MODALITY. A pathway for acquiring sensory information. Auditory, visual, tactile, and kinesthetic are the most common modalities through which learning occurs.

MULTISENSORY APPROACH. Generally refers to teaching methods that rely simultaneously on several sensory modalties—visual, auditory, kinesthetic, and tactile.

NORM-REFERENCED TEST. Objective test standardized on groups of individuals. Compares a student's performance to the performance of other students who are the same *chronological age.* Using norm-referenced tests, for example, Jill's reading can be assigned a grade-level score of 3.2 on a standardized reading test. In other words, the test tells how Jill is doing compared with other students. Contrast with *criterion-referenced test.*

ORTON-GILLINGHAM TECHNIQUE. A method of teaching reading that is highly structured and phonetically oriented and that stresses a *multisensory approach* (visual, auditory, and kinesthetic).

POSTTEST. A terminal evaluation of the student's status on completion of specific instructions or training. *Pretests* and posttests make it easier to measure progress in the course of remedial work.

PRETEST. A preliminary test used to establish a baseline of performance in a specified area.

RATE OF READING. A speed-of-reading score comparing the time required for a student to read a selection with standard rates obtained from cases in the standardization population. Generally expressed as the number of words read per minute.

RATIO SCORE. Refers to *criterion-referenced* testing, where the score can be expressed as a ratio. The total number of skills mastered divided by the total number of skills required:

$$\frac{\text{Number of skills mastered}}{\text{Number of skills required}} = \text{Score in percent}$$

For example, if Mary has learned 180 words out of a total of 200 words on a reading test, her score would be 180/200, or 90 percent.

SCREENING. A fast, efficient measurement for a large number of students. The purpose of screening is to identify students from the general population who need further diagnostic testing because of suspected deviance in a specific area.

SEQUENCING. A distinctive, fairly automatic function of the mind related to the serial ordering of stimuli. For example, remembering a series of movements within a skill, recalling the pattern of letters in a spelling word, or remembering the sequence of sounds within a word.

STRUCTURAL ANALYSIS. Breaking a word into its component parts, such as word families, rhyming aspects, roots, prefixes, and suffixes.

TACHISTOSCOPE. An apparatus that exposes visual material for brief, controllable periods of time. Practice with this device is designed to improve rate and span of the visual perception of words and phrases.

WORD ANALYSIS. A reading term that refers to the analysis of an unlearned word in terms of known elements for the purpose of identification.

WORD RECOGNITION. Identification of a word presented in isolation, either through the use of form configuration or skill in phonetic analysis. Indicates accurate decoding ability, but does not tap knowledge of word meaning.

VISUAL AND VISUAL-PERCEPTUAL MOTOR PROCESSING

COPY. Direct reproduction of a form with a pencil. Involves the ability to look at a figure and reproduce it without any additional clues. Contrast with *imitation.*

FAR-POINT COPYING. Copying with constant access to a model placed at a distance (for example, copying from a blackboard). Requires visual perception in association with a kinesthetic-motor response. Contrast with *near-point copying.*

IMITATION. A process used in learning copying skills by demonstration. First the student watches the examiner demonstrate how to draw the form; then the student imitates the examiner's movements. Contrast with *copy*.

NEAR-POINT COPYING. Copying with constant access to a model placed close at hand (for example, copying from a textbook). Requires visual perception in association with a kinesthetic-motor response. Usually, an easier task than *far-point copying*. Contrast with *far-point copying*.

VISUAL-MOTOR INTEGRATION. The ability to associate visual stimuli with motor responses. Coordinating vision with the movements of the body or parts of the body.

VISUAL PERCEPTION. Ability to identify, organize, and understand sensory stimuli received through the eye.

ORAL LANGUAGE AND AUDITORY PROCESSING

AUDITORY PERCEPTION. Ability to identify, organize, and understand external auditory stimuli, such as environmental sounds, music, or speech.

DISTINCTIVE FEATURE. A distinguishing acoustic or articulatory feature of a *phoneme*, such as voicing, stop, nasality, or place of articulation.

DYSPHASIA. Impairment of the ability to acquire symbols for a language system. The partial or complete loss of ability to comprehend spoken words (receptive dysphasia) or to speak words (expressive dysphasia). Associated with injury, disease, or abnormality of the speech centers.

ECHOLALIA. The parrotlike, senseless repetition of sounds, words, phrases, or sentences spoken by another person, without understanding the meaning of the language.

EXPRESSIVE LANGUAGE. The ability to produce language for communication purposes. Speaking and writing are the expressive language skills.

GRAMMAR. The study of word classes, their inflections, and their functions and relationship in sentences. A part of *syntax*.

HEARING VOCABULARY. Recognition vocabulary, generally measured through a picture vocabulary test. More heavily weighted with *receptive language* than with *expressive language*. Provides a rough estimate of verbal *intelligence*.

LANGUAGE. A conventionalized system of audible and visible signs (symbols) by which thoughts are conveyed.

LINGUISTICS. The scientific study of the form and function of *language*.

MORPHEME. The smallest unit of speech that is meaningful. For example, *farm*, the *er* in *farmer*, and the *ing* in *farming* are all morphemes.

MORPHOLOGY. The aspects of *linguistics* that deals with the study of and the rules for the formation of words in any particular language (for example, the formation of plurals, possessives, and compounds).

PHONEME. The smallest unit of sound in a language. Each phoneme is made up of a set of *distinctive features*. Each individual letter sound or blend, such as /p/ or /ch/, are phonemes.

PHONOLOGY. The study of the linguistic system of speech sounds in any language.

PRAGMATICS. Rules governing the use of language in context; that is, language as communication. Such features as conversational turn-taking and topic maintenance are examples of pragmatic skills.

PSYCHOLINGUISTICS. The study of the psychological and linguistic aspects of the language process.

RECEPTIVE LANGUAGE. The ability to comprehend the spoken or written word. Listening and reading are the receptive language skills.

SEMANTICS. The study of meaning in language, including the relationship among language, thought, and behavior.

SYNTAX. The study and science of the grammar system of a language. The linguistic rules of word order and the function of words in a sentence (sentence structure).

FINE AND GROSS MOTOR SKILLS

BILATERAL INTEGRATION. Integration of the sensorimotor function of the two sides of the body, including such factors as the ability to smoothly coordinate the two hands (or two legs) in bilateral (two-sided) motor activities. The tendency to cross the midline of the body, and the ability to distinguish the right side of the body from the left.

BODY IMAGE. The concept and awareness of one's own body. Includes the impressions one receives from internal data as well as feedback resulting from contact with others.

FINE MOTOR SKILL. The development of small muscle skills (for example, the use of eye-hand coordination in cutting, writing, tying shoes, and other tasks).

GROSS MOTOR SKILL. The development of large muscle skills (for example, walking, running, climbing, throwing, and other activities).

KINESTHESIA. Movement sense. Perception of position, direction, and speed of movement of the body or part of the body. Principal receptors are in the joints, ligaments, and inner ear.

MOTOR PLANNING. See *praxis*.

POSTURAL MECHANISMS. Motor responses, generally automatic, that allow an individual to maintain a desired position in relation to gravity and the earth's surface. An example is the shifting of body weight necessary to maintain sitting balance on a moving object.

PRAXIS (Motor planning). The ability to plan and to execute unfamiliar skilled motor tasks.

SENSORY INTEGRATION. The organization of incoming sensory information by the brain. Also a specific type of perceptual-motor training.

TACTILE PERCEPTION. The ability to recognize and give meaning to sensory stimuli that are received through the sense of touch.

VESTIBULAR SYSTEM. Detects sensations related to equilibrium and position. Sensitive to both movement (linear, angular, and rotational, acceleration and deceleration) and position of the head in relation to the pull of gravity.